The Fourth Reich

Ever since the collapse of the Third Reich, anxieties have persisted about Nazism's revival in the form of a Fourth Reich. Gavriel D. Rosenfeld reveals, for the first time, these postwar nightmares of a future that never happened and explains what they tell us about western political, intellectual, and cultural life. He shows how postwar German history might have been very different without the fear of the Fourth Reich as a mobilizing idea to combat the right-wing forces that genuinely threatened the country's democratic order. He then explores the universalization of the Fourth Reich by left-wing radicals in the 1960s, its transformation into a source of pop culture entertainment in the 1970s, and its embrace by authoritarian populists and neo-Nazis seeking to attack the European Union since the year 2000. This is a timely analysis of a concept that is increasingly relevant in an era of surging right-wing politics.

Gavriel D. Rosenfeld is Professor of History at Fairfield University. He has published widely on the Third Reich, the Holocaust, and the Second World War, including *Hi Hitler! How the Nazi Past is Being Normalized in Contemporary Culture*, which won the Sybil Halpern Milton Memorial Book Prize for the best book dealing with Nazi Germany and the Holocaust.

The Fourth Reich

The Specter of Nazism from World War II to the Present

Gavriel D. Rosenfeld

CAMBRIDGE UNIVERSITY PRESS

CAMBRIDGE
UNIVERSITY PRESS

University Printing House, Cambridge CB2 8BS, United Kingdom

One Liberty Plaza, 20th Floor, New York, NY 10006, USA

477 Williamstown Road, Port Melbourne, VIC 3207, Australia

314–321, 3rd Floor, Plot 3, Splendor Forum, Jasola District Centre, New Delhi – 110025, India

79 Anson Road, #06–04/06, Singapore 079906

Cambridge University Press is part of the University of Cambridge.

It furthers the University's mission by disseminating knowledge in the pursuit of education, learning, and research at the highest international levels of excellence.

www.cambridge.org
Information on this title: www.cambridge.org/9781108497497
DOI: 10.1017/9781108628587

First published 2019

Printed in the United Kingdom by TJ International Ltd, Padstow Cornwall

A catalogue record for this publication is available from the British Library.

Library of Congress Cataloging-in-Publication Data
NAMES: Rosenfeld, Gavriel David, 1967– author.
TITLE: The Fourth Reich : the specter of Nazism from World War II to the present / Gavriel D. Rosenfeld.
DESCRIPTION: Cambridge ; New York, NY : Cambridge University Press, 2019. | Includes bibliographical references and index.
IDENTIFIERS: LCCN 2018042760 | ISBN 9781108497497 (alk. paper)
SUBJECTS: LCSH: Germany – Politics and government – 1945–1990. | Germany – Politics and government – 1990– | Germany – History – Errors, inventions, etc. | National socialism – History. | Nazis – History. | Right-wing extremists – Germany. | Political culture – Germany. | Collective memory – Western countries. | Fear – Political aspects – Western countries. | Political culture – Western countries.
CLASSIFICATION: LCC DD257.4 .R67 2019 | DDC 320.53/3–dc23
LC record available at https://lccn.loc.gov/2018042760

ISBN 978-1-108-49749-7 Hardback

CONTENTS

ILLUSTRATIONS

PREFACE

> What kind of person would write about something that he
> knows doesn't exist?
>> Philip K. Dick

There is no Fourth Reich. There never has been. So why would
anyone write a historical study about it? Philip K. Dick's question
implies that the author of such a study must be something of
a contrarian. I do not consider myself to be such a person. But I have
nonetheless been fascinated by the idea of the Fourth Reich for a very
long time. I first came across the idea while writing my books,
*The World Hitler Never Made: Alternate History and the Memory of
Nazism* (2005) and *Hi Hitler! How the Nazi Past is Being Normalized
in Contemporary Culture* (2015). Both dealt with the subject of counterfactual history – with "what if?" narratives about the Third Reich.
In researching these studies, I occasionally came across works of literature, film, and television that imagined postwar Nazis trying to return to
power and establish a "Fourth Reich." At the time, I refrained from
thinking deeply about this scenario as it was outside of my area of focus.
It did not so much examine what might have happened in the past as
what might still happen in the future.

Gradually, however, I realized that the concept of a Fourth
Reich was deeply historical. Over the course of the last decade,
I noticed how the concept kept surfacing in media coverage of current
events. Following the eruption of the Great Recession of 2008,
European commentators accused the German chancellor, Angela

Merkel, of imposing a Fourth Reich on Europe by forcing other EU countries to embrace austerity measures. Leftist political activists branded the Israeli government a Fourth Reich because of its military actions in Gaza and Lebanon. And American commentators raised the alarm that President Donald Trump was threatening to establish a Fourth Reich in the United States. Given all of these trends, I became curious why critics were articulating their political fears in such polemical fashion and began researching the Fourth Reich's origins as a concept. I soon realized that it had a long and complex history. The fear of a Nazi return to power had been a constant presence in postwar western political, intellectual, and cultural life.

Studying this fear historically is complicated, as it places us in the difficult position of passing judgment on people who had no way of knowing whether or not their concerns were legitimate. Today, we enjoy the benefit of hindsight and can easily view postwar anxieties about a Nazi return to power in Germany – or anywhere else – as overblown. Those who lived in the early postwar years, however, had no idea how the future would unfold. To place ourselves back into the mindset of those people, to identify with their fears despite our subsequent knowledge, is challenging. But it is doable.

All of us have been held hostage by fear at one point or another in our lives. I think back to my years growing up in the bucolic college town of Bloomington, Indiana. In the summer of 1983, I returned from a month away at summer camp to learn the shocking news from my parents that our local synagogue had been damaged in an arson attack. Unknown assailants had started a fire at the base of the Torah ark, from which it spread to the sanctuary before being extinguished, leaving tens of thousands of dollars of damage.[1] Without any break in the case, unease persisted. Then a year later, in October of 1984, there was another shock: a Jewish fraternity house on the campus of Indiana University, less than a ten-minute walk from my house, was set on fire, killing one student and injuring thirty-four others.[2] Having grown up with a father who was a professor of Holocaust literature and the director of the university's Jewish Studies program, I was well aware of the history of antisemitism and was convinced that a wave of anti-Jewish violence was upon us. My fears were somewhat alleviated by the revelation that the perpetrator of the fraternity attack had been involved in a drunken brawl with several members earlier that night and was seeking revenge rather than acting on antisemitic motives.[3] But they were reinforced when the FBI subsequently arrested a white supremacist group for the synagogue attack.[4] Fortunately, the group's members were swiftly brought to justice, and the threat was neutralized. Before long, I recognized that my fears of an antisemitic wave had been exaggerated. The constellation of local events had been a coincidence, not a harbinger. My knowledge of the tragic Jewish past had distorted my view of the future.

Ever since those childhood experiences, I have been sensitive to the paradoxes of historical memory. I am well aware of George Santayana's famous claim that those who forget history are condemned to repeat it. But I am equally aware of Otto Friedrich's observation that "those who cannot forget the past are condemned to misunderstand it."[5] Just as we should not be overly naive about the possible recurrence of historical threats, we should also not be overly alarmist. This is an admonition that is especially difficult to heed these days. We are living in an era of omnipresent fears – of economic instability, social dislocation, political upheaval, and cultural conflict. The clash between globalists and nationalists, the potential "clash of civilizations" between the western and Muslim worlds, the resurgence of authoritarian populism, the possible return of fascism – all of these things have left us profoundly uncertain about our collective future. Unsure how things will turn out, we prefer to err on the side of vigilance and highlight the "lessons" of the past in order to guard against their repetition.

It is particularly timely, therefore, to revisit how earlier generations responded to their own fears by analyzing the postwar history of a nightmare that never happened – the creation of a Fourth Reich. It may be comforting to recognize how people not too long ago were paralyzed by concerns that proved to be groundless. Perhaps we, too, will one day look back on our present-day anxieties and sheepishly admit that we worried for nothing. On the other hand, studying the Fourth Reich helps us realize that postwar fears of a Nazi return to power were also grounded in real dangers – ones that might have been realized had circumstances been slightly different. By revealing how contingencies can determine history – by reminding us that our world was hardly inevitable – this book warns against complacency. By revealing how our worst fears have gone unrealized, it cautions against hysteria. By examining how people have contended with fears in the past, it shows how they might cope with fear in the present.

INTRODUCTION

The forests of Taunus were flooded with a dark human tide . . . .

After nightfall, fires flared at regular intervals along the hillside. Each time a new light pierced the blackness, thousands of loud-speakers roared: 'The goal is in sight.' Many were dressed in 'festive shepherds' garb' and wore ornamental badges. There were also many uniforms similar to those of the former Wehrmacht, except that the swastika had been replaced by a shepherd's staff with a ribbon, the ends of which were gripped in the beaks of doves.

Ten minutes before midnight, Friedolin appeared on a clearance where a pile of wood had been prepared. He was accompanied by the Shepherds, five field marshal generals, two grand admirals, and one air general . . . .

In the clearing a few hundred guests of honor – Germans as well as foreigners – were waiting . . . .

A field marshal general held a silver microphone. Thousands of loudspeakers transmitted Friedolin's shrill cry: 'The Fourth and Eternal Reich is in sight!'

Then the pile of wood in the clearing flared up. The human mass roared; power gathered like a thunderhead.[1]

As World War II was winding down in the fall of 1944, the American-based Austrian writer, Erwin Lessner, published a dysto-pian novel, *Phantom Victory*, that gave voice to a burgeoning fear among many people in the English-speaking world. The novel's plot, set in the years 1945–60, portrayed a humble, but charismatic shepherd named Friedolin replacing Adolf Hitler as Germany's new Führer and leading the nation in a renewed bid for world power. *Phantom Victory* reflected growing concerns that the dangers of the recent past might return in the near future. At the time of the novel's publication, Allied forces were rapidly driving the Wehrmacht back into German territory. The novel's conclusion, however, implied that military might would not be enough to guarantee a final triumph. Unless the Allies remained vigilant about preventing the revival of Nazi ideas, the impending defeat of the Third Reich might prove fleeting – a "phantom victory" – and be followed by the rise of an even deadlier Fourth Reich.

Lessner's narrative was one of the first to articulate a fear that has hovered over the entire postwar era. Ever since the collapse of the Third Reich in 1945, a specter has haunted western life – the specter of resurgent Nazism. Throughout Europe and North America, anxieties have persisted about unrepentant Nazis returning to power and establishing a Fourth Reich. These anxieties have been expressed not only in novels like Lessner's, but in political jeremiads, journalistic exposés, mainstream films, prime-time television shows, and popular comic books. They have imagined a range of threats – political coups, terrorist attacks, and military invasions – emanating from a variety of settings, including Germany, Latin America, and the United States. Fears of a Fourth Reich have fluctuated over time, swelling in certain eras and ebbing in others. But the nightmare they have envisioned has never come to pass. Thus far, the prospect of a revived Reich has remained confined to the imagination.

It may initially seem pointless to examine the history of the Fourth Reich. After all, history is commonly understood as the documentation and interpretation of events that actually happened. Yet, as Hugh Trevor-Roper eloquently observed more than a generation ago, "history is not merely what happened: it is what happened in the context of what might have happened."[2] It is a fact that no Fourth Reich came into being in the years following World War II. But could it have? Can reflecting on such a counterfactual question teach us anything about real history? This book suggests that the answer is yes.

From today's perspective, postwar fears of a Fourth Reich appear grossly exaggerated. Germany did not descend into dictatorship after 1945. Instead, the country became a stable democracy. It is entirely appropriate, therefore, to view postwar German history as a success story. Yet doing so runs the risk of portraying the country's democratization as more or less inevitable. It implies that a Fourth Reich was destined to remain an unrealized nightmare. Whether or not this claim is true is hard to say. Until now, there has been little serious research on the subject of the Fourth Reich. As a result, historians have remained ignorant about its complex postwar history. They have generally overlooked the fact that in every phase of the Federal Republic's existence, fears persisted throughout the western world that a new Reich was on the horizon. They have neglected to examine the reasons for these fears. And they have failed to ask – let alone answer – the question of whether these fears had any basis in reality. This latter omission is particularly problematic, for there were more than a few episodes after 1945 when Germany faced serious threats from Nazi groups seeking to return to power. All of these efforts ultimately failed. But it is worth investigating whether they might have succeeded. By revisiting these episodes and imagining scenarios in which they might have unfolded differently, we can better gauge the validity of postwar anxieties.

By examining the history of what might have happened, moreover, we can better understand the memory of what actually did. The evolution of the Fourth Reich as an idea in postwar western intellectual and cultural life reflects how people have remembered the twelve-year history of the Third Reich. The idea's evolution, however, does not merely show how people have passively remembered the events of the past. It shows how they have actively employed those memories to shape the future. The fear of a Nazi return to power has long driven public efforts to prevent such a possibility from actually transpiring. The fear has galvanized people to prevent a Nazi revival not only in Germany, but anywhere in the world. Over the course of the postwar era, the Fourth Reich has become universalized into a global signifier of resurgent Nazism and fascism. In the process, the idea has functioned like a self-fulfilling prophecy in reverse. By inspiring popular vigilance, its existence in the realm of ideas has prevented its realization in reality. In order to understand this paradoxical phenomenon, it is necessary to examine the origins and evolution of the Fourth Reich in western consciousness. In so doing, we can see how postwar history has been shaped by a specter.

Historicizing the Fourth Reich

There has been little systematic research thus far on the Fourth Reich. As a result, most people have been exposed to the topic through sensationalistic stories in the mass media. For decades, but especially since the turn of the millennium, European newspapers in countries from Spain to Russia have warned of a Fourth Reich – none more frequently than British tabloids, which have regularly published stories with excitable headlines, such as "MI5 Files: Nazis Planned 'Fourth Reich' in Post-War Europe" and "Dawn of the Fourth Reich: Why Money is Fuelling New European Fears of a Dominant Germany."[3] Similar stories have appeared in the American press, particularly since the election of Donald Trump in 2016, with one recent journalist dramatically declaring that the efforts of left-wing "antifa" groups to combat the "alt-right" were part of a larger campaign to "guard … against a Fourth Reich."[4] Further contributing to this sensationalizing trend have been non-academic studies that have linked the idea of a Fourth Reich to various global conspiracies. Books such as Jim Marrs' *The Rise of the Fourth Reich: The Secret Societies That Threaten to Take Over America* (2008) and Glen Yeadon's *The Nazi Hydra in America: Suppressed History of a Century – Wall Street and the Rise of the Fourth Reich* (2008) have made outlandish assertions that have done little to shore up the topic's claim to academic credibility.[5]

The proliferation of such sensationalistic texts helps explain why historians have shied away from studying the Fourth Reich. This is not to say that they have entirely avoided it. In fact, scholars and other writers have produced monographs, journal articles, and opinion pieces with eye-catching titles prominently featuring the phrase "The Fourth Reich."[6] Yet, after grabbing readers' attention, these works have generally failed to explain the idea in any significant depth and show how it was perceived, used, and exploited. Similar shortcomings have marked academic studies that have mentioned, but never sufficiently defined, the idea of the Fourth Reich. In her book, *A History of Germany 1918–2008*, for example, Mary Fulbrook asserted that, after the end of World War II, "many [Germans] saw the occupation by the Allies as a 'Fourth Reich,' no better than the Third."[7] Similarly, in his study, *The Nazi Legacy*, Magnus Linklater declared that, after 1945, "the German people, totally exhausted by war and politics, thought only of survival: a kilo of potatoes … mattered more than dreams of a Fourth Reich."[8]

These two passages employ very different understandings of the Fourth Reich; yet because neither goes on to interpret the concept in any further depth, its significance remains unclear.[9] The failure of scholars to advance our understanding of the Fourth Reich has been compounded by historians who have dismissed the concept altogether. In his book, *The Third Reich at War,* Richard Evans flatly declared that "history does not repeat itself. There will be no Fourth Reich."[10] In *The Nature of Fascism*, Roger Griffin dismissed "fears ... [of] a Fourth Reich in Germany" as "hysterical."[11] And in *The Spirit of the Berlin Republic*, Dieter Dettke concluded that "it is inconceivable that the Berlin Republic will ever be a Fourth German Reich."[12] These curt responses are understandable given the sensationalistic invocations of the concept. But by dismissing its seriousness, they discourage efforts to probe its deeper history.

In light of how the Fourth Reich has been under-theorized and under-documented, it is high time for it to be historicized. Doing so requires uncovering the term's origins and tracing its evolution in western intellectual, political, and cultural discourse. This task entails examining the ways that the Fourth Reich has been imagined by intellectuals, politicians, journalists, novelists, and filmmakers. It necessitates explaining how the idea's evolution has reflected broader political and cultural forces. Finally, it involves understanding how the concept relates to broader questions of history and memory.

The Fourth Reich as Symbol

The first step towards historicizing the Fourth Reich involves recognizing its semantic ambiguity.[13] At the most basic level, the Fourth Reich is a linguistic symbol – that is to say, a word or a phrase that employs description or suggestion to communicate some kind of meaning in relation to some external entity.[14] The Fourth Reich is also a metaphor, a phrase that means one thing literally, but is used figuratively to represent something else. Most importantly, the Fourth Reich is a slogan. It is a highly rhetorical signifier that employs an attention-grabbing phrase in order to inform and persuade. The phrase can be aspirational or oppositional, positive or negative, but it reformulates complex social and political ideas into more simplified terms. In so doing, a slogan forges solidarity among people of varying political views by giving them a common idea to rally around. At the same time, a slogan can also foster social polarization by sparking opposition from groups whose members believe differently.[15]

From its inception up to the present day, the Fourth Reich has displayed nearly all of these characteristics. As an omnipresent symbol, metaphor, and slogan in postwar western life, it has long been defined by ambiguity. This is especially true in a temporal sense. As a term, the Fourth Reich has mostly been used to refer to the future – to a reality yet to come. But it has also been used to refer to the present – to a reality that (allegedly) has already come to be. The Fourth Reich is also ambiguous in a spatial sense. It has mostly been employed to refer to a future or present-day Germany, but it has been applied to other countries as well. In both realms – temporal and spatial – the Fourth Reich has communicated denotative as well as connotative meaning. It has been used literally, symbolically, and metaphorically to describe a current or future reality – whether democratic or totalitarian – in multiple locales. It has also been employed rhetorically to evoke competing views about that reality. These views have been both positive and negative; they have expressed fantasies as well as fears. In both cases, the idea of the Fourth Reich has galvanized support as well as opposition. In doing so, it has won the allegiance, and aroused the enmity, of millions of people in Germany and around the world. For all of these reasons, tracing the history of the Fourth Reich provides a deeper understanding of one of the postwar era's more influential, albeit under-examined, ideas.

The Fourth Reich and Postwar German History

Historicizing the Fourth Reich opens up new perspectives on postwar German history. It is especially useful in helping us rethink the Federal Republic's main "master narrative." Scholars have traditionally portrayed Germany's postwar development as a "success story" (*Erfolgsgeschichte*).[16] They have attributed this success to a range of factors, including the reconstructionist thrust of the western Allies' occupation policy, the prosperity generated by the country's economic miracle (*Wirtschaftswunder*), the stability afforded by Chancellor Konrad Adenauer's pursuit of western integration (*Westbindung*), and the salutary effects of the country's overall "modernization." Politicians have long embraced the belief that this combination of factors made Germany a model to emulate – most notably, Chancellor Helmut Schmidt, who, in 1976, coined the famous campaign phrase, "*Modell*

Deutschland."[17] The "success story" narrative has also been institutio-
nalized in museums, such as the Haus der Geschichte in Bonn, whose
permanent exhibit presents an unmistakable story of progress from
dictatorship to democracy.[18] Despite this consensus, however, some
issues remain debated. Scholars have disagreed about *when* postwar
Germany became stabilized once and for all, with conservatives pointing to the mid 1950s and liberals dating it to the country's liberal
"second founding" in the 1960s and 1970s.[19] Most agree, however,
that with German reunification in the years 1989–90, the country's
success was clinched. By this point, Germany's deviant historical path
of development (or *Sonderweg*) finally came to an end.[20]

There is nothing inherently false with the "success story" narrative, but it has sometimes lent the Federal Republic's success an aura
of inevitability. Few historians have made this claim explicitly, but the
tendency of some to portray the country's democratization as proceed-
ing in uninterrupted fashion makes the thesis vulnerable to certain
interpretive pitfalls.[21] One potential problem is "hindsight bias." This
common fallacy uses our knowledge about the final outcome of a
historical event to portray it as overdetermined and essentially inevitable; in so doing, it reproduces the familiar problems associated with
teleological or "whiggish" views of history.[22] To cite one example:
hindsight bias clearly informed a speech delivered by Federal President
Horst Köhler in 2005, in which he praised the "success" of Germany's
postwar "democratic order," concluding that "hindsight shows clearly
that all [the] . . . decisions [that were made] were right."[23] Hindsight bias
is closely related to the equally problematic narrative strategy of "backshadowing," in which historical events, decisions, and phenomena are
portrayed – and, more importantly, judged – as smoothly progressing to
inevitable outcomes that "should" have been visible to contemporaries.[24] Both of these interpretive shortcomings are related to the larger
problem of "presentism."[25] The tendency to view the past exclusively
from the vantage point of the present brings with it inevitable distor-
tions of historical perspective. Besides promoting deterministic thinking, it ignores the existence of alternate paths of development and
neglects to imagine how history might have been different.

In recent years, historians have called attention to the presentist
features of postwar Germany's master narrative. They have done so,
fittingly enough, because of important changes in present-day German
life. The "success story" narrative peaked in the years leading up to, and

immediately following, German unification in 1990 – a time when many Germans viewed their country's postwar development with unadulterated pride.[26] Since the turn of the millennium, however, new concerns about contemporary problems – economic stagnation, social decline, and cultural anomie – have led scholars to critically rethink the "success story" narrative. Some have called for questioning the postwar era's underlying "myths" and "dark sides."[27] Others have bemoaned the fact that Germany's success is taken for granted and have called for challenging its aura of inevitability.[28] Still others have criticized the paradigms of "westernization," "modernization," and "democratization" for being overly "whiggish."[29] From these critics' perspective, none of Germany's postwar achievements *had* to happen. "Other paths of development," one observer has declared, "were ... conceivable."[30]

Yet while scholars have admitted there were alternative paths for postwar Germany's development, few have explored *how* they might have actually unfolded. Few have speculated at length about what specific alternatives existed. Fewer still have wondered what their consequences would have been. Would alternative decisions have made things better? Or would they have made them worse?

Counterfactual History

To answer these speculative questions, it helps to employ counterfactual reasoning. In recent years, scholars in the humanities and social sciences have increasingly explored "what if" questions in their academic work. They have produced extended, "long form counterfactuals" devoted to speculating on such varied subjects as Darwin's theory of evolution, World War I, and the Holocaust.[31] They have interjected briefer, "medium form counterfactuals" into narratives on the rise of the west, the Enlightenment, and the dictatorship of Joseph Stalin.[32] And they have produced fleeting, "short form counterfactuals" on a myriad other topics. In so doing, scholars have challenged the view that history pertains only to events that actually happened and have instead explored events that *never happened*. They have produced "fantasy scenarios" to show how events could have turned out better; they have imagined "nightmare scenarios" to show how events might have been worse; and they have entertained "stasis scenarios" to show how history ultimately had to happen as it did. In the process, they have embraced diverse rhetorical strategies to convince readers of their scenarios' plausibility. They have employed *causal, emotive, temporal, spatial, existential,* and *manneristic* counterfactuals in order to appeal to readers' emotions and reason.[33]

This recent scholarship makes clear that counterfactual reasoning is indispensable for understanding historical causality. Counterfactuals are embedded in all causal claims: when we declare that "x caused y," for instance, we implicitly affirm that "y would not have occurred in the absence of x."[34] Counterfactuals can also help us differentiate between different levels of causality: between immediate, intermediate, and distant causes; between exceptional and general causes; and between necessary and sufficient causes.[35] To be sure, it can be difficult to distinguish between the relative importance of such causes, but as Max Weber argued over a century ago, we can determine a single factor's significance in causing a historical event by imaginatively eliminating (or altering) the former and speculating on how doing so would affect the latter.[36] By revealing the relationship of events that did and did not happen, counterfactuals enable us to sort out the relative influence of contingency and determinism in historical events. Counterfactuals enable us to rethink teleological views of history – in particular, the distorting effects of hindsight bias and backshadowing – and reveal the alternative paths that history might have followed.[37] Ultimately, counterfactual history provides historians with a new and important arrow in their methodological quiver as they pursue the elusive ideal of historical truth. Skeptics may question whether exploring events that never happened can bring us closer to this ideal. But as John Stuart Mill pointed out long ago, we acquire a "clearer perception and livelier impression of truth" once it is brought into "collision with error."[38] Similarly, we can better understand what actually happened in the past by examining it alongside *what might have happened.*

Pursuing this unconventional path of analysis is not only profitable, but timely. We are living in an era that is inclined to counterfactual thinking. Speculative thought thrives in periods of rapid change. While orthodox views of the past are easy to maintain in periods of stability, revisionist challenges gain support in eras of upheaval. It is easy to take history's course for granted – to perceive it as deterministically preordained – when the existing order is not threatened by any looming alternatives; by contrast, when the status quo begins to break down in the face of new forces, alternative paths of development become increasingly clear.[39] The current interest in counterfactuals reflects this same trend. Although "what ifs?" were hardly unknown during the cold war, they proliferated after its conclusion. The end of the comparatively stable, bipolar world brought about a new era of uncertainty marked by unexpected crises. They began in the 1990s with the Yugoslav Civil War, intensified after the turn of the millennium with the global "war on terror," and reached a climax after 2008, with the eruption of the Great Recession and the rise of right-wing and left-wing populism. All of these developments cast doubt upon previous certainties – especially the efficacy of capitalism and the inevitability of democracy – and stimulated the tendency to speculate about how the past and present might have turned out differently.[40]

Counterfactuals and Postwar German History

This new climate has shaped perceptions of postwar German history. Until recently, the validity of the Federal Republic's "success story" narrative was more or less taken for granted. When the narrative became solidified in the years leading up to the Federal Republic's fortieth anniversary in 1989, there was little reason to question West Germany's commitment to democracy and the western alliance; there was even less reason to question these commitments during the euphoric period following unification in 1990, when Francis Fukuyama's claims about the inevitable triumph of liberalism made postwar Germany's democratization seem equally inevitable.[41] The growing uncertainty of the contemporary world, however, has challenged this deterministic viewpoint. It has also helped us appreciate the insecurities of the early postwar era. Because at the time of this writing (2018) we do not know the ultimate outcome of the "war on terror," the future of the post-Brexit EU, or the fate of the United States under President Donald Trump, we can better grasp the concerns of people who, after 1945, feared that Germany's young democracy might be threatened by a Fourth Reich. Aware as we are about our own world's contingent character, we are more likely to entertain "what ifs?" about the postwar period.

It may sound unorthodox to speculate about events that might have happened, but German scholars have long sensed the potential in such an enterprise. Already a generation ago, Hans-Peter Schwarz argued that postwar German history could profitably be explained through the concept of "the catastrophe that never was."[42] By examining what failed to happen, he suggested, historians could better understand what did – namely, why postwar German history ended up being so stable. Other scholars have echoed this claim and called for an "imaginary history" of the Federal Republic – a history of "that which was expected, but never arrived."[43] Thus far, however, few have done much to advance this goal.

How might it be done? To begin with, it helps to adopt an alternative perspective on postwar Germany's "success story." Whereas most historians typically explain the country's success by focusing on what went right, we can focus instead on what did not go wrong; rather than examining why Germany succeeded, we can focus on why it did not fail. Put simply, we can investigate why the Federal Republic never fell to a Fourth Reich. Reframing the story of postwar German history in this way is not a matter of slippery semantics. It is about examining two sides of a causal relationship. Historical events typically result from the interplay between existing "systems" and external "forces."[44] The more stable the system, the more difficult it is for an external force to affect it; the less stable the system, the easier it is for an external force to affect it. Historians have often applied this mode of reasoning to explain the rise of the Nazis. Heinrich August Winkler, for instance, has endorsed the argument that "Hitler came to power ... not because the National Socialists ... [were] so numerous ... but because there were not enough democrats ... to defend [the Weimar Republic]."[45] Scholars who have analyzed the postwar Federal Republic have shared this focus on the existing "system," rather than on oppositional "forces," preferring to examine the policies that stabilized the postwar state rather than Nazi efforts to challenge it.[46]

This tendency reflects the widespread belief that Nazism was an extremely weak force in postwar Germany. As early as the 1950s, journalists insisted that there was "no [chance of] reviving the National Socialist corpse" in the Federal Republic, while in the 1960s, historians confidently dismissed the "fear that there may be a recurrence of the events of 1933."[47] Many recent scholars have advanced similar claims, declaring that Nazism after 1945 was "crushed" as a political tradition, "failed entirely" as a movement, and "never [posed] a serious threat to democracy in West Germany."[48] Convinced that Nazism appealed only to isolated "cranks" after 1945, scholars have insisted that "an antidemocratic right had no chance in the Federal Republic."[49]

While these statements are factually accurate, they enjoy the benefit of hindsight and marginalize the instances after 1945 when Nazi forces threatened to overturn German democracy. These efforts first erupted in the occupation period, when conspiratorial campaigns to resist the installation of a democratic order were launched by fanatical Werewolf insurgents, unrepentant Hitler Youth leaders, committed SS men, and unbowed Wehrmacht veterans. In the early years of Chancellor Konrad Adenauer's administration, between 1949 and the early 1950s, fears of "renazification" were sparked by the rise of the Socialist Reich Party (*Sozialistische Reichspartei*, or SRP) and the uncovering of the infamous "Gauleiter Conspiracy" headed by former Nazi Propaganda Ministry deputy Werner Naumann. Soon thereafter, the eruption of the "swastika wave" of 1959–60 revived concerns about the persistence of Nazi loyalists in West Germany, as did the rise of the National Democratic Party (*Nationaldemokratische Partei Deutschlands*, or NPD) in the years 1964–69. In the 1970s and 1980s, the appearance of extreme right-wing demagogues, such as Manfred Roeder and Michael Kühnen, fanned fears of resurgent Nazism. And in the decades after German unification, concerns about growing right-wing extremism were stoked by the rise of neo-Nazi skinhead groups and New Right organizations affiliated with Hans Dietrich Sander's journal, *Staatsbriefe*, the German College (Deutsches Kolleg), and the Reich Citizens' Movement (*Reichsbürgerbewegung*).

Historians are familiar with all of these movements and have examined them with varying degrees of thoroughness. But they have overlooked their ties to the idea of a Fourth Reich. This oversight is surprising, given the idea's frequent invocation by both its supporters and opponents. Throughout the postwar period, Nazi and other radical right-wing activists energetically pursued the creation of a new Reich and employed the concept as a rallying cry to inspire their adherents. Their critics in Germany and abroad, meanwhile, raised the alarming prospect of a Fourth Reich as a means to mobilize popular resistance to it. Empirically documenting the concept's usage in postwar political discourse is the first step towards writing the history of the Fourth Reich. The second step is equally important, but more challenging – namely, interpreting the concept's overall significance. It is common knowledge that all the Nazi efforts to create a Fourth Reich failed. Yet, to fully understand why, we need to ask how close they came to succeeding.

Employing counterfactual reasoning and examining scenarios in which history might have turned out differently helps address this important question. To be sure, this task represents a methodological challenge for the obvious reason that it is impossible to prove anything about events that never happened. Nevertheless, if we explore counterfactual scenarios responsibly by carefully considering their plausibility, we can ensure that the task of speculation is not overwhelmed by an excess of imagination. In part, this requires positing different points of divergence from the established historical record and imagining their varied consequences. Counterfactual reasoning, however, does not have to be a purely subjective enterprise. The rich secondary literature on postwar German history contains a surprisingly large number of short-form counterfactual claims by scholars that can also be employed in attempting to answer various "what if" questions. The task of synthesizing new and old speculative assertions is challenging, but worth the effort. By examining how narrowly the Federal Republic avoided a Fourth Reich, we can acquire a new perspective on the reasons for the country's postwar stability.

By imagining how history might have happened differently, we can further address the important question of whether postwar fears of a Fourth Reich were warranted. Strictly speaking, the question answers itself. Because the Nazis never achieved their goals after 1945, fears of a Fourth Reich would appear to be exaggerated. Yet it would be wrong to dismiss them as entirely groundless. Doing so, first of all, would both reflect and perpetuate the chief weakness of the "success story" narrative – namely, its suggestion that Germany's postwar democratization was more or less inevitable. Today, we know the ending of the dramatic story of Germany's postwar recovery from military defeat. But what is now a settled past once lay in the future. In the years after 1945, Germany's postwar narrative was still open-ended – a fact that caused anxiety throughout the western world. Putting ourselves in the position of contemporaries and taking their fears seriously enables us to better understand the factors that shaped the era's events. Fears have long been an active force in history. As is shown by the ways in which modern political movements, such as nineteenth-century conservatism or twentieth-century fascism, exploited anxieties about looming revolution, fears about possible future events have often shaped the events that actually transpire.[50] Some historians have endeavored to apply this insight to the postwar Federal Republic and have called for framing the country's postwar history as a "history of fears."[51] Others have sought to explain why the intensity of these fears were out of proportion to the country's stable reality.[52] Building on these approaches, we can profitably assess the legitimacy of postwar fears of a Fourth Reich.

The Fourth Reich and the Memory of Nazism

In so doing, we can better understand the role that memory played in the Federal Republic's postwar "success story." Since the collapse of the Nazi regime in 1945, countless observers have urged the Germans to remember the "lessons" of the Third Reich in order to prevent history from repeating itself. In attempting to determine whether or not the Germans successfully fulfilled this task, scholars have examined how they pursued the difficult work of "coming to terms" with the Nazi experience. The scholarship on *Vergangenheitsbewältigung*, as it is known in Germany, is vast and has been advanced from many methodological perspectives.[53] To date, however, few scholars have recognized that the postwar discourse on the Fourth Reich was a crucial part of this larger process of confronting the recent past.

In the years after 1945, the Fourth Reich was a signifier of competing positions on memory. The question of how to respond to the Nazi experience divided people both in Germany and abroad. Some, mostly on the left-liberal wing of the political spectrum, called for remembrance, demanding that the crimes of the Nazi era be documented and their perpetrators brought to justice. Others, typically on the center-right, argued for amnesia and amnesty, insisting that Nazi-era misdeeds be forgotten and their perpetrators integrated into postwar society. These opposing views about Germany's past were directly correlated with worries about whether a new Reich loomed in the country's future. On the one hand, "alarmists" in Germany and abroad were committed to remembrance and consistently stoked fears about the possibility of a Nazi return to power. On the other hand, "apologists" believed that Nazism had been permanently consigned to the past and dismissed postwar fears to the contrary as unwarranted. Examining how both groups employed the idea of a Fourth Reich reveals that it was influenced by different motives – some pure, others less so. Among the alarmists, some sincerely believed that a new Reich represented a serious possibility, while others instrumentally exploited the concept for ulterior motives. Among the apologists, some genuinely doubted that Nazism posed a real postwar threat, while others deliberately underplayed it to help boost Germany's international image. Comparing the two groups' intense debate on the Fourth Reich helps us understand how present-day forces shaped views of the past.

Studying the Fourth Reich as a reflection of memory, moreover, allows us to understand not just German, but also global, trends in remembrance. Starting in the 1960s, the concept of the Fourth Reich became increasingly normalized. Rather than being viewed as a signifier of a Nazi revival in Germany, it became universalized into a metaphorical harbinger of global fascism. Starting with the swastika wave of 1959–60 and the capture and trial of Adolf Eichmann in 1960–61, many people became convinced that the Nazi threat could emanate from places outside of Germany – whether Latin America, the Middle East, or the United States. Shortly thereafter, left-leaning political activists and intellectuals in the US and Europe – including H. Rap Brown, James Baldwin, and Régis Debray – employed the concept of a Fourth Reich to attack racism against African-Americans, the war in Vietnam, and the Watergate scandal. During the 1970s and 1980s, the term became further globalized to refer to other authoritarian states, whether Greece's military junta or South Africa's Apartheid regime. Since German unification in 1990, finally, the Fourth Reich has become further inflated into a signifier of global malfeasance. Right-wing European nationalists in Britain, Russia, and Poland have employed the idea to attack European integration, globalization, and westernization. Left-leaning activists in the US, meanwhile, have employed the term to attack symbols of authoritarian populism, such as Great Britain's decision to leave the EU and Donald Trump's election as president of the United States.

In addition to becoming universalized, the Fourth Reich has become aestheticized. Starting in the late 1960s and 1970s, the idea of a renewed Reich was increasingly featured in popular novels, films, television shows, comic books, and even punk rock songs. The more prominent examples included best-selling novels (and later hit films), such as Frederick Forsyth's *The Odessa File*, Ira Levin's *The Boys from Brazil*, and Robert Ludlum's *The Holcroft Covenant*; episodes of the television shows *Mission Impossible*, *The Man from U.N.C.L.E.*, and *Wonder Woman*; issues of DC and Marvel comic books, such as *Batman* and *Captain America*; and songs by the Dead Kennedys and the Lookouts. This trend has continued up to the present day, whether in ironically minded films, such as *Iron Sky*, or ambitious Internet dramas, such as Amazon's *The Hunt*.[54] These works have been inspired by a variety of motives, but many of them have exploited the premise of a Nazi resurgence for profit and entertainment, thereby dimming its moral thrust. As a result of these normalizing trends, the idea of the Fourth Reich has become unmoored from its original referent – the idea of a Nazi return to power in Germany – and become an all-purpose signifier of evil. Through this process, it has lost some of its admonitory credibility.

The Fourth Reich in History and Memory

This book examines the evolution of the Fourth Reich in post-war western life by adopting both a chronological and a thematic approach. The first part of the book focuses on the Fourth Reich's origins in, and impact on, Germany from the early 1930s to the early 1950s. Chapter 1 shows how the idea emerged as an anti-Nazi rallying cry among a wide range of dissident groups, including left-leaning German-Jewish exiles, conservative Wehrmacht officers, and renegade National Socialists. In response, Nazi government officials sought to suppress the concept, a fact that initially led British and American observers to view the Fourth Reich as the hopeful symbol of a future democratic Germany. As the Second World War neared its conclusion, however, Anglo-American fears that Nazi loyalists were going underground to resist Allied forces transformed the Fourth Reich into an admonitory symbol of unrepentant Nazi fanaticism. Chapter 2 focuses on the ensuing Allied occupation of Germany from 1945 to 1949 and describes how American and British military officials, journalists, civilian lobbying organizations, novelists, and filmmakers continued to warn about the prospect of a Fourth Reich unless the Allies purged Nazism from all areas of German life. This fear reflected the fact that committed Nazis during this period actively sought to overthrow the Allied occupation and revive the Reich. They included the Werewolf insurgency of 1945–46, the attempted coup led by Hitler Youth leader Artur Axmann in 1945–46, and the "Deutsche Revolution" plot led by SS and Wehrmacht veterans in 1946–47. Allied forces ultimately suppressed the revolts, but by imagining certain counterfactual scenarios, it is possible to see how they might have succeeded. Chapter 3 examines how Nazi resistance movements continued after the creation of the Federal Republic of Germany in 1949 by examining the rise of the SRP and the uncovering of the Gauleiter Conspiracy in the years 1950–52. Like the coup attempts of the occupation period, these threats were also crushed. But had circumstances been slightly different, they might have been more successful. In recognizing West Germany's vulnerability to the Nazi threat during this period, it becomes clear that fears of a Fourth Reich were hardly baseless.

The second part of the book covers the 1960s up to the present and explores how the idea of a Fourth Reich spread beyond, but ultimately circled back to, Germany. Chapter 4 describes how fears of a Nazi comeback in the Federal Republic were revived by the eruption of the "swastika wave" in 1959–60 and the rise of the NPD from 1964 to 1969. These fears ultimately proved to be unwarranted, but they did not entirely disappear. Around the same time, new concerns arose that Nazism was emerging in the United States. During the 1960s, the rise of the American Nazi Party, the racist backlash against the Civil Rights Movement, the escalation of the war in Vietnam, and the scandalous behavior of the Nixon administration prompted left-liberal Americans to claim that a Fourth Reich was dawning in America. These claims played an important role in normalizing the Fourth Reich by universalizing its significance. The normalization process was also promoted by the aestheticization of the Fourth Reich in popular culture. Chapter 5 explains how, during the "long 1970s," the fear of a Nazi return to power was transformed into a source of mass entertainment in Anglo-American works of literature, film, and television. This cultural turn represented a major development in the postwar evolution of the Fourth Reich, but it was abruptly halted in 1989–90, with the collapse of the Berlin Wall and the unification of Germany. Chapter 6 shows how, starting in the 1990s and continuing after the turn of the millennium, the Fourth Reich was "re-Germanized" and became a topic of renewed political concern. All across Europe, worried observers voiced the fear that the Federal Republic was heading in a right-wing, if not neo-Nazi, direction. Some of the claims were grounded in legitimate concerns, as right-wing German intellectuals were busy theorizing the political basis for a future Fourth Reich. Yet other claims, especially those articulated in the wake of the 2008 financial crisis in countries like Greece, Italy, and Russia, were more tendentious and expressed cynical domestic and foreign policy calculations.

How the Fourth Reich will evolve in the future is uncertain. But the book's conclusion explores the possibility that it will remain an appealing signifier in a world of growing uncertainty. To date, the term has largely served as an ominous slogan of admonition. But there is no saying it will not evolve into a term of inspiration. Given the ways in which Nazi groups have kept the term alive since 1945, it is conceivable that under the right conditions, the idea of a Fourth Reich could one day experience a popular renaissance.

1 BETWEEN FANTASY AND NIGHTMARE: INVENTING THE FOURTH REICH IN THE THIRD REICH

> The Fourth Reich is a Reich of peace. It consciously regards itself as a European Reich. It seeks to be an active member of a League of Nations in which all the people of the Earth work together in democratic equality to defend each nation against those who would disturb the peace.[1]
>
> > Georg Bernhard, "Draft of a Constitution for the Fourth Reich" (1936)

> The real question regarding Hitler's end, real or simulated, is the use to which the Nazis intend to put it.
>
> Days before ... Admiral Doenitz announced the Führer's death, Nazi spokesmen feverishly began to [establish] ... the legend of a ... self-sacrificing leader who was prepared to give up his life for his country and ultimately did.
>
> [The] ... Nazis are monumental liars .... But they lie with a purpose .... [In] this instance ... [it is] to save from the wreckage of Hitler's plans something upon which they ... [can] build a Fourth Reich at some future time.[2]
>
> > Barnet Nover, *The Washington Post* (May 3, 1945)

During the years of the Third Reich, many people actively contemplated the possibility that Hitler's regime would one day be replaced by a Fourth Reich. In Germany and abroad, politicians, journalists, and academics actively imagined what a post-Nazi state might look like. Their motives and conclusions varied considerably. As was shown by the draft constitution written by the German-Jewish émigré journalist Georg Bernhard in 1936, some people in the years before World War II optimistically hoped that Hitler's eventual fall from power would enable the creation of a progressive, democratic Fourth Reich, superior in every way to the Third. As the war advanced and the Allies became increasingly convinced of their eventual victory, however, other critics envisioned a more worrisome future for Germany. The anxious comment by American journalist Barnet Nover in May of 1945 expressed the fear that, following the Third Reich's collapse, unrepentant Nazis would attempt to return to power by establishing a state in the spirit of its predecessor. During the years of the Nazi dictatorship, in short, the prospect of a Fourth Reich inspired both fantasies and nightmares in the western imagination.

The Fourth Reich's Foil: The Idea of the Third Reich

The idea of the Fourth Reich was conceived during, and developed in reaction to, the Third Reich. Explaining the origins of the former thus requires discussing the origins of the latter. In conventional usage today, the Third Reich refers to the years of the Nazi dictatorship from 1933 to 1945. Yet nothing is as simple as it seems. Disagreement persists about the appropriateness of using the phrase "Third Reich" to describe the historical era in question. Some scholars contend that doing so validates the Nazi regime's propagandistic usage of the phrase. As a result, they prefer to surround it with quotation marks (referring to the "Third Reich" instead of the Third Reich) or avoid it altogether in favor of moralistic designations, such as the "National Socialist Terror Regime" (*Nationalsozialistische Gewaltherrschaft*).[3] These strategies are well intentioned, but have drawbacks. Abstaining from referring to the "Third Reich" can backfire by granting the phrase the kind of aura that is common to all taboos. Avoiding the phrase in the hope of demythologizing it, moreover, may also reduce our capacity to understand its original propagandistic function. To be sure, referring to the Third Reich naively, without any awareness of its fraught history, is also inadvisable. But employing it in a scholarly sense does not mean endorsing it.

Given the politics of usage that surrounds the concept, the Third Reich is best understood by historicizing it within the larger context of German history. The easiest place to begin is with the term "Reich" itself. Translated into English, the German word "Reich" broadly means "realm," but it is most often translated as "empire" or "kingdom." The term is thus both a spatial designation and a signifier for a political formation. In the context of German history, the term "Reich" has been applied to several states that have existed over the span of a thousand years. The first was the Holy Roman Empire, usually dated as lasting from its founding by the Frankish king, Charlemagne, in the year 800 (or, in other accounts, by his Saxon successor, Otto I, in 962) until its dissolution by Napoleon Bonaparte in 1806. The second was the Wilhelmine Empire, known as the *Kaiserreich*, which lasted from 1871 until its collapse in 1918. The third was the Nazi regime. This tripartite definition regularly appears in surveys of German history. However, the definition is incomplete, as it reduces the term "Reich" to a mere political designation.

In truth, the idea of the Reich also has profound spiritual – indeed mystical – connotations. These connotations are deeply rooted in Christian theology, particularly in the chiliastic idea of God's eventual Kingdom (*Reich*) on Earth. According to the latter chapters of the Book of Revelation, this kingdom would take the form of a thousand-year period of peace (known as the "millennium") that would both precede and follow Jesus's battle with Satan. The corresponding belief that this kingdom would represent a *third* Reich, in turn, arose during the Middle Ages, courtesy of the twelfth-century Italian theologian Joachim of Fiore, who viewed it as the final stage of Christian eschatology. Inspired by the idea of the Holy Trinity and expressing a long tradition of triadic thinking in western thought, Joachim defined the Third Reich as the expected third, and final, phase of world history. The first and original era, he argued, was the Kingdom of the Father, meaning the era of the Hebrew religion. The second Kingdom was that of the Son and referred to the birth of Christianity. Still to come was the third and final Kingdom of the Holy Spirit, which would arise following an apocalyptic confrontation between the forces of evil and their opponents, the "spiritual men," who were destined to inaugurate a millennial era of perfection. Through this titanic battle, the arrival of the Third Reich would represent the end of earthly history altogether.[4]

Over time, the idea of the Third Reich expanded beyond its original religious meaning and became secularized. By the dawn of the modern era, the idea began to accommodate a range of disparate visions. In the nineteenth century, the expectant belief in a coming "third age," as it was often termed, appealed to many European intellectuals, ranging from the French utopian socialist Henri de Saint-Simon to the Italian nationalist Giuseppe Mazzini.[5] But it particularly spoke to Germans, thanks to their historic lack of national unity. During the Middle Ages and into the early modern era, many Germans viewed the Holy Roman Empire, with its joint rule of pope and emperor, as "the forerunner of the Kingdom of God on earth."[6] Yet the Empire's gradual decline in the wake of the Reformation and its ultimate disappearance following the invasion of Napoleon's armies in the early 1800s made this view increasingly difficult to sustain. Painfully aware of the liabilities of internal division, Germans seized upon the concept of the "nation" as a new source of popular unity. As part of this process, the idea of the Reich became nationalized into a vehicle of German rebirth. Convinced that the German *Volk* deserved its own *Vaterland*, German nationalists began to conceive of different strategies of unifying the German people in a new Reich. Two visions emerged: the first was a universal, *grossdeutsch* empire, encompassing both the territories of the Germanic Confederation and the Austrian lands of the Habsburg monarchy; the second was a more particularistic, *kleindeutsch* empire ruled by the Hohenzollern monarchy of Prussia. As fate would have it, the latter solution emerged victorious. Following Prussia's military victories over Austria and France in the years 1866–70, the second German Empire was finally proclaimed on January 18, 1871 in the Hall of Mirrors at Versailles.

The second Reich was a secular political construct, yet it retained a quasi-religious dimension. This became clear a few years after the Reich's founding when the euphoria that initially surrounded it began to wane. The catalyst for this development was the financial crash of 1873 and ensuing economic depression. With this traumatic event, certain Germans began to lose faith in the new state and started to question its foundations. These critics felt that the *Kaiserreich* was overwhelmingly defined by materialistic forces – primarily free-market capitalism and political liberalism – and lacked a deeper, spiritual dimension. In response, they conceived of utopian visions for a new Reich that would replace the one that had just been established. Many of these visions were conceived by right-wing, *völkisch* activists, such as Paul de Lagarde, Julius Langbehn, and Heinrich Class. With a few exceptions, they did not refer explicitly to the future Reich with the adjective "Third" but instead used the terms "new" or "next."[7] They affirmed that it would be an imperialistic "Greater German Reich," ruled by a Führer, and committed to the old "Teutonic" virtues of freedom, equality, and selflessness. Around the same time, other right-wing thinkers, such as Guido von List, Lanz von Liebensfels, and Houston Stewart Chamberlin, added racist and antisemitic elements to this vision, demanding that the Reich be purged of foreigners and minorities and united on the basis of blood.[8] This conception of the Reich was generally secular. Yet the missionary zeal of its supporters expressed a millenarian spirit.

This desire for a new Reich intensified further following the calamitous events of 1914–18. During the First World War, the phrase "Third Reich" occasionally surfaced in a spiritual, pacifistic context.[9] But following Germany's military defeat, the phrase was mostly embraced by representatives of the political right. Shaken by the collapse of the Hohenzollern monarchy in November 1918 and enraged by the revolutionary Weimar government's ratification of the Treaty of Versailles in July of 1919, conservative and *völkisch* Germans believed that a radical response was necessary to help their country emerge from its unprecedented crisis. Starting in the early 1920s, various writers adopted a millenarian perspective and called for the creation of a "Third Reich." The most important figure to do so was the conservative writer Arthur Moeller van den Bruck, whose famous book, *Das Dritte Reich* (1923), gave the previously religious concept a distinctly political interpretation.[10] Building upon the medieval thought of Joachim of Fiore, Moeller asserted that, following the rise and fall of the Holy Roman Empire and the *Kaiserreich*, a third Reich was destined to follow. It would be established, he argued, via a conservative revolution that would reconcile the contradictions of nationalism and socialism and find a third way between them. As in Joachim's scheme, Moeller believed that this process would involve a struggle between the forces of good and evil. The latter, Moeller believed, was epitomized by liberalism, but it included all forms of Marxist thought and, more broadly, the Weimar Republic itself.[11] He further implied that the new order could only be created through violence. In the end, though, Moeller believed that the Third Reich would remain true to its medieval origins and stand as an "idea of eternal peace."[12] With its creation, the German people would "fulfill its destiny on earth" and inaugurate an era of German national dominance.[13]

While Moeller was the most famous exponent of the Third Reich during the Weimar Republic, he was not the first. He was preceded in embracing the concept by the right-wing poet and founding member of the Nazi Party, Dietrich Eckart. Eckart lent the Third Reich an antisemitic cast by viewing it as the utopian telos of Germany's world historical struggle against Jewish evil.[14] Eckart hated the Jews for a variety of political and economic reasons, but he merged them all into a comprehensive, apocalyptic vision. As he made clear in a series of essays published in his journal, *Auf gut Deutsch*, in the years 1919–20, Eckart viewed the Jews as nothing less than the Antichrist. It was Germany's sacred mission, he believed, to destroy them and thereby redeem the world. As he famously put it in July of 1919, "there is no people on earth more qualified ... to realize the Third Reich than ours!"[15]

It remains unclear how and when the idea of the Third Reich entered into Nazi ideology. Hitler seems to have been influenced by Eckart as well as Moeller. The Nazi leader acknowledged the former as his political mentor, but he was introduced to the latter by one of his fellow party members, Otto Strasser, who himself endorsed the need for a "Third Reich."[16] Whatever the case may be, Hitler and other leading members of the Nazi Party (National Socialist German Workers Party, NSDAP) were surely aware of the phrase as it gained popularity across Germany during the 1920s. That said, the phrase was not monopolized by the Nazi Party in this period; indeed, it found articulation in a wide range of political circles. Traditional conservative thinkers, for instance, envisaged the Third Reich as a revived monarchy under the Hohenzollerns or Habsburgs.[17] Further to the right, supporters of General Erich Ludendorff's militaristic Tannenberg Union (*Tannenbergbund*) and Alfred Hugenberg's German National People's Party (DNVP) called for a Third Reich as well.[18] There were also literary articulations of the Third Reich by lowbrow *völkisch* novelists and highbrow poets.[19] Given the widespread appeal of the Third Reich as an idea, leading Nazi ideologues predictably embraced it as well. After Otto Strasser, the most prominent was Joseph Goebbels, who wrote the treatise *Paths to the Third Reich* in 1927, and Alfred Rosenberg, who invoked "the rising Third Reich" in his *Myth of the Twentieth Century* in 1930.[20] For his part, Hitler does not seem to have employed the concept of the Third Reich very often in the 1920s, but he probably sympathized with the idea. On page 1 of *Mein Kampf* he called for a new (and implicitly a third) Reich when he declared, "one blood demands one Reich." Later in the book, he channelled the concept's mystical dimensions when he expressed the desire for "an ideal Reich."[21] Neither Hitler nor any other Nazi leader, however, bothered to give the idea of the Third Reich any specific political content. Rather than serving as a clear blueprint for a future government, it served mostly as a rallying cry for national regeneration.

The term's galvanizing function became increasingly clear the closer the Nazis came to seizing power. While the phrase "Third Reich" seldom appeared in the mainstream German press during the 1920s, it became more common following the NSDAP's breakthrough performance in the Reichstag elections of 1930.[22] It is untrue that the idea of a "Third Reich" was largely popularized by the foreign media.[23] Although it was mentioned in the Anglo-American press beginning in 1930, the phrase appeared just as often in German newspapers.[24] This reflected the fact that the Nazis themselves increasingly began to use it as a campaign slogan. Calls for a Third Reich appeared in the pages of Nazi press organs, such as the *Völkische Beobachter* and *Der Angriff*.[25] They were voiced in the speeches of Nazi politicians.[26] And they were expressed in gatherings of rank-and-file party members.[27] These expressions of support for the Third Reich, moreover, were not mere political rhetoric. They articulated the millenarian yearnings of ordinary Germans.[28]

Not all invocations of the Third Reich, however, were meant to be positive. The Nazis' political opponents often invoked the idea in order to disparage it. In 1930, the *Hamburger Anzeiger* dismissed the Nazis' "rapturous adoration of the legendary Third Reich" as a far-fetched "utopia."[29] Campaign posters produced by the Social Democratic Party (SPD) for the 1932 Reichstag election illustrated the phrase "The Third Reich" with images of gravestones and skeletons (Figure 1.1).[30] In 1931, the Rowohlt Verlag, a major German publishing firm, found itself in a legal battle in the Berlin district court with the publisher of Moeller van den Bruck's book, *The Third Reich*, after producing a tongue-in-cheek book by the same title that made "the spiritual meaning of National Socialism laughable."[31] Such critiques did not only emanate from the left but also came from the right. In 1932, Erich Ludendorff attempted to tar the notion of the Third Reich with the brush of homosexuality, condemning Hitler's decision to retain his (openly gay) SA-Chief Ernst Röhm by saying: "It is well known that

Figure 1.1 This SPD-produced poster for the German Reichstag election of 1932 predicted that, under a Third Reich, Germany would become a massive cemetery, strewn with gravestones (Source: Landes-Archiv Baden-Württemberg).

those who prefer their own sex are called the 'third sex.' How senseless is it, therefore, to call the Hitler party the 'Third Reich!'"[32] Given the manifold critiques of the phrase in this period, it may not be surprising that Hitler shied away from using it himself. Although he explicitly employed it as early as 1930, he left the job of promoting it to his underlings.[33]

This changed after Hitler became chancellor in 1933, however. The day after his appointment by President Paul von Hindenburg on January 30, the *Völkischer Beobachter* triumphantly declared that the decision had "laid the foundation for the Third Reich."[34] With the new Reich now closer to reality, Hitler increasingly embraced the term.[35] As is shown by Max Domarus's comprehensive compilation of the Nazi leader's speeches, Hitler repeatedly invoked the idea of the Third Reich in the early years of his dictatorship.[36] In May of 1933, for instance, he informed the First Congress of the German Labor Front of the importance of winning over the loyalty of the German *Volk* "for the coming Reich, our Third Reich" (thereby making clear that it had not yet been established).[37] In subsequent speeches, Hitler invoked "the baptismal water of the Third Reich" (Munich, 1934), hailed the "flag of the Third Reich" (Coburg, 1935), and referred to Germany as "the National Socialist Third Reich" (Nuremberg, 1936).[38] By 1937, he implied that the Reich had finally arrived, telling the Reichstag on January 30 that new Nazi organizations, such as the SA, SS, and Hitler Youth, had become "bricks in the proud structure of our Third Reich."[39]

In the years that followed, however, Hitler's use of the Third Reich declined. Following Germany's annexation of the Sudetenland in the fall of 1938, Hitler increasingly de-emphasized the term in favor of more expansive designations, such as "Greater German Empire" (*Grossgermanisches Reich*).[40] Then, in the summer of 1939, Hitler ordered the Propaganda Ministry to ban the "Third Reich" from all official communications.[41] The reasons remain murky, but it is possible that the term had become viewed as too pacifistic.[42] Given that the original Christological notion of a "Third Reich" suggested an era of peace and harmony, its continued use by the Nazi regime may have implied that the regime had no plans for further revolutionary action. Such a prospect, however, was far from Hitler's mind. By the late 1930s, the Nazi leader was bent on seizing *Lebensraum* through war. To mobilize support for this objective, a new term was required. In June of 1939, therefore, Hitler instructed the German media to employ the phrases "Germanic Empire of the German Nation" (*Germanisches Reich deutscher Nation*) and "Greater German Empire" (*Grossgermanisches Reich*). Both terms were preferable, he explained, as Germany was destined to become a "conqueror state."[43] From this moment on, references to the Third Reich largely disappeared in Nazi Germany. Although the German press continued to use the phrase in the first years of the war, and while Hitler occasionally did so as well, it gradually faded from German public discourse.[44]

The Origins of the Fourth Reich

Another reason the Nazis abandoned the Third Reich as a phrase was the fact that the regime's opponents had rhetorically devalued it by promoting the alternative concept of a Fourth Reich.[45] Building upon older precedents, the idea of the Fourth Reich originally emerged as a rallying cry for the anti-Nazi resistance after 1933. In Germany as well as abroad, the progressive left and the reactionary right both embraced the concept as an idealistic slogan promising a hopeful, post-Nazi future. The Fourth Reich, however, was not viewed solely as the antithesis of the Third Reich during this period. While it retained positive connotations within anti-Nazi circles prior to 1939, the eruption of the Second World War gradually lent the concept a more ambiguous significance. Particularly among Allied observers, the Fourth Reich became more associated with fears than fantasies.

The Fourth Reich before 1933

Like its predecessor, the idea of the Fourth Reich has deep religious roots. It can be traced back to the biblical Book of Daniel, specifically its 2nd and 7th chapters, which introduced into western thought the influential concept of the four world monarchies or kingdoms (*Reiche*, in German). In chapter 2, Daniel interprets a dream of the Babylonian king, Nebuchadnezzar II (c. 634–562 BCE), in which the latter witnesses an enormous statue made of four metals (gold, silver, brass, and iron) being destroyed by a large rock. Later, in chapter 7, Daniel describes one of his own apocalyptic dreams, this time of four beasts (a lion, bear, leopard, and beast with ten horns) emerging from the sea and ultimately being destroyed by God's judgment (Figure 1.2). In both chapters, the number four possesses important political symbolism relating to the Book of Daniel's immediate historical context. Composed by Jews living under the oppressive rule of the Greek Seleucid monarchy in the second century BCE, the Book broadly

Figure 1.2 The idea of the Fourth Reich traces its roots back to the biblical Book of Daniel, which predicted the rise and fall of four world kingdoms (*Reiche*, in German). This image from around 1750 portrays the colossus of royal rule, made of four metals and surrounded by four mythical animals portraying the four world kingdoms. At the top right, a massive boulder sent by God falls from on high to topple human rule by divine justice (Source: Getty Images).

condemned the four monarchies that had oppressed the Jewish people throughout history. The first three were traditionally held to be those of the Babylonians, Medes, and Persians; the fourth kingdom – the *viertes Reich* in German – was that of the Greek king, Antiochus IV Epiphanes

(c. 215–164 BCE). By allegorically alluding to this latter kingdom's destruction, the tales in the Book of Daniel provided oppressed Jews with an uplifting, anti-imperialistic message about the triumph of good over evil and the imminence of divine deliverance.[46]

In the post-biblical era, Christian thinkers reinterpreted the Book of Daniel and profoundly altered its message. Throughout Late Antiquity, the Middle Ages, and the early modern era, religious figures in Europe used the biblical narrative to periodize universal history and make sense of their own historical realities. Their main concern was to determine which historical monarchy the biblical Fourth Kingdom referred to. Early Christian thinkers changed the traditional interpretation of the Fourth Kingdom from the Greeks to the Romans; this interpretation reflected the Roman Empire's initial oppression of the Christian sect and preserved the *negative* connotations of the "Fourth" Kingdom. Yet, as Christianity gradually became the state religion of Rome, the anti-imperialist message of the Book of Daniel was inverted into a *positive* endorsement of the imperial status quo. Rather than signifying the last phase of suffering prior to a climactic moment of liberation, the Fourth Kingdom came to be seen as the last bulwark against an apocalypse of destruction.[47]

As time progressed, this narrative was embraced by the German-speaking world. In the early Middle Ages, Germans came to see themselves as having inherited the legacy of Imperial Rome. Although the Western Empire's collapse in the fifth century CE theoretically should have brought about the expected apocalypse, the Germans employed the principle of *translatio imperii* ("transfer of rule") and declared that the Empire lived on in the new Holy Roman Empire of Charlemagne and Otto I.[48] From this juncture, the idea that the Holy Roman Empire represented the Fourth Kingdom, or *Reich*, evolved in a consistent direction. During the Protestant Reformation, religious dissenters, such as Luther, Calvin, and Melanchthon, adopted a presentist view of the Fourth Reich and used the term to defend the Empire against new representatives of the "Antichrist," such as the Ottoman Turks.[49] During the Wars of Religion, the French Revolution, and the Napoleonic Wars, the concept of the Fourth Reich retained its rhetorical appeal for Germans seeking to defend the existing imperial order against new apocalyptic threats.[50] As the nineteenth century progressed, however, the Fourth Reich lost much of its prophetic power. The rise of secular modes of political thought and historical inquiry stripped the concept of its prior relevance – so much so, that by the early twentieth century, it had become reduced to an arcane religious notion of interest only to clerics and academics.[51]

Only in the early 1930s did the Fourth Reich evolve into a more secular political concept. This transformation commenced with the appearance of Kurt van Emsen's book, *Adolf Hitler und die Kommenden* (*Adolf Hitler and Those Who are Still to Come*).[52] Published in 1932 on the eve of the Nazi seizure of power, the book was an extended, if highly idiosyncratic, meditation on the role that both a Third *and* Fourth Reich were destined to play in Germany's political future. The book's author (who, in reality, was the German physician and sanatorium director Karl Strünckmann) was influenced by an eclectic array of ideas, including Christian apocalypticism, astrology, numerology, occultism, racial science, *völkisch* thought, pan-Germanism, and the philosophical works of Hegel, Marx, and Nietzsche.[53] Van Emsen's point of departure was the messianic belief that Germany was destined to give rise to "the Fourth Reich of 'those who are still to come.'"[54] This resonant phrase, included in his book's title, highlighted how van Emsen altered the traditional meaning of the Fourth Reich from a present-day reality to a future-oriented ideal. "The task for the day after tomorrow in the Fourth Reich," he asserted, was for Germans to "become pioneers of new transnational creations, bearers of a federal form of 'universalism' in state, church, and economy."[55] This utopian vision resembled Moeller van den Bruck's notion of the Third Reich, insofar as it conceived of a redemptive, world-historical mission for the German people. Yet van Emsen's vision differed in one important sense. Conceived nearly a decade *after* Moeller's book, it reflected the fact that the Third Reich was no longer available as a signifier for his desired utopia, having already been appropriated by the Nazi Party. Van Emsen thus had to refer to his future vision as a *Fourth* Reich, which could only be established in the wake of its still-to-be-created Nazi predecessor.

In mapping out this process, van Emsen employed a dialectical philosophy of history, predicting that Germany's future would be determined by a series of revolutionary events initiated by none other than Adolf Hitler. As the "drummer of the German revolution," Hitler was destined to heal Germany's chronic class, religious, and racial divisions by establishing a "Prussian–Greater German Third Reich" that would finally reconcile nationalism and socialism, and integrate the "fourth estate" (the proletariat) into the "social organism."[56] Yet while van Emsen saw Hitler as "the beginning of a turning point," he was merely "the symbol of the transitional phase"; "once his role is fulfilled," van Emsen wrote, "others will follow in his place."[57] Hitler's "small German revolution" would merely be a particularistic, "*völkisch*" prelude to the more universal "world revolution" that was due to come at the end of the twentieth century (Figure 1.3).[58] This would bring about the "great rebirth" that would heal Germany's historic religious divisions by creating a new "Communistic-Christian brotherhood" and facilitating the emergence of the "Fourth Reich, the Reich of God."[59]

This process would entail a violent, Nietzschean process of creative destruction. "The last bastions of the past," van Emsen declared, "will have to be entirely destroyed" before the Fourth Reich could emerge.[60] Quoting the *Elder Edda* from Old Norse poetry, he wrote that the Germans would have to suffer "through the deepest depths of hell" and make it through the "era of the axe [*Beilzeit*]" before they arrived at the "the era of healing [*Heilzeit*]."[61] In the initial era, the Germans would forge a nationally unified colonial empire in Central and Eastern Europe "through blood and iron."[62] But, thereafter, they would pursue a more peaceful process of cultural unification, in which they would "build bridges" to "Hindu cultural circles" in Asia and connect with "the oldest spiritual and religious homeland of the 'Aryans.'"[63] The result would be the establishment of a final "Armanist–Atlantic Reich of the German Nation" and the creation of a "new humanity."[64] As he mystically put it:

> Today, we are experiencing the catastrophic transition from the Age of Pisces to the Age of Aquarius. We stand at an eonic turning point, as in the age of Jesus's birth … when an ancient world declined and a new one arose: that of the Christian Occident. After two thousand years, another rise and fall is upon us: the decline of the West and the rise of the new Atlantic world. It is the role of the Third Reich to dismantle the dying remnants of the occident. It is the task of the Fourth Reich to help form the new Atlantic cultural world.[65]

The Fourth Reich would ultimately inaugurate an era of universal peace, a "Pax teutonica." A "new earth" would emerge and Germany would be its "guardian angel."[66]

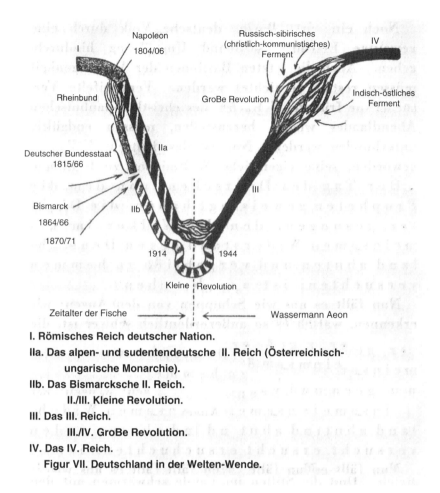

I. Römisches Reich deutscher Nation.
IIa. Das alpen- und sudentendeutsche II. Reich (Österreichisch-
    ungarische Monarchie).
IIb. Das Bismarcksche II. Reich.
    II./III. Kleine Revolution.
III. Das III. Reich.
    III./IV. GroBe Revolution.
IV. Das IV. Reich.
    Figur VII. Deutschland in der Welten-Wende.

Figure 1.3 Kurt van Emsen's 1932 book, *Adolf Hitler and Those Who are Still to Come*, mystically prophesied a Fourth Reich. This biomorphic diagram entitled "Germany in World Transition" (p. 129), portrays Germany's evolution through four phases of existence: "I) the Holy Roman Empire of the German Nation; IIa) the Alpine and Sudeten-German Second Empire (Austro-Hungarian Monarchy); IIb) the Bismarckian Second Empire (small revolution); III) the Third Reich (great revolution); IV) the Fourth Reich."

After 1933: The Fourth Reich in Foreign Incubation

It is unknown how widely van Emsen's book was read, but it provided an enduring slogan for anti-Nazis after 1933. German émigrés were the first to promote the concept of a Fourth Reich. An early figure in this effort was the Bavarian Catholic aristocrat, Prince Hubertus zu Loewenstein (1906–84). Scholars have claimed that Loewenstein promoted the idea of a "post-Nazi Fourth Reich" in several books he wrote after leaving Germany for Los Angeles in 1933.[67] Loewenstein was an active figure in German-American circles, helping to found the Hollywood Anti-Nazi League in 1936 and writing numerous books in support of a future Reich. But he never referred to his future Germany as a Fourth Reich; instead, he viewed it as a reformed Third Reich. In his 1934 book, *After Hitler's Fall: Germany's Coming Reich,* Loewenstein made clear from the outset that "after the collapse of the present pseudo-Reich, we must be ready for the true Coming Third Reich; that is, the third historical incarnation in a people of the Idea of the West."[68] In explaining his rationale for this future state, Loewenstein traced the idea of the Reich back to ancient Rome and defined it in platonic terms as the idea of a "European cultural community" committed to a vision of "universal responsibility towards humanity."[69] As embodied in the Holy Roman Empire, it was devoted to the Christian idea of "service and love," a fact that explained why the Nazis' Third Reich "has no connection to it," since "the idea of the Reich can never be realized where violence rules ... [and] freedom and justice have been destroyed."[70] The coming Reich would thus be a spiritual idea predicated on the "universal brotherhood of man."[71] As was true of Moeller van den Bruck's earlier vision of the Third Reich, Loewenstein believed that Germany would have "a special part to play" in creating it. Just as the country led the Holy Roman Empire for one thousand years, Germany would be responsible for guarding the essential idea of the Reich – "the content of the West" – and serving the future of Europe by laying a foundation of peace, freedom, and justice.[72]

In contrast to the conservative Loewenstein, other supporters of the Fourth Reich hailed from the left-liberal wing of the political spectrum. One of the most outspoken was the journalist and former SPD Reichstag representative, Georg Bernhard (Figure 1.4). In 1933, Bernhard left Germany for Paris, where he helped establish the major German exile newspaper, the *Pariser Tageblatt.* As editor, Bernhard was devoted to the paper's mission of being "a sharp spiritual weapon of the Germans living abroad against the barbarism [*Unkultur*] of the Third Reich."[73] Much of his work was devoted to alerting the western powers about the Nazis' aggressive foreign policy goals and "unveiling the lie" underpinning Nazi propaganda. But Bernhard also saw himself as part

Figure 1.4 While in French exile in the years 1935–37, the Jewish journalist and former SPD Reichstag representative Georg Bernhard collaborated with other German émigrés to produce a "Draft of a Constitution for the Fourth Reich." He hoped that this future Germany would be committed to "global democracy and equality" (Source: Wikimedia Commons).

of an exiled "intellectual vanguard" that could formulate a political alternative to National Socialism.[74] In the years 1935–37, he partici-pated with other leading émigrés – including Heinrich Mann, Lion Feuchtwanger, and Konrad Heiden – in the larger, communist-sponsored effort to bring leftist and liberal forces together into an anti-

Nazi *Volksfront*.[75] As part of this effort, Bernhard and his fellow journalist, Leopold Schwarzschild, were appointed to a subcommittee known as the Lutetia commission and volunteered to produce draft constitutions for a new Germany.[76]

Significantly, Bernhard called his version a "Draft of a Constitution for the Fourth Reich."[77] The highly detailed document was liberal in its principles, being committed to "freedom of conscience ... and the equality of all classes and races." It was furthermore devoted to "purging all signs of [Nazi] barbarism" from the future state, insisting that "no one will be able to hold office in the Fourth Reich who was a leader of the Nazi party."[78] The document included many details about the reorganization of the military, bureaucracy, judiciary, school system, and economy. Linking all of these recommendations was a rejection of violence. "The Fourth Reich," according to Bernhard's document, would be "a Reich of Peace" that rejected any form of "pan-German nationalism" and "colonial policy" as "criminal." Instead, it committed itself to "global democracy and equality."[79] Predictably, Bernhard's document, like Schwarzschild's "draft constitution" of the same period, sparked vigorous debate among the *Volksfront*'s liberal and communist factions.[80] But it was ultimately moot, for, as long as the Nazis remained in power, the draft constitution remained a dead letter.[81]

The idea of the Fourth Reich was not merely political. The fact that both Bernhard and Schwarzschild – like many other exile journalists – were Jews showed how the idea also came to acquire a Jewish inflection.[82] In this period, German Jews generally viewed the idea of a Fourth Reich with a degree of hope and, at times, even humor. German-Jewish refugees, in particular, were naively hopeful that Hitler's fall was imminent and tried to see the positive aspects of their plight. Among the many German-Jewish immigrants who fled to the United States, many congregated in New York City, especially in Washington Heights.[83] At a certain point in the late 1930s, the area acquired the nickname "The Fourth Reich." The nickname's precise origins are unknown, but it appears that German Jews themselves bestowed the appellation on their new neighborhood – albeit in "facetious," "ironic," or "sarcastic" fashion.[84] That said, the name's significance probably went deeper than what Ernest Stock, after the war, called "heavy-handed jocosity."[85] There is little doubt that the phrase represented something of a coping mechanism. German Jews in

Washington Heights strove to preserve as many of their cultural traditions as they could in their new home. By calling their neighborhood the Fourth Reich, German-Jewish refugees employed black humor in linking their new home to the one they had fled.[86] This is suggested by the appearance of a well-known "whisper joke" (*Flüsterwitz*) during the Nazi era that went as follows: "A Jew visits one of his relatives who succeeded in immigrating to New York. To his surprise he found a portrait of Hitler in the living room. Inquiring into the meaning of its presence, he was told by the owner 'it's to ward off homesickness.'"[87] In light of this reality, the ironic nickname, "Fourth Reich," can be seen as reflecting German Jews' hope that Nazi regime would be finite in duration.

This hope informed some of the references to the Fourth Reich that appeared in the Jewish press in the 1930s. In the fall of 1935, the American Jewish Labor leader and manager of the *Forward* newspaper, Baruch Charney Vladeck, confidently proclaimed that the Third Reich of the Nazis would soon be replaced by a more progressive state composed of democratic forces. Asserting that the "Socialist movement in Europe ... is definitely recovering from the first shock ... of Hitlerism and ... has taken the offensive," he predicted the rise of a "mass movement" of labor and liberal elements against fascism. The upshot, he predicted, was that "The Fourth Reich ... is going to be a union of labor and the middle classes, based on equality and democracy."[88] The same kind of hope found expression the following year in an essay published in the weekly American-based German-Jewish newspaper, the *Aufbau*. In January 1936, the paper published a futuristic fictional recap of a New Year's Eve Celebration in New York City in 1956. After describing the imaginary event, which included a live "television broadcast of the first act of Wagner's Parsifal from the great National Opera of Tel Aviv," the report optimistically noted that "among the attendees ... were German General Consul, Dr. Wolfgang Isidor Nathan ... accompanied by the chief editor of the New York *Staatszeitung*, Dr. Hadubrand Krause, whose courageous support for democracy and socialism in the Fourth Reich has earned him all of our sympathy."[89] By showing Germans and Jews as having reconciled with one another, the *Aufbau* presented an appealing fantasy of German-Jewish reconciliation. This hope was articulated with an added dose of defiance in another *Aufbau* article published in August of 1939. Occasioned by the Nazis' removal of a statue of the philosemitic eighteenth-century

Enlightenment thinker, Gotthold Ephraim Lessing, from Vienna's Judenplatz, the article resolutely declared: "And rightly so! The author of *Nathan* [*the Wise*] does not need to be a hero for the Nazis," adding that the crime would be rectified "only in the Fourth Reich!"[90] Finally, the hopes that Jews associated with the idea of the Fourth Reich were expressed in Rabbi (and later US Naval Chaplain) Charles Shulman's book, *Europe's Conscience in Decline* (1939). In the volume, which was an indictment of contemporary antisemitism, Shulman empathetically wrote that the Jews of Germany "thought that with the end of the [First] World War ... hate had come to an end. They realized that they were again mistaken as they witnessed the rise of Hitler ... In Germany and in exile they have not accepted the Nazi regime as the Germany envisaged by their ultimate hopes. They are waiting for the Fourth Reich."[91] In Jewish usage, in short, the Fourth Reich symbolized the hope for an ideal future version of Germany.

Once the war began, moreover, the Jewish press predicted that the next German Reich would be a progressive state. To ensure this possibility, some newspapers insisted that any future peace settlement would need to avoid the problems of the Treaty of Versailles and treat Germany leniently instead of punitively. In 1940, Ben Mordecai declared in the *Jewish Advocate* that, "despite all that we have suffered at Hitler's hands ... if we insist on shackling the new Germany ... the Fourth Reich, with a huge bill for all the sins and depredations of its predecessor government, we shall succeed only in making impossible a normal life for that unfortunate country ... Agitators will then ... point out that it is Jews who are retarding the reconstruction of Germany."[92] This stance of self-restraint may seem surprising in light of subsequent Jewish demands after 1945 to punish Germany for its wartime crimes. But at the time that Mordecai was writing, the worst of the Nazi regime's persecutions of the Jews had not yet taken place. Moreover, American Jews were sensitive to the charge that they were "warmongers" trying to embroil President Franklin D. Roosevelt's administration in a foreign war opposed by American isolationists. Articles in the Jewish press thus endeavored to appear optimistic about a future Fourth Reich.

A similar aversion to vengeance was expressed in a fantasy story written by Martin Panzer and published in the *Jewish Exponent* in the spring of 1941 about "what might happen to Hitler after the war is over." Panzer's vision was a mild one in which the Führer received a mere slap on the wrist for his crimes. Set in a future world "three months after the peace treaty ... and five months after ... the Fourth Reich had begun to function almost smoothly," the new German government captures Hitler and puts him on trial for his crimes. Weeks of testimony and cross-examination ensue, but the unexpected result is that Hitler emerges as "a pathetic figure in his loneliness," so much so, that people begin to view him as "an underdog." When the time comes to announce the verdict, Hitler is found guilty but merely given a suspended sentence. Surprisingly, few people find the sentence unjust, for they regard "the old wreck" as essentially "powerless." The fantasy ends with a scene of poetic, if farcical, justice:

> Several producers offered Hitler fat sums to appear on the stage and on the screen. From a large insurance company came an offer of fifty thousand dollars annually if Hitler would accept a vice-presidency. But Hitler heeded none of the offers. He rented a little room over a delicatessen shop and wrote interminably. Around him grew a small party called the Future German Party. A policeman stood guard before the building to protect him.[93]

Panzer's tale was far from prescient in predicting Hitler's postwar reputation. But it underscored American Jewish sensitivities at a time when their country was still neutral and their loyalties still suspect. By portraying themselves as being willing to forgive Germany for its crimes and trust the new postwar government to pursue the cause of justice, American Jews endorsed the idea of a Fourth Reich.

The Fourth Reich in Germany: Visions from the Right

Back in Germany, the effort to imagine a Fourth Reich emerged from a very different wing of the political spectrum. Prior to the eruption of the Second World War, most alternatives to the Nazi regime were conceived in right-wing circles. One of the most prominent visions of a future Reich was advanced by the renegade ex-Nazi Otto Strasser (Figure 1.5). Strasser joined the NSDAP in 1925 but quit in 1930, believing that Hitler had abandoned the party's socialist principles in favor of an alliance with reactionary capitalist forces. Strasser went on to found the "Black Front" splinter movement to promote what he believed was a genuine form of "German Socialism." The Black Front

Figure 1.5 Otto Strasser, seen here in Parisian exile in 1939, broke with the Nazi Party in 1930 to form the "Black Front" splinter movement, which he hoped would oust Hitler from power and establish a new German Reich (Source: Getty Images).

has long been seen as belonging to the "conservative revolutionary" or "National Bolshevik" camp by virtue of its desire to blend nationalist and socialist principles.[94] Not surprisingly, Strasser's organization ran afoul of the Nazis soon after their seizure of power in 1933. Following the murder of his brother, the longtime Nazi second-in-command, Gregor Strasser, on the Night of the Long Knives (June 30, 1934), Otto escaped to Czechoslovakia before moving to Paris in 1939. In 1940, he left Europe entirely, eventually settling in Canada, where he remained for the duration of the Second World War. During this period, Strasser received considerable attention in the English-speaking world as the ruler of a possible Fourth Reich thanks to several books published in 1940: his own autobiographical volume, *Hitler and I*, and British journalist Douglas Reed's sympathetic biography, *Nemesis? The Story of Otto Strasser and the Black Front*.[95]

Strasser did not explicitly refer to a "Fourth Reich" in his writings, but he nonetheless came to be associated with the concept in Great Britain and the US thanks to Reed's repackaging of Strasser's political vision. Reed employed the idea of a new Reich throughout

Nemesis?, claiming that Strasser "often spoke of the new Germany that he would like to build as The Fourth Reich."[96] Reed personally believed that the future state would be better served by an entirely "new name ... than a revised edition of discredited old one," but he nevertheless endorsed the idea of a Fourth Reich in discussing Strasser's agenda.[97] Reed explicitly supported Strasser's goal of overthrowing Hitler and building up a "new order" by employing the Black Front to launch a "revolution from above" and create a "German Socialism."[98] Drawing on Strasser's 1930 book, *The Structure of German Socialism* (which was updated and published in English in 1940 as *Germany Tomorrow*), Reed explained that the Black Front's vision for the new Reich entailed a mix of radical and reactionary policies, including the abolition of private property and the reintroduction of guilds; an authoritarian political system ruled by a Reich president appointed for life; and a federal structure with a diminished role for Prussia. Finally, the new Germany would reject Hitler's "repugnant" methods of solving the "Jewish question" by enabling Jews to "lead a dignified existence," while simultaneously limiting their "immoderate ... influence."[99]

Strasser himself did not describe this vision as a Fourth Reich, but he implied that the future German state could be considered as such. He frequently noted that Germany after Hitler would continue to be a Reich.[100] In *Hitler and I*, Strasser recalled how, in a discussion with Hitler two decades earlier in 1920, the latter claimed to constitute the Third Reich himself, to which Strasser replied: "No ... Möller van den Bruck said the First Reich was Charlemagne's Christian and federal Holy Roman Empire, the second was that of William and Bismarck, and the third must again be federal, Christian, and European."[101] Like Hubertus zu Loewenstein, Strasser believed that a future German Reich had to be part of a broader European community. For this reason, he committed himself to fighting the chief enablers of Hitler's version of National Socialism – "Pan-German industrialists ... [and] Prussian Junkers" – and pledged eternal loyalty to what he called the true "National Socialist Programme" of "making Germany a member of the great European family."[102] In so doing, Strasser sought the support of the German people. Arguing that "ten million human beings [in Germany] have suffered personally from Hitler's methods," he predicted that the Germans were primed to support "a national and social revolution" by "destroying the roots of ... Pan-Germanism" and pursuing "the spirit of European unity ... [instead] of European domination."[103]

Yet while Strasser may not have personally employed the Fourth Reich as a phrase in his own writings, others associated him with it. As early as 1930, the German media mockingly described his split with Hitler as part of "Strasser's Third or Fourth Reich."[104] Similar accusations came from Nazi circles as well. In 1935, the SS journal, *Das Schwarze Korps*, attacked Strasser – who was then in Czech exile – for accepting funds from German émigrés in Prague, declaring that "in order to camouflage his financial sources ... Strasser is collecting 'building stones' for his 'Fourth Reich' [that will] ... be 'paid back' as soon as the 'Black Front' has seized power."[105] Finally, Anglo-American reviews of *Hitler and I, Germany Tomorrow*, and *Nemesis?* echoed the assessment of *The New York Times* that Strasser was pursuing the goal of "forming a Fourth Reich."[106]

Beyond Strasser, other dissident Nazis, conservative revolutionaries, and National Bolsheviks were linked to the prospect of a Fourth Reich. One of the most prominent was the radical SA leader, Ernst Röhm. Prior to the Night of the Long Knives, Röhm was rumored to be planning a new Reich as part of an alleged rebellion against Hitler's rule. That, at least, was the contention of Hermann Goering, who, at the Nuremberg Trials in March of 1946, claimed that "a few weeks before the Röhm Putsch, a low-ranking SA leader confided in me that ... an action against the Führer ... was being planned to replace the Third Reich as expeditiously as possible by a final Fourth Reich, an expression that these people used."[107] It is difficult to know whether Goering was being truthful or merely trying to justify Röhm's murder after the fact. But his claim was not merely a postwar projection. Already in 1934, Otto Strasser himself insisted that "Röhm was only a military man. He knew nothing at all about politics. To say he was plotting a Fourth Reich is to give him an importance he never possessed."[108]

Apart from the SA, other supporters of the Nazi Party's socialist principles were linked to the possibility of a Fourth Reich. In 1941, *The New York Times* reported that the one-time Nazi supporter and conservative revolutionary, Hermann Rauschning, was planning to "erect a Christian Fourth Reich built on a traditional conservative, legitimate base."[109] For his part, Rauschning used the phrase in his 1941 book, *The Conservative Revolution*, observing, with considerable self-pity, that the future German state would seek to scapegoat Prussia for the rise of Nazism, concluding: "We Prussians are destined to the be Jews of the Fourth Reich."[110] Around the same time, the former left-winger turned National Bolshevik, Ernst Niekisch, was described as having "advocated the creation of a 'Fourth Reich' that would … eliminate all bourgeois elements and … cooperate with Soviet Russia."[111] Finally, the right-wing writer Ernst von Salomon was described in 1944 as a "prophet of the Fourth Reich" who, after the war, hoped to establish a regime along National Bolshevik lines.[112]

Beyond these radical representatives, traditional conservatives flirted with the idea of a Fourth Reich as part of a restored monarchy. In the fall of 1933, the *Vossische Zeitung* used the convening of the German Catholic Congress in Vienna as an opportunity to condemn certain "troubadors" who were allegedly hoping to create a Habsburg-led "fourth Reich" under the rule of Archduke Otto.[113] Several years later, as Hitler was developing plans for Austria's annexation, Joseph Goebbels' newspaper, *Der Angriff*, condemned the prospect of a Habsburg return to power, accusing Archduke Otto of plotting to "destroy the unity of Germany and wait in Vienna as the future monarch of a Catholic 'Fourth Reich.'"[114] Such claims in Nazi government newspapers are difficult to corroborate and should be viewed with suspicion, given how the regime instrumentally used the phrase to discredit political opponents. But they explain how the Fourth Reich developed into an anti-Nazi term in Germany.

This trend was further visible in reports of plans allegedly being hatched by the German military. In 1935, Gestapo agents anxiously reported that Reichswehr veterans were overheard chanting a martial poem ending with the lines: "In the Third Reich we are marching, in the Fourth Reich we will be ruling!"[115] That same year, the English-language press reported that, among "younger members" of conservative military circles, there was "talk of a Fourth Reich in which the Reichswehr and Stahlhelm would rule with a General as Chancellor."[116] Other stories quoted German military officers grumbling about Nazi interference in the army and predicting that "once we have sufficient young men in our ranks and [can] … teach them our point of view, we shall have taken a great step towards a Fourth Reich."[117] Such reports reflected the Allied fantasy that the Nazis could be toppled internally without going to war. Even after hostilities began in the fall of 1939, such wishes continued to be expressed. Following Georg Elser's failed assassination attempt against Hitler on November 8, 1939, the British press speculated that, if the attempt had succeeded, Hermann Goering would have "formed a temporary Government" and "asked the Allies to stop the war in order to facilitate the task of reorganizing the 'Fourth Reich.'"[118]

As the Second World War progressed, the German resistance increasingly embraced the idea of the Fourth Reich as a galvanizing principle. Members of the liberally oriented Bosch Circle around German industrialist Robert Bosch (1861–1942) employed the idea of a new Reich in secret meetings with American consular officials to help the anti-Nazi resistance bring an early end to the war.[119] The Cologne-based Catholic resistance did so as well, as was shown by the invocation of a Fourth Reich by the Dominican provincial Laurentius Siemer and the Jesuit priest Alfred Delp, both of whom led vigorous discussions about the principles underpinning a post-Nazi state.[120] Former Leipzig mayor and member of the Kreisau Circle, Carl Goerdeler, was widely reported to be the designated chancellor of the Fourth Reich.[121] The American Office of War Information (OWI) official and later political scientist Gabriel Almond reported that, in 1944, an anti-Nazi resistance group in Dresden sent an anonymous letter to local Nazi officials bearing the signature "The Provisional Government of the Fourth Reich."[122] Finally, near the war's end, Wehrmacht officer and resistance member Hans Bernd Gisevius wrote in his diary that the foreign intelligence chief of the Nazi Security Service (SD), Walter Schellenberg, was "seeking to link up to the opposition ... [and] save himself by going over to the Fourth Reich."[123]

The concept of the Fourth Reich allowed ordinary Germans to practice a more subtle form of oppositional *Resistenz*. The famed Dresden literature professor and diarist Victor Klemperer pointed out how the concept had found its way into popular, anti-regime "whisper jokes."[124] While temporarily imprisoned in late June of 1941, Klemperer recalled that "a very old Third Reich joke ... gave me real consolation. Questionnaire of the fourth Reich: 'When were you imprisoned under the previous government? If not, why?'"[125] The joke's appeal was clear; it expressed the hope that in the near future, the Nazis' warped conception of criminality would be reversed and a proper moral balance reestablished. Other Germans used the Fourth Reich as a symbol of perseverance. In her memoir, *Berlin Underground*, the journalist and resistance figure Ruth Andreas-Friedrich recalled an exchange she had in the spring of 1941 with her friends Erich and Karla

Tuch, who were due to leave Berlin for a Foreign Office assignment in the Far East. In saying farewell, Mr. Tuch started to say, "We'll be seeing you in … " before being overcome with emotion and failing to complete his sentence. In response, Andreas-Friedrich thought to herself: " … the Fourth Reich, we finish silently for him. And nod to show him we understand."[126] These and other encounters in Andreas-Friedrich's memoir showed how the prospect of a new Reich bound the opponents of the Hitler regime to one another.[127]

The growing association of the Fourth Reich with the anti-Hitler resistance predictably prompted the Nazis to suppress it. In 1934, government officials disparaged talk "about an imminent Fourth Reich" as "emigrants' drivel."[128] Several years later, the authorities began using more strident language. On March 4, 1936, in a speech in Altona, Gauleiter Wilhelm Kube warned "those who dream of a Fourth Reich" that they "no longer have any say in our Volk's destiny," adding that "the 'Fourth Reich' has been suspended for all time behind the walls of the concentration camps."[129] Still later, the Nazis tried to suppress the idea with more punitive measures. In 1940, the British press published a story (perhaps apocryphal) of how a German musician was taking a state qualification examination when she was asked the question: "What will come after the Government of the Third Reich in Germany?" The newspaper story went on to report: "Having a sense of humour, she wrote 'The Fourth Reich' and was failed as a result. The answer that she should have given was 'I do not know what will come after eternity.'"[130] More ominously, in 1944, the Nazi *Volksgerichtshof* sentenced White Rose member Hans Leipelt to death for his anti-Nazi activities, including his eagerness to "disparage National Socialism" by drafting and publicizing a satirical "Questionnaire in the Fourth Reich."[131]

As the war dragged on, the Nazis employed the concept of the Fourth Reich more aggressively as a propaganda weapon. They especially used it to instill a fighting spirit in the German people by frightening them about Allied plans for vengeance. Claiming that Allied occupation plans for postwar Germany were driven by "an extermination program of international Jewry," the Nazi press predicted that "a Fourth Reich would not likely receive any better [peace] terms than the Third can expect."[132] In other reports, the regime emphasized Allied mercilessness by saying that "after the defeat of the Third Reich, neither a Fourth Reich, indeed nor any Reich of the Germans, would be permitted whatsoever."[133] These uses of the term were meant to counter the German people's eagerness to surrender to the Allies as the latter entered German territory. For good measure, the Nazis also used terror to extinguish any popular hope for the creation of a post-Nazi state. As the war wound down, foreign journalists reported on several occasions that the Nazis were seeking to "liquidat[e] ... all persons ... suspected of ... building up a Fourth Reich" or any other "capitulation regime."[134]

The Fourth Reich in the Allied Imagination

While the idea of the Fourth Reich was demonstrably anti-Nazi in Germany, its meaning in the Allied nations was more ambiguous. During the early and middle years of the war, many people used the term as a progressive designation for the next Germany. Yet, as the war wound down, certain critics began to associate the Fourth Reich with the prospect of a restored Nazi state. The diverging views about the nature of the Fourth Reich reflected the larger uncertainty within the Allied nations about how to treat Germany after the war's conclusion. During the last years of the conflict, debate raged within the American and British governments, the Anglo-American media, and the German exile community about whether to impose a soft or a hard peace on Germany. Much of the indecision reflected profound disagreement about the character of the German people – specifically, whether they were capable of democratic rehabilitation and should be treated mildly, or whether they were incorrigible militarists who should be punished for their crimes. In advancing their views, the supporters of each position employed different concepts of a Fourth Reich. The proponents of a soft peace tried to retain the concept's progressive meaning, insisting that Germany's turbulent twentieth-century history was the result of contingent factors and recommending that the country be reconstructed with a generous peace settlement. By contrast, proponents of a hard peace argued that the Germans were a rabidly militaristic and anti-democratic people who needed to be punished lest they establish a Fourth Reich and launch a Third World War.[135]

Proponents of a soft peace, especially among German émigrés, expressed their hopes in the English-language media by putting a positive spin on the idea of a Fourth Reich. In March of 1939, following the German occupation of Bohemia and Moravia, Otto

Sattler, the socialist émigré leader of the New York-based German-American League for Culture, expressed his shame about the "rape of Czecho-slovakia" and his hope that a revolution would help a "Fourth Reich . . . arise: a Reich for freedom and culture, united with mankind's tireless march towards . . . universal peace."[136] In the spring of 1940, *The New Leader* published the views of the left-wing Viennese journalist Johann Hirsch and the former Weimar-era Minister of the Interior, Wilhelm Sollmann, both of whom cautiously hoped that the "German socialists would . . . be given the opportunity, by a world tired of war, to build the Fourth Reich into a stable European center."[137] One year later, in his 1941 book, *Thinker versus Junker* (1941), the left-wing German journalist Will Schaber reprinted German novelist Heinrich Mann's 1931 essay, "Deutsche Entscheidung," with a new title: "Outlook on the Fourth Reich." In this short essay about Germany's political future, Mann – who, by then, had acquired the nickname as the "uncrowned President of the Fourth Reich" – equated the future German state with democracy, predicting that it would triumph "by fighting" against the Nazi regime and overthrowing it "in bloodshed."[138] Around the same time, Heinrich Mann's brother, the Nobel Prize-winning Thomas Mann, was described in *The New Yorker* as "the ideal president of the Fourth Reich, once the Nazis are defeated."[139] The German refugee socialists who produced the edited volume *The Next Germany* in 1943 assumed that Germany would enjoy a "democratic system of government in a Fourth Reich."[140] Finally, the German-Jewish (and later Catholic convert) émigré journalist R. G. Waldeck's 1943 book, *Meet Mr. Blank: The Leader of Tomorrow's Germans*, cautiously anticipated "a great future for liberalism in Germany" and predicted that faith in liberal ideas would be "strongest among the young who . . . will play the decisive role in the Fourth Reich."[141]

Many of these German exiles found support in American circles. Writing in *The Boston Globe*, the influential columnist, and later proponent of a soft peace, Dorothy Thompson cited unnamed Germans "who occupy important positions in the Third Reich . . . [and who] have been preparing to the [time] after Hitler" to assure her readers that "the Fourth Reich which they envisage is not Communist . . . [but rather] a democratic republic."[142] American journalist and Office of Strategic Services (OSS) officer Wallace Deuel asserted in *The New York Times* in 1944 that the postwar German state would be "a free and democratic

Fourth Reich with which the world can live in peace."[143] Finally, in February of 1945, the OSS's black propaganda project, "Operation Musac" (which beamed fake German-language pop songs from the British-based Soldatensender Calais, or "Soldiers' Radio Calais," into Germany), broadcast a new song entitled, "In the Fourth Reich," which concluded with the following upbeat lyrics:

> Yes, in the Fourth Reich
> the Lord God comes to stay
> while Goering moves away,
> for the Fourth Reich
> will be home to justice in time.
> Once the Nazis are broken,
> Germany will have awoken,
> and be resurrected as well,
> for in this lovely Fourth Reich,
> there'll be no more Goebbels, that lying cheat,
> no more radio spouting deceit,
> no more of Hitler's tantrum shouts,
> no more of Himmler's violent rubouts,
> no more of Schirach's bossy grief,
> no more of Ribbentrop, that thief,
> no more Rosenberg panting,
> or Ley's drunken ranting –
> in the Fourth Reich
> they all will go to straight to hell![144]

In contrast to these optimistic predictions, more skeptical observers feared that a future German Reich would be Nazi in orientation. Some were convinced that, as the war came to a close, the Nazi regime's leaders would not accept defeat but would go into hiding until they could return to power. In 1944, the German émigré writer Curt Riess's book, *The Nazis Go Underground*, warned that the Nazi Party leadership would abstain from violently resisting the Allied occupation in favor of establishing "underground cells" of party loyalists who could infiltrate postwar German life and undermine it from within.[145] According to Riess, Heinrich Himmler had already assembled "a group of some 200,000 to 300,000 men" in Germany and "an army of millions of sympathizers" in countries such as Argentina and Spain.[146] Their job was to wait "until the world has had time to forget what the Nazis did in Germany," at which point they could begin "whisper[ing] of the good old times ... under Hitler" until the time came to strike.[147] Riess was unwilling to predict who would be "the head man in the Fourth Reich," but he had no doubt that the Nazi leadership's ultimate goal was "to come to power so ... they can start World War III."[148]

The same suspicion informed British journalist Gordon Young's fictional essay from 1944, "Mein Zweiter Kampf."[149] Published in the London *Daily Express,* the essay speculated what a second volume of *Mein Kampf* would look like if Hitler were to write it. In the imaginary text, Hitler soberly identifies the varied reasons for Germany's military defeat ("bad intelligence," insufficient resources, and the like), but shrewdly outlines a plan "for every loyal German to work ... for the third and final conflict which will at last give the Reich world power." Arguing that Germany failed to achieve this end via military force, Hitler declares that "The Fourth Reich will have to succeed ... by appearing to be more democratic than the democracies" themselves. "In the guise of promoting world science and culture," Germany would send forth its cultural and intellectual elite "to every international congress," but would simultaneously work to spy "on what our enemies do and say." Ex-military men would fraternize with their foreign colleagues, while the "General Staff must work under cover" to "evolve new weapons of war." In the second volume of *Mein Kampf*, Hitler even concedes that "the New Germany will have to cultivate the favor of the Jews" by offering them "reinstatement, compensation, and support for all their claims." The ultimate goal, however, was clear: "while this new 'reformed' Germany holds up a giant mask to the world, we can organize at home our secret Fourth Reich, which will prepare our final war."

Riess's and Young's fears that postwar Nazis would act like wolves in sheep's clothing were shared by other Anglo-American observers. In June of 1944, Vincent Church wrote in the *Daily Mail* that "certain members of the Gestapo, the Party and the Army will ... go to ground ... and prepare in secret for a Fourth Reich."[150] In October of 1944, Maxwell McCartney and J. H. Freeman made the same point in *The Times Literary Supplement,* observing, "The Fourth Reich is already casting its shadow over the world, and at this moment the Germans are probably better prepared to win the third German war than are the allies to win the peace."[151] Similarly, American journalist

Barnet Nover saw the danger that a day would arise "when a new Hitler at the head of a Fourth Reich will launch a Third World War."[152]

Other observers warned that the Nazis would try to lay the foundation for a Fourth Reich by creating a mythologized view of Adolf Hitler. Following the failed July 20, 1944 assassination attempt against Hitler, OSS intelligence officer Wallace Deuel wrote to his boss, William Donovan, that "one of the most interesting ... angles of the past days' developments ... is that the Fourth Reich now has its alibi for the present war." In making this observation, Deuel implied that unrepentant Nazis would blame Germany's impending military defeat on "the disloyalty of a small group of traitorous generals" and would absolve Hitler of any political responsibility, thereby paving the way for his rehabilitation.[153] Similarly, in February of 1945, the British diplomat and hard peace supporter, Robert Vansittart, predicted that Hitler was destined for a mythic form of "stardom" in the postwar world because of the German people's penchant for charismatic, authoritarian leaders. Convinced that the Germans were unconcerned that "corporal Hitler ... failed as a Fuehrer," Vansittart warned that "he may be of great use as a Myth to back up a Fourth Fuehrer and a Fourth Reich," concluding that the word "Reich" should be entirely "prohibit[ed] if we are wise."[154]

Of all the warnings against the emergence of a Fourth Reich, however, the most strident was Austrian émigré writer Erwin Lessner's 1944 novel, *Phantom Victory* (Figure 1.6). Subtitled *The Fourth Reich, 1945–60*, the book was a frightening future history of a world in which the Nazis snatch victory from the jaws of defeat. As the novel opens, World War II is nearing its conclusion and the German leadership adopts a stance of superficial cooperation with the Allies. Leading this effort is a newly established fraternal order called the "Potsdam Bund," which is made up of the leaders of the German General Staff. The Bund instructs Wehrmacht soldiers to lay down their weapons and orders the German population to engage in passive resistance. Without having any army to negotiate with, the Allies forge a separate peace in exchange for the Germans abandoning their passive resistance. As a condition of the Pact, the Bund surrenders Hitler to Allied control, but, in a hint of future duplicity, he turns out to be a double. Unable to locate the real Führer, the Allies soon abandon the program of denazification. Although they compel ordinary Germans to fill out questionnaires about their past political behavior, the resulting 62 million forms is so large that

Figure 1.6 The Austrian writer Erwin Lessner's 1944 novel, *Phantom Victory*, was influential in associating the Fourth Reich with the fearsome prospect of a Nazi return to power (Source: Random House).

processing them would require "the legal machinery of the United Nations ... to suspend all its other tasks for five and a half generations."[155]

Against this unpromising backdrop, the novel goes on to show how Allied disagreement about occupying Germany paves the way for disaster. Two American journalists personify this disagreement: the cautious hard-liner Donald Donnelly, who wants to hold all Germans accountable for their nation's crimes, and the naively hopeful Rose Flag, who appeals to the German people in a radio broadcast to do penance and earn their rehabilitation. In response to Flag's appeal, the novel's central character, a modest but charismatic shepherd from the Taunus Mountains named Friedolin, emerges to lead a mass movement of German "penitents." Wearing recycled Swastika armbands "stamped over with a 'B'" for *büssen* (to atone), the members of the penitent movement gradually display quasi-Nazi traits, greeting each other with the salutation, "*Buss Heil!*" (Hail penance!). As a wave of contrition spreads across Germany, American officials become convinced that the country has sufficiently completed the process of self-examination to be ready for economic revival. The United States is particularly eager for this to take place as it remains at war with Japan and needs Germany's armaments to triumph in the Pacific theater.[156]

The US's dependence on Germany proves fatal, however, as it gives Friedolin the leverage he needs to gain power. Donald Donnelly is the first to recognize this threat, lamenting to a bartender midway through the novel "that we will give [Friedolin] whatever he demands – and we shall bleed in Asia while the Germans enrich themselves ... Then a new act in the Friedolin farce: the Fourth Reich. Every new Reich starts a war. I ask you to forgive my prophecy, but we don't win the Third World War."[157] Soon enough, Donnelly's fears become reality as Friedolin exploits the US's growing economic weakness to regain Germany's national sovereignty, forcing American troops to leave the country by 1947. Even though the US eventually defeats Japan, the country's indebtedness to Germany enables Friedolin's government to force economic union upon its European and African neighbors. Hailing the creation of "Eurafrica," Friedolin's "Council of Shepherds" in 1950 boasts that Germany "has accomplished by peaceful methods more than what former German governments dreamed of accomplishing by armed might!"[158] By 1952, Friedolin organizes a massive propaganda spectacle in a meadow near the Taunus Mountains, where he appears in shepherd's garb and announces the proclamation of the "Fourth and Eternal Reich."[159] Spouting new slogans such as "one flock, one pasture, one shepherd" and brandishing the new German emblem of "two shepherd's staffs crossed," the new Germany emerges as a latter-day version of the Nazi dictatorship.[160]

From this point on, the Allies experience an unending series of disasters. The new Reich uses its economic might to compel European, Asian, and Latin American nations to join its renamed "German Union," sponsors anti-colonial uprisings against the British Empire, and, by 1960, launches a successful military invasion of the United States. With "squadrons of enemy bombers ... spreading death and destruction" over American cities, Donald Donnelly frantically tries to mobilize resistance, but he is ultimately shot and killed by a pro-Nazi teenager in Manhattan's heavily German-populated neighborhood of Yorkville. As the novel concludes, Friedolin delivers a speech in "Greater Yorkville" (the new name for New York City) and reveals that he is a former SS man who trained for the day when the Nazis would return to power. He also announces the stunning news that Hitler is still alive and will soon be "taking his place at my side." In his final mocking comment, he boasts: "The re-educators wanted us to do penance. Now they reap what they sowed. They shall serve as our flocks for the duration of the Fourth Reich – for all eternity!"[161]

A blatantly propagandistic work of literature, *Phantom Victory* employed the concept of the Fourth Reich to garner American support for imposing a hard peace on postwar Germany. The novel was published at a pivotal time in American policymaking. Throughout 1944, American lobbying organizations, such as the hard-line Society for the Prevention of World War III, had been warning of another armed conflict with Germany unless the country's military might was permanently destroyed. Simultaneously, US government officials were contemplating the punitive Morgenthau Plan for Germany's deindustrialization. In this climate, *Phantom Victory* urged a punitive course. For his part, Lessner supported a tough peace for personal reasons. An Austrian journalist who had fought with Germany in World War I, he actively opposed the Nazi regime after Hitler's rise to power, eventually fleeing Austria in 1938 for Czechoslovakia and, later, Norway, where he was captured and tortured by the Gestapo. After escaping to the United States in 1941, he became a vocal spokesman for eradicating German militarism as a chief precondition for postwar peace.[162] Lessner's tough stance was visible in *Phantom Victory's* final chapter, which was comprised of a single sentence that read, "And for the rest, I say that Germany should be destroyed."[163] This allusion to Cato the Elder's famous remark, "*Carthago delenda est*" ("Carthage must be destroyed," which was uttered during the Punic Wars to express the Roman Republic's determination to eliminate Carthage as a future military threat), made clear that Lessner supported a Carthaginian peace for Germany that would prevent it from threatening the western powers. His nightmare of a Fourth Reich was meant to ensure that the future Germany would never become a revived Nazi state.

Phantom Victory enjoyed a wide and generally supportive reception. *The New York Times* praised the novel's plot as "exceedingly ingenious," while other journalists concluded that it "leaves the reader with the shuddery after-feeling of a particularly gruesome nightmare."[164] Not all reviews were positive: one commentator doubted that Lessner's call for Germany's destruction would "dispose ... of the spiritual menace that is Naziism," while another rejected his portrayal of American gullibility in the face of German penance, insisting they would be able "to see through the German game."[165] On the whole, however, critics appreciated Lessner's message of vigilance. *The Hartford Courant* wrote that *Phantom Victory* was "a healthful tonic for those who ... feel that the war is behind us and that we can move back into that dream-state which characterized our thinking before Pearl Harbor."[166] *Life Magazine* made a similar point, declaring in a prominent profile of the book in May of 1945 that its "fantastic predictions had jumped ... into today's ... headlines" and had "give[n] ... US readers ... plenty to think about."[167] These positive responses to *Phantom Victory* testified to its importance in alerting Americans to the potential danger of a Fourth Reich.

Conclusion

During the years of the Nazi dictatorship, and especially over the course of the Second World War, the idea of the Fourth Reich evolved dramatically as the signifier for an alternative Germany. The visions of this future state varied considerably. It was originally conceived at the beginning of the Nazi regime by a diverse array of Germans: foreign émigrés and domestic dissidents, Jews and Christians, liberals and conservatives, mainstream socialists and schismatic Nazis.

In most of their visions, the Fourth Reich represented a post-Nazi state linked to humanistic values and guided by the rule of law. The fact that the Nazi regime tried to suppress the concept made clear that the Fourth Reich was generally regarded as a progressive signifier that stood on the "right" side of history. With the outbreak of World War II, however, the concept underwent a transformation. Although the idea of a Fourth Reich retained support and was embraced by the German resistance, it also acquired new critics. As Allied victory became increasingly likely, observers in the Anglo-American world began to worry that the Nazis would not accept military defeat and would go underground in the hope of making an eventual comeback. The idea of the Fourth Reich thus became associated with future peril. In the ensuing occupation of Germany during the years 1945–49, these competing visions of Germany's future would continue to clash.

2 FROM WEREWOLVES TO DEMOCRATS: THE FOURTH REICH UNDER ALLIED OCCUPATION

> With the demise of the Prussian army, the German situation is now
> rather different from what it was in 1919, when the German High
> Command managed to survive the debacle . . . intact and went on . . . to
> regain control of the nation. This time . . . there is a golden chance for
> the anti-Nazi civilians to fill in the vacuum left by the Junkers and
> establish, once and for all, a non-militaristic, non-aggressive, non-
> imperialistic Fourth Reich.[1]
> *Commentary* (July 1, 1947)

> The French remind us that, if we let the Germans get back to their
> mines, their smokestacks and their test tubes, there is a danger of
> a Fourth Reich goose-stepping forth to war with weapons hidden
> again under smokestacks . . . A thousand years of French history make
> the reminder more than plausible. The danger is there.[2]
> *The Dallas Morning News* (June 27, 1947)

With the beginning of the Allied occupation of Germany, the
concept of the Fourth Reich entered a new phase of evolution. During
the years 1945 to 1949, disagreement persisted about how to view the
future German state. As is shown by the dueling newspaper editorials
above from the summer of 1947, some observers continued to associate
the Fourth Reich with a new, progressive Germany while others linked it
to a Nazi return to power. Both perspectives coexisted during the course
of the occupation. Over time, however, the latter gained increasing
influence over the former. Critical observers in Western Europe and

the United States cited ongoing Nazi activism in the American, British, and French occupation zones as evidence that a future Fourth Reich would be dictatorial in character. So did communist officials in the Soviet zone, many of whom used the concept to attack the "fascist" resurgence in the west. These charges, fueled by intensifying cold war tensions, led to a flurry of western counterclaims that an authoritarian Fourth Reich was actually emerging in communist-occupied eastern Germany. Yet, like the scattered efforts to preserve the concept's neutrality, these claims did not prevail. By the time that the West and East German states were created in the fall of 1949, the discourse had shifted. The concept of the Fourth Reich had become firmly linked to the prospect of a Nazi revival.

As we know today, these fears proved to be unfounded. No Nazi Fourth Reich ever came into existence during the occupation years. Instead, the transitional period ended with the creation of the liberal, democratic Federal Republic of Germany (FRG) and the communist German Democratic Republic (GDR). This outcome makes it easy to dismiss early postwar concerns as the product of irrational anxieties or cold war politics. That said, the concerns were not entirely groundless. While the prospect of a communist Fourth Reich was the chimerical product of a rhetorical war of words between east and west, the same cannot be said of the possibility of a Nazi Fourth Reich. There were more than a few genuine right-wing threats to the Allied effort to rebuild Germany into a democratic state in the years 1945–49. During the early occupation, unrepentant Nazis strove to exploit bleak postwar conditions for their own political ends, hatching various conspiracies to return to power. Thanks to quick Allied action, the conspiracies were suppressed. But their failure was not inevitable. By examining the plots' origins and speculating about how they might have unfolded differently, we can better appreciate the depth of early postwar fears and understand why history ultimately transpired as it did.

Debating the Prospect of a Fourth Reich

As the Allies set about occupying Germany, debate resumed about whether the country would eventually become a Fourth Reich. The debate had been intense already during the war years, but it was sharpened by early postwar tensions. From 1945 to 1947, the Allies struggled mightily to restore order in Germany. The overwhelming material destruction across the country – ruined cities, mangled infra-structure, acute food shortages – was daunting in its own right. But it was compounded by additional problems: mass social dislocation in the form of millions of German refugees, Jewish Holocaust survivors, and European slave laborers trying to find their way to old and new homes; acute economic desperation in the form of mass joblessness and poverty; and burgeoning political discontent over the Allies' punitive policies of denazification, demilitarization, and non-fraternization. Finally, a combustible mix of traumatic memories and emotions – humiliation, guilt, and denial – made for a volatile psychological and cultural cli-mate. It was against this dispiriting backdrop that postwar debate about the Fourth Reich resumed.

One reason for the debate was the ambiguity of the Reich's legal status following the war. With the surrender of German armed forces to the Allies on May 8, 1945, the Nazi regime of Adolf Hitler came to an ignominious end. The German Reich, however, technically continued to exist. For several weeks, Hitler's designated successor, Grand Admiral Karl Doenitz, presided as Reich President (*Reichspräsident*) over a caretaker "German Reich government" (*Deutsche Reichsregierung*) in Flensburg that enjoyed temporary Allied toleration (though not official recognition) until it was disbanded at Soviet insistence on May 23, 1945. Doenitz and his entire Reich cabinet was subse-quently imprisoned, and a power vacuum ensued until the Allies issued the Berlin Declaration of June 5, which formally stripped sovereignty from Germany and placed "supreme authority" in the hands of the four occupying powers. The Allies thereafter assumed that the Reich had ceased to exist and subsequently referred to "Germany" instead of the "Reich" in official documents. In daily life, however, most Germans acted as if the Reich survived: political parties, ranging from the Christian Democratic Union (CDU) to the Communist Party of Germany (KPD), drafted new platforms for the "Reich's" future, while ordinary citizens bought goods with Reichsmarks, journeyed by rail on the *Reichsbahn*, and followed various laws (*Reichsgesetze*) that implied the Reich's persistence.[3] Only in the years 1948–49 would the question of the Reich's formal existence be directly addressed – and even then, it would not be decisively resolved.

Given this initial ambiguity, early postwar observers often viewed the concept of a Fourth Reich in neutral, if not favorable, terms. Some used the phrase as a numerically logical, if hypothetical, placeholder to designate the Third Reich's eventual successor. Two days after VE Day, on May 10, 1945, a London-based correspondent for the Australian press reported: "It will be years before there is a Fourth Reich, because in the immediate future, Germany will be under Allied military occupation, which may conceivably continue as long as 10 years."[4] In July of 1945, the British press reported that the upcoming Potsdam conference would probably differ from the earlier Yalta conference, because the latter dealt with occupation plans while the former "will raise the issue ... of a 'Fourth Reich.'"[5] By September, *Time* magazine reported that the "outlines of a Fourth Reich" seemed to be emerging in occupied Germany.[6] The question of the future country's capital was a particular focus, with observers debating whether Berlin or some other German city "would ... become the capital of the 'Fourth Reich.'"[7] Germany's future borders were still undetermined, although one story identified the Oder-Neisse line as the "permanent eastern frontier of the Fourth Reich."[8] To some degree, the idea of the future Reich was still being shaped by outside influences. Reporting on the ongoing Allied effort "to settle Germany's future" at the Moscow foreign minister's conference in March of 1947, *The New York Times* realistically acknowledged that the participants were all seeking "to fashion the Fourth Reich more or less in their own image."[9] Less than two years into the occupation, the concept remained an open-ended abstraction.

By contrast, more pessimistic observers cast the idea of a Fourth Reich in a more negative light and portrayed the future Germany as beholden to the destructive traditions of militarism, imperialism, and nationalism. On VE Day, *The Cleveland Plain Dealer* celebrated the Allies' victory, but warned that "confronting a revived and rearmed Fourth Reich" would remain the one of major challenges facing "the next generation of the free world."[10] A few weeks later, *The New York Times* noted that there was a consensus among the Allies "that Berlin, cradle of German imperialism, shall never again rise from its ashes as the capital of a Fourth Reich."[11] Nearly a year into the occupation, however, growing Allied squabbling and the growth of a "German national movement" led the British Foreign Minister, Anthony Eden, to warn that "it will not be long before Germans think that they see in Allied disunity the Fourth Reich's opportunity."[12] Those who feared this prospect did not always agree on how it might manifest itself. The British journalist Sefton Delmer predicted that the effort to "build up Germany into a new ... militant Fourth Reich" would be "based on Vienna instead of Berlin."[13] By contrast, the French President of the Pan European Union, Richard Coudenhove-Kalergi, worried about a German-dominated European Union, noting in 1946 that "none of Germany's neighbors would be willing to join a European federation around a Fourth Reich ... out of the fear that it might resume the policies of its predecessors."[14]

The most acute fear, however, was that the Fourth Reich could be used as a rallying concept by intransigent Nazis. In his posthumously published book, *Hitler and Beyond* (1945), the politician and former Weimar-era government minister Erich Koch-Weser (1875–1944) warned that stubborn "elements among the German people" were refusing to recognize "the blood guilt of National Socialism" and continuing to "dream of a fourth Reich to endure a thousand years."[15] Similar concerns were expressed one year later at the Nuremberg Trials in 1946, when the Soviet media criticized the Allied military tribunal for allowing convicted Nazi war criminals to make farewell speeches before their executions, declaring that they could create a "new myth for a Fourth Reich."[16] These concerns were later amplified in the fall of 1946, when the press reported the sensational news that one of the main defendants at Nuremberg, Hitler's former deputy, Rudolf Hess, was secretly "drawing up plans for Fourth Reich."[17]

Many of these comments were made in passing, but there were also sustained reflections on the dangers of a right-wing Fourth Reich. One of the first appeared in 1946 with the publication of Swiss historian Friedrich Gaupp's book, *Deutsche Fälschung der abendländischen Reichsidee* (*The German Falsification of the Occidental Idea of the Reich*).[18] An effort to address the serious challenges facing the early postwar world, Gaupp's study sought to debunk what he believed was the dangerous idea of the German Reich. While he believed that the "aggressive military state" of Germany had been destroyed in the war, he asserted that the idea of "the German Reich" had survived and retained the capacity to cause mayhem.[19] "Does one not realize what a mystical, religious, irrational allure the word 'Reich' has long possessed?" he asked.[20] Convinced of its inherent destructiveness, Gaupp argued that "it is high time to clearly expose the ... Reich idea ... [as] one of the greatest falsifications of history ... ever foisted upon humanity."[21]

To expose the lie, he offered a historical survey of the Reich idea's evolution from the ancient empire of Alexander the Great to the modern dictatorship of Nazi Germany. For Gaupp, the fateful moment came in the Middle Ages, when German nationalism corrupted the original notion of the Reich as a non-partisan, transnational, and culturally cosmopolitan entity. Thanks to the "coup" launched by the Saxon king, Otto I, in 962, the Reich was transfigured from a universal, humanistic concept into a particularistic German one, a trend that culminated with Prussia's authoritarian appropriation of the Reich idea in 1871.[22] Through this process, Gaupp argued, "the greatest ... lie in all of western history" took shape: namely, the notion that "the continental Reich idea was a German idea" that "justified the Germans' claim to rule over other peoples and races."[23] This development had catastrophic consequences. "In the hands of the Germans," Gaupp wrote, "the notion of the Reich became the mortal enemy of everyone."[24] "No other idea today ... is so associated with guilt, blood, destruction, and inhuman crimes as the concept of the Reich."[25] Having "cost millions of people their lives," the idea had to be eliminated.[26] The "concept of the Reich," he concluded, "does not deserve to survive. Even the word should not be permitted to be used."[27]

Yet, despite his warnings, Gaupp feared that postwar Germans might nevertheless flirt with the possibility of a Fourth Reich. Part of the threat emanated from the laxity of the Allies. Although they controlled Germany, he argued, "it is to be feared that they underestimate [the Reich idea's] ... power to survive."[28] For this reason, he asked, "how can one hope to democratically 'reeducate' the Germans" or "pursue the creation of a Federated Republic of European states" as long as one permits "the phantom ... of the 'Reich' to survive?"[29] There was little doubt that the Germans "will remain dangerous as long as they are allowed to call themselves a 'Reich.'"[30] He was particularly concerned that a "new falsification" of the Reich idea might take hold "in the minds of younger generations" and manifest itself in a successor state.[31] As he put it, the possibility existed that "out of the physical and psychological collapse of the Third Reich, at some point a fourth Reich will emerge, a new embodiment of the transnational Reich idea established by the German sword." Gaupp thought it was a bad omen that people continued to "speak ... of an emerging 'Fourth Reich,' despite the absence of a 'Reich government' ... [and] a unified 'Reich administration.'" For this reason, he reiterated, the "elimination [of the Reich idea]

Figure 2.1 In 1946, the German journalist Dolf Sternberger sought to explain why Germans were exclaiming, "God, please grant us the Fifth Reich. The Fourth is just like the Third" (Source: Getty Images).

is as important to the future of humanity as all other international problems."[32]

Yet while many people associated the Fourth Reich with right-wing thought – if not Nazism itself – many conservative Germans refused to associate themselves with the concept. This was made clear in a radio speech delivered in early 1946 by the liberal German journalist and later political scientist Dolf Sternberger (Figure 2.1). Entitled "Contemporary Disappointments," the speech sought to explain the appearance of a "humorous popular saying" (*Volkswitz*) that was making the rounds of Germany at the time. Expressing what Sternberger called the "vox populi," the saying assumed the form of a "little prayer" and went as follows: "God, please grant us the Fifth Reich. The Fourth is just like the Third."[33] In interpreting the saying's meaning, Sternberger observed that it was not "without humor," insofar as it mocked how "holy and noble" the "magical phrase of the Third

Reich once sounded."[34] But he feared that the prayer's despairing tone "expressed a decisive unhappiness with the current situation in Germany."[35] The "hopelessness" of many Germans, he wrote, reflected their recognition that the "widely praised and long yearned for freedom of our Fourth Reich" had not come to pass and probably would never become a new "golden age."[36] These disappointed expectations were rooted in the Germans' dawning recognition that they had not been liberated, but instead had been conquered, by the Allies. Even though many anti-Nazi Germans "had wished for the defeat of their own nation," the Allies had "thrown [them] into the same pot" with those who had supported the regime. "Even the Americans," Sternberger noted, "did not come to us, the oppressed Germans, as friends." The Americans forced the Germans to realize that "it was not just Hitler and the NSDAP that lost [the war] but the German nation." The disappointment also reflected the recognition that the Germans' new "democracy" had not come from "an inner upheaval," but had "been steered ... from outside" of Germany. "There is no avoiding the fact," Sternberger declared, "that we did not bring about the overthrow [of the Nazi regime]." The "cause of these disappointments," he concluded, "lies, first and foremost, in ourselves."[37]

Sternberger went on to note that the Germans' refusal to recognize their own failures had produced a worrisome response. It had led them to relativize the crimes of the Nazis by comparing them to misdeeds allegedly committed by Allied occupation forces. Sternberger criticized the fact that many Germans were claiming that "denunciations are again rife, only now by others ... that there is once more a secret police, but only among the Americans ... that people ... are being ... excluded from voting – in the name of ... democracy." Such relativizing claims, according to Sternberger, explained the popularity of the *Volkswitz* about the Fifth Reich. By comparing the Fourth Reich (understood to mean the era of Allied occupation) to the Third Reich, the *Volkswitz* allowed Germans to assume a self-pitying stance of victimization and refrain from confronting their own culpability in the Nazi regime's crimes. Sternberger did not accuse the Germans who held these views of being Nazis, but he nevertheless spoke out against them by concluding his essay with the following exhortation:

> There is no such thing as the "Fourth Reich," since we are not living in a Reich at all, but in a condition of dependence, which

is entirely different from that of the Third Reich, but which unfortunately reminds us every day ... of the Third Reich's origins ... Moreover, we are living in a condition that should lead us to finally adopt a stance of ... independent responsibility in our far-from-ideal ... reality. This is the reason why we should not jokingly ask God ... for a Fifth Reich ... but instead accept our fate.[38]

Sternberger's speech revealed that the idea of the Fourth Reich remained in flux during the early occupation. Although Allied observers associated the idea with the German far right, Germans on the conservative wing of the political spectrum avoided using the Fourth Reich themselves. In 1946–47, English-language papers reported that German nationalists were expressing their opposition to Allied rule by calling for a "Fifth Reich."[39] *The New York Times,* for example, noted that unrepentant Nazis had altered the phrasing of the *Volksswitz* discussed by Sternberger to read: "Dear Lord, please give us a Fifth Reich that will look like the Third."[40] Meanwhile, the Australian press reported that liberated concentration camp prisoners had been threatened with an anonymous letter telling them that they had better "mind your step under the Fourth Reich. If not, you will be hanged under the Fifth."[41] As these competing views revealed, the meaning of the Fourth Reich remained unstable in the early occupation. Yet, whatever it was called, the possibility that inveterate Nazis might try to return to power remained a real fear.

The Werewolves and the Threat of a Nazi Insurgency

The first Nazi threat appeared with the Werewolf movement. This violent partisan insurgency emerged during the last months of the war but continued well into the occupation. Between 1945 and 1947, Nazi insurgents launched hundreds of attacks against Allied forces and alleged German collaborators. These attacks claimed the lives of several thousand people, destroyed key infrastructure, and created a climate of fear among political leaders, the press, and the general public in the Allied nations and Germany itself. Strictly speaking, the Werewolves did not set out to create a Fourth Reich. They were originally committed to defending its still-existing predecessor by slowing the Allies' invasion of Germany, delaying its military defeat, and gaining it time to arrange a separate peace. The Werewolves failed to achieve their goal. But they adjusted their objectives after Germany's surrender and worked to shorten the ensuing occupation.[42] Here, too, the Werewolves met with failure, as the Allies remained a firm presence in German life until the creation of the FRG and GDR in 1949. In a sense, however, the Werewolves succeeded in their larger mission of ensuring Nazism's survival. Even after the movement disbanded, many of the original participants went on to form underground groups that pursued a Nazi return to power.

Scholars have overlooked the full significance of the Werewolf movement. Of the few who have studied it, most have agreed that it was a complete failure.[43] One reason for this view is the desire to repudiate neo-Nazism. Perry Biddiscombe and Volker Koop, for example, have sought to tell the "real story" about the Werewolves in order to counter the recent effort of neo-Nazis to romanticize the movement and justify its violent deeds.[44] Other scholars have sought to demythologize the Werewolf movement in order to counter conservative political attempts to inflate its historical significance. During the Iraq War, American Secretary of Defense Donald Rumsfeld and Secretary of State Condoleeza Rice cited the Allied defeat of the Werewolves in 1945 to reassure anti-war critics that US forces would inevitably crush the Iraqi insurgency that erupted following Saddam Hussein's defeat in 2003.[45] Finally, the scholarly response is also a reaction against recent media reports that have hyped the Werewolf movement – for instance, British tabloid stories revealing the movement's plan to fight the Allies with James Bond-style weapons, including poison sausages and toxic cigarette lighters.[46]

The effort of scholars to demythologize the Werewolf movement is understandable, but it has had the effect of underplaying its significance. For one thing, it has reinforced the problematic phenomenon of hindsight bias and made the movement's defeat by the Allies appear to be all but inevitable. This viewpoint obscures the contingent nature of the era's events and prevents us from recognizing how things might have turned out differently. It also keeps us from understanding the sincerity, and assessing the legitimacy, of the fears generated by the movement at the time. To address these pitfalls, counterfactual reasoning is of considerable value. By exploring "what ifs" related to the Werewolf movement we can recognize that its defeat was hardly a foregone conclusion. In so doing, we can better appreciate how the

Figure 2.2 In 1944, Heinrich Himmler (left) tasked *SS-Obergruppenführer* Hans-Adolf Prützmann (right) with assembling "Werewolf" guerilla units to fight the Allies (Source: Getty Images).

Allies' success in combating it contributed to Germany's postwar recovery.

The origins of the Werewolves date back to the fall of 1944, when the Nazi government decided to form a resistance movement to counter the imminent arrival of Allied forces in Germany. The most important figure in this effort was SS chief Heinrich Himmler, who instructed *SS-Obergruppenführer* Hans-Adolf Prützmann to coordinate the regional assembly of guerilla units to fight the Allies (Figure 2.2). Prützmann was not a particularly effective leader, but by the end of

1944, he had gathered a group of some 5,000 fighters.[47] At the same time, other Nazi officials tried to shape the movement. The Hitler Youth (HJ) leader, Artur Axmann, Propaganda Minister Joseph Goebbels, Deputy Propaganda Minister Werner Naumann, and *Der Stürmer* editor Julius Streicher worked on recruitment and publicity.[48] Hitler's secretary, Martin Bormann, German Labor Front (DAF) head Robert Ley, and Reich Security (RSHA) chief Ernst Kaltenbrunner weighed in on operational matters.[49] And military consulting was provided by *SS-und Polizeiführer* Jürgen Stroop (noted for crushing the Warsaw ghetto uprising of 1943), and German *SS-Standartenführer* Otto Skorzeny.[50]

The Werewolves' overall goal was to bolster the morale of Germany's civilian population and counteract any sense of defeatism by launching attacks against the approaching Allies. They followed in the tradition of earlier guerilla movements in German history, such as the partisan bands of the Seven Years War, the *Landsturm* of the Napoleonic Wars, and the Freikorps after World War I.[51] More ominously, they also drew on the precedent of medieval vigilante courts (known as *Vehme*) and used terror against the German population to keep them from surrendering.[52] To add the movement an extra aura of menace, the Nazis selected the name *Werwolf*, drawing on German writer Hermann Löns's bestselling 1914 novel, *Der Wehrwolf*, about partisan warfare in the Thirty Years' War, which the regime republished in 1944.[53] All of these elements were visible in a fiery inaugural speech broadcast on Joseph Goebbels' Werewolf radio network on April 1, 1945. It began:

> We are the voice of the German freedom fighters ...
>
> The enemy has thrust into our home and has raped the holy soil of our Fatherland. German men and women have had to endure desecration and murder ... In this fateful hour for our people, in both the occupied west and east, countless men and women, boys and girls, have united into a National Socialist resistance under the name Werewolf. We have joyfully resolved never to submit to the enemy ...
>
> Beware, Englishmen, Americans, Jews, and Bolsheviks! ...
>
> Hatred is our prayer and revenge our battle cry.
>
> Thrice woe to traitors who place themselves at the enemy's disposal. Werewolves, do not spare the lives of the enemy who wishes to destroy the lives of our people ...

Go to work, werewolves, and fight for our people's freedom and honor! Long live the National Socialist Werewolf movement! Long live our Führer Adolf Hitler! Long live our people![54]

Inspired by this exhortation, Werewolf bands in the last phase of the war launched numerous attacks against the Americans, British, and French in the west and the Soviets in the east.[55] The attacks mostly entailed acts of sabotage against communication and transportation networks: blowing up bridges, laying out trip wires on roads, disrupting supply lines, and bombing military installations.[56] But there were also deadly sniper shootings and individual assaults against Allied troops.[57] All of these attacks prompted fierce Allied countermeasures, including mass arrests, curfews, and executions. Most Werewolf attacks, however, were directed against the German people.[58] The murder of the American-installed mayor of Aachen, Franz Oppenhoff, on March 24, 1945, was the first high-profile killing claimed by the Werewolves, with Goebbels heralding it as a warning to potential German collaborators. In reality, this infamous attack was not a Werewolf operation, but was carried out by the SS. Nevertheless, many genuine Werewolf attacks were launched against other German "defeatists," ranging from minor local politicians to ordinary workers.[59] In certain instances, the killings were large-scale, as with the so-called "Penzberg murder night," on April 28, 1945, when the fanatical Nazi activist Hans Zoeberlein led a Werewolf massacre of sixteen members of the anti-Nazi uprising, known as the Freedom Action Bavaria, outside of Munich.[60] By the end of the war, Werewolf attacks and Allied reprisals had caused the deaths of several thousand people.[61]

When news reports of the Werewolves began to proliferate in the Anglo-American press in April of 1945, many Allied observers feared the worst.[62] The reports were ominous. Some asserted that Nazi Party officials were "abandon[ing] their posts ... [to] take up underground stations in the 'werewolf war.'"[63] Others claimed that the Germans had positioned 200,000 troops in an impenetrable "Alpine redoubt" in Bavaria to fight a prolonged struggle against Allied forces.[64] Still others insisted that the Werewolves were so fanatical that they "will not cease their work when the war ends [but] ... will carry on their political terrorism until the last one is run down and exterminated."[65] Allied officials widely believed these stories. Supreme

Allied commander Dwight D. Eisenhower told President Franklin D. Roosevelt in April of 1945 that "a very large number of troops" would be needed to suppress German "guerilla warfare."[66] Only by crushing the Werewolf "underground army," he believed, could the proper conditions be established for a successful Allied occupation.[67]

By contrast, other commentators viewed the Werewolf threat as exaggerated. In early April, American newspapers dismissed stories of the Werewolves as "wild tales" that could have been "lifted from the pages of Sherlock Holmes," while the British press suspected that "the organization ... exists only in the imagination of ... Berlin broadcasters."[68] By the end of the month, *The New York Times* observed that the Werewolf campaign had "complete faded out" and dismissed it as Hitler's "last failure."[69] In explaining why the Werewolves had been a "flop as effective guerilla opposition," some journalists reported that they were mostly "teen-aged desperadoes," no more than 15 years of age, who were ill-prepared to rally other "kindergarten killers" to take on Allied forces.[70] Further bolstering this skeptical perspective were reports that the German people themselves were "sneering" at the notion of the Werewolf movement.[71] Perhaps the most indicative sign that the Werewolf threat was not taken seriously was the appearance of American songwriter Irving Caesar's song parody in April of 1945. Written in response to the Nazis' own "Werewolf Song" performed by "Lily the Werewolf," Caesar's lyrics mocked the Werewolf threat by defiantly declaring:

> Who's afraid of the big bad werewolf,
> High in his mountain lair?
> By day he growls, by night he howls,
> But GI Joe don't scare.
> He hides in caves, and rants and raves
> This super Aryan.
> But thanks to Ike, he's dying like
> A real barbarian.
> Who's afraid of the big bad werewolf?
> No one goodness knows.
> We only fear to get too near
> To a skunk in werewolf's clothes.[72]

Stuck between these competing views of the Werewolf threat were observers who could not decide how seriously to take it. When

Joseph Goebbels credited the insurgent group with murdering the mayor of Aachen in the spring of 1945, Allied officials suspected a German "trick," believing the regime was trying to evade responsibility for a targeted assassination by blaming it on the actions of "spontaneously" forming groups.[73] *New York Times* reporter Drew Middleton also doubted the strength of the insurgency, writing that Germany would not be able to "sustain an underground movement of any strength" because no larger German army could support it. Yet he remained cautious and insisted "once the Germans see the chance to strike back" against the Allies, they would take advantage of the "hour of revenge" and do so.[74] *The Los Angeles Times* took a similar stance, noting that while the Werewolves had so far been "a flop as [an] effective guerilla opposition," they still needed to be taken seriously, for they might end up becoming "a new murder society ... which might take years to stamp out."[75] Summing up this position, *The Oregonian* concluded that the Werewolves represented a "strange ... combination of ludicrousness and ... evil."[76]

With the end of the war, however, Allied fears of the Werewolves began to ebb. The formal announcement by Hitler's successor, Karl Doenitz, on May 5, 1945 that all Werewolf activity would come to an end diminished Allied expectations of a prolonged insurgency.[77] The suicides of Heinrich Himmler and Hans-Adolf Prützmann further robbed the movement of its main leaders.[78] By May and June of 1945, the Allies increasingly believed that the Werewolf threat had been a "hallucination."[79] American occupation officials reported that the killing of Aachen's mayor had "little effect on German officials working for allies."[80] And they were relieved to note that "the Werewolves appear to be quiet as yet."[81] Fears further declined after US officials were told by captured German leaders that the Werewolf threat was "pure nonsense" and could be "stamped out promptly" wherever it flared up.[82] In fact, after the surrender of May of 1945, Werewolf killings – either of Allied soldiers or German collaborators – became exceedingly rare.[83]

Within certain circles, however, suspicions persisted. While Werewolf activity declined immediately after VE Day, it increased as the occupation dragged on. Deepening economic misery and resentment towards denazification sparked new cases of vandalism and sabotage across Germany, and even inspired scattered killings in the Sudetenland.[84] Continuing press reports about the arrests of

Werewolf bands and discoveries of weapons caches further kept the movement in the public eye.[85] These cases made clear that the Werewolves retained a presence in German life. Even though Military Government officials publicly spoke of the "collapse of the Werewolves" in the late summer, they simultaneously announced their suspicions that a "Nazi underground propaganda agency" was spreading rumors and disinformation against the Allies.[86] Well into the fall, commentators continued to warn that the Werewolves remained a long-term threat. In October of 1945, the Society for the Prevention of World War III declared that it was "naïve" to suspect that the "anti-Allied underground would begin immediately after the military defeat." Instead, it noted, the "real problem will arise in the years ahead, when the pressure of Allied occupation is relaxed and Werewolf leaders consider the time ripe for starting action." Rather than "laugh[ing] off ... the Werewolves as ... some 'Walt Disney cartoon,'" the editorial admonished readers to "double our vigilance" in order to avoid "trouble ahead."[87]

What observers feared in the fall of 1945, however, never came to pass; the Werewolves never made good on their threats to seriously challenge the Allied occupation of Germany. But was their failure inevitable? Most scholars seem to say yes. Koop, for instance, argues that the Werewolves' actions were "condemned to failure from the beginning."[88] Other scholars are less definitive, but have nevertheless claimed that the Werewolves faced long odds in trying to realize their objectives. Planning started late.[89] The leadership was chaotically divided between the SS and rival party and state organizations.[90] Resources were scarce.[91] The German population was exhausted, demoralized, and in no mood to continue hostilities.[92] Finally, the Nazis were ideologically incapable of organizing a guerilla insurrection for the simple reason that the party "assumed that it could not die."[93] Unable to imagine the possibility that the Third Reich would fail to last for one thousand years, the NSDAP leadership was inept at contingency planning and neglected to grant itself the means for future survival. Given all of these factors, it would appear that Allied fears were unfounded.[94]

And yet we can imagine ways in which the Werewolves might have been more successful. Especially in light of the prolonged rebel insurgency that erupted against Allied forces in Iraq after 2003, it is possible to envision counterfactual scenarios in which the Allied occupation of Germany could have turned out worse than it did in reality.[95] Certain historians have flirted with some of these nightmare scenarios. Koop has speculated, for instance, that "the Werewolf [campaign] could have been more successful from the Nazi leadership's perspective had it been planned and built up in more timely fashion."[96] Biddiscombe has wondered about the disastrous effect that Werewolf attacks would "likely … have had" if the Allies had not been so "harsh" in responding to the movement.[97] These claims reflect a sense of relief that history unfolded as it did. But they stop short of exploring the full extent of how things might have been different.

We can realize the full potential of these hypothetical possibilities by posing certain imaginary scenarios. For instance: what if Germany had not been subjected to divided Allied occupation? In reality, the division of Germany into separate zones shaped the nature of Werewolf resistance. Following the end of World War II, Werewolf activity was more common in eastern than western Germany. This was largely due to the greater severity of violence on the eastern than the western front. During the war itself and then in the initial postwar period, violence was intense between the Red Army and Wehrmacht, as well as between Soviet soldiers and German civilians (many of whom were also attacked by their Polish and Czech neighbors). Murder, rape, and expulsion were common. Many Germans thus joined the Werewolves in the east because of their desire to avenge crimes committed against them.[98] This response was further fueled by the violent response of Soviet troops to Werewolf attacks, which included shooting civilian hostages, burning down villages, and organizing mass arrests.[99] This cycle of violence in the east, in turn, may have shaped German civilian behavior in the west. German awareness of the Red Army's brutality may have deterred large-scale Werewolf resistance against British, French, and American occupation troops. Already during the war, German awareness of Red Army atrocities had prompted civilians and soldiers to flee to the comparative safety of the western part of the country in the expectation of softer treatment.[100] Similarly, after the war's end, Werewolf resistance in the west may have been milder due to the German people's relative relief about their situation and their awareness that they would suffer more if the Soviets were to replace Anglo-American forces as their occupiers. In short, many Germans may have remained passive in the west because it was their best option to maintain their security.

But what if the Soviets had taken all of Germany? Would more Werewolf opposition have arisen? The harsh collective punishment imposed by the Soviets would have ensnared many more innocent Germans and potentially driven them into the resistance, thereby enlarging it. Without the ability to flee to other Allied occupation zones, many Germans might have felt they had nothing to lose by joining the Werewolf movement. As it was, most Germans had been conditioned to fear Bolshevism for more than a generation – even prior to the Third Reich. Moreover, a punitive Soviet occupation would have partly redeemed the NSDAP by ostensibly validating the party's anti-Bolshevik stance. It is impossible to know how many Germans would have given Nazism a second chance, following the Third Reich's collapse in 1945, but a brutal Soviet occupation would have added fuel to any Nazi insurgency.

Intriguingly, the same thing also might have transpired if the western Allies had conquered all of Germany after D-Day. Had the Germans only been under western Allied control and not had to fear a harsh Soviet alternative, they might have rebelled more actively against them. Many Germans had been fed a steady diet of anti-British and anti-American propaganda by the Nazi regime, and resented Anglo-American forces after their arrival on German soil. The possibility that they might have rebelled more violently is partly suggested by the course of the Iraqi insurgency.[101] One contributing factor to the eruption of the long-term Sunni and the short-term Shiite rebellions against Allied coalition forces in Iraq was the fact that the insurgents were able to direct their aggression against a single occupying force and did not fear that their actions might pave the way for a worse occupation by a nearby outside power.[102] Because Iraq was not divided into separate occupation zones, there was no equivalent of the Soviet Red Army administering one part of the country and acting as a deterrent to potential insurgents in another. Indeed, if anything, the opposite was true: neighboring countries, such as Saudi Arabia and the Gulf states, contributed to the rise of Iraq's Sunni insurgent groups, while Iran supported local Shiite militias. (Conversely, the Werewolves' inability to find support from any of Germany's neighbors after 1945 contributed to the movement's failure.) These comparisons reveal something important about the Allied occupation of Germany. The fact that the four powers adopted a policy of dividing and conquering the country was crucial for limiting Werewolf resistance. By effectively playing a version of "good cop" and "bad cop," the western Allies and the Soviets helped make the German people docile instead of rebellious.

To be sure, these scenarios raise basic questions of plausibility. Could either the Soviets or the western Allies have occupied Germany exclusively by themselves? It is unlikely, but not impossible. It is well known that the Allies agreed to divide Germany into separate occupation zones before the end of the war. In the fall of 1944, at the London foreign ministers conference, Allied officials in the European Advisory Commission laid out three zones, which were later expanded to four at the Yalta Conference in February of 1945. For political reasons, it was more or less inevitable that Germany was going to be under divided rule. Nevertheless, we can imagine scenarios in which the Soviets – and perhaps also the western Allies – could have occupied Germany all by themselves.

In the summer of 1944, while Anglo-American troops were still in France, Red Army forces had reached the eastern outskirts of Warsaw and were poised to move into Germany. At this point, however, Stalin ordered some of his forces to halt (allowing the Nazis to crush the Warsaw uprising of August 1944) while simultaneously sending others into the Balkans to occupy Romania, Bulgaria, Yugoslavia, and Hungary.[103] Had the Soviets decided otherwise, they could have sped up their march into Germany and conceivably taken most of the country on their own. Stalin himself had fantasies of making it all the way to France.[104] The British and Americans, meanwhile, had been aware of such a scenario ever since the Soviets' victory at Stalingrad and opened up a second front in Normandy in June of 1944 partly to prevent it from occurring.[105] Concerns that the Soviets might take most of Germany also prompted the western Allies to convene the Yalta conference in February of 1945 (it was intended to commit the Soviets to the pre-arranged occupation zones at a time when the Red Army was only 50 miles from Berlin and the western Allies were still recovering from the grueling Battle of the Bulge). British and American behavior in the years 1944–45, in short, reveals that a total Soviet conquest of Germany was plausible.[106]

The same can be said about the possibility of the western Allies taking Germany entirely by themselves. If Great Britain and the US had devoted less time and resources to invading North Africa and pursuing strategic bombing over Germany in the years 1942–43, they could have opened a second front in France two years before they ultimately did. Had they done so, according to Jacques Pauwels, they "might have penetrated much deeper ... into Germany ... and found themselves ensconced in Berlin and perhaps as far as Warsaw" at war's end.[107] Other writers, such as Caleb Carr, have imagined the Allies invading Germany with a Blitzkrieg-style "deep strike" strategy (instead of a "broad front" approach) that might have enabled them to seize Berlin and compel a German surrender by November of 1944, thereby preventing a Soviet presence in the Reich.[108] Still another possible scenario involves the Allies succeeding with Operation Market Garden in September of 1944. If they had been able to cross the Rhine and seize the industrial capacity of the Ruhr, the western Allies might have taken all of Germany more quickly and ended the war by Christmas of 1944, before making any final concessions at Yalta.[109] All of these scenarios would have required greater Anglo-American sacrifice and likely would have led the Soviets speed up their own westward push. But they might have enabled an exclusively Anglo-American occupation of Germany and, with it, a more aggressive Werewolf guerilla campaign.

It is impossible to know whether these outcomes had any chance of being realized, but they are more than instances of idle speculation. In fact, they enable us to understand better what really happened after 1945. At the most obvious level, contemplating such alternate scenarios helps us appreciate how Allied policy in Germany spared the postwar world the nightmarish kind of insurgency that erupted in Iraq. In other words, the scenarios allow us to appreciate how history could have been worse. Yet they can also prompt us to wonder how history might have turned out better. At the conclusion of his book *The Last Nazis*, Perry Biddiscombe explains how the ultimate significance of the Werewolf movement lies in the realm of events that never transpired. The Werewolves, he writes, were crucial for adversely affecting the early political history of postwar Germany, for:

> at the very dawn of the ... "Zero Hour" ... when Germans would have been most open to change, the Allies were so busy wielding the instruments of oppression that they could hardly encourage such a process, nor ... allow it to emerge spontaneously from German sources. Thanks at least partly to the Werewolves, the political, social, and cultural

revolution of 1945 became the great non-event of modern German history.[110]

By encouraging an Allied crackdown, the Werewolves prevented the Germans from pursuing a truly new beginning. This claim is certainly debatable, as a range of factors were involved in maintaining continuities between the occupation era and the subsequent Federal Republic. But the case of the Werewolves reminds us that even failed movements can shape history. The stillborn insurgency reveals how difficult it was for postwar Germany to make a clean break with the past. It certainly could have been worse. But, even in failure, the Werewolf movement reveals that Nazism did not die in 1945, but survived into the occupation.

Early Postwar Nazi Conspiracies and Allied Responses

The Allies were made painfully aware of this fact in early 1946 when they encountered new efforts by unrepentant Nazis to assert themselves in occupied Germany. Representing disparate, but ideologically committed groups of ex-party leaders, SS-officers, military figures, and Hitler Youth members, these efforts took the form of conspiracies to infiltrate the nascent institutions of occupied Germany with loyalists eager to exploit popular disaffection with Allied rule and facilitate a Nazi return to power. In 1946 and 1947, Allied intelligence officials became aware of these conspiracies and launched two important arrest campaigns, "Operation Nursery" and "Operation Selection Board," to suppress them. Both were successful. But they exposed the ongoing influence of Nazi ideas and lent credibility to fears about the prospect of a Fourth Reich.

The Hitler Youth Conspiracy and Operation Nursery

The first conspiracy was associated with the longtime Nazi and Hitler Youth leader, Artur Axmann (Figure 2.3). A party member since 1931, Axmann replaced Baldur von Schirach as Hitler Youth (HJ) chief in 1940 and was quickly admitted into Hitler's inner circle. In the last weeks of the war, Axmann spent considerable time in the Berlin Führerbunker, helping to coordinate the city's defense by channeling Hitler Youth members into the Volkssturm and Waffen-SS. After

Figure 2.3 In 1946, the former Hitler Youth leader, Artur Axmann, led an abortive coup attempt of unrepentant Nazis against Allied occupation forces. The revolt was crushed by the Allies in "Operation Nursery" (Source: Getty Images).

Hitler's suicide on April 30, Axmann fled the bunker, together with fellow Nazi loyalists Werner Naumann and Martin Bormann, under heavy fire from Red Army troops. In the chaos, the men were separated, but Axmann eventually made it to the state of Mecklenburg in the Soviet zone. At this point, he disappeared and was thought by the Allied authorities to be dead. In reality, Axmann had changed his name to Erich Siewert and gone underground to begin implementing the first stages of a postwar resistance plan.[111] Drafted in the early spring of 1945, the plan was based on the assumption that Anglo-American and Soviet forces would split at the war's conclusion, thereby providing an opportunity for Hitler Youth fighters to join the former against the latter. To advance this goal, Axmann ordered 35,000 HJ leaders in the spring of 1945 to travel to the mountainous terrain of south Germany, where they would support the Werewolf movement and await orders to pursue further resistance activity.[112]

Although this agenda grew out of Axmann's involvement with the Werewolf movement, it focused less on actively resisting Allied rule militarily than subverting it from within.[113] Immediately after the war, while in north Germany, Axmann instructed Hitler Youth leaders in the south, such as HJ *Oberbannführer* Willi Heidemann, to use designated funds to set up business operations – especially trucking firms – that were meant to "become influential in the new economic life of Germany."[114] At the same time, other HJ members were told to find employment with military government officials and earn their trust. The plotters' plan was to lie low, slowly amass economic strength, and then move to "influence existing parties along Nazi principles."[115] For his part, Axmann remained particularly committed to the *Führerprinzip*, which he intended to employ in a new version of the Hitler Youth.[116] His ultimate goal was to resurrect the Nazi Party and become Germany's new leader.[117] In so doing, he and his fellow conspirators hoped to show that the twelve years of the Third Reich had "not [been] in vain."[118]

Before Axmann's group could further develop their plans, however, American and British intelligence officials put an end to them with Operation Nursery. Named for the young age of the individuals targeted for arrest, the operation had been in the works for ten months, during which time Allied officials collected information provided by former Nazis who had infiltrated the group as spies.[119] Much of the information was discovered thanks to the growing rift between two factions of the group that had begun to squabble over strategy.[120] In December of 1945, counterintelligence forces made a first wave of arrests, netting Axmann and over 200 other persons, although the news was initially kept secret. Then, in March of 1946, some 7,000 Allied troops fanned out across more than 200 towns in the western occupation zones and arrested more than 1,000 suspects from the HJ rank and file. In many cases, gunfire was exchanged between Allied soldiers and Germans on the arrest lists. Allied troops also recovered more than 1 million Reichsmarks in Nazi funds and were alerted to the locations of ammunition caches in secret mountain locations.[121]

When news of the raids broke in the US and Britain, sensationalistic newspaper headlines, such as "Raids Smash Plot to Re-Nazify Germany," emphasized the importance of the Allied action. Many press reports quoted US Brigadier General Edwin Sibert's claim that the arrests had halted a major effort to "revive ... the Nazi ideology in

Germany" and select a "new Führer."[122] US officials reassured the public that the conspiracy had been interrupted while it was still non-violent, adding that it was not "destined for combative action in the sense of the French Maquis."[123] But they pointed out that "it was the most dangerous threat to our security ... since the war." Indeed, even though many newspapers cited Sibert's confident statement that "the back of the movement has been broken," they continued to urge vigilance.[124] Many stressed the need for Allied troops to remain in Germany. In the US, one newspaper spoke of danger of the "Germans ... bring[ing] forth a reinvigorated, and perhaps camou-flaged, new Nazi program," while another stressed the need for the Allies to continue the effort "to uncover and destroy ... this evil."[125] The Australian press colorfully referred to the persistence of a "jackal Underground movement" made up of "Nazis ... still fighting like cor-nered Dingoes."[126] In occupied Germany, meanwhile, diverging responses coexisted: one newspaper in the American zone apologetically cited the hardships of daily life under Allied rule as the reason ordinary Germans believed that "the Werewolf Nazis could improve conditions and Axmann and his comrades were patriots"; by contrast, another paper expressed relief at the "near miss" and self-critically speculated that "if [Axmann's] ... plans had become reality, Germany's population would have ceased to ... have any right of existence in the world."[127] Finally, the communist press in the East German zone concluded that the ongoing efforts of unrepentant Nazis to "hatch ... conspiracies" a year after Germany's defeat proved that they were hopelessly incap-able of recognizing their role in the country's "catastrophe."[128]

Was the threat really so dire? At first glance, the answer would appear to be no. The literature on the Allied occupation of Germany has largely ignored the conspiracy.[129] The same is true of the obituaries of Axmann that appeared following his death in 1996.[130] This lack of attention suggests that, for many observers, the conspiracy was doomed to failure and unworthy of being remembered. Of late, however, the Hitler Youth leader's subversive agenda has received new attention, with Scott Selby's book, *The Axmann Conspiracy*, claiming that it was part of a larger "plan for a Fourth Reich."[131] This renewed interest in the conspiracy reminds us how seriously contemporaries viewed the threat of a Nazi revival.

As early as the winter of 1945–46, the Allies recognized that the bleakness of life under occupation was keeping Nazi ideas alive among certain Germans. Forecasts for the German economy at this time ranged from gloomy to dire. Food shortages were so acute that the British press predicted that more people were destined to die than had been killed by "the first two bombs of the atomic epoch."[132] In March of 1946, the reduction of daily rations to around 1,000 calories in the British zone sparked riots in Hamburg, with multiple acts of looting, burglary, and vandalism.[133] In response, the British employed mass arrests and announced that "they were prepared to use military armor to quell German hunger rioters."[134] These threats did little to stop the crisis, however.[135] By late 1946, the English-language press was publishing lurid reports about fanatical Nazi "cannibals" murdering people to make "human sausages" for sale on the black market.[136] It was not merely food shortages that contributed to the climate of despair. Homelessness and unemployment continued to plague millions of Germans, particularly expellees, refugees, and soldiers returning from Allied captivity. Small wonder that Allied political officials warned that the economic situation could have "explosive potentialities" and "swing large masses of the German people to the extreme political camps of both Right and Left."[137] This political nightmare appeared increasingly likely in light of the Allies' inability to decide whether they were more interested in "making Germany impotent or making Germany democratic."[138] Many commentators feared that the political situation could easily be exploited by "surviving Nazis" who would "find their opportunity" by playing one side off of the other.[139]

By the spring of 1946, the Allies realized that, despite the success of Operation Nursery, Nazi ideas had merely been "scotched – not killed."[140] Allied political observers and journalists were well aware of the fact that younger Germans – especially women and girls – remained drawn to Nazi ideas.[141] A few weeks after Operation Nursery, *The New York Times* published an attention-grabbing story entitled "Nazi Virus Thrives in American Zone," which claimed that, throughout Bavaria, representatives of the Nazi "underground resistance" were "quietly reorganizing for a return to power by capturing control of the democratic institutions we have created." Because American military government officials had naively relied upon the personnel recommendations of "conservative elements" who were "sympathetic" to the Nazis, right-wing Germans were "infiltrating [key] positions" in the American zone and quietly biding their time until "conditions are favorable" for undermining Allied rule. Only the presence of the US military was keeping "chaos" at bay.[142]

This bleak assessment, which was echoed by various American and German observers, raises the counterfactual question of whether the crisis could have escalated into a revolutionary situation and enabled a Nazi comeback.[143] Economic despair, social unrest, and political disillusionment have long been preconditions for revolutionary unrest. Germany had all of these things in abundance in 1946. The only missing ingredient was a catalytic act of violence to propel deeper structural problems over the tipping point into dramatic, epoch-making events.

In fact, violence in Germany intensified in the months that followed. On October 19, 1946, several bombs exploded at a denazification tribunal building and US military police jail in Stuttgart. That same day, another bomb exploded at a denazification board building in the nearby town of Backnang, while, a week later, a bomb blew up in the nearby town of Esslingen. These attacks, which caused structural damage but no injuries, raised fears of intensifying Nazi radicalism.[144] *The Boston Globe* described the bombs as "the first openly violent attack on American military and German civil police by the Nazi underground" and claimed they represented a "serious" development.[145] Many observers surmised that the attacks represented protests by surviving Werewolf cells against the Allied denazification program, with some suspecting they were meant to derail the nearby trial of former Reichsbank chief, Hjalmar Schacht.[146] This impression was bolstered by the appearance of nationalistic posters in the area claiming that the Nuremberg Trials were "not a judgment, but murder."[147] The spike in violence was alarming in and of itself, but it became even more worrisome after American officials declared in October of 1946 that they "expected more bombings ... against the denazification program."[148] Before long, these fears were borne out, for in January and February of 1947, explosions in Nuremberg damaged offices of denazification officials who were entrusted with prosecuting former German chancellor and Hitler supporter, Franz von Papen.[149] Still other attacks struck denazification courts in Munich and Kassel around the same time, while, shortly thereafter, a denazification trial court (*Spruchkammer*) prosecutor was murdered in the Württemberg town of Öhringen.[150]

Had the violence continued unopposed, Germany's future development might have gone in a different direction, but as matters turned out, the reaction was swift and strong. First, many Germans strongly opposed the attacks. In Stuttgart, 75,000 workers staged a short general strike on October 22 to protest the efforts of "former Nazis" to challenge the postwar order.[151] Other union-led protests were held in Nuremberg.[152] The German press widely condemned the attacks, with communist East German newspapers highlighting the ongoing threat of fascist "reactionaries" and "Werewolves."[153] Critically, the Allies also exhibited a strong response. Within a short time, the American authorities were able to track the perpetrators of the Stuttgart area attacks to a cell of Nazi fanatics led by a 23-year-old former SS man named Siegfried Kabus. His goal was to rally popular anger against denazification and launch a movement for Germany's national revival with himself as the country's new Führer. The Allies were also able to catch the culprits behind the Nuremberg attacks, which were perpetrated by another radical Nazi, former Waffen-SS soldier and Werewolf activist, Alfred Zitzmann. Both Kabus and Zitzmann were young men, whose Nazi-era activism left them few prospects for the immediate future. Their supporters were all mostly former Hitler Youth and Waffen-SS members with equally minimal options. Kabus and Zitzmann's violent actions ultimately led nowhere.[154] But they testified to the survival of Nazi ideas among segments of the German population. To be sure, certain German observers tried to dismiss Kabus as an aberration by pointing to his eccentricity (he wildly embellished his war record and claimed to be in touch with Martin Bormann).[155] Other Germans, however, worried that Kabus's ensuing conviction and ensuing death sentence (later commuted) might turn him into a "martyr" who could inspire other fanatics to radical action.[156] These fears were echoed in the United States, where news stories about Kabus pursuing "elaborate plans for a 'fourth Reich'" stoked anxieties about a Nazi comeback.[157]

The Deutsche Revolution and Operation Selection Board

The desire to prevent this prospect partly explains why, in early 1947, Allied officials in the western zone launched Operation Selection Board. The campaign was specifically directed against a Nazi underground group known as the "Deutsche Revolution."[158] This movement

Figure 2.4 *SS-Hauptsturmführer* and former Gestapo chief of Lyon Klaus Barbie took part in the failed rebellion of the "Deutsche Revolution," which Allied forces crushed in "Operation Selection Board" in February of 1947 (Source: Getty Images).

was made up several loosely affiliated groups of ex-SS-officers and Wehrmacht veterans in the British and American occupation zones. The main group was the Deutsche Revolution itself, which was also known as the Organization for German Socialism (*Organisation für den Deutschen Sozialismus*) and led by *SS-Oberscharführer* Bernhard Gericke. Joining it was the Organization South Germany (*Organisation Süddeutschland*), led by former *SS-Oberführer* Kurt Ellersiek, and two unnamed cells of SS- and Wehrmacht officers led by *SS-Hauptsturmführer* (and former Gestapo chief of Lyon) Klaus Barbie, *SS-Brigadeführer* Christof Naumann, and Wehrmacht officer Ernst Gunther Jahnke (Figure 2.4). The groups originated independently but found their way to one another thanks to shared personal connections and ideological principles. Scholars have argued that the group's members saw themselves as "the nucleus of a new Nazi movement, the spearhead of a Fourth Reich."[159] But, as with the Axmann conspiracy, there is no evidence that the cells employed the concept of a Reich in their plotting. That said, they supported returning Nazism to power.

The conspirators believed that, with certain adjustments, National Socialism could retain its validity for the postwar world. According to Gericke, who was the conspiracy's main theoretician, Hitler's ideas had been overly nationalistic and racist, a drawback that could be redressed by striving for a more cosmopolitan kind of Nazism – what Gericke called "German Socialism" – committed to a united, anti-Soviet, European bloc.[160] The conspirators were realistic enough to recognize that, in the war's immediate aftermath, violent methods would get them nowhere, so they instead sought to infiltrate like-minded supporters into German life.[161] Ellersiek, for example, drew on his experience in the prewar SS university student organization known as the "team houses" (*Mannschaftshäuser*) and sought to insert former SS men into postwar German academic institutions; Gericke sought to place Nazis into the postwar political establishment; and Barbie used black marketeering, robbery, and forgery to help former SS comrades to establish new identities and evade Allied arrest. In pursuing these covert activities, the conspirators not only expressed an enduring commitment to Nazi ideals, they revealed their inability to accept the reality of the new postwar order. Because their compromised pasts excluded them from mainstream German life, the conspirators felt they had little choice but to "justify ... their inevitable underground existence," as American Counterintelligence Corps (CIC) officials put it in 1947, by maintaining their existing belief system.[162]

The Deutsche Revolution's immediate goal was to convince the western Allies, especially the British, to join forces with them in a new alliance against the Soviets. Attempting to exploit intensifying east–west tensions and leverage their experience in wartime anticommunist intelligence work, the group hoped to trade their collaboration for a series of Allied concessions: most notably, an end to denazification, the release of Nazis from internment camps, the return of Germany's eastern territories from Poland, and an end to economic reparations.[163] In late 1946 and early 1947, the conspirators, led by Ellersiek, tried to establish contact with British officials who were thought to be sympathetic and convince them to collaborate.[164] Unfortunately for the conspirators, the Allies had already penetrated their organization with spies who were regularly reporting on the conspiracy's progress. The British and Americans allowed planning to continue up until early 1947. But in January of that year, their hand was forced by new developments. At the end of the month, the publication of a headline-grabbing report by a private international lobbying organization, the International Committee for the Study of European Questions, claimed that shadowy Nazi underground groups were sabotaging denazification efforts in the western zone.[165] Fearing that the Soviets would use the information to gain a propaganda advantage at the upcoming Moscow foreign ministers conference, which was set to discuss Germany's fate in early March, the Allies decided to act.[166]

On the night of February 22, several thousand Allied troops fanned out across the western occupation zones in frigid weather to arrest more than one hundred suspects associated with the Deutsche Revolution.[167] Many of the most important leaders, such as Ellersiek and Gericke, were caught, as were dozens of former SS-officers, Wehrmacht officials, and mid-range Nazi Party leaders, including the head of the Hitler Youth in Poland, General Walter Schimmelpfennig, and the former Gauleiter of Württemberg, Helmut Baunert. Allied troops also arrested other Nazis who were not directly connected to the conspiracy. Most notable was the detainment of several officials associated with the Wehrmacht's "Group for Bacteriological Warfare Research," Hans-Georg Eismann and Karl Rosenberg, on the separate charge of threatening Allied forces with germ warfare. These arrests notwithstanding, the operation was not a complete success. Certain major figures, such as Klaus Barbie, evaded capture, and others went underground.[168]

Following the announcement of the arrests, the Anglo-American press expressed shock and alarm. Featuring headlines such as "Sudden Swoop by Allies Smashes Nazi Plot," a deluge of news stories described the conspiracy as more dangerous than the Hitler Youth plot crushed one year earlier in Operation Nursery.[169] Most articles breathlessly reported that the plotters had deliberately "aimed to revive ... Nazism," with *The New York Times* declaring that they represented "the most ambitious German underground movement to build a new dictatorship on the Nazi ruins."[170] Some went so far as to claim that the conspiracy was part of a Nazi "world plot" to "open ... an attack on civilization" itself.[171] These strident claims were partly rooted in the worrisome revelation that the conspirators possessed "a secret bacteriological weapon," which they planned on using to "blackmail the Western Allies" into "adopt[ing] an anti-Russian policy."[172] According to press accounts, "the gang envisaged the introduction of anthrax and plague bacilli into England and the United States" by sending specially trained agents equipped with powdered and liquid forms of the germs hidden in walking sticks, umbrellas, and briefcases to British and American cities, where they were to be released over a five-day period – in subway stations, restaurants, and other public sites – and "infect 12,000 people daily."[173] Despite Allied reassurances that the plot had been entirely defeated, the revelations gave rise to alarmist headlines, such as "Nazi Germ Threat to Britain," and heightened public anxieties.[174]

In occupied Germany, the reaction was divided. Most newspapers in the western zone dutifully reported the facts of the conspiracy, but denied that it posed any real danger. *Der Spiegel* dismissively referred to the Deutsche Revolution's inept effort to create a "second edition of the Third Reich," while other papers asserted that the conspirators did not speak for the majority of the German people.[175] This skeptical view was confirmed by CIC surveys of public opinion, which reported that Germans were nonplussed by the news of the Allied crackdown, believing that it had been launched to preempt Soviet criticism of lax Anglo-American denazification policies.[176] At the same time, dissenting views were heard among West German newspapers, some of which cautioned against "minimizing" the fact that "Nazi conspirators ... [were] trying to spin connections across the [occupation] zones."[177] The communist press in the East German zone emphasized this point, claiming that the arrests proved that there were still "circles that wanted to employ reactionary forces to revive the Hitler system."[178]

Given the massive press coverage of Operation Selection Board, it is surprising that the episode has received relatively little attention in the scholarly literature on the Allied occupation.[179] Much of this neglect probably reflects the belief that the Deutsche Revolution represented a minor threat that never seriously endangered Allied rule. This inattention is unjustified, however. Seen from the perspective of early 1947 – a time when Germany's reconstruction was barely underway and its democratization far from assured – fears of a Nazi comeback were hardly irrational. Indeed, it is easy to imagine ways in which the conspiracy might have been more successful.

This is especially true given the willingness of both contemporary and subsequent observers to employ counterfactual reasoning to explain the crackdown. In assessing the results of the operation in the summer of 1947, American CIC officials speculated that if the conspirators had

> been successful ... [in] obtaining British acquiescence to what appeared to be an innocuous political theory, the result would have been to consolidate the ranks of those in sympathy with Nazi idealists who would eventually have infiltrated into and infected those more respectable movements enjoying similar political sentiments. Sooner or later this sort of development would probably have faced the allied administration with a problem correspondingly more difficult to solve.[180]

The German press argued similarly, with the *Kasseler Zeitung* declaring that without Allied intervention, the conspirators might be able to "attract a large number of fellow travelers from the ranks of unhappy Nazi fanatics" and "grow into a powerful movement that could pose a dangerous threat for the security of the occupation."[181] Scholars have echoed Allied fears that the plot "might have had a considerable effect on sections of the [German] population" had it continued.[182] Perry Biddiscombe, for one, has speculated that "without Allied intervention, the Deutsche Revolution might have emerged as a powerful force on the German right, with the potential to turn back the clock."[183]

This claim is suggestive, but it begs the question of what might have kept the Allies from cracking down on the movement when they did. A hint, however, can be found in their failure to arrest Klaus Barbie. Evidence suggests that he was already being recruited by the CIC to help in the American intelligence effort against the Soviet Union and may have been deliberately allowed to escape the Operation Selection Board dragnet.[184] This may have occurred *despite* the fact that Barbie remained an unrepentant Nazi – a man whom CIC official (and Barbie's later recruiter) Robert S. Taylor described as "a Nazi idealist who believes that ... his beliefs were betrayed by the Nazis in power."[185] Barbie also never broke ties with his SS comrades, even though doing so was a condition for working with the Americans.[186] Barbie's case was hardly exceptional, moreover. At the time, the Americans and the British showed few moral scruples about making common cause with former enemies. They were especially interested in recruiting Nazi intelligence agents, most famously Abwehr chief on

Soviet affairs, Reinhard Gehlen, who was given permission by Alan Dulles and William Donovan to keep his intelligence network intact and have its members work for the Americans. Given this example and others, it is theoretically possible that the Allies might have worked *with* the Deutsche Revolution and supported their desire for a joint campaign against the Soviets.[187] Had this happened, right-wing forces would have been strengthened.

As events transpired, however, the conspirators' timing was off. In principle, conditions were right for the plotters to make their move. The winter of 1946–47 was the coldest on record, and economic conditions across the western occupation zones were abysmal. Public discontent was growing and the Allies were on the defensive as never before. Yet the plotters approached the Allies too soon. In early 1947, with the Moscow foreign ministers conference looming, the Americans and British had not yet abandoned the possibility of jointly administering Germany with the Soviets. Had the conspirators waited until east–west tensions had intensified – say, by the time of the Berlin crisis one year later – they might have had more leverage and been able to infiltrate more of their members into the nascent German establishment and advance their ideological agenda. In the end, impatience proved to be the Deutsche Revolution's undoing. The movement failed to change the course of postwar German history. That does not mean that it was without significance, however. The movement's existence provides further evidence that Nazi ideas were not extinguished with the end of World War II, but stubbornly survived well into the occupation period. It further helps us appreciate the Allies' crucial role in preventing these ideas from jeopardizing Germany's nascent democratization.[188]

Operation Selection Board was the last major instance during the occupation when the Allies used the stick instead of the carrot to confront the threat of a Nazi resurgence. Although many observers continued to believe that Germany needed to be punished for reasons of morality, they came to recognize that rehabilitation was more likely to promote democracy. In late February of 1947, *The New York Times* declared that while the arrest of Nazi leaders was important, it was insufficient simply to use "overwhelming ... force ... to make resistance appear hopeless." Because "the real danger lies in the mental state of the German people which makes them easy victims of such leaders," the former needed to be given "an outlet for their energies in the service of ... reconstruction" and shown "a way to their rehabilitation as respected members of the family of nations."[189] A similar point was made in 1947 by the British intelligence officer and historian, Hugh Trevor-Roper, who said that in order to counteract the "real danger" that a "new form of Nazism" could exploit popular "discontents" and rally support for a "totalitarian" state, the German economy had to be restored."[190]

As these and similar stories began to proliferate, the western Allies decided to adopt a reconstructionist occupation policy.[191] Following the proclamation of the Joint Chiefs of Staff (JCS) Directive 1779 in July of 1947, which declared that "an orderly, prosperous Europe requires the economic contributions of a stable and productive Germany," the Allied authorities increased food shipments and other supplies to their zones, delivering some 14 million metric tons of military materiel, seeds, and agricultural equipment between 1947 and 1949.[192] Without this shift, historian Harold Zink counterfactually noted in 1955, "there would ... have been mass starvation" in Germany, adding: "In the absence of the most extensive food relief program ever undertaken, it is almost impossible to imagine what might have happened."[193] Zink's unwillingness to speculate about the political ramifications of the Allies not revising their occupation policies probably reflected a psychological reluctance to dwell on the frightening consequences of a disaster only recently averted. But seen from today's perspective, there is little doubt that if the Allies had not made the policy switch that they did, Nazi agitation would have continued and probably found a more receptive audience. In the end, the policy adjustment proved crucial for stabilizing life in Germany.

The Fourth Reich in Early Postwar Culture

The shift in Allied policy, however, did not entirely banish concerns about a Nazi revival. Fears of a Fourth Reich also suffused early postwar culture. Films gave particular attention to the Nazis' ongoing capacity to sow mayhem around the world. During World War II, Nazi malevolence was a common theme in American and British films, and some that were released near the war's end, such as *The Master Race* (1944), pointed to the future by depicting Nazi militarists plotting a comeback after Germany's defeat. Postwar films seamlessly picked up on this theme. In the years 1945–48, British and American films portrayed Nazism as an enduring danger. Many did so

Figure 2.5 Orson Welles's 1946 film, *The Stranger*, profiled an Allied War Crimes investigator attempting to track down a Nazi war criminal who has changed his identity and gone into hiding in rural Connecticut (Source: Wikimedia Commons).

by embracing the increasingly popular film noir premise that evil lurked behind the façade of normality. Even if Germany was safely under Allied occupation, the potential for a Fourth Reich remained constant.

One of the first prominent films to remind viewers of the enduring Nazi threat was the major Hollywood production from 1946, *The Stranger* (Figure 2.5). Directed by Orson Welles, the film profiles an Allied War Crimes investigator, Mr. Wilson (Edward G. Robinson) attempting to track down a Nazi war criminal, Franz Kindler (Welles), who has changed his identity and gone into hiding as a prep school teacher named Charles Rankin in the small town of Harper, Connecticut. So successful is Rankin's dissembling that he becomes engaged to Mary Longstreet (Loretta Young), the daughter of a Supreme Court justice. Rankin's world comes undone on the day of his wedding, however, when a former Nazi associate, Konrad Meinike, pays him a surprise visit. After fleeing Germany for Latin America after the war, Meinike experiences a religious conversion and wants Kindler to join him in rediscovering God's mercy. Kindler, however, defends his own new identity, declaring that "[my] camouflage is perfect. Who would think to look for the notorious Franz Kindler ... surrounded by the sons of America's first families?" Ominously, Rankin adds: "And I'll stay hidden ... till the day when we strike again." When Meinike responds, "Franz! There will be another war?" Rankin replies, "Of course," and, shortly thereafter, he kills his former comrade and buries his body in the woods.

As its plot unfolds, *The Stranger* makes clear that the Nazi threat must be met with vigilance. Most of the film portrays Mary's difficulty in recognizing and accepting her husband's true identity. Handicapped by her naiveté – she blithely declares at one point that "In Harper, there's nothing to be afraid of" – she is nearly killed by Rankin, who tries to get her to climb a sabotaged ladder leading up to the town's church tower. In the end, *The Stranger*'s main message is an inversion of its title. Although ostensibly warning that danger comes from outside, the film reveals that it can emanate from within. In a key exchange, Mary indignantly tells Mr. Wilson that her husband cannot be a war criminal, noting, "I've never so much as even seen a Nazi." In response, the Allied official declares: "Well, you might without your realizing it. They look like other people and act like other people – when it's to their benefit." At the film's conclusion, Rankin meets a just end when he falls to his death from the clock tower. The villain is vanquished, but the message remains disquieting: the Nazis have a long-term plan that must be resisted.

In making the film, Welles had clear political intentions.[194] A left-leaning opponent of fascism, he was shocked about Germany's wartime crimes and sought to keep them in the public eye.[195] *The Stranger*, in fact, was the first Hollywood production to show concentration camp footage (Mr. Wilson shows Mary film clips to teach her about Kindler's crimes).[196] Welles wanted to prevent a fascist resurgence in Germany. Yet he also had concerns about America. When he began work on the screenplay in the summer of 1945, early signs of the country's anticommunist turn were being expressed by politicians, such as the Mississippi Democrat, antisemite, and former KKK supporter, John E. Rankin, who used the House Un-American Activities Committee (HUAC) to investigate communists in American life, especially the film industry. Welles believed that Rankin's "phony fear of Communism" was "smoke-screening the real menace of

Figure 2.6 The British film *Snowbound* (1948) depicted an ex-Nazi Gestapo agent trying to recover looted gold from an abandoned Italian ski lodge in order to fund the creation of a Fourth Reich.

renascent Fascism," which he also saw embodied in the racist treatment of Black veterans in the South and atomic testing on bikini atoll.[197] To counteract this trend symbolically, Welles named his film's arch villain after the Mississippi politician. In so doing, Welles universalized the idea of a Nazi revival by warning that it was not restricted to Germany, but possible anywhere in the world.

By contrast, the British film *Snowbound* (1948) offered a more particularistic portrayal of a Nazi revival (Figure 2.6). Directed by David MacDonald, the film is set in an isolated ski lodge high in the Italian Dolomites, where a group of British and Southern European characters have ostensibly gathered to enjoy the crisp mountain air. Yet, as in *The Stranger,* the characters all have a hidden agenda – they are seeking gold looted by the Nazis in World War II. Much of the film portrays the characters tip-toeing around their secret identities, but before long a Greek character, Keramikos, admits that he is actually a German named von Kellerman, who served as the Gestapo chief of Venice and ordered the transfer of Italy's gold reserves to the Reich near the war's end. He explains that he entrusted a subordinate with transferring the gold, but the latter instructed his soldiers to bury it beneath the lodge. Kellerman goes on to declare that he has returned for the gold and proceeds to force two of the British characters, Wesson and Blair, to search for it beneath the hut.

Kellerman wants the gold not for economic, but rather political, reasons. Like *The Stranger*'s Franz Kindler, he is a man fanatically committed to the Nazi cause. During a showdown in the hut, Kellerman screams to Engles, "Germany is destroyed now, but one day she will be rebuilt ... One day, you can be sure, fascism will triumph again. We'll see to that." Shortly thereafter, the hut accidentally catches on fire, and when Kellerman goes to investigate, one of the British characters, Wesson, yells: "Leave the door open, will you? There's a bit of a smell down here!" His friend Blair thereupon chimes in, "The remains of the Third Reich!" In response to this snide comment, Kellerman defiantly replies,

> Go on digging! And underneath the remains ... of the Third Reich, you will find the gold which will help to found its successor ... You find that funny ... Well, so do I. It's very funny that the enemies of the Third Reich should be so helpful in founding the Fourth. Well, make no mistake, my British friends, there will be another Reich, only this time it will spread all over the world!

Predictably, Kellerman fails to achieve his goal, and the conflagration swiftly consumes him. Viewers, however, understand that a new Reich remains a real possibility.

Like other postwar films, *Snowbound* provided a cautionary tale about Great Britain's need for continued foreign policy vigilance after 1945. At one juncture in the film, Kellerman warns Blair, "This is not your law-abiding ... little island of England. This is Europe ... after seven years of war, where people ... hate and go on fighting. It's a jungle. Here it is no good to meddle in matters that do not concern you." Coming from the film's arch villain, the demand that England remain out of Europe's affairs validated the country's wartime intervention in World War II and its postwar occupation of Germany. *Snowbound*'s ultimate lesson was simple: only by remaining involved in the world and not ceding control of the continent to its defeated rival could Britain prevent Germany from becoming a future threat.

A similar message was offered by another British film released in 1948, *Counterblast*. Directed by Paul L. Stein, the movie was probably inspired by the sensational events of Operation Selection Board the year before, particularly the revelation that German scientists had been part of a larger plot to launch germ warfare against Britain and the United States. As the film opens, a Nazi scientist and war criminal, Dr. Bruckner (the "Beast of Ravensbrück"), has escaped detention in England with the help of a British-based Nazi underground movement. Bruckner wants to flee to Latin America, but he is told that he first has to help the Nazis launch a bacteriological war against its former enemies. In attempting to fulfill his mission of developing a vaccine that can protect the German people, Bruckner murders, and then takes the place of, a newly arrived Australian scientist named Forrester in order to gain access to laboratory equipment at a research institute near Oxford. He then enlists two young laboratory assistants, Paul Rankin and Tracy Hart, to assist him. Bruckner keeps his real identity and mission secret, but explains to Tracy that German scientists have figured out how to weaponize bacterial cultures of cardiac plague, warning that "any defeated or weak nation could sap the strength of a greater nation. It's the next war – undeclared and in the dark. The microbe. The invisible weapon." While this proclamation actually reflects his goals for Germany, Bruckner lets Tracy think that the project of creating an "effective vaccine" is meant for the British people. As events unfold, however, Bruckner fails in his mission. Although he develops a vaccine by using Tracy as a volunteer guinea pig, his suspicious assistant (and Tracy's lover), Rankin, discovers his true identity. Following an extended manhunt, Bruckner ultimately meets his demise in an act of poetic justice. After stowing away on a ship going overseas, he ends up being asphyxiated when the vessel is fumigated with poison gas to eliminate a rat infestation. With this conclusion, *Counterblast* echoed *The Stranger* and *Snowbound* in urging continued vigilance against the hidden German threat.

Mild by comparison in its depiction of the German threat was the film *Berlin Express* (1948). Directed by Jacques Tournier, the film features a motley group of Allied and German characters who, while traveling by train from Paris to Berlin, suddenly find themselves confronting murder and political intrigue. The journey begins peacefully enough, but once the train leaves French territory and enters the German town of Sulzbach, a rigged grenade explodes in the compartment of the famous German peace activist, Dr. Heinrich Bernhard. Only after the train's passengers have all been questioned by the American occupation authorities in Frankfurt are they told the shocking news that Professor Bernhard has actually survived (he is journeying under an assumed name and is actually one of their traveling companions) and that the deceased man is actually an agent assigned to protect him. At this point, Bernhard resolves to continue his mission, which involves traveling to an Allied-sponsored conference in Berlin and presenting his plan to bring the Allies together on the subject of German unity. Before he can do so, however, a shadowy group kidnaps him at Frankfurt train station and whisks him away.

The resistance group is portrayed ambiguously. On the one hand, it is depicted as a serious threat. When Dr. Bernhard insists on traveling to Berlin despite the attempt on his life, his secretary, Lucienne, admonishes him: "The danger is by no means over. Hasn't that affair taught you what we're up against? An underground, which is determined to stop at nothing." On the other hand, *Berlin Express* never actually depicts Dr. Bernhard's opponents as Nazis, but merely as "fanatics" and "the enemy." The film further shows that there are good Germans. When the main American character, Lindley, initially encounters a German passenger on the train, he thinks to himself: "There he was, his first German. You know ... you've licked him in two wars and you're still not so sure you've got the upper hand. You could be wrong, though. He could be a right guy." This nuanced portrait of the German people reflected the cold war shift in Allied occupation policy and the growing belief that the Germans needed to be enlisted in the fight against the Soviets. Nevertheless, *Berlin Express* depicted Nazism as an ongoing threat. At the film's conclusion, one of the train's passengers, a seemingly upstanding French entrepreneur, is unmasked as a member of the Nazi underground and the perpetrator of the original assassination attempt against Dr. Bernhard. *Berlin Express* thus reminded viewers of the Nazis' capacity for deception.

In addition to receiving top billing in early postwar films, unrepentant Nazis also appeared as background villains. Beyond infiltrating postwar American, British, and German life, Nazis were often portrayed plotting in Latin America. In Alfred Hitchcock's classic film, *Notorious* (1946), Cary Grant and Ingrid Bergman battle a cell of Brazil-based Nazis who are stockpiling uranium in order to build an atom bomb and return to power. Rita Hayworth's debut film, *Gilda* (1946), featured Argentinian-based Germans hoping to exploit a tungsten monopoly to "rule the world." The film *Cornered* (1945), starring Dick Powell as a Canadian air force veteran seeking vengeance for the wartime murder of his wife in Vichy France, is set in a Buenos Aires populated by fascists who "do not consider themselves defeated."[198] These films did not focus primarily on the prospect of a Nazi return to power and often used the premise as a secondary dramatic context for the primary plots involving romantic relationships. The Nazi threat, in other words, often functioned as what Hitchcock called a "Macguffin," a storytelling device that was more or less incidental to the larger plot.[199] Still, even if the Nazis received second billing, their cinematic ubiquity confirmed them as an enduring danger.

This view was further confirmed by the reception of the era's films. The most widely reviewed was *The Stranger*, which was hailed in the English-language press as a "socko melodrama" and praised for showing an unrepentant Nazi "preparing for the Fourth Reich."[200] Many reviewers of *Snowbound* also mentioned the prospect of a "Fourth Reich" in endorsing the film's narrative.[201] *Counterblast*'s plot, meanwhile, was praised as "not only topical, but … disturbingly plausible."[202] By contrast, other films were criticized for underemphasizing the Nazi threat. *Berlin Express* was faulted for reducing the Nazi underground to a bunch of "ragged hoodlums."[203] *Gilda* was panned for its muddied plot about "some sort of Nazi cartel."[204] And the Nazi villains of *Notorious* were dismissed as "routine."[205] These complaints suggested that western viewers expected Nazism to be portrayed as an enduring threat. At the same time, however, the comments revealed that the threat was being diminished by new political concerns.[206]

The Fourth Reich in the Cold War

In the late 1940s, the intensification of the cold war began to shape western views of the Fourth Reich. This development came to a head in the years 1947–48, when the western Allies embraced a more reconstructionist policy by approving the Marshall Plan and the Soviets responded with the Berlin Blockade. As tensions deepened, the communist press rhetorically employed the concept of the Fourth Reich to attack the nascent West German state. As early as February 1947, the *Berliner Zeitung* polemically labeled a West German judge a "judge of the Fourth Reich" for finding a German soldier guilty of deserting "Hitler's army" during the war.[207] Several months later, *Neues Deutschland* reported that the Soviet newspaper *Isvestia* had called the incipient effort to create a federation of Germany's western zones a "battle program for a Fourth Reich" that reflected the ambition of British and American industrialists to create a hegemonic "world monopoly."[208] Finally, during the early stage of the Berlin Blockade in September of 1948, Soviet Colonel Serge Ivanovich Tulpanov sent a thinly veiled warning to the western powers by ominously declaring that "the Soviet Union will destroy those ... who attempt to create a Fourth Reich."[209]

In North America and Western Europe, meanwhile, observers used the idea of the Fourth Reich to describe developments in the eastern zone. In 1946, *The New Leader* argued that an anti-Russian form of communism known as National Bolshevism was taking root in an East German "Fourth Reich."[210] In April of 1947, *The New York Times* claimed that "The Soviet Union wants a highly centralized Fourth Reich," a point also made by British diplomat Robert Vansittart who warned of "the Russians ... want-[ing] to set up the Fourth Reich as their greatest ... satellite."[211] Several months later, *The Times* expanded upon this claim in a story about the Ruhr, speculating that "a Fourth Reich might well grow up among the ruins of the Third Reich if the productive forces of this part of western Germany were at the disposition of a group of men who, for Marxist or non-Marxist reasons, rejected the principles of domestic liberty."[212] In France, scattered observers expressed the fear that "a centralized German government might ... end in Berlin as a totalitarian 'Fourth Reich' under Red patronage."[213] In the West German occupation zones, finally, news of an East German decision to draft young men for two-year terms into the *Volkspolizei* was described as a "Path to the Fourth Reich."[214]

Ironically, western fears about a Fourth Reich were echoed by an important German resident of the Soviet occupation zone, the Dresden literature professor Victor Klemperer (Figure 2.7). As was shown in his early postwar written work, Klemperer did not take long after VE Day before associating life in the eastern zone with the notion of a Fourth Reich. In his postwar diary – later published as *The Lesser Evil: The Diaries of Victor Klemperer, 1945–1959* – the scholar saw many similarities between the "language of the Third Reich" (what he had referred to during the years of the Nazi regime as the "LTI," or "*lingua tertii imperii*") and what he called the "language of the Fourth Reich" (the "LQI," or "*lingua quarti imperii*"). On July 4, 1945, Klemperer wrote that "the LTI lives on" in the press of the eastern

Figure 2.7 In his postwar diary, the Dresden literature professor Victor Klemperer identified a new "language of the Fourth Reich" (an "LQI," or "*lingua quarti imperii*") (Source: Getty Images).

zone in the form of "analogies between Nazisistic and Bolshevistic language," particularly the penchant for superlatives. "In the articles about Stalin," he noted, "the supreme commander of the Soviet Union is the most brilliant general of all times and the most brilliant of all men living."[215] These and other examples showed Klemperer that while the East German authorities were making serious efforts at "eradicating the fascist mentality," they were allowing "the language of the Third Reich ... to survive in ... certain characteristic expressions [that] have ... [become] a permanent feature of the German language."[216] The repeated presence of "dubious phrases" in the communist press, such as "'orientation,' 'action,' and 'militant,'" revealed there was "no difference ... between LTI and LQI."[217] This insight was dispiriting for Klemperer, who had hoped that communism would offer Germany the best chance for postwar redemption. Yet despite his observation in November of 1945 that "the equivalence of LTI and LQI ... is horrifying!" he never left East Germany.[218]

The End of the Occupation and the Specter of Renazification

As matters turned out, the association of the Fourth Reich with East German communism was short-lived. As the cold war continued and the three western zones forged closer economic and political ties, the prospect of political union came onto the agenda. The ensuing discussions about drafting a constitution for an independent West Germany raised the question of whether the new state would be a Reich or a Republic. At the same time, the Allies' decision to allow political parties to form at the national level in 1947 raised the possibility that extreme right-wing parties might emerge and receive public support. The fact that some of them did, in turn, led the concept of the Fourth Reich to shift from the left back to the right.

In the fall of 1948, the Parliamentary Council responsible for drafting West Germany's constitution debated whether to call the future state a Reich or a Republic. Since most of the representatives wanted to emphasize that the future West German state reserved the right to speak for the entire country (half of which was still under communist rule), they refused to formally declare the Reich abolished; at the same time, they recognized that embracing the term "Reich" in the new country's name would be politically controversial. In a discussion on October 6 about drafting the constitution's preamble, SPD politician Carlo Schmid (Figure 2.8) declared that there were "psychological reasons ... for avoiding the term. For our neighbors, the word 'Reich' has an aggressive accent to it ... and is perceived as implying a claim to domination." Schmid expressed his preference for the word "Republic," noting that its "associations ... are directed inwardly, while [the word] 'Reich' makes outward-oriented claims." In response, CDU politician Jakob Kaiser objected that "if we abandon the concept of Reich and switch over to more sober formulations, within a few years a movement will arise within our people calling for the Reich's return."[219] Describing the word Reich as "a very beautiful word," Kaiser implied that preserving it could help prevent the resurgence of German nationalism. Several weeks later, on October 20, Hans-Christoph Seebohm of the right-wing German Party (*Deutsche Partei*), took up Kaiser's idea by submitting a motion calling for the constitution's preamble to "preserve the old name, German Reich" for the German state.[220] In response, Schmid again rejected the name "German Reich," noting that it had become

Figure 2.8 In the fall of 1948, as the members of the Parliamentary Council responsible for drafting West Germany's constitution were debating the future name of the West German state, SPD politician Carlo Schmid expressed his preference for the term "Republic" and declared there were "psychological reasons" for avoiding the term "Reich" (Source: Getty Images).

"surrounded by certain undertones ... that have had a disastrous effect in recent years." Instead, he reiterated the need to select a name like "Republic ... which can inspire the Germans to great deeds of peace."[221] No decision was made in the fall of 1948. But the matter was finally resolved on May 6, 1949, when, during the second reading of West Germany's Basic Law (*Grundgesetz*), Seebohm renewed his call for preserving the "Reich idea."[222] Schmid responded that, while the name "German Reich" had an "honorable tradition," the "memory of the misdeeds that were perpetrated in its name by the National Socialist dictatorship is still too fresh and the danger too large that the old name could cloud the new reality with ... romantic claims that no longer belong to our century."[223] In the ensuing vote called by Konrad Adenauer, the measure was defeated and the new German state turned its back on the Reich.[224]

This decision sent a strong signal, but during the interval when the matter remained unresolved, western observers, such as

The New York Herald Tribune, wondered whether "western Germany [would] be known as the 'Fourth Reich?'"[225] This speculation intensified on several other occasions: the approval of the *Grundgesetz* on May 8, the proclamation of the Federal Republic on May 23, and the first Federal elections on August 14, of 1949. In this transitional period, French leaders, including Charles De Gaulle, hoped that the future Germany would be "a federation of German states, but not a Fourth Reich" beholden to nationalist forces.[226] In Britain, the *Daily Mail* worried about the fact that "Germans [were] ... thinking of a Fourth Reich" and argued that "we should beware of anything ... that dismays the French."[227] Even after the new German state was proclaimed as a Republic, *The Los Angeles Times* said in August of 1949 that "already in name if not in form, the Fourth Reich is in existence."[228]

These comments invoked the concept neutrally, but others expressed the fear that the Fourth Reich would be right-wing in orientation. By 1949, certain commentators claimed that the western decision to integrate Western Germany into the larger anticommunist bloc risked heightening the German people's nationalistic tendencies. On the convening of the Bundestag in September of 1949, *The Los Angeles Times* opined that the new assembly would "launch the Fourth Reich," adding that it was "all set to fight Bolshevism in the name of western civilization, but also [in the name] ... of a future German Reich."[229] A few months later, *The Christian Science Monitor* asked if Western Europe could be "saved from the Soviet Union ... without giving Europe to some unregenerate Fourth Reich?"[230] Predictably, many journalists answered in the negative. One left-leaning Australian newspaper claimed that Konrad Adenauer's "nationalist[ic]" and "anti-British" government had disappointed hopes that it would be "moderate" and try to "heal the ugly wounds left by Nazism"; instead, the paper concluded, "the world is witnessing the birth of the Fourth Reich."[231]

These allegations were not merely rhetorical, but reflected western concerns about the rise of right-wing parties in Germany's political landscape. When Allied officials allowed the licensing of political parties at the regional level in 1946, right-wing groups were able to form and disseminate their agendas to the German electorate. These parties foreswore any allegiance to the outlawed NSDAP, but their political platforms, leaders' backgrounds, and appeals to ex-Nazi voters drew the anxious attention of Allied observers. This was especially true once the parties began to achieve electoral successes. In the British zone in 1948, the German Conservative – German Right Party (*Deutsche Konservative Partei* – *Deutsche Rechtspartei*, DKP–DRP), led by the right-wing nationalists Adolf von Thadden and Franz Leonhard Schlüter, tallied impressive vote totals in parts of Lower Saxony, especially the cities of Göttingen and Wolfsburg, where the party's opposition to denazification and support for POWs and expellees appealed to ex-Nazis, former Hitler Youth members, and revanchistic refugees.[232] The party extended these totals in the Bundestag election of 1949, where it received five seats in the Bundestag from Lower Saxony.[233] In the American zone, the National Democratic Party (*Nationaldemokratische Partei*, NDP), led by extreme nationalist Heinrich Leuchtgens, former Waffen-SS man Carl C. Heinz, and Hitler Youth leader Karl-Heinz Priester, also registered similar success. In 1948, the party got at least 10 percent of the vote in nearly all of Hessen's electoral districts and 26 percent (the third largest total) in Wiesbaden. In the 1949 Bundestag elections, Allied proscriptions forced the NDP into a coalition with the Free Democratic Party (FDP), but the party nevertheless received the second-highest vote total (28 percent) in the American zone.[234] Finally, another right-wing party, the German Bloc (*Der Deutsche Block*, DB), led by ex-Reich Labor Service company commander Karl Meissner in Bavaria, sparked widespread concerns by organizing Nazi-style propaganda rallies, replete with *völkisch* slogans, martial music, imperial flags, and jackbooted bodyguards.[235]

In light of these developments, fears grew that a Nazi revival might be in the offing. American Military Governor Lucius Clay gave them credence in January of 1949, when he warned that "Nazi-minded nationalist groups" were on the march in Germany.[236] A few months later, *The Wisconsin Jewish Chronicle* complained about the passive response of the American authorities to the German Right Party by polemically accusing the US of "expediting the establishment of a Fourth Reich."[237] Around the same time, the Australian press raised the possibility that "the Fourth Reich . . . [might] really . . . [be] as bad as the previews indicate," while the British *Daily Mail* warned that the "western powers should . . . be on their guard, otherwise a new German Nazism . . . will be reborn."[238]

Of all the alleged threats arising in this period, none received as much attention as the one-time Nazi renegade, Otto Strasser. Since emigrating to Canada in 1941, Strasser had been waiting for the right moment to return to Germany and revive the Black Front. In the fall of 1948, he permitted his followers in Bad Kissingen to establish the "League for Germany's Renewal" (*Bund für Deutschlands Erneuerung*), whose platform was based on Strasser's 1946 manifesto, *Germany's Renewal (Deutschlands Erneuerung)*. In this work, Strasser issued a "Call to the Fighters of the Black Front!", in which he absolved his movement of any responsibility for Germany's postwar plight, declaring: "the Black Front is not responsible for this misery ... and tried to prevent it." Its job now is to "heal it." As he proclaimed, "after the era of the axe [*Beilzeit*] comes the era of healing [*Heilzeit*]! This is the new motto of the Black Front."[239] *Germany's Renewal* was mostly a restatement of Strasser's prewar ideas, although it made a conservative turn towards embracing Christian values.[240] The manifesto even flirted with the notion of a Fourth Reich.[241] Although Strasser never invoked the phrase explicitly, his call for all the "Germanic tribes" to forge an "eternal union" in a "new German Reich" suggested his support for the concept.[242]

In late 1948 and early 1949, the western press began to run stories about the possibility of Strasser's return to Germany. Featuring ominous headlines such as "Black Front Rises in Reich," newspapers reported that Strasser had applied for a passport and was planning to travel from Canada to Germany to resume his political career.[243] Few had any illusions about his intentions. While most newspapers did not go as far as the Australian media's warning that Strasser was pursuing a potential "Fourth Reich," they found plenty to be concerned about.[244] *The New York Times* noted that Strasser's followers called for embracing "the 'better' aspects of National Socialism."[245] The Scottish press warned that "the sinister Otto Strasser" was "welcoming ex-Nazis as members" into his party and dismissing democracy as a "mummified corpse."[246] In Germany itself, the SPD's press service claimed that Strasser was telling former Nazis that he had "come as the new Führer and will lead the Germans to freedom."[247] East German newspapers, meanwhile, blamed Strasser's newfound prominence on the West German SPD's willingness to permit the survival of "heavy industry."[248]

How realistic were concerns that Strasser might revive a new Nazi movement in postwar Germany? Given the prominence that he and his brother, Gregor, enjoyed in the 1920s and early 1930s, the fear was not unfounded. Allied intelligence officials were well aware of

Strasser's charismatic appeal, declaring in 1948 that "his great sugges-tive power in the field of agitation" made him a "smaller-scale model of Hitler."[249] Calling Strasser "'more papal than the Pope' as far as his Nazism is concerned," CIC officials kept close tabs on his plans for a political comeback, as well as on the activities of his followers in Germany.[250] They knew the latter were circulating thousands of pamphlets "preach[ing] ... a demagogic incitement of the worst kind" against Allied rule – telling Germans, for example, that they were "living in concentration camps [KZ's]." CIC officials feared that Strasser's return to the German political stage "would cause ... tremendous confusion."[251] Had Strasser been permitted to return to Germany in 1949, he may have been able to unite many of the disparate right-wing groups under his leadership and forge a more solid front opposed to West Germany's nascent democratic order. This scenario was on the minds of British officials, who estimated that a united right-wing bloc could claim one-sixth of the vote in their zone.[252] That said, Strasser would have had to contend with internal dissension within his move-ment. After the war, his embrace of Christianity, dilution of socialism, and imperious leadership earned him growing opposition from his followers in Germany. As matters turned out, the Allies denied Strasser's "League for Germany's Renewal" a license in several states, deeming the organization undemocratic.[253] They repeatedly rejected his request to return to Germany until 1955.[254] The possibility of a Strasser-led Nazi revival was thus eliminated. Recognizing its possibi-lity, however, underscores the importance of the Allies as a backstop guaranteeing Germany's political stability.

Conclusion

Knowing what we do today about the Federal Republic of Germany's development after 1949, it is easy to describe the Allied occupation as a success. Yet it would be a mistake, rooted in hindsight bias, to view that success as inevitable. Although the end of World War II marked a significant setback for Nazism, it did not extinguish it entirely. The ongoing effort of unrepentant Nazis to undermine the occupation, prevent the creation of a stable democracy, and plot a return to power revealed that Nazism had survived into the postwar era. The scholarly tendency to overlook key moments in the occupation era when Nazi cells sought to act on their beliefs obscures how vulnerable the occupation really was in the years 1945–49. Thanks to key instances of Allied intervention, such as Operation Nursery and Operation Selection Board, the Nazi threat was neutralized. But the response of observers at the time shows that the era's anxieties were genuine. Significantly, these anxieties were increasingly expressed in references to a future "Fourth Reich." Although the term's meaning was contested at the occupation's outset, the era's political developments gradually led it to become associated with the political right. To be sure, those who feared the term employed it more than those who supported it; in fact, the Nazis themselves shied away from it during this period, leaving it to their opponents to use as a term of vigilant admonition. By the turn of the 1950s, however, this trend began to change in the face of new Nazi conspiracies.

3 THE FOURTH REICH TURNS RIGHT: RENAZIFYING GERMANY IN THE 1950S

[Yesterday in] Dannenberg, Lower Saxony ..., former state
representative [Hermann] Heimhardt announced at a gathering of the
Socialist Reich Party that the SRP has made the creation of a 'Fourth
Reich' one of its goals. 'We aim to ensure that Germany once again
becomes a proud and free land, one that is respected throughout the
world,' the speaker said, without noting the irony that the party
leadership had to arrange security for the venue in case of a tumult.[1]
    Mittelbayerische Zeitung (February 25, 1950)

Not long after the Federal Republic's founding in 1949, fears of
a Nazi return to power intensified in Europe, North America, and other
parts of the western world. These fears were expressed in the increasing
concern that West Germany was experiencing a surging wave of "renazification." Growing out of trends that began at the end of the occupation period, concerns about renazification grew acute in late 1949 and
persisted into the middle of the 1950s.[2] They found abundant expression in alarmist newspaper reports, journalistic exposés, and mono-
graphic studies, all of which found a wide readership. These accounts
focused on the increasing efforts of ex-Nazis in the Federal Republic to
form new political parties and hatch conspiracies to return to power.
This new right-wing activism, critics claimed, signified a renewed Nazi
push to replace West Germany's new democracy with a Fourth Reich.
In making this sensational charge, critics were taking ex-Nazis at their
word. As was revealed by the proclamation of the Socialist Reich Party
member and ex-*SA-Sturmbannführer*, Hermann Heimhardt, the former

supporters of the Third Reich had placed the creation of a Fourth Reich at the center of their political agenda for the first time since the end of the war.

Predictably enough, the claim that ex-Nazis were mobilizing to create a Fourth Reich did not go uncontested. In fact, it sparked a larger debate about the extent to which the Federal Republic was truly in danger of being renazified. In response to the spread of alarmist allegations promoting this view, more apologetic defenders of the Federal Republic dismissed the threat as wildly exaggerated. Both in West Germany and abroad, they insisted that popular support for Nazism in the Federal Republic was weak and posed little danger to the country's new democratic system of government. With the German people having committed themselves to their new Republic, there was little chance of them once more embracing a Reich.

Knowing what we do today about West Germany's political evolution during the Adenauer era, the alarmists clearly exaggerated the danger that renazification posed to the country. Most scholars agree that the Federal Republic of Germany was never at risk of being replaced by a Fourth Reich in the 1950s.[3] Yet, whatever its undeniable merits, this view displays several shortcomings: it whiggishly projects the success of West Germany's democratization back into earlier periods when it was more uncertain; it fails to fully explain the intensity of the era's fears about a Nazi revival; and it underestimates the Nazi movement's real strength at the time. In fact, fears about West Germany's possible renazification were not unfounded. Unrepentant Nazis were seriously committed to overturning the Federal Republic's democratic order in the early 1950s. Had circumstances been somewhat different, they might have come close to succeeding. By revisiting the Nazi effort to establish a Fourth Reich in the counterfactual context of what might have happened, we can arrive at a deeper understanding of how and why contemporaries viewed the Nazi threat as they did.

In the process, we can determine how competing memories of the Third Reich influenced the Federal Republic's postwar evolution. The renazification debate of the 1950s was not just about the West German present, but the Nazi past. The alarmists and apologists held different views on the merits of memory. The former believed in the virtues of remembrance, insisting that the only way to prevent a repeat of the Nazi disaster was to compel the German people to reflect upon the magnitude of the Third Reich's unprecedented crimes. The latter, by contrast, viewed remembrance as a liability, arguing that memories of the Nazi past were distorting the reality of the German present and leading people abroad to doubt the country's commitment to democracy. As matters turned out, the latter view prevailed. From the moment he ascended to the chancellorship in 1949, Konrad Adenauer avoided a full reckoning with the crimes of the Third Reich and chose to integrate its former supporters into the new democratic polity. Thanks to the Federal Republic's successful democratization in the 1950s, many scholars have vindicated this approach as having been correct. Yet others have questioned its wisdom and suggested that alternate strategies could have been pursued. What their results would have been cannot be determined with any certainty. But by exploring paths that were not taken and speculating about where they might have led, we can render a more comprehensive verdict on what actually happened.

The Origins of the Renazification Debate

The renazification debate took place during a sensitive time in the early history of the Federal Republic. Although West Germany had regained an important degree of autonomy in 1949, it had yet to regain full sovereignty. From 1949 to 1955 – the years of the Allied-run High Commission for Occupied Germany (HICOG) – Adenauer's government was busy negotiating with the Allies over the terms of the General Treaty (*Generalvertrag*), which finalized the end of the occupation statute and brought the Federal Republic into the western alliance.[4] These negotiations were especially difficult because of the controversial Anglo-American plan to rearm West Germany and admit it into the proposed European Defense Community (EDC). While many viewed German rearmament as an urgent necessity, especially following the eruption of the Korean War in 1950, others were unsure whether the Federal Republic had become a trustworthy democratic ally. These skeptics were concerned that, in rebuilding West Germany into a bulwark against Soviet communism, the Allies had made it susceptible to a revival of Nazism. As they abandoned their early policies of denazification, demilitarization, and decartelization, the Allies allowed members of the Third Reich's elite – former Nazi Party members, Wehrmacht generals, and captains of industry – to regain influential positions in the new West German state. This trend had already begun in the last years of the occupation and found scattered mention in the western media, especially in the publications of watchdog organizations, such as the Society for the Prevention of World War III.[5] But their popular reach was relatively small. Once news of ex-Nazis returning to West German life were more widely reported in the press following the declaration of West Germany's independence, however, the stage was set for a public outcry.

Starting in late 1949, observers in the United States and Great Britain raised the alarm about West Germany's alleged "renazification." In the US, *New York Times* journalist Drew Middleton inaugurated the discussion in November by publishing a series of articles (subsequently published at the end of 1949 in a slim volume entitled *The Renazification of Germany*) that called attention to the "return of ... former Nazis to power" in West German life.[6] Pointing to industrialists, teachers, and journalists, Middleton noted that the same people who had supported the bygone German dictatorship were being given important responsibilities in the new democracy. In early December, *The New York Times* editorial page endorsed Middleton's position in an article entitled "Renazification," warning that if "convinced Nazis ... [are] making a comeback ... we have lost the war."[7] Earlier that fall, another *New York Times* journalist, Delbert Clark, published a scathing book, *Again the Goose Step*, which gloomily predicted that, following the withdrawal of Allied troops from West Germany, the Germans would be "ready to follow the new Führer when he appears."[8] In Great Britain, there was a similar sense of pessimism. Sefton Delmer, the most famous reporter at the world's largest newspaper, the *Daily Express,* ominously proclaimed that the "spirit of the swastika" was returning to West Germany and threatening to call forth "the Nazi that lurks in every German's heart."[9] The reason, he noted, was the transfer of power from the Allies to the Germans, an event that symbolized the fact that the latter were now "safely launched on the road to Nazism."[10] In future elections, he predicted, "Nazis will appear on the scene and ... will ... have substantial backing." By early 1950, other journalists joined the chorus. William Shirer blamed US cold war policies for "rebuilding the Nazi Military-Industrial Monster which almost enslaved the world," thereby ensuring that "Germany ... is reverting to Nazism."[11] And in the summer of 1950, the Society for the Prevention of World War III condemned the staffing "of the German

Civil Service ... with pro-Nazi bigwigs" and "the training of ex-Nazi diplomats to take over where they left off under Hitler."[12]

Besides liberal journalists, left-wing organizations and Jewish groups also expressed concerns. Starting in 1950, they published a series of informational pamphlets, including: *Nazis Preferred: The Renazification of Western Germany* (1950), by the communist Jewish activist, Moses Miller (Figure 3.1); *Shadow of the Swastika: German Rearmament & Renazification. The Road to World War III* (1950), by the left-wing, Los Angeles-based West Side Committee against Renazification of Germany; and *Germany's New Nazis* (1951) by the London-based Anglo-Jewish Association.[13] All of these publications decried capitalist interests for reindustrializaing and rearming Germany, thereby paving the way for ex-Nazis to return to power. Left-wing journals advanced similar arguments. In 1950, *The Nation* blamed the Nazi revival on the same "sinister financial interests, which were directly responsible for ... the Nazi regime," while *Jewish Life* declared that "the renazification of Western Germany constitutes one of the supreme dangers to humanity ... today."[14] The American Jewish Committee and Anti-Defamation League also expressed alarm about "renazification" in press releases.[15]

German critics weighed in on the discussion as well. The West German and East German press both employed the term "renazification" as early as 1948 and continued to do so in news stories following the independence of the FRG and GDR in 1949.[16] Leading intellectuals also commented on the threat. In September of 1949, novelist Thomas Mann observed that "developments are quickly headed towards renazification under Anglo-American auspices. In two years, I believe we will have a fully fascist West Germany."[17] That same year, the journalist and Buchenwald survivor Eugen Kogon pessimistically speculated that "were Hitler to return, many would follow him anew."[18] Even conservative West German politicians alluded to the reality of renazification – although they blamed it on the Allies, a point that was made in a 1950 Bundestag debate by FDP representative August-Martin Euler, who attributed it to the United States' "overzealous denazification" program.[19]

Many of these observers linked the new renazification to the prospect of a Fourth Reich. Writing in *The Nation* in April of 1950, J. Alvarez Del Vayo attributed "the resurgence of Nazism" to the cold war, which he said was "preparing the Fourth Reich" to fulfill Hitler's

Figure 3.1 In 1950, the communist Jewish activist Moses Miller directed attention to the problem of "renazification" with his pamphlet, *Nazis Preferred*.

original "mission of leading Europe against the East."[20] In the *Christian Science Monitor*, Ernest Pisko worried that Nazism was lurking "behind the scenes in Germany" and that "alarmists" were right in fearing that "in the Fourth Reich, as in the second and the third, the dark spots will grow over the bright patches."[21] Similarly, the Anglo-Jewish

Association's publication, *Germany's New Nazis*, warned that the survival of "Nazi beliefs" in "quarters which are ostensibly democratic" might eventually lead to the larger "attempt to re-create a Fourth Reich."[22]

Not all observers shared these fears. Following the September 1949 elections, London's *Daily Mail* soberly reported that the Bundestag delegates were convening to "form the Fourth Reich," thereby echoing the early postwar claim that such a state could be democratic.[23] In December of 1949, the *Dallas Morning News* insisted that there was no need "to start tearing out our hair just because some right-wing Germans are now talking about a Fourth Reich." As the paper explained, it was "not the name itself" that was a problem, but the fact that "right-wing extremists [were] misusing [it]." The goal, therefore, "should be to help the Germans read the right meaning into their historic word for the German nation."[24] This attempt at reassurance, however, was the exception to a growing rule. With news spreading about the presence of ex-Nazis in the new German democracy, concerned commentators increasingly feared that a future Fourth Reich would stand on the far right.

The Postwar Right and the Quest for a Fourth Reich

These concerns were magnified by the simultaneous emergence of neo-Nazi political parties. Prior to the Federal Republic's establishment in 1949, Allied licensing requirements had generally prevented the emergence of extreme right-wing parties. In March of 1950, however, the lapsing of these requirements enabled such parties to form and gain prominence.[25] Some of them were on the extreme nationalist and irredentist right, such as the League of German Expellees and Those Deprived of Rights (*Bund der Heimatvertriebenen und Entrechteten*, BHE), which represented refugee and expellee interests; and the German Community (*Deutsche Gemeinschaft*, DG), which, for a time, served as the BHE's coalition partner in Bavaria. Others, however, were classified as neo-Nazi thanks to their members' political backgrounds and efforts to revive Nazi ideals. In March of 1950, the Society for the Prevention of World War III presented a list of ten different "Neo-Parties of Today" that bore watching.[26]

The first of these parties to attract attention was the German Reich Party (*Deutsche Reichspartei*, or DRP). It was formed in early

1950 from a merger of the German Conservative – German Right Party (*Deutsche Konservative Partei – Deutsche Rechtspartei*, DKP-DRP) and the National Democratic Party (*Nationaldemokratische Partei*, NDP). As was visible in its name, the DRP was one of the first postwar parties in the Federal Republic to explicitly embrace the idea of the Reich and rehabilitate it for postwar use. Like many right-wing parties, the DRP assumed a strongly nationalist stance, condemning the Allies' "crimes" against the German people – especially the "expulsion of millions ... from arch-German Eastern territories" – and demanding the restoration of "the German Reich in which all Germans who so desire may find their homeland."[27] The party first achieved notoriety in 1950 thanks to its scandalous association with the ex-Nazi politician Wolfgang Hedler. A longtime Stahlhelm and NSDAP member, Hedler made national headlines as a Bundestag representative of the right-wing German Party (*Deutsche Partei*, DP) on November 26, 1949, when he gave an inflammatory speech that defamed members of the conservative German resistance and expressed antisemitic opinions about the Holocaust.[28] Although he was expelled by the DP and put on trial for libel in early 1950, his ensuing acquittal by a Neumünster court staffed by ex-Nazis – and his subsequent admission into the DRP – caused a national scandal.[29] Many German and western critics were concerned by Hedler's popularity in right-wing circles and were appalled by the spread of the evocative phrase "Heil Hedler!" among some of his supporters. The East German press went so far as to describe Hedler's rise as proof of the Federal Republic's "march into the Fourth Reich!"[30]

At the very same time, another DRP member, Franz Richter, provided further evidence that a right-wing Fourth Reich might be in the offing. Richter resembled Hedler in being a longtime NSDAP member. But like Charles Rankin in *The Stranger*, he was also hiding a secret identity: in reality, he was the former Nazi Propaganda Ministry official, Fritz Rößler, who had assumed the fake identity of Richter after 1945 in order to avoid denazification.[31] In early 1950, Richter's true background was still unknown when he made international headlines by doing something no other right-wing German politician had done since the end of World War II. As was widely reported in the American, British, and German press, Richter delivered a speech in January of 1950 in which he openly pledged support for a "Fourth Reich."[32] Not surprisingly, Richter ended up being described as a "new Hitler" and came under heightened public scrutiny.[33] Before long, this attention led to Richter's unmasking and dismissal from his political position.[34] But it confirmed the growing belief, expressed by *The New Republic*, that "neo-Nazism grows with the country's recovery, is well-organized, and has serious leaders."[35] More importantly, it showed a new readiness of right-wing politicians to embrace the idea of a Fourth Reich.

The Rise and Fall of the Socialist Reich Party

This readiness became increasingly clear later in 1950 with the sudden rise of the Socialist Reich Party (*Sozialistische Reichspartei*, or SRP). Between its creation in early October of 1949 and its prohibition in 1952, the SRP sparked fears in Germany and abroad that it was seeking to revive the NSDAP. In fact, the SRP had many ties to the old Nazi Party. Seventy percent of the SRP's political leaders were former Nazis, with most hailing from the middle and lower echelons of the NSDAP leadership. After 1945, many of them were embittered, having suffered temporary internment and difficulty finding employment in the new West German state.[36] A case in point was the SRP's founding leader, Fritz Dorls. A longtime NSDAP member and SA man, Dorls was interned after the war and subsequently struggled to find work as a journalist. In 1949, he joined the DKP-DRP, but was expelled after allegedly making contact with Otto Strasser and voicing unseemly opinions about the Nazis' persecution of the Jews.[37] Making a similar journey was Dorls's deputy and fellow DKP-DRP member, Otto Ernst Remer (Figure 3.2). A longtime Wehrmacht officer, Remer gained national fame during the Third Reich for his role in suppressing the conservative German resistance's effort to assassinate Hitler and seize power in the failed military coup "Operation Valkyrie" on July 20, 1944.[38] Remer's actions earned him Hitler's gratitude (not to mention a promotion to the post of major-general) and made him a committed supporter of the regime. After the war, however, Remer was arrested and interned until 1947, at which point he struggled to make his way as a bricklayer. With his years of glory behind him, he eventually returned to the movement that originally made him famous. By 1949, Remer had joined the SRP and quickly became its most charismatic leader. Around the same time, the party welcomed Franz Richter/Fritz Rößler into its ranks, as well as other former Nazis, such as the former Reich Press Chamber (*Reichspressekammer*) official and SS member Wolf Graf von Westarp and the postwar leader of the Deutsche Revolution (suppressed in Operation Selection Board), Bernhard Gericke.[39] The SRP also

Figure 3.2 In the years 1950–52, the Wehrmacht general and unrepentant Nazi Otto Ernst Remer became one of the most charismatic representatives of the far right-wing Socialist Reich Party (SRP) (Source: Getty Images).

included one major Nazi official as a member: the former Interior Ministry Secretary, Wannsee conference attendee, and convicted war criminal, Wilhelm Stuckart. Finally, the SRP maintained close connections with ex-Wehrmacht generals and SS-officers through the latter's semi-secret cadre organization known as the *Bruderschaft*, which was founded in 1949 to advance a radical, nationalist political agenda.[40]

Besides its leaders and members, the SRP embraced a political program that showed continuities with the Nazi Party.

Although the SRP's leaders denied that it was a "successor to the NSDAP" or was pursuing its "restoration," they fully embraced Nazi principles.[41] In describing the party's outlook, one spokesman, the former Reich Labor Service (*Reichsarbeitsdienst*) official and SA man, Ulrich Freiherr von Bothmer, declared that the party "had the same blood type as the NSDAP."[42] The SRP openly sought support among former NSDAP members. In 1949, Remer admitted "I do not conceal the fact that we are making an appeal especially to the former Nazis. We want them; we need them, and we know that they were not always such bad fellows."[43] To gain their support, Remer not only opposed denazification, but expressed his commitment to "preserving and building upon the good contained in National Socialism."[44] This included such Nazi principles as the people's community (*Volksgemeinschaft*), the belief in a collectively oriented economic order (*Deutscher Sozialismus*), and the embrace of an authoritarian form of democracy (*Führungsdemokratie*).[45] Remer conceded that the NSDAP, like many revolutionary movements, had embraced flawed methods and ultimately degenerated into a dictatorship.[46] For this reason, he and other party leaders officially rejected antisemitism (they blamed the Holocaust on Nazi careerists rather than idealists).[47] These mistakes, however, did not prevent the SRP from unabashedly evoking nostalgia for the Third Reich. As Remer asked his supporters: "were not things better under Hitler?"[48]

To emphasize this point, the SRP tried to shift postwar German resentments away from the Nazis and onto the Allies. The party denied Germany's war guilt and tried to exonerate the NSDAP for the country's military defeat by creating a new postwar "stab in the back" legend.[49] Remer frequently condemned the July 20, 1944 plotters as traitors and argued that, were it not for their actions, Germany would not have lost the war.[50] In seeking to exploit the grievances of Germans who had suffered due to the conflict, the SRP portrayed itself as part of a "national resistance" against the joint rule of the Allies and the Adenauer government.[51] The SRP was adamantly opposed to the West German government's embrace of western integration and rearmament. Instead, it wanted Germany to become a "third force" and assume a neutral role of mediating between East and West.[52] The SRP thereby gave expression to enduring nationalist sentiments among right-wing Germans.

One of the more important goals that the SRP used to rally nationalist forces was the creation of a new German Reich. As suggested by the party's name, the concept of the Reich stood at the heart of the SRP's agenda.[53] It was expressed in the very first point of the SRP's "Programme for Action," which proclaimed that "all Germans must be united into a single German Reich."[54] Many other references to the Reich appeared in the document: from the party's invocation of "loyalty to the Reich" to its affirmation of the "Reich concept" as the preferred "organizing principle of the Germans."[55] In advancing these claims, the SRP avoided explaining how their view of the Reich related to the bygone one of the Nazis. On the one hand, the party abandoned the Nazi effort to identify the Reich with any racial notions of Aryan superiority; this implied that their call for "reestablishing" the Reich sought to create something new.[56] At the same time, however, the SRP's leaders believed in the postwar *de jure* existence of the Third German Reich under the leadership of Hitler's successor, Karl Doenitz, arguing that it had been illegally disbanded by the Allies following the collapse of the Nazi regime.[57] This claim suggested that the SRP recognized the ongoing existence of the *Third* Reich and sought to reestablish it in the present.[58] It is unclear to what degree the party's leaders cared to resolve the question of their preferred Reich's numerical identity. But it is significant that some of them invoked the idea of a "Fourth Reich" in campaign appearances and speeches. Franz Richter was not yet a member of the SRP when he first used the phrase in January of 1950, but in February of the same year SRP spokesman Hermann Heimhardt delivered a talk in which he called for "the merging of all German regions, even those not presently under German control, into a 'Fourth Reich.'"[59] Remer called for a Fourth Reich in campaign speeches as well.[60]

In presenting their domestic and foreign policy agenda, the SRP employed many Nazi methods. The party's campaign rallies used abundant visual imagery, displaying banners featuring the party's symbol, a black eagle on a red background, evoking the color scheme of the Nazi swastika flag (Figure 3.3). Martial music was often played, such as the Badenweiler march, which was much beloved of the NSDAP's members. This imagery, combined with fiery speeches, deliberately evoked the pathos-laden mood of Nazi campaign rallies. The SRP's public events attracted large crowds – sometimes numbering over 1,000 people – and often led to violent riots, as was true of Weimar-era Nazi

Figure 3.3 This SRP poster, featuring a Reich eagle and the black, white, and red color scheme favored by the Nazis, appealed to voters with the message: "Whoever loves his homeland, wants the Reich, and refuses to sacrifice German blood for others, will ignore lies, terror, and the threat of prohibition to vote for the Socialist Reich Party" (Source: Bundesarchiv).

rallies. In 1950, bloody clashes erupted at SRP events in Wilhelmshaven, Wolfsburg, and Berlin.[61] On some of these occasions, left-wing protesters attacked Remer as a "fascist dog" and threatened him with bodily harm.[62] The SRP also mimicked the Nazis in creating a range of subsidiary organizations: the *Reichsfront*, which resembled the SA; the *Reichsjugend*, which mimicked the HJ; and the *Frauenbund*, which mirrored the Nazi *Frauenschaft*.[63] The party also sought to recruit famous German military figures from the Third Reich, such as General Heinz Guderian and Luftwaffe ace Hans-Ulrich Rudel, and pursued alliances with fascists abroad.[64] In employing these methods, the SRP strove for nothing less than the toppling of the West German state. In 1952, Fritz Dorls anticipated that within two years, the party would be "strong enough to take over the Reich government."[65]

In 1951, the SRP took a first step towards achieving its goal by registering notable successes in regional elections. The party's first breakthrough came in May, when it received some 400,000 votes (11 percent of the total) in Lower Saxony. In certain districts, the party received upwards of 30 percent of the vote and actually attained an absolute majority in thirty-five small communities.[66] Several months later, in the fall of 1951, the party received 7.7 percent of the vote in Bremen. The SRP also did well in Lüneburg, where, together with the BHE, it received between 40 and 50 percent of the vote. During this period, the party attracted sizable crowds, with some exceeding 2,500 onlookers.[67] At the same time, party leaders claimed that they had between 30,000 and 40,000 members.[68]

The SRP's electoral success reflected the party's popularity among disaffected Germans. Lower Saxony had a history of voting for the NSDAP before 1933, with its rural and lower-middle-class Protestant population embracing a right-wing *völkisch* worldview.[69] After 1945, Lower Saxony had many serious economic and social problems. The state had an unemployment rate of 14 percent, and many people sympathized with the SRP's agenda.[70] Most of the SRP's voters had suffered in the war and were critical of the new West German state. They were predominantly young and male (few women supported the party) and included Wehrmacht veterans, former Nazi Party members, farmers, and expellees.[71] War veterans and party members resented their experiences of internment and denazification.[72] Farmers, who had profited handsomely in the early postwar years when there were food shortages, lost ground after the 1948 currency reform allowed free trade and foreign competition.[73] Finally, expellees were a major constituency in Lower Saxony (making up one-third of the population, which had increased by 50 percent after 1945) and yearned for their lost homes in the east.[74] These groups' difficulty in finding postwar security boosted their support for the SRP. Around 30 percent of SRP members were unemployed.[75] Prior to 1949, these disaffected voters had given their support to right-wing parties, such as the DRP and DP (they avoided the Christian Democratic Union, or CDU, as too Catholic). But because these parties failed to deliver, they turned to the SRP, making it a successful protest party.[76] Had the party not had to compete against the BHE, it would have won even more votes.

The SRP's electoral successes set off alarm bells in the media. Writing in *The New York Times* in July of 1951, Drew Middleton observed that the SRP had convinced discontented German voters that Nazism "could be tried again and succeed – without the mistakes Hitler made."[77] Many other newspapers equated the SRP's leaders with Hitler, singling out Remer for wanting to become a "new Hitler" or a "new Führer."[78] Certain journalists saw parallels between Hitler's rise to power and the uncompromising strategy embraced by Remer. *Reader's Digest* fretted that "even if Remer should go to jail ... he would [not] be unduly distressed ... [because] Adolf Hitler was arrested and sent to jail, too ... but came out to conquer Germany."[79]

Many commentators asserted that the SRP was eager to establish a Fourth Reich. One of the most important was Sefton Delmer, who advanced this claim in a series of sensationalistic articles for the *Daily Express* in July of 1951. In a July 6 essay entitled "Is a New Hitler Rising?" Delmer called Remer "the active prophet of a fourth Nazi Reich," and, in a subsequent piece several days later, urged his readers not to underestimate the SRP leader, noting that he "found Remer far more impressive than I had ever found Hitler at the same stage of his career."[80] In June of 1951, the British magazine *Picture Post* featured an article entitled "Are the Nazis Coming Back?" which profiled the SRP leadership and asserted that "although the Nazi Party died with Hitler and the Third Reich in the spring of 1945 ... [that] doesn't mean that there aren't a number of ex-Nazis planning the Fourth."[81] North American media sources made similar claims. *The Seattle Times* wrote that Remer "campaigns for the rebirth of a greater Germany united in a Nazi Fourth Reich."[82] *Collier's* pointed to Remer's flirtation with the Soviet Union and declared that "Germany's resurgent Nazis will play ball with anyone who will help them build up a Fourth Reich."[83] And famed American Jesuit, John Lafarge, insisted on the need to resist a "Fourth Reich united under a revived Hitlerism."[84]

In the Federal Republic and the German Democratic Republic, the situation was mixed. The West German media largely avoided invoking any possible Fourth Reich in calling for action against the SRP.[85] But in East Germany, the state-controlled media liberally used the term, with *Die Neue Zeit* scornfully declaring in February of 1950 that people in West Germany were stridently "marching into the 'Fourth Reich'" with the goal of reviving "all that was good in the NSDAP."[86]

The growing media alarm placed great pressure on the German political establishment. Adenauer recognized the danger of the SRP, yet for most of 1950–51 his administration ignored the party in the hope that it would fade as the country's economy improved.[87] This practice reflected the chancellor's strategy of integrating ex-Nazis into the polity of the Federal Republic, but it risked legitimizing the SRP. In mid 1951, the CDU in Lower Saxony actually flirted with forging a coalition with the SRP and DP in the effort to displace the state's ruling SPD government.[88] By contrast, the SPD warned that "tolerating the party would amount to national suicide."[89] The Social Democrats were not blameless in allowing the SRP's rise, however. The SPD-run government of Lower Saxony decided not to ban the party, even though it had incriminating material against it, because the SRP drew votes away from the CDU and kept conservatives divided.[90] Rather than forging a united front against the SRP, the mainstream parties tried to manipulate it for their own purposes.

For their part, the western Allies faced a difficult situation. The Americans and British sought to play down alarmist media reports about the SRP in order to show faith in Adenauer, while simultaneously making sure that the Germans did not entirely dismiss the threat. Initially, High Commissioner John McCloy denied that the SRP represented an immediate problem and dismissed its success as unrepresentative of the larger German electorate.[91] By early 1952, however, he became convinced that the party represented a "potential danger" and demanded the Germans "repudiate" all neo-Nazi trends, insisting that the US would intervene if needed.[92] Foreign policy concerns largely shaped this shift, specifically the fear that the SRP would aid the Soviet Union's goal of blocking Germany's integration into the western alliance.[93] The Allies were also concerned about the threat that the party posed to German democracy. In 1951, US Secretary of State Dean Acheson went so far as to ask McCloy, "What would happen if the

SRP carried out a coup?"[94] The British, meanwhile, believed the SRP's rise represented an "extremely critical phase" in Germany's postwar evolution and needed to be addressed as soon as possible. Both the US and the British were especially eager to intervene, as they realized that their control over German affairs was diminishing with the country's growing military importance. As a result, they pressed Adenauer to accelerate the creation of the Federal Republic's Constitutional Court, which could take legal action against the party.[95]

In the face of Allied pressure, the Adenauer government moved to muzzle the SRP. Minister of the Interior Robert Lehr led the effort, convinced that the SRP wanted "to promote a revolt against the State."[96] By contrast, only a minority of ordinary Germans (23 percent) wanted to ban the party.[97] Early measures to combat the SRP included regional speaking prohibitions and decrees outlawing subsidiary organizations, such as the *Reichsfront*, in 1950–51; the Federal government also declared the party "hostile to the state" (*staatsfeindlich*) at this time.[98] Remer himself was subjected to several libel trials in 1951–52 and sentenced to short jail terms for defaming the Federal government and the anti-Nazi conservative resistance.[99] Finally, Adenauer decided to ban the party altogether. Following discussions between the Justice and Interior Ministries, the government submitted its request for a ban on November 16, 1951 to the Federal Constitutional Court in Karlsruhe, which had been established two months earlier. On October 23, 1952, the court delivered a verdict prohibiting the party as unconstitutional by virtue of its "affinities" with National Socialism.[100] By then, the SRP was already dead and gone. Several weeks earlier, the party voluntarily dissolved itself in anticipation of the ban in an effort to evade police raids and survive underground.[101] This plan went nowhere, however. Although the party's leaders sought to join other like-minded right-wing parties, internecine squabbling doomed their efforts, and the SRP disappeared from German political life.[102]

Following the party's dissolution, observers in Germany and abroad reacted with a mix of relief and triumphalism. Representatives of the alarmist camp expressed satisfaction that the "Nazi threat of a comeback" had been "exploded."[103] The West German communist party credited the Constitutional Court with ensuring the "failure of the Fourth Reich."[104] Many observers remained wary, however, endorsing *Die Welt*'s admonition that Germans "needed to remain watchful" against future right-wing movements.[105] By contrast, the apologist camp considered itself vindicated for having dismissed the seriousness of the SRP threat all along. *Die Zeit* declared that the party had "popped like a soap bubble" and insisted that its dissolution proved that "it was based on nothing from the beginning."[106] Around the same time, Hugh Trevor-Roper dismissed the SRP as "a mere flash in the pan," while Fritz René Allemann later declared that it had "dissolved overnight."[107] At this stage in the renazification debate, the SRP's fate seemed to vindicate the position of the latter camp. But as matters turned out, it was too early for them to claim victory.

The Naumann Conspiracy

Within a matter of months, an even more serious Nazi threat to Germany's young democracy erupted. On the morning of January 16, 1953, the British authorities arrested half a dozen prominent ex-Nazis who were said to be plotting the overthrow of the West German government. Leading the plot was the former state secretary in the Reich Ministry of Propaganda, Werner Naumann, and an array of other figures belonging to the so-called "Gauleiter Circle" of Nazi loyalists based in Düsseldorf and Hamburg. In contrast to the SRP, which embraced rabble-rousing tactics in pursuing a new German Reich, the Naumann conspiracy, as it came to be known, used more covert measures against the German political system. Like earlier Nazi plots during the occupation period, this conspiracy also ended in failure, but not before raising further questions about West Germany's relationship to its Nazi past.

The leader of the conspiracy, Werner Naumann, was one of the most prominent ex-Nazis in the Federal Republic. A member of the NSDAP since 1928, Naumann held prominent positions in the SA, SS, and Reich Ministry of Propaganda, where he served as state secretary directly under Goebbels, gaining sufficient influence to be named his successor in Hitler's last will and political testament (Figure 3.4).[108] Late in the war, Naumann was one of the few party stalwarts remaining in the Berlin Führerbunker, where he took a leading role writing propaganda for the Werewolf movement.[109] On May 2, he fled the bunker together with Martin Bormann and Artur Axmann, before eventually making his way to south Germany. For the next five years, he remained underground, evading denazification and working as a bricklayer.[110]

Figure 3.4 In the years 1951–52, the former Nazi Deputy Reich Ministry of Propaganda, Werner Naumann organized a conspiracy of former Gauleiters and other Nazi Party members to topple the government of Chancellor Konrad Adenauer. The conspiracy was crushed by the Allies in "Operation Terminus" (Source: Ullstein Bild via Getty Images).

In 1950, after the passing of the first amnesty law, Naumann resurfaced in northwest Germany as the manager in a Düsseldorf-based export firm owned by the ex-Nazi and Wehrmacht propaganda officer Herbert Lucht.[111]

From this point, Naumann sought to return to the world of politics by reestablishing contact with former colleagues in the NSDAP. In doing so, he built upon the infrastructural foundation established by the semi-clandestine right-wing *Bruderschaft* organization. Since its founding in 1949, the *Bruderschaft* had linked many prominent ex-Nazi officials and Wehrmacht officers, who abstained from the overt political activities of the SRP in favor of waiting until the expected decline of the West German political system offered them the opportunity to act.[112] Naumann was personally connected with many of the *Bruderschaft*'s members and, when it disbanded due to factional infighting in 1951, he brought them into his large circle of contacts. Estimated at more than 1,000 people, Naumann's network included a small "inner circle" and a larger "outer circle."[113] Among his intimate confidants in the former – which was based in Düsseldorf and known as the "Gauleiter Circle" – were the former Gauleiter of Salzburg and the designated Minister of Culture in Hitler's last will and testament, Gustav Scheel; the former Gauleiter of Hamburg, Karl Kaufmann; the former Gauleiter of Düsseldorf, Friedrich Karl Florian; and the former Gauleiter of Cologne-Aachen, Josef Grohé. It also included a variety of other Nazi functionaries, including the *SS- und Polizeifuhrer*, Paul Zimmermann, the racial theorist Heinrich Haselmeyer, Propaganda Ministry official Karl Scharping, Nazi *Ortsgruppenleiter* Heinz Siepen, and Hitler Youth official Friedrich Karl Bornemann.[114] The outer circle, which was steered by Scheel from Hamburg, comprised a variety of military men and right-wing political organizations representing hundreds of lesser ex-Nazis. Outside of these two groups, Naumann was in frequent contact with other members of the Third Reich's elite. They included major figures in Germany, such as Artur Axmann, former Reichsbank chief Hjalmar Schacht, Hitler's court sculptor, Arno Breker, Wehrmacht Generals Heinz Guderian and Hermann Ramcke, and Waffen-SS commander Paul Hausser. They also included former Nazis and fascist collaborators overseas, such as Otto Skorzeny and Hans-Ulrich Rudel, Propaganda Ministry official and antisemite Johann von Leers, British Union of Fascists chief Oswald Mosley, and Belgian Rexist leader Léon Degrelle.[115] All of them expressed support for Naumann's agenda.

Early in 1952, members of Naumann's group began to plot their strategy. Like the SRP, they sought to rehabilitate National Socialism and create a mass right-wing political movement dedicated to reestablishing the German Reich. Naumann remained a true believer in Nazi principles. "One cannot simply abandon an ideal that one has believed in so long, as I have," he wrote in 1950.[116] "Perhaps more values remain [buried] in the ruins of the Reich Chancellery than hasty critics believe."[117] Convinced that the Nazi regime had produced "great works of social welfare" that had benefited the *Volksgemeinschaft*, Naumann dismissed the regime's criminal "excesses" as the "disagreeable effects of puberty." He added that they paled in comparison to the regime's "gigantic successes" in the realm of foreign policy.[118] This being the case, Naumann promoted a "purified National Socialism" that would continue the battle against Bolshevism, reestablish a unified "National Socialist Reich," and assert Germany's dominance in a "common European order."[119]

Unlike the SRP, Naumann did not explicitly employ the concept of a "Fourth Reich" in outlining his vision. The reason probably had less to do with any ideological aversion to the concept – which he implicitly endorsed by calling for a revived Reich – than with tactical considerations. In light of the SRP's banning in early 1952, Naumann realized that he had to avoid the party's aggressive methods in pursuing his agenda.[120] Rather than employing a traditional "propagandistic" strategy, he sought to recast Nazi ideas in a "new style" – one that was "strict, objective, and serious" – and slowly introduce them into the Federal Republic's political culture.[121] Any premature entry into the political system would elicit foreign protests and domestic repression.[122] For this reason, Naumann recommended using "evolutionary" rather than "revolutionary methods" in creating a unified national political party.[123] He hoped to remain behind the scenes before returning to public view in time for the Federal elections of 1957.[124] At that point, he believed, the "day of decision" would arrive, and he could finally act "to resurrect the Reich as an ordering force in Central Europe and a bulwark ... against the East."[125]

Naumann took his first steps towards this goal by exploring the possibility of working with representatives of the center-right Free Democratic Party (*Freie Demokratische Partei*, or FDP). In August of 1950, the prominent Essen-based lawyer and FDP politician Ernst Achenbach approached Naumann and inquired about his interest in infiltrating ex-Nazis into the party. A NSDAP member since 1937, Achenbach was closely tied to the Nazi state, having served as an attaché in the diplomatic staff of the German Ambassador to Vichy France, Otto Abetz, in Paris, where he participated in the deportation of Jews to camps in the east.[126] After the war, Achenbach defended various Nazi officials standing trial in Nuremberg and affiliated himself with right-wing groups. By 1950, he began to work with the FDP chairman of North Rhine-Westphalia and deputy national party chair, Friedrich Middelhauve, to shift the party decisively to the right. A longtime critic of Weimar parliamentarism, Middelhauve wanted the FDP to establish a new conservative bloc known as the "National Rally" (*Nationale*

Sammlung), which would stand to the right of the CDU and constitute a third major party on the West German political scene.[127] Middelhauve envisioned bringing the FDP into an alliance with the DP and BHE and court their base of ex-Nazi voters.[128] Achenbach, meanwhile, was interested in using Naumann to bring ex-Nazis into leadership positions within the FDP.[129]

In the period that followed, Naumann recruited a new group of prominent ex-Nazis into his expanding circle and affiliated them more closely with the FDP.[130] One of the most important was the international law professor, ex-Nazi, and ardent antisemite Friedrich Grimm, who in 1951 worked with Achenbach to establish the "Office for a General Amnesty," which lobbied the Allies to approve a sweeping amnesty program for all convicted Nazi war criminals. Thanks to this connection, Naumann forged contacts with two particularly prominent employees of Achenbach's and Grimm's office: former Gestapo official, deputy chief of Heydrich's Security Service (*Sicherheits Dienst*, or SD), and *Reichskommissar* for Denmark, Werner Best (recently released from a four-year Danish prison term), and former *SS-Obergruppenführer* and Reich Main Security Office (*Reichssicherheitshauptamt*, or RSHA) official responsible for "enemy research," Franz Alfred Six.[131] Grimm and Achenbach further helped engineer the hiring of former *SS-Standartenführer*, Propaganda Ministry official, and committed antisemite Wolfgang Diewerge to be Middelhauve's personal secretary and FDP party whip.[132] Finally, Grimm brought Naumann into contact with the former radio chief of the Propaganda Ministry and postwar Nuremberg Trials defendant, Hans Fritzsche, and *Reichsjugendführer* and Waffen-SS member, Siegfried Zoglmann, who promoted Naumann's effort to disseminate pro-Nazi articles in the German-language print media, especially the FDP's weekly journal, *Die Deutsche Zukunft*.[133]

Against the backdrop of this activity, Achenbach increasingly undertook measures to move the FDP to the right. The key step was the presentation of a new party manifesto, known as the "German Program," at the FDP party congress in Bad Ems in November of 1952. Drafted by Zoglmann, Best, Grimm, Diewerge, and Fritzsche, it outlined a strong nationalist course, demanding an end to Germany's western integration, the adoption of a "third way" foreign policy between the cold war superpowers, the end of denazification, the approval of restitution for ex-Nazis, and a "general amnesty" for imprisoned war criminals.[134] The document also explicitly embraced the idea of the reestablishing a German Reich. Although the German Program avoided using the adjective "Fourth," the document implicitly endorsed it at the outset by declaring, "we pledge loyalty to the German Reich as our Volk's inherited way of life and the realization of its unity."[135] The program further called for reestablishing the Reich as a "unitary state" that would allow the German people to "realize their individuality," "overcome the catastrophe that befell us," and once more "gain world respect."[136] The German Program was supported by the FDP state committees of Hesse and North Rhine-Westphalia, but it was opposed by other states' party representatives, who countered with a more liberal program. The FDP's eventual refusal to embrace the German Program and growing liberal opposition to the party's right-wing drift led Naumann to doubt whether the FDP could truly become the vehicle for a Nazi resurgence.[137] But he nevertheless resolved to push on with his agenda by pursuing talks with other right-wing parties, including the BHE, DP, and DRP. He hoped that the coming 1953 elections would "be the last … Bundestag" to be democratically elected.[138]

None of Naumann's subversive goals came to pass, however. By mid 1952, British occupation officials and the Adenauer government had become aware of Naumann's plans.[139] Initially, they disagreed about how to proceed. The former wanted to intervene immediately against the conspirators, while the latter wanted to secure sufficient evidence before doing so. By the end of the year, however, British High Commissioner Sir Ivone Kirkpatrick unilaterally decided to crush the Naumann Circle once and for all.[140] On the night of January 14–15, 1953, British officials launched "Operation Terminus," arresting Naumann at his home and seizing thousands of documents in an effort to prove the Gauleiter Circle's conspiratorial agenda. They simultaneously arrested five other members of the circle the same day and several others in the ensuing weeks. In explaining their actions, British officials declared in a public communiqué that "a group of former leading Nazis have been plotting to regain power in western Germany" and made clear that the occupation statute authorized the British to intervene in order to prevent a "threat to the security of Allied forces."[141] They further described the Naumann Circle as a threat to the Basic Law, European unity, and western defense.[142]

When news of the arrests broke, the Anglo-American press responded with shock. The return of what *The New York Herald Tribune* called a "New Nazi Specter in Western Germany" was cause for major alarm.[143] In a front-page story, *The New York Times* described the conspiracy as "the first known serious plot for the restoration of Nazi power in Germany" and issued an editorial declaring that, while "neo-Nazism is very much of a minority movement ... given time and a certain chain of circumstances, a form of nazism could again rise to power in Germany."[144] In Great Britain, the *Daily Mail* reported on the "plot to build a new Nazi regime from the smouldering ashes of the old," while *The Times* of London said Naumann envisioned himself as "Führer of the future."[145] In France, *Le Monde* wrote of "the old Nazis rearing their heads in West Germany."[146] Jewish groups, such as the American Jewish Committee, were especially concerned, as were watchdog organizations, such as the Society for the Prevention of World War III, which pointed to the "Naumann Circle Menace" as further proof of "the re-nazification of Germany."[147]

As with the coverage of the SRP, many newspapers stressed that the Naumann Circle was committed to establishing a Fourth Reich. Writing at a time when the details of the plot were still unconfirmed, Sefton Delmer noted that "it is by no means impossible that Naumann regards Hitler's will as a sacred trust to rebuild the Fourth Reich. Naumann may well have taken the first steps in that direction."[148] *The Jerusalem Post* described the arrests as "the first major plot to establish a 'Fourth Reich' since the war."[149] In the United States, *The Cleveland Plain-Dealer, The Los Angeles Times*, and *The Boston Globe* published similar reports – albeit with the erroneous claim that Naumann's vision for a "Fourth Reich" was "communist-supported."[150] Subsequent media reports about the efforts of other right-wing groups in West Germany to forge a "Fourth Reich," together with the disclosure of HICOG poll results revealing growing popular support for Nazism among ordinary Germans, lent further credence to the fear that the Federal Republic was facing the real prospect of a revived Reich.[151]

By contrast, the West German response to the Allied operation was more critical. German journalists complained that the arrests had been carried out by the British instead of the German authorities, thereby violating the latter's sovereignty; they alleged that the British authorities violated *habeas corpus* rules in arresting the plotters; they suspected that the British were deliberately reviving the specter of resurgent Nazism to delay Germany's integration into the western military alliance; and they speculated that the arrests were meant to discredit the CDU's ally, the FDP, and force Adenauer's party into a grand coalition with the SPD.[152] All of these critics doubted that the Naumann group represented a serious threat to the Federal Republic. *Die Welt* opined that the plotters were little more than "pathological clowns."[153] And *Der Spiegel* compared Operation Terminus to Operation Selection Board, insisting that both were politically motivated campaigns directed against minor plots.[154] As the magazine concluded, the inability of foreign journalists to realize that the Gauleiter Circle was little more than a "nostalgia society" led them to distort West Germany's democratic face into a "Nazi death's head" (*Totenschädel*).[155]

Despite this criticism, West German politicians supported the British authorities' actions. Predictably, SPD leaders used the arrests to criticize the CDU's laxness in confronting the Nazi threat.[156] CDU officials also expressed concern, however. Interior Minister Thomas Dehler argued that Naumann was a dangerous "custodian of National Socialist ideas," who needed to be countered as "a rallying figure for people [seeking] … a new authoritarian state of a National Socialist character."[157] Even Adenauer was supportive. Although he publicly complained about being bypassed by the British, he confided to others that the arrests spared him the obligation of acting against the Naumann group, which could have cost the CDU the support of right-wing voters in the coming 1953 elections. Without having to worry about shoring up his right flank, the chancellor was confident that the Federal Republic had dodged a bullet and would be in better shape going forward. In fact, he believed that the danger of a future Nazi revival had been decisively halted.[158]

The crushing of the Naumann conspiracy seemed to bear out critics' claims that it never posed a real threat to the Federal Republic. After the British turned the task of prosecuting the Naumann Circle over to the Adenauer government in March of 1953, the ensuing investigation by the German authorities failed to turn up sufficient evidence proving the existence of a "National Socialist organization" threatening Allied forces.[159] The charges were eventually dropped, and Naumann and his colleagues were released on July 28, 1953. This decision appeared to confirm doubts that there had ever been a neo-Nazi conspiracy. At this juncture, Naumann sought to capitalize on his newfound national prominence by running for political office. After stylizing himself into a patriotic victim of Allied intrigue in a hastily published book in the summer of 1953, entitled *Nau Nau Threatens the Empire* (*Nau Nau gefährdet das Empire*), he decided to run in the upcoming Federal elections on the right-wing DRP ticket, together with Hans-Ulrich Rudel and several other candidates.[160] Naumann went on the campaign trail and drew large crowds to his rallies, prompting western newspapers to ask whether he represented yet another "new Hitler."[161] He ultimately met with disappointment, however.[162] After being pelted with rotten eggs and tomatoes at an appearance in Kiel, he was subjected to belated denazification proceedings by the state government of North Rhine-Westphalia in late August, which classified him as an "offender" and stripped him of the right to run for office.[163] As with the banning of the SRP, the decision to remove Naumann from the ballot revealed the West German government's commitment to defending democracy against right-wing threats.

The ensuing elections in September confirmed the weakness of neo-Nazi forces in West Germany.[164] The CDU won handily, improving on its 1949 performance by earning 45.2 percent of the vote. By contrast, the right-leaning parties, including the FDP, DP, DRP, and BHE, all lost support.[165] This outcome showed the difficulty of establishing a "national opposition" party to the right of the CDU.[166] Adenauer had succeeded in luring many of the voters who had previously gravitated to right-wing parties like the SRP.[167] The West German electorate thereby showed that it rejected right-wing radicalism. This message notwithstanding, Naumann refused to give up and, after being cleared of all charges in 1954, tried to reenter political life. By that point, however, it was too late. He ultimately retreated into the private sector, becoming hired as a director of the electrotechnical firm Busch Jaeger by Joseph Goebbels' stepson, Harald Quandt.[168] The immediate danger of a Nazi infiltration of the West German political system had passed.

Resuming the Renazification Debate

In banning the SRP and suppressing the Naumann conspiracy, the Adenauer administration avoided a major crisis, but the two episodes predictably revived the renazification debate. From 1952 until the middle of the decade, critics and defenders of the Federal Republic published a wave of books and articles about the degree to which the country was threatened by unrepentant Nazis. This was a debate not merely about how to assess the politics of the present, but about how to remember the past. Those who remained suspicious of Germany insisted on the need to preserve the lessons of the Third Reich by holding former Nazis accountable for their past actions. By contrast, the defenders of the Federal Republic insisted that the country's democratic prospects were best served by Adenauer's policy of amnesty and amnesia. As the debate unfolded, it dovetailed with the ongoing discussion of whether the Federal Republic would become a Fourth Reich.

One of the most critical accounts appeared in 1953 with the German émigré journalist T. H. Tetens' book, *Germany Plots with the Kremlin*.[169] Drawing on news reports about the presence of ex-Nazis in the West German government, the rise of the SRP, and Adenauer's extraction of concessions from the Allies in exchange for rearmament, Tetens warned that the Federal Republic was secretly pursuing a cunning plan to "establish a Fourth Reich free from the control of the Allies."[170] It was the height of foolishness, Tetens argued, to believe that the Germans' "political outlook ... [has] changed or that they can be considered a reliable ally."[171] In the short term, West Germany might be happy to accept American aid in order to rearm and regain its economic strength, but it would eventually abandon the western alliance and cut a deal with the Soviets to become a "third power bloc" independent of the superpowers.[172] For Tetens, the plan to create a unified Europe dominated by Germany dated back to the Nazi era, where "it was a strategic objective of Hitler's Third Reich."[173] The plan gained added momentum at the war's end when the High Command realized that if all European countries after 1945 "[gave] up their sovereignty," Germany would "automatically gain equality and the stigma would be removed from the Fatherland."[174] For Tetens, the continuity in personnel from the Third Reich to Adenauer's government proved that the chancellor was "executing ... [a] Nazi blueprint."[175] "Neo-Nazi movements are gaining strength daily," he warned, "and many of them boast that by 1956 a Nazi dictatorship will be re-established."[176] The lesson, for Tetens, was clear: as he put it in the book's foreword, entitled an "Open Letter to President Eisenhower," "We have not learned our lessons from the past. Twice within a generation we went to war to stop German aggression .... If the Germans have their way it will happen again . . . and the United States will . . . be faced with the greatest disaster in her history."[177]

Around the same time, Hungarian-Jewish journalist Hans Habe advanced a similar argument in his book, *Our Love Affair with Germany* (1953).[178] Like Tetens, Habe criticized Allied occupation policy and pointed out how it had "sowed the seeds of the new Nazism" in the Federal Republic.[179] He was especially critical of the Allied decision to rearm Germany as part of the western alliance, writing that the nation's "remilitarization is identical with its renazification."[180] Habe, however, was also concerned about domestic political trends in the Federal Republic. The rise of the FDP, DP, BHE, and SRP proved that "the Nazis are back already" and were committed to "overthrowing the government."[181] Their strategy was to "tunnel underground" and infiltrate the Federal Republic's existing parties until the day that they were ready to "come to the surface."[182] By that time, the Federal Republic would be Europe's most powerful country and would "return to a form of government which may not call itself National Socialistic, but which will basically correspond to this description."[183] The only way to avoid this outcome, Habe asserted, was to embrace memory. Only if the US rejected "a general amnesty" for ex-Nazis and prohibited them from joining the armed forces would it be possible to "prevent renazification."[184]

Both Tetens' and Habe's books found a wide readership and earned their share of supporters, but their arguments did not go unopposed.[185] While the two authors insisted that the indifference to remembrance had led western observers to overlook the threat of a Nazi revival, critics countered that an excess of memory had led them to exaggerate it. Leading the charge was the German émigré journalist, Norbert Muhlen, who, in his book *The Return of Germany* (1953), as well as in a series of essays around the same time, insisted that Nazism had been rendered impotent in the Federal Republic.[186] According to Muhlen, beyond a "small hard core of Nazis," most Germans had been "passive non-Nazis" during the Third Reich and constituted the "apolitical majority" of people in the Federal Republic.[187] For this reason, there was little reason to fear any threat emanating from the SRP, a party whose lack of strong leadership and a mass base made it "destined to failure."[188] Muhlen was concerned that western observers nevertheless continued to exaggerate the strength of neo-Nazism in Germany. This alarmist impulse, he argued, was rooted in the psychological need to compensate for their failure to "take Nazism very seriously . . . in the 1930s" and to make sure they did not become "guilty of tolerating a new Nazi regime in Germany" today.[189] Although well intentioned, the desire to remember the lessons of the recent past promoted a distorted view that "Germany [was] forever Nazi," thereby obscuring the country's new democratic reality.[190] Worse still, West Germany's democratization was hampered every time the American media displayed an "undiscriminating hostility to things German," for it provided right-wing Germans with an excuse to avoid democratic reform by allowing them to claim: "See, the Americans . . . have no faith in us, no matter what we do!"[191] As Muhlen concluded: "we cannot hope for a stable, free Germany if we see her primarily in fearsome stereotypes based on the crimes of the Nazi regime; by treating the German nation as a permanently unregenerate criminal, we abort the real possibility of regeneration."[192]

Other critics echoed Muhlen's concerns. In a November 1953 essay in *Commentary*, Swiss journalist Peter Schmid complained that too many American and German observers tended to "spy Nazism lurking everywhere, unchanged under the democratic mask and waiting only for another chance to raise its head." This was the only reason, he argued, "why Werner Naumann . . . could be taken for a political figure of importance." This overreaction, together with the panicked Allied response to Otto Ernst Remer, reflected the tendency of foreign observers to fall victim to "optical illusions" and "inflate . . . a third-rate Nazi into a new Hitler."[193] Yet this practice could backfire by promoting a self-fulfilling prophecy in which the past would repeat itself. In a February 1952 *Commentary* article, the Swiss journalist Herbert Lüthy suggested that the tendency of foreign observers to question the wisdom of integrating the Federal Republic into the western alliance risked calling forth the very nationalism they feared. Were this to happen, it would perversely enable the world to justify "the opinions it always held on a Germany eternally incorrigible."[194] Writing in *The New Leader*, Richard Lowenthal echoed this view following the Naumann affair, arguing that unless the British provided real evidence of a threat, "nationalist politicians in Germany" would brand the arrests as part of an "anti-German" campaign to smear the Federal Republic's name in world opinion.[195] The West German journalist Paul Sethe went even further, arguing in the *Frankfurter Allgemeine Zeitung* that the Naumann arrests actually promoted support for

Nazism among the German people.[196] The implication was clear: only by allowing the Germans to forget the past and focus on the present could they become politically stable.

In response, the alarmist camp insisted on the necessity of memory. In Great Britain, Sefton Delmer sparked controversy in 1954 by publishing a series of articles in the *Daily Express* exposing the presence of ex-Nazis in the West German political establishment.[197] Starting with his attention-grabbing essay "How Dead is Hitler?", Delmer alleged that a "secret camarilla" of former NSDAP members and SS men in Adenauer's cabinet – including Minister of Refugees Theodore Oberländer, Minister for Special Assignments Waldemar Kraft, Minister for Housing Victor Preusker, Communications Minister Hans-Christoph Seebohm, Federal Chancellery Director Hans Globke, and later Federal Intelligence Service chief Reinhold Gehlen – were striving to ensure that "the germs of democratic freedom are already being extinguished even before the new machine is born."[198] These stories infuriated the West German government, which attempted to discredit Delmer by divulging information about his role in spreading "black propaganda" for the British government during the Second World War.[199] But Delmer's reporting was echoed by other publications. In 1954, Lord Russell of Liverpool's book, *The Scourge of the Swastika* (1954), vividly chronicled how Hitler's Nazi henchmen perpetrated "war crimes … on an unprecedented scale" as part of a "preconceived … plan to terrorize" any groups "who might oppose the Germans' plan of world conquest."[200] Two years later, British journalist Alistair Horne's more measured study, *Return to Power: A Report on the New Germany* (1956), revisited the scandals surrounding the SRP and the Naumann Circle, concluding that if conditions did not improve in West Germany, similar-minded nationalists "might well have a better chance next time."[201]

As the debate about renazification continued, many critics worried that the Federal Republic was in the process of becoming a Fourth Reich. These concerns were prompted by the difficult negotiations for the General Treaty and EDC in the early 1950s and intensified as West Germany approached full sovereignty in 1955. In 1952, Jacques Soustelle wrote in *Foreign Affairs* that, with the "outlines of the Fourth Reich appear[ing] on the horizon," the French were becoming anxious that "German chauvinism is in full renaissance."[202] That same year, British historian Sir Lewis Namier argued in his book *Avenues of History* that "once the Germans regain strength and freedom of manoeuver," they would "found their Fourth Reich" by exploiting the east–west conflict to their advantage.[203] In 1955, *The Nation* questioned the west's decision to "rearm … a fourth Reich to 'defend civilization'," when in reality the Germans had "less to contribute" than any other people due to their tendency to wallow in "self-pity, fear, hate, cowardice, and escapism."[204] Finally, *The Pittsburgh Press* concluded that "with the ratification of the Paris pacts, the Fourth Reich comes into existence," warning that it might "some day" be vulnerable to "a Nazi type revival."[205]

The most alarmist assessments appeared in East Germany, where observers declared that a Nazi Fourth Reich had already arrived. This was made clear by the appearance of an anthology of scathing political cartoons by the French communist artist Louis Mitelberg entitled *The Fourth Reich* (Figure 3.5).[206] Published in 1955, at a time when the East German government was intensifying its propaganda campaign against West German "renazification," the book featured approximately five dozen cartoons on a variety of topics.[207] Most of them equated West Germany with a restored Nazi state, depicting Adenauer working with sinister Nazi officials, ghoulish SS men, and Prussian Wehrmacht generals on behalf of western integration. In explaining Mitelberg's agenda in the book's preface, the East German writer, publisher, and later film director Walter Heynowski wrote that the cartoons expressed "the solidarity … of the French working class … with the West German population" and its "intensifying fury … against the Fourth Reich."[208] According to Heynowski, Mitelberg believed "satirical cartoons were the 'art of vigilance'" and intended his "critiques of the 'Fourth Reich'" to sway "German eyes, minds, and hearts." As he put it, "Mitelberg is a radiologist who illuminates his 'patients' against their will by placing them in front of the screen of truth. His x-ray drawings of the 'Fourth Reich' … allow the rotten flesh of the [West German] economic miracle … to fall away and reveal … the skeleton of a militaristic and Nazistic organism." By alerting readers to this reality, Heynowski concluded, Mitelberg could help the book's prophetic theme – "The Fourth Reich – Rise and Fall" – come to pass.

Figure 3.5 In 1955, an East German press published the French communist artist Louis Mitelberg's collection of anti-West German political cartoons under the title *The Fourth Reich*. On the cover, West German Chancellor Konrad Adenauer is depicted calmly playing a harp made out of barbed wire.

Assessing the Renazification Debate: What Ifs?

After reaching its peak in the mid 1950s, the renazification debate subsequently declined. In the process, it left a contradictory legacy. While the debate was marked by increasingly explicit concerns about a Fourth Reich, none of them ever were ever realized. West Germany never succumbed to a Nazi revival. For this reason, scholars have viewed the fears of the 1950s as exaggerated.[209] Most have argued that the demise of the SRP and Naumann conspiracy proves that the Federal Republic was never in danger of being replaced by a Fourth Reich. The suppression of the Nazi threat vindicated Konrad Adenauer's policy of integrating ex-Nazis into the postwar West German democratic order. Recent scholars, however, have questioned this view. They have treated the Nazi threat more seriously and have raised questions about whether there might have been alternatives to Adenauer's policy of amnesty and amnesia. In presenting their arguments, both groups have employed counterfactual modes of argumentation. Adenauer's defenders have employed "deterministic" counterfactuals rooted in "stasis" scenarios to argue that history would have been no different if an alternate approach had been adopted; they have also submitted "close call" counterfactuals rooted in "nightmare" scenarios to argue that it might have been worse. In so doing, they have validated history as it actually unfolded. Adenauer's critics, by contrast, have questioned the real historical record by employing "missed opportunity" counterfactuals rooted in "fantasy" scenarios to show how things might have been better. While both groups' claims are suggestive, they have mostly been made in passing and have not explored the full range of counterfactual possibilities. By supplementing them with further "what if" scenarios, we can develop their full potential and better determine how history might have been different.

Adenauer's Advocates

According to many historians, Adenauer's policy of integrating ex-Nazis into the West German state was a highly effective method of ensuring the Federal Republic's democratization.[210] Some have even spoken of an "intergration miracle" comparable to the country's "economic miracle."[211] When Adenauer assumed the chancellorship in the fall of 1949, he appealed to right-wing German voters by promising to end the widely hated Allied program of denazification (Figure 3.6).[212] Especially after the 1949 election results revealed the existence of a rightist voting bloc of ex-Nazis and revanchist expellees, Adenauer recognized the importance of winning them over to the CDU and

Figure 3.6 In the 1950s, West German Chancellor Konrad Adenauer approved a generous amnesty program to integrate ex-Nazis into postwar German society on the condition that they pledge loyalty to the postwar democratic order. Questions remain as to whether there were alternatives to this trade-off (Source: Getty Images).

keeping them from embracing the new far-right parties.[213] He offered right-leaning voters a simple, if strict, deal: the new West German government would forgive them for supporting the Third Reich by approving a generous amnesty program that would allow them to find employment in the postwar Federal Republic.[214] In exchange, ex-Nazis had to abandon their allegiance to Nazi ideas and commit themselves firmly to democracy.[215] For their part, many former party members eagerly accepted the deal, especially once the Federal Republic began to stabilize economically in the early 1950s. Given that the collapse of the Third Reich represented the greatest failure of their careers, most ex-Nazis wanted to put the past behind them and welcomed the chance to regain a level of economic security.[216] Indeed, after right-wing parties failed to register much success in the elections of 1953, most ex-Nazis gradually lost interest in political activism and retreated into private life.[217] From this point on, German democracy was secure. Fears of a Nazi comeback were no longer warranted.

For some time, this claim has been bolstered with counterfactual arguments. In the mid 1980s, the Swiss-German philosopher Hermann Lübbe offered perhaps the best-known formulation, when he advanced the controversial thesis that "a certain silence [about the Nazi past] was the social-psychological and political precondition for the transformation of our postwar population into the citizenry of the postwar Federal Republic." According to Lübbe, the fact that "a majority of the population ... had embraced Nazism" meant that the "postwar order could not have been established against the will of this majority."[218] Their desire to avoid discussion of the recent past thus had to be respected. This was especially true, Lübbe added, since, without the participation of ex-Nazis, "it would have been impossible for organizational reasons to rebuild civil society."[219] Lübbe's thesis is an example of a deterministic counterfactual, a hypothetical expression of the belief that history's course was inevitable. Many scholars have supported this view in counterfactual terms. Christian Meier has written that it is doubtful whether "West German society had any other choice ... but to be silent about what happened," while Götz Aly has argued that "without silence and repression, a new beginning [for Germany] would have been impossible."[220] Such comments implicitly credit Adenauer for having made a wise policymaking decision.

Other scholars, by contrast, have endorsed Lübbe's thesis in more qualified fashion by pointing out that the chancellor had no choice but to integrate ex-Nazis into postwar German society. Norbert Frei has argued that, given their immense size and desire for amnesty, ex-Nazis were able to dictate the terms of their postwar integration.[221] Still other scholars have argued that, while Adenauer's strategy was unavoidable, it entailed certain costs. Thomas Schmid has conceded that there was "no alternative to silence," but has added that it was nevertheless "shameful."[222] Taking a slightly different perspective, Edgar Wolfrum has argued that Adenauer only acted as he did because of Allied pressure, speculating that "had the Allies not been constantly admonishing German politicians to be more restrictive [on the question of amnestying ex-Nazis], the result would have presumably been more generous and worrisome."[223] Adenauer, according to these claims, should not be overly credited for doing what could not be avoided.

Lübbe's thesis did not merely rest upon a deterministic counterfactual, however, but on an implicit nightmare scenario. His thesis implied that if West Germans had not been silent about the Nazi past during the 1950s – for example, had they moralistically ostracized former party members – Germany's democratization would have been imperiled.[224] Many observers have endorsed this view, both at the time and since. In the early 1950s, the American Military Governor, General Lucius Clay, argued that "if the nominal [Nazi] Party members had not been given back their civil rights and the possibility of leading a normal life, a serious source of political unrest would have developed sooner or later."[225] Historian Hans-Ulrich Wehler later supported this conclusion, speculating that a "rigorous break with the past" might have generated "an enormous potential of dissatisfied, aggrieved ... [people] that could have merged into a ... highly explosive political force" and endangered West Germany's young democracy.[226] If the Allies had "really tried to punish all the people," Fritz Stern has added, then "half the German[s] ... would have stood in front of a court," and it would have been impossible "to make them into democrats."[227] Worse still, according to Klaus Epstein, if ex-Nazis had been "pushed into a ghetto of misery and despair," then "there was a genuine danger that [they] ... would be driven into neo-Nazism."[228] Ordinary Germans might also have been adversely affected. For this reason, Rudolf Augstein concluded, "no chancellor could have succeeded if he had placed the monstrousness of the recent past in the center of his activities and ideas."[229] Adenauer's strategy was thus the correct one.

Supporters of this position argue that its wisdom was confirmed by Adenauer's successful handling of the threat posed by the SRP and Naumann Circle in the early 1950s. In making this claim, they have employed counterfactual "stasis" scenarios to show that, thanks to larger deterministic forces, history was unlikely to turn out very different from how it actually transpired. Henning Hansen has argued that, even without any intervention on the part of Adenauer or the Allies, "the air would have eventually gone out of the SRP and it would not have posed a threat to the Federal Republic."[230] As for the Naumann conspiracy, scholars say that it, too, would have faded away by itself even if the British had not intervened. Beate Baldow has observed that it is "questionable" whether Naumann would have gained much electoral support had he not been prohibited from running for office in 1953.[231] Günter Trittel has added that we can "assume that Naumann's backwards-looking [plan] ... would have failed even without the intervention [of the British]," for he "grotesquely overestimated" his ability to inspire ex-Nazi voters to reembrace a "whitewashed" version of National Socialism and the willingness of the Adenauer regime to "effectively combat enemies from the right."[232] All of these claims maintain that Adenauer's integration policy ensured that the Nazi threat never amounted to much.

Other scholars have advanced a more qualified version of this thesis. While they agree that Adenauer's amnesty and integration policy ultimately worked, they view the threat posed by ex-Nazis more seriously and argue that it was only suppressed thanks to the vigorous support of Allied occupation forces.[233] These scholars have floated close-call counterfactuals to reflect on how history might have turned out worse. In doing so, they have echoed the claims of Sir Ivone Kirkpatrick, who was instrumental in crushing the Nazi threat at the time. In his memoirs, Kirkpatrick explained his decision to arrest Naumann by noting that the latter's "attempt to enter politics had [not] been an isolated phenomenon," but was part of a broader "resurgence of Nazism," associated with Remer's SRP, concluding:

> if I failed [to act] ... we should never be in a position later to complain to an independent German Government of tolerance towards a revival of Nazism. Moreover, with the passage of time Naumann's political activities would become more widely known and supine acquiescence on the part of the British authorities would be a source of dangerous discouragement to the democratic forces in Germany.[234]

Subsequent observers have echoed this position. In the late 1960s, K. P. Tauber argued that Naumann's Nazi agenda "might well have succeeded had the cadres not been dispersed [by the British] before they were firmly established."[235] More recently, Norbert Frei has written that it remains an "open question whether, on its own, the early West German republic's political class would have consistently been able to control ... nationalism [and] ... neo-Nazism."[236] "Without the permanent intervention of the Allies," he argued, "the risk of an organizational merging of nationalist and Nazi political currents would have been far greater. And at the time, no one could say for sure whether the outcome would have been a final brown trickle or a fresh dark fountainhead."[237]

Still other scholars have gone further and imagined dire possibilities without an Allied presence in Germany. Kristian Buchna has written that, without Allied pressure, the Germans would not have intervened against the Naumann plot, thereby enabling the FDP to establish a populist "nationalist party to the right of the CDU" that would have supported the "Reich idea."[238] Still others have raised the possibility that, if the time period had been less stable, the ex-Nazis' plans might have had a greater chance at success. Ulrich Herbert has pointed out that the SRP generally did not attract major Nazis, most of whom preferred to forego political objectives for economic objectives in the booming FRG; yet he admits that the hypothetical question "cannot be answered ... how these circles would have behaved in times of political and social upheaval."[239] Similarly, Trittel has noted that it is an "open" question whether "an acute foreign or domestic crisis" might have "given momentum to national socialist ideas" and enabled them to "pose a serious threat to the new [German] democracy" in the form of a "renewed kind of neo-fascism."[240] To be sure, all of these claims vindicate how history actually transpired. At the same time, they highlight the contingency, rather than the inevitability, of the outcome.

The Chancellor's Critics

By contrast, other scholars have challenged the deterministic claim that there were no alternatives to Adenauer's approach and have advanced counterfactual fantasy scenarios that imagine history turning out better. These critics have emphasized the high costs of Adenauer's amnesty strategy. To begin with, they note that the presence of ex-Nazis in major places in German life established West Germany's democracy upon an immoral foundation of forgetting and injustice. The integration of ex-Nazis further enabled right-wing sentiments to seep into postwar society, thereby weakening its democratic foundations.[241] These trends, critics add, fostered deep distrust among foreign observers towards the Federal Republic for decades after the end of the Second World War. Moreover, in West Germany itself, the amnesty strategy ultimately sowed the seeds of social division that eventually exploded in the generational rebellion of the 1960s. Ever since, critics contend, the Federal

Republic has been bitterly divided about how to deal with "a past that will not pass away."[242]

These commentators insist that there were alternatives to Adenauer's policy. Already in the early postwar period, Hannah Arendt and Walter Dirks decried the "restorationist" direction of the Federal Republic and wondered whether a "revolution" might have been possible.[243] Ever since, scholars have offered variations on this claim. In the early 1980s, Hans-Ulrich Wehler disputed Hermann Lübbe's thesis about the inevitability of silence by arguing that "the criminally implicated could have been brought to justice ... The social costs would have been seen in the efficiency of the administration, the justice system, and the economy. But it would have been defensible ... [given] the barbarism of National Socialism."[244] Similarly, Wilfried Loth has criticized the fact that the political elites of the 1950s "succumbed to the threats of the [Nazi] perpetrators and their lobbyists," arguing that Adenauer could have taken more risks in confronting the Nazi era without jeopardizing the nation's stability. As he put it, there is no reason to think that "greater consultation with German exiles would have endangered democratization."[245] Peter Graf Kielmansegg has added that it was one of Adenauer's "major omissions" not to have subjected civil servants – especially judges – to the strict screening that it imposed on officers and generals in the *Bundeswehr*.[246] And Klaus Epstein has written that Adenauer could have integrated ex-Nazis "by methods short of cabinet appointments."[247]

According to some scholars, the best chance for an alternate approach would have been if Konrad Adenauer had never become chancellor in the first place. They have floated the possibility that history would have turned out better if his SPD rival, Kurt Schumacher, had become chancellor instead (Figure 3.7). According to Jeffrey Herf, Schumacher could have pursued "a different path to democratization in West Germany ... [that] combine[d] rule by the people with a sharp moral and legal confrontation with Nazi criminality."[248] Similarly, Jason Dawsey has noted that "one could imagine a very different cultural and political climate for *Vergangenheitsbewältigung* in the FRG had Kurt Schumacher, and not Adenauer, prevailed."[249] Peter Merseburger, finally, has written that "if the Social Democrats had won the first federal elections and Schumacher had become chancellor," his "new approach, both politically and culturally, would have been much more decisive."[250]

Figure 3.7 If SPD leader Kurt Schumacher had become chancellor instead of Konrad Adenauer, would Germany's postwar democratization have been more, or less, successful? (Source: Getty Images).

Weighing the "What Ifs?"

It is impossible to determine the "truth" of these competing counterfactual claims, but we can assess their relative plausibility by asking additional "what if?" questions. To evaluate the success of Adenauer's amnesty policy, for instance, we can speculate about ways that it might have backfired. We can also explore the question of whether Schumacher's approach – had it been tried – would have made things better or worse. Finally, we can ask whether either of these alternate scenarios might have enabled a Nazi return to power. The more the answer appears to be yes, the more that postwar fears of a Fourth Reich would appear to be justified.

A Failed Adenauer Chancellorship?

While Adenauer's policy had undeniable merits, it came with clear risks. For one thing, it probably underestimated the potential danger of Nazi subversion. For much of the postwar period, scholars dismissed the possibility that ex-Nazis posed a threat to the West German state because of the topic's links to communist propaganda and pulp fiction thrillers.[251] In recent years, however, scholars have taken the topic more seriously and exposed the shockingly large number of ex-Nazis who worked in the early postwar West German political establishment. To cite merely a few examples: an estimated 80 percent of the country's judges (and roughly a similar percentage of the personnel of the Federal Supreme Court, or *Bundesgerichtshof*) were former NSDAP members; two-thirds of the leadership of the Federal Criminal Police (the *Bundeskriminalamt*, or BKA) were former SS men; and much of the personnel of the Federal Intelligence Service (*Bundesnachrichtendienst*, or BND) had worked for the Gestapo, SS, and SD. Many ex-Nazis were also employed in the Foreign Office (*Auswärtiges Amt*, or AA) and the Federal Office for the Protection of the Constitution (*Bundesamt für Verfassungschutz*, BfV).[252]

The numbers are stunning, but their significance is difficult to interpret. Some scholars have concluded that the presence of ex-Nazis "in no way posed a danger to the functioning of the democratic ... state."[253] By contrast, others have questioned this reassuring claim by showing how ex-Nazis subtly compromised the integrity of West Germany's postwar institutions. Officials in the judiciary, for example, were consistently lenient in judging ex-Nazis – even war criminals – after 1945.[254] Personnel in the BND, BKA, BfV, and AA helped ex-Nazis, such as Adolf Eichmann and Klaus Barbie, evade detection and arrest abroad.[255] Finally, the presence of ex-Nazis working for West Germany's most important news magazine, *Der Spiegel*, helps explain its habitual downplaying of the Nazi threat in the early 1950s and raises questions about the objectivity of early postwar German news coverage.[256]

All of these examples raise questions about the effectiveness of Adenauer's integration strategy. While it has been judged a success, it may have been less effective than assumed. It obviously failed to integrate the unrepentant, ideologically committed Nazi supporters of the SRP and Naumann Circle, none of whom accepted the Federal

Republic's legitimacy. It also may not have entirely integrated some of the "fellow travelers" who had joined the NSDAP for opportunistic reasons. It remains unclear how committed to democracy these former party members really were. Much of the support shown by ex-Nazis for the Federal Republic was motivated by economic considerations and lacked genuine political conviction.[257] Indeed, some ex-Nazis in the postwar political establishment led "double lives," outwardly pledging support to democracy while inwardly remaining committed to right-wing principles.[258] Despite such evidence, few scholars have considered the possibility that these ex-Nazis' embrace of democracy – and their abandonment of Nazism – might have been temporary instead of permanent.[259] Few have considered scenarios in which former party members might have reconsidered their commitment to the Federal Republic and reverted to their old ways.

For example, what if the German economy had not improved in the early 1950s? The economic miracle (*Wirtschaftswunder*) was crucial for integrating ex-Nazis and other skeptics into the new democracy.[260] But the economic upswing was far from inevitable. "It should not be forgotten," Dirk van Laak reminds us, "that the early Federal Republic rested upon a precarious foundation."[261] At the start of 1950, West Germany's economy was in terrible shape. Although there was a brief boom after the currency reform of 1948–49, the turn of the decade witnessed a dramatic about-face. Energy shortages (due to structural weaknesses in the Ruhr coal region) limited industrial production, caused a major budget deficit, and slowed economic growth. By early 1950, wages were stagnating and unemployment was at 13.5 percent. The German economy was further weighed down by the obligation to pay back a foreign debt of some 30 billion DM and the substantial costs of Allied occupation, which amounted to an estimated 35 percent of the total state budget.[262] Finally, Adenauer's government also faced the massive expense of absorbing more than 8 million ethnic German refugees into West German society. Given these challenges, rumblings of political discontent became louder at the beginning of 1950. On the left, the SPD declared the social market economy a failure and demanded Adenauer's resignation.[263] On the right, the SRP appealed to disaffected German voters by invoking the vision of a new German Reich.

Several events were important for defusing this potentially destabilizing situation. The first was the role of the Korean War in producing the so-called "Korea Boom." Although the war in East Asia initially sparked shortages and inflation, by the middle of 1951 it had boosted worldwide demand for precisely the kind of industrial goods – machine tools, automobiles, electrical and chemical products – that Germany was in a position to produce and export.[264] From this point on, the West German economy was on its way to record postwar growth. The second key event was the renegotiation of Germany's foreign debt, which in early 1953 cut in half the amount of Weimar-era debt that the Federal Republic owed to foreign nations.[265] Without these important developments, West Germany's economic miracle likely would have been delayed and the country's democratization adversely affected.[266]

There was no guarantee, however, that these developments had to happen as they did. The Korean War might have been avoided in any number of ways: if the United States had convinced the Soviet Union and China that it would resist a communist incursion in Korea; if the US had maintained its combat readiness after 1945 instead of downsizing its armed forces; or if Chiang Kai Shek's Kuomintang army had defeated Mao's communist forces and won the Chinese Civil War.[267] As for Germany's debt problem, the London debt negotiations of 1952 nearly failed to resolve it because of the opposition of conservative politicians (and the German public) to the United States' insistence on linking debt reduction to the payment of reparations to Israel.[268]

If these measures had delayed or prevented West Germany's economic recovery, the country probably would have lurched to the political right. Adenauer would have had much more difficulty attracting right-wing Germans to the CDU and integrating them into the new democratic order. This certainly held true for millions of former NSDAP members. Without the economic miracle, many ex-Nazis would have remained unemployed and bitter towards the new state. Moreover, without the debt agreement of 1952, Germany might have had to pay even larger reparations at a later date, a reality that, according to Adam Tooze, would have further exacerbated "the nationalist resentment that continued to boil beneath the surface" of West German life.[269] In short, the opposition to democracy would have only increased. The very same people who had ostensibly been co-opted into the democratic system might have been transformed into Trojan horses seeking to undermine it from within.

Beyond impeding the integration of ex-Nazis, a stagnant economy would have prevented Adenauer from integrating expellees. In real
history, they ended up being absorbed thanks to the Law for the
Equalization of Burdens (*Lastenausgleich*), which, after being passed
in August of 1952, placed a capital levy on German property owners in
order to compensate Germans who had lost their possessions in the
war.[270] Yet, the law was only made possible by the economic miracle.[271]
Without it, the expellees might have remained impoverished and
become a disruptive element willing to support the BHE's radical political vision.[272] The party's official representatives, Waldemar Kraft and
Egon Hermann, would have pushed harder to regain lost eastern lands
and forced Adenauer, who frequently indulged such fantasies, to
endorse them more emphatically for fear of ceding the issue to the far
right.[273] In a climate of economic insecurity, a less integrated refugee
population would have been driven to take desperate measures. They
might even have given support to the Nazi fringe.[274]

This development could have had major consequences for the
actions of the SRP and Naumann Circle in the early 1950s. While it may
seem far-fetched to imagine scenarios in which either group was more
successful than they were in real history, it is important to realize that
ex-Nazis themselves often thought in counterfactual terms and
employed "what if?" scenarios to rehabilitate their political philosophy.
Some, such as Otto Ernst Remer, fantasized that if the July 20, 1944
plotters had not "betrayed" the German army, the Nazis could have
won the war.[275] Others, such as Werner Naumann, employed nightmare scenarios to justify the Nazis' crusade against Bolshevism, arguing
that "without January 30th 1933, Europe would have long since
become Bolshevik," adding that, while there were millions of communists in Germany in 1933, there were none in 1945.[276] Summing up the
Nazi penchant for postwar self-justification, Theodor Adorno wrote in
1959 that "the surviving sympathy for National Socialism does not need
to employ much sophistry to convince itself . . . that things could just as
well have turned out differently; that what happened was, in fact, due
only to mistakes, and that Hitler's downfall was a world historical
accident that the world-spirit might still correct."[277]

In a climate of economic insecurity, West Germans might have
found these counterfactual claims convincing. Although only 20 percent
of the population after 1945 reportedly believed that the Nazis might
have won the war, greater domestic insecurity in the early 1950s would

have sharpened cold war fears and convinced a greater number that the Nazis had been right about communism.[278] Whether or not they would have given neo-Nazi parties another chance to shape West Germany's political future would have partly depended on the ex-Nazis who occupied influential positions in the German state. It is possible that in more unstable circumstances, the West German judiciary, police, and intelligence services – all of which were staffed by ex-Nazis – might have been more sympathetic towards, and reluctant to suppress, the SRP and Naumann Circle. Had either group, let alone both, been able to develop their plans further, the impact on the West German political system might have been destabilizing. Had the Naumann Circle's members been able to infiltrate the FDP and DP, they might have been able to exploit the electorate's economic anxieties, and their parties would have done better in the elections of 1953. If this had happened, Adenauer either would have had to forge a coalition with them – thereby further alienating foreign opinion – or forge a grand coalition with the SPD, something he had already rejected in 1949.[279] Had he made the former choice, the country would have shifted dangerously to the right. Eventually, the Allies would have had to intervene and fulfill their role as Germany's backstop against political reaction. What the consequences would have been are hard to say, given the difficulty of projecting long-range counterfactuals far into the future. But West Germany's democratic development probably would have suffered. Had this happened, Adenauer's strategy of integrating ex-Nazis into the Federal Republic would have been regarded as a colossal mistake.

A Successful Schumacher Chancellorship?

Had these events transpired, many Germans might have wished that Kurt Schumacher had become chancellor instead. Would it have made a difference? Historians have explored various ways in which the SPD leader might have become the leader of the West German government.[280] To begin with, he might have become chancellor outright in the Federal elections of September 1949. At first glance, this scenario appears to be plausible. Going into the election, the SPD had high expectations that it would do well. Schumacher viewed himself and his party as claiming the moral authority to lead the country after the horrific Nazi experience.[281] Schumacher's personal history as a strident anti-Nazi who had served more than ten years in concentration camps (including Dachau and Neuengamme) underscored his status as a martyr for the cause of social democracy, which he believed offered Germany the only path forward. As matters turned out, the SPD did worse than Schumacher hoped, but the party's vote total nearly matched the CDU's. The CDU received 31 percent of the vote and 139 seats in the Bundestag, while the SPD received 29.2 percent and 131 seats. In the ensuing elections for chancellor, moreover, Adenauer only won by a single vote – his own.[282] In fact, even this single vote was almost not enough. Adenauer benefited from the actions of a breakaway Bayernpartei politician, Johann Wartner, who disobeyed his party (which wanted to extract concessions from the CDU) by refusing to abstain from voting for Adenauer.[283] If Wartner had acted as ordered, Adenauer might not have won. That said, an Adenauer defeat would not have translated into a Schumacher victory. Many Bundestag representatives abstained from voting in the election's first round (which was narrowly won by Adenauer), but would have voted for him in a hypothetical second or third round of voting.[284] The only way Schumacher could have won is if the deputies from left-leaning, but non-voting states, such as Berlin (then excluded from the Federal Republic) and the Saar (then under French control), had been allowed to vote.[285] There was no chance of this happening at the time, however.

A second possibility of making Schumacher chancellor was in a coalition government. Many politicians in the SPD and CDU wanted such an arrangement following the close elections of 1949.[286] But Schumacher flatly rejected the possibility. The SPD leader, embittered and physically weakened from his years in concentration camps, believed his party had the moral right to govern West Germany by itself without any coalition partners.[287] He also believed that the Federal Republic needed a strong opposition party for the good of the country's democracy. Ultimately, he hoped that Adenauer's CDU-led government would be temporary.[288] Might there have been a way for Schumacher to consider a coalition government? Perhaps if he had avoided being imprisoned in Nazi concentration camps – say, by going into exile like later SPD leader Willy Brandt – he would have been more flexible and considered the possibility. But the prospect of a coalition remains doubtful, especially given Adenauer's own autocratic reluctance to share power.

A third possibility is that Schumacher could have become chancellor if – as outlined in Chapter 2 – the western Allies had somehow taken control of all of Germany and denied the Soviets an occupation zone at the end of World War II. Because the five states that ended up comprising the German Democratic Republic were heavily working class and leaned socialist, their inclusion in the unified national elections of 1949 might have allowed the SPD to win the election and make Schumacher chancellor. To be sure, this scenario is less likely than the others already discussed. Such a dramatic point of divergence would have changed so many other things in the history of the early postwar period – including the course of the cold war – that it is difficult to speculate on how it would have unfolded.

The final and most likely way that Schumacher could have become chancellor would have been if Adenauer had been forced to resign from the post in the early 1950s. Hans-Peter Schwarz has argued that in light of the country's "heterogeneous coalition, the lousy economic situation, [and] the difficult international constellation – it was certainly possible that Adenauer could have failed at any point before 1952."[289] In 1951, his approval ratings had fallen below 23 percent.[290] Moreover, he nearly fell victim to scandal. In April of 1950, Adenauer violated his administration's position on rearmament and secretly offered to create a 30,000-man German Federal police force (*Bundespolizei*) to help the US defend West Germany's eastern border in the event of a Soviet invasion. Two years later, word leaked out that this secret offer had, in the interim, led to the formation of paramilitary "Technical Service" units made of up soldiers who had been recruited from the ranks of the Waffen-SS, some of whom had allegedly composed a list of communist and SPD politicians who were to be assassinated in the event of war with the Soviets. Predictably, the news sparked a furor in West Germany, with sensationalistic headlines describing plans for "the resurrection of Hitler's werewolves."[291] Schwarz speculates that "if the social Democrats [had] learned about this in August, November, or December of 1950, Adenauer would have been eaten alive and had to resign as Federal chancellor."[292] In this scenario, new elections would have been held, the CDU would have lost votes to the SPD, and Schumacher could have forged a coalition government with the FDP and other smaller parties on a nationalistic platform.[293] To be sure, Schumacher would not have had a long tenure at the helm of the Federal Republic; he was in poor health and ended up dying in August of 1952. But he would have had more than a year and a half to have an impact on West German life.

How might Chancellor Schumacher have confronted Germany's Nazi past? At first glance, it is easy to imagine him pursuing a more vigorous approach than Adenauer. As opposition leader, he bravely spoke out after 1945 about the German people's need to confront their guilt for the Third Reich, railed against neo-Nazism, and criticized the presence of former NSDAP members in West Germany's foreign office and military establishment.[294] He also condemned anti-semitism, foregrounded German culpability for the Holocaust, and led the push to grant reparations to the State of Israel.[295] Yet while Schumacher behaved honorably towards the Nazis' Jewish victims, he was more ambivalent on the question of what to do with the perpetrators. Despite his moralistic speeches, he supported much of Adenauer's integration policy and probably would have behaved similarly as chancellor.[296] Like his CDU rival, Schumacher spoke out against the sweeping nature of the Allied denazification program and the shortcomings of the Allied war crimes trials.[297] He realized the need to incorporate "small Nazis" – especially former members of the Hitler Youth – into the state, going so far as to demand inclusion of members of the Waffen-SS.[298] He also supported Adenauer's "Law 131" from 1951, which granted pensions and voting rights to former NSDAP bureaucrats, policemen, and other officials.[299] He even protested the execution of the last major Nazi war criminals in Landsberg in 1951.[300] Schumacher believed it would be morally wrong, and potentially dangerous, to permanently ostracize ex-Nazis and far preferable to win them over to social democracy. This pragmatic strategy risked branding Schumacher a hypocrite, but it reflected his nationalistic desire to convince German voters that the SPD was more committed to defending the national interest than the pro-Allied policies of Adenauer's CDU. Schumacher also had to overcompensate for the liabilities of his personal biography. As Ina Brandes has written, Schumacher's "very existence for the German people was a constant reminder of a sordid past. In his physical appearance, this damaged but fiery man was a symbol of the guilt they had heaped upon themselves. He measured them according to his unattainably high moral standards and ceaselessly reminded them of how they had failed as individuals."[301] Deep down, Schumacher surely knew this. Recognizing that the German people would resist a more thorough reckoning with the Nazi legacy, he responded by endorsing their nationalist sentiments. On the domestic front, in short, Schumacher as chancellor probably would not have done much more than Adenauer.

Yet in foreign policy the story might have been different. One of the most famous counterfactual questions in postwar German history is whether West and East Germany might have been able to reunify sooner if Adenauer had seriously entertained – or even accepted – the famous "Stalin note" of March, 1952.[302] Offered at a juncture when West Germany was in the midst of delicate negotiations over its unresolved economic, political, and military status, the note held out the tantalizing possibility of a unified Germany if the Allies removed their occupying forces and allowed the country to assume a neutral status between western and eastern blocs. Scholars have debated this question for years without resolving the issue. But it raises the related question of how Schumacher would have responded if he had been chancellor. It is well known that the SPD leader was more eager than Adenauer to consider the Soviet offer.[303] Schumacher believed that the German people would only truly embrace democracy within a unified country and feared that if 18 million East Germans were denied their freedom, the very concept of democracy in Germany would be saddled with an aura of impotence, as it had been in the Weimar era.[304] Given Schumacher's views, what were the odds that he would have accepted Stalin's offer and been able to reunify Germany?

Although the scenario is an enticing one, the odds were stacked against it. In all probability, Stalin did not intend to follow through on the offer and merely floated it to sabotage the United States' goal of integrating a rearmed West Germany into the western alliance.[305] Even if the Soviet leader had been serious, the US would have placed immense pressure on Chancellor Schumacher to reject the deal. Schumacher probably would have resisted the pressure and explored the deal's viability, but in the end it would have been doomed by the question of timing. It is doubtful that any agreement could have been negotiated before Schumacher's death several months later in August of 1952. On the Soviet side, meanwhile, Stalin's death and the ensuing succession crisis the following March would have also inhibited a possible deal. Given the political uncertainty in both countries, it is doubtful that either would have been able to follow through on a plan that was already a long shot.

What would have been the political consequences for the Federal Republic? In all likelihood the ensuing elections of 1953 –

without the disgraced Adenauer as a candidate – would have pitted Schumacher's successor, Erich Ollenhauer, against a candidate from the CDU, possibly former East Berlin CDU chief, Jakob Kaiser. Kaiser's support for Schumacher's nationalist foreign policy might have given him an edge over the uncharismatic bureaucrat, Ollenhauer; there might even have been the chance of forging an SPD–CDU coalition, as both parties' leaders agreed on the importance of unification.[306] Regardless of who won the election, the new chancellor would have had to contend with more assertive right-wing parties, which would have vented their anger at the government for failing to realize the goal of national unity. This right-wing anger would have been more or less voluble depending on the state of the West German economy, but in any event, West Germany's new chancellor would have had to move to the right in order to co-opt that political faction's nationalist message. Foreign observers would have been alarmed by this turn of events, but it is probable that the new chancellor would still have worked to align the Federal Republic more closely with the west. This is especially true given the likelihood that the June 17 worker uprising in East Berlin would have taken place as it did in real history, thereby heightening anticommunist sentiment in West Germany and moving the country more firmly into the American-led, anti-Soviet camp.[307] If, as would be expected, cold war forces continued to bolster the West German economy, the ensuing course of events would have probably followed the real trajectory of economic expansion and political stabilization. The outcome would have been an example of a "reversionary counterfactual," one in which history veered back onto its existing course.

Conclusion

What do these hypothetical scenarios allow us to conclude about the renazification debate of the early 1950s? To begin with, they suggest that there were probably few viable alternatives to the Federal Republic's strategy of dealing with the Nazi past after 1945. Regardless of whether Adenauer or Schumacher had been chancellor, the policy of integrating ex-Nazis into the postwar social and political order was probably unavoidable. The way that history actually turned out, as well as the possible ways that it that might have been different, validate the course of events as they actually happened. They vindicate the wisdom of Adenauer's integration strategy as a means of promoting Germany's democratization.

This does not mean, however, that the renazification debate was without purpose. In a sense, both sides came away with a victory. On the one hand, the defenders of West Germany's fledgling democracy were proven right in demanding that skeptics trust the new republic. On the other hand, the critics who feared that West Germany remained vulnerable to a Nazi takeover were not entirely wrong. In fact, they were correct in viewing the Federal Republic's defenders as overly complacent about the reality of the Nazi threat. Although their fears may seem exaggerated today, that is only because we know in hindsight that they never came to pass. Given the era's tremendous uncertainty, they were entirely prudent. There were no guarantees in the early 1950s that the Federal Republic would become an economic and political success story. Had circumstances been somewhat different, West Germany might have moved in a more right-wing direction. This fact justifies the insistence of foreign skeptics about the need to remember the Nazi past. In expressing the concern that the Federal Republic was becoming renazified, foreign observers sought to keep the German people on historical probation. They made clear that if the Germans themselves proved reluctant to confront their Nazi past, foreign opinion would remind them. For foreign observers, memory was an insurance policy. Thankfully, they could rely on the Allies as their agents. More than anything else, the renazification debate underscored the importance of the Allies as a stabilizing presence in the early Federal Republic. Given the fact that in real history, the Allies had to intervene on several occasions in the early 1950s to suppress Nazi threats to West Germany's democratization, it is clear that in their absence the country would have been in a more precarious situation. Their presence – and their commitment to remembrance – ensured that early postwar German history did not transpire otherwise.

In the end, the renazification debate had a paradoxical impact on the idea of the Fourth Reich. At the precise time that West German democracy was becoming solidified – at the precise time that the country was becoming *less* likely to fall victim to a Nazi comeback – public fears to the contrary were intensifying. The fear that West Germany might one day become a Fourth Reich was solidified by the efforts of unrepentant Nazis associated with the SRP and the Naumann Circle to replace the Federal Republic's democratic order with a revived Reich.

The suppression of these efforts reinforced the stability of West German democracy, but it cemented the connection between the idea of a Fourth Reich and renewed right-wing radicalism. By the time of West Germany's entry into NATO in 1955, the notion of a Fourth Reich had moved decisively to the right. Despite being halted in actuality, it loomed ever larger in western consciousness. This gap between perception and reality persisted well beyond the crisis years of the early 1950s. Although fears of a Fourth Reich ebbed following the middle of the decade, they did not disappear. With the dawn of the 1960s, they began to evolve in a new and unexpected direction.

FROM GERMANY TO THE UNITED STATES: 4 UNIVERSALIZING THE FOURTH REICH IN THE TURBULENT 1960S

On Friday evening, more than 5,000 people in Munich –
predominantly students . . . and young union members – protested in
a mile-long demonstration against neo-fascism and the NPD.
The demonstrators marched from the Königsplatz to the Siegestor
carrying banners with slogans reading, "We Do Not Want a Fourth
Reich."[1]

Neues Deutschland (November 19, 1966)

The Blackman in America must realize that integration of the Black
and white races in the U.S. will never work . . . Black people in America
are a nation within a nation, a colonialized captive African nation.
    America is an enemy of all freedom-loving peoples of the world . . .
It is an international racist criminal. It is the Fourth Reich, worse than
Nazi Germany.[2]

Max Stanford (March, 1968)

With the dawn of the 1960s, new events began to transform
western views of the Fourth Reich. West Germany's growing economic prosperity and political stability during the 1950s boosted
international confidence in the country and brought a halt to the
renazification debate. The halt, however, proved temporary. Not
long after the turn of the decade, the eruption of new events
rekindled interest in West Germany's Nazi past. In late 1959 and
early 1960, the eruption of anti-Jewish vandalism known as the
swastika wave revived western fears about German antisemitism.

The Israeli Mossad's capture of *SS-Obersturmbannführer* Adolf Eichmann in Argentina in May of 1960 refocused world attention on the Nazi regime's crimes against the Jews. And the rise and electoral success of the far-right National Democratic Party (*Nationaldemokratische Partei Deutschlands*, NPD) in the years 1964–69 renewed concerns about the persistence of Nazi ideas in the Federal Republic. As was shown by the 1966 protest against the NPD in Munich, fears returned that the Federal Republic might still become a Fourth Reich. In a notable new development, however, these fears were not directed solely towards West Germany. The angry declaration by the American Black nationalist, Max Stanford, in March of 1968 showed that the idea of the Fourth Reich had made its way into new settings and had come to denote new dangers. Like the broader significance of the Nazi legacy, the idea of the Fourth Reich was becoming universalized.

This development reflected the turbulent events of the 1960s. Already in the early years of the decade, but especially during its second half, growing numbers of people in the United States and Europe became convinced that Nazism was not solely a German phenomenon. The fact that the West German swastika wave spawned copycat attacks worldwide convinced many observers that Nazism and antisemitism enjoyed support outside of the Federal Republic. Similarly, while the rise of the NPD revived western concerns about the health of West Germany's democracy, anxious observers perceived "fascist" tendencies in other countries as well. The belief that fascism was an increasingly universal danger reflected the decade's deepening sense of political polarization. Throughout the western world, the onset of economic recession, the explosion of generational revolt, and the emergence of the counterculture widened the gulf between the left and right, and led both camps to apply the idea of the Fourth Reich to new concerns. This development was predictably visible in the Federal Republic, where left-wing students invoked the idea in debating their country's political future. In a surprising turn, however, the idea of the Fourth Reich was invoked even more frequently in the United States, where radical leftist groups – ranging from college Marxists to Black nationalists – employed the term to condemn the Vietnam war, American racism, and the Watergate scandal. In the process, the Fourth Reich became transformed into an all-purpose signifier of contemporary evil.

Reviving the Renazification Debate

Few observers at the beginning of the decade could have predicted the coming turmoil over the Nazi past. By the end of the 1950s, the renazification debate seemed to be over. In the Federal elections of 1957, Adenauer's CDU gained 50 percent of the vote and a comfortable majority of seats in the Bundestag, a result that showed the strength of the political center and the weakness of the far right. The Federal Republic's impressive stability appeared to confirm the contention of many observers that the country had extinguished the last vestiges of Nazism. The former US High Commissioner for Germany, James Conant, summed up the consensus in 1958 when he declared that Nazism was "dead and buried."[3]

In this new climate, alarmist references to a Nazi Fourth Reich began to decline. To a degree not seen since the late occupation period, more neutral invocations of the concept began to appear. As early as 1955, the usually critical Germany-watcher and *New York Times* journalist Drew Middleton foresaw the possibility of a "united, prosperous and powerful Fourth Reich" coming into existence in the future.[4] A few years later, the conservative historian William Henry Chamberlin wrote in the *Wall Street Journal* that "neo-Nazi movements ... have flopped dismally" in "the Fourth 'Reich' of Konrad Adenauer."[5] The creeping normalization of the concept was further visible in a 1960 *New Yorker* review of the German romance film, *Rosemary*, which the magazine breezily described as focusing on "the *nouveaux riches* of the Fourth Reich."[6] The same trend was visible among West German journalists. During the late 1950s, various magazines and newspapers published articles employing anodyne references to the Fourth Reich as the successor state to the Third Reich, thereby lending the term a sense of democratic legitimacy.[7] Scattered West Germans even began to employ the concept to critique the East German regime. In 1959, the comedic Berlin theater company The Porcupines made headlines when it satirized the premise of Bertolt Brecht's play *Fear and Misery of the Third Reich* (1938) by changing it to *Fear and Misery of the Fourth Reich*, transforming the original play's Gestapo agents into spies serving the East German communist regime.[8] Similar references to a communist Fourth Reich in newspaper articles and academic books revealed that the concept did not refer exclusively to the Federal Republic.[9] This shift in discourse suggested that West Germany was finally emerging from the shadow of the Nazi past and could focus squarely on the future.

Around the same time, however, new signs of uncertainty appeared. In the late 1950s, diplomatic relations between the US and West Germany grew increasingly tense. Although the two nations had jointly resisted Soviet attempts to undermine the process of western military and economic integration, they began to disagree at the end of the decade about pursuing a policy of *détente*. The US under President Dwight D. Eisenhower wanted to reduce east–west tensions by negotiating disarmament agreements and recognizing the European territorial status quo. West Germany, however, stuck to the Hallstein Doctrine and refused to recognize the German Democratic Republic in order to hold open the possibility of reunification. These diverging interests became visible with the eruption of the Berlin crisis in the years 1958–61. In November of 1958, Soviet premier Nikita Khrushchev responded to the accelerating exodus of East Germans to West Berlin by demanding that western forces abandon their sectors of the city within six months or have the Soviets award full control to the East German government. Since the US did not want to jeopardize the chances of superpower accommodation, it ignored West German opposition and pursued a series of diplomatic summits meant to settle the city's status. None of them ended up working, as was made clear by the East German government's decision to erect the Berlin Wall in August of 1961. But throughout the tense three-year period, West Germans were in a constant state of anxiety about how the great powers might determine their fate.[10]

They were particularly concerned that western confidence in the Federal Republic might be shaken by new revelations about the country's Nazi past. Although West Germany was increasingly viewed as a success after the mid 1950s, it had to contend with sporadic controversies involving the legacy of the Third Reich. The presence of ex-Nazis in the postwar state remained a particular issue of concern. Not only did critical attention persist towards Adenauer's cabinet members Hans Globke, Theodor Oberländer, and Hans-Christoph Seebohm, it began to extend to the West German legal, educational, and medical establishments. The presence of Nazis in the judiciary was highlighted by the Nieland–Budde affair of 1958–59, when an ex-Nazi judge, Enno Budde, exonerated a Hamburg businessman, Friedrich Nieland, for publishing an antisemitic pamphlet condemning world Jewry. Around the same time, the presence of Nazis in the West German school system was highlighted by the Zind affair, when a right-wing schoolteacher, Ludwig Zind, received widespread support from his fellow citizens of Offenburg while on trial in 1958 for spewing antisemitic invective at a Jewish businessman during an altercation in a local restaurant. Not long thereafter, the arrest of the Flensburg medical doctor Werner Heyde (also known as Fritz Sawade) for his wartime involvement in Hitler's T4 "euthanasia" campaign revealed how Nazi doctors had found their way back into the medical profession. These cases, in addition to the resumption of war crimes trials for SS Einsatzgruppen members and concentration camp guards from Buchenwald and Sachsenhausen in 1958, received considerable news coverage in West Germany and, to a lesser degree, abroad. Yet, until the turn of the decade, none of these episodes sufficed to revive the renazification debate.

The Swastika Wave

This changed dramatically at the end of 1959, however, when an unprecedented wave of antisemitic vandalism erupted throughout the Federal Republic.[11] On Christmas Day, in the city of Cologne, unknown perpetrators painted black swastikas and the phrase "Jews Get Out" on the exterior of the city's newly restored synagogue (Figure 4.1).[12] Vandals also defaced a nearby memorial to victims of the Gestapo. This public display of hatred was shocking enough in itself, but it deepened the next day when the perpetrators were apprehended and revealed to be young members of the right-wing DRP. Even more alarming was the fact that they appeared to be motivated by Nazi ideas. Although they denied being antisemitic, they openly criticized what they called the "German people's [tendency to] be self-besmirching" and insisted on the need to recognize the "many positive aspects [of National Socialism]."[13]

The episode in Cologne was only the beginning. In the days and weeks that followed, hundreds of copycat actions were recorded across West Germany. In Berlin, Nuremberg, Hanover, and dozens of other localities, vandals painted swastikas, SS runes, and Stars of David on synagogues, schools, and shop windows. They often added antisemitic slogans, such as "Death to the Jews" and "Heil Hitler."[14] In certain instances, they even targeted individual Jews, as in the town of

Figure 4.1 On Christmas day, 1959, in the city of Cologne, Germany, unknown perpetrators painted black swastikas and the phrase "Jews Get Out" on the exterior of the city's newly restored synagogue (Source: Getty Images).

Scheinfeld, where the house of a Jewish businessman was smeared with the slogan "Filthy Jew," and in Hesse, where an elderly Jewish survivor of Terezin was anonymously threatened with crucifixion.[15] Still other individuals were caught singing Nazi songs, chanting Nazi slogans, and distributing antisemitic pamphlets.[16] There were even cases of attempted arson against synagogues in Bavaria.[17] Altogether, 833 cases were registered nationwide between December of 1959 and mid February 1960 – more than twenty a day.[18] Subsequent episodes were registered well into 1961.[19]

The foreign response was immediate. The press in the United States devoted considerable coverage to "The Swastika Syndrome," with newspapers reporting every new instance with deep concern.[20] Governments in Western Europe, North America, and Israel energetically condemned the "Neo-Nazi Outrages."[21] Public dismay was also expressed in the form of mass demonstrations in London and other cities.[22] This surge of attention far exceeded that given to earlier instances of postwar German antisemitism. The swastika wave's unprecedented scope and its eruption against the backdrop of the deepening Berlin crisis revealed that foreign opinion remained distrustful of the Federal Republic. As the German Foreign Office admitted in a March affidavit, the reaction to the swastika wave revealed that "nothing has been forgotten in the West" and that "the name of Germany is still associated with concentration camps and gas chambers."[23] To be sure, Anglo-American observers did not view the swastika wave as a serious threat to West German democracy.[24] Yet the vandalism convinced foreign critics that the Federal Republic had failed to adequately confront its Nazi past.[25] Many commentators contended that the young age of the perpetrators – most were in their teens and 20s – exposed serious shortcomings in the country's educational system.[26] Critics raised further concerns that ex-Nazis were increasingly "turning up in high places, in both East and West German governments."[27]

In the Federal Republic, the response to the swastika wave was divided. Adenauer worried that the episode had "damaged Germany's international image" at a time of growing east–west tensions over Berlin.[28] In responding, therefore, he bluntly described the wave as a "source of shame for the whole German people" and vowed to combat it. At the same time, his administration defensively offered up politically expedient explanations for the antisemitic vandalism. Government officials commonly claimed that it was part of a premeditated conspiracy hatched by the communist East German regime to "defame West Germany's image in the eyes of the world."[29] Other observers dismissed the vandalism as the spontaneous actions of young and often inebriated "rowdies." These explanations insisted that the wave did not reflect any deeper antisemitic or antidemocratic sentiments.[30] By contrast, the political opposition, led by the Social Democratic Party (SPD), Jewish groups, and liberal media, connected the swastika wave to Adenauer's integration of ex-Nazis into the postwar establishment.[31] They charged that the presence of Globke, Oberländer, and others in his cabinet revealed that the government had done more for the Nazi regime's collaborators than their victims. Younger Germans amplified these charges by organizing protest marches and demanding that Adenauer remove ex-Nazis from government positions.[32] These protests placed new pressure on Adenauer and stimulated renewed calls to confront West Germany's Nazi past.[33] In so doing, they revived the renazification debate.

The Renazification Debate: The Alarmists

As was true in the early 1950s, the renewed debate of the early 1960s featured the publication of alarmist books that revisited old concerns about the Federal Republic's trustworthiness. The first of these books was William L. Shirer's worldwide bestseller, *The Rise and Fall of the Third Reich*. Although not directly tied to the renazification debate, the book influenced it profoundly.[34] Published in October of 1960, Shirer's study benefited from its impeccable timing, appearing less than half a year after the ebbing of the swastika wave in February and a few months after the capture of Eichmann in May. These events, in addition to the ongoing Berlin crisis, lent the book heightened immediacy and revived memories of the Nazi era abroad. These facts by themselves made many West German elites concerned about the book, but they were even more alarmed by its underlying "Luther to Hitler" thesis, which located the Third Reich's roots deep in German history. Even though Shirer made few direct connections between Germany's recent history and its present-day reality, there was little doubt, given his background as a founding member of the Society for the Prevention of World War III and his critical wartime and postwar journalism, that he remained wary of the Federal Republic. For this reason, West German observers condemned his book as an "anti-German" diatribe.[35] Their hyperbolic reaction, however, only deepened international interest in the Nazi era and enlarged the audience for other alarmist studies.

Two such books were T. H. Tetens' *The New Germany and the Old Nazis* (1961) and John Dornberg's *Schizophrenic Germany* (1961). Tetens' book revisited some of the arguments of his earlier study, *Germany Plots with the Kremlin*, arguing that the "Nazis have had a quiet comeback everywhere" and were "only waiting for a change in the political wind" before they made their move. Tetens interpreted the swastika wave bleakly, arguing that 7 to 8 million Germans were "fanatical supporters of old Nazi concepts" and a "restored German Reich."[36] Most Germans, he concluded, were "waiting for a new Führer."[37] Dornberg's book, by contrast, offered a more nuanced assessment. He described West Germany as a "bewildering ... society of contradictions," noting that its citizens were "neither [able] to remember [n]or forget [the Nazi past]." As a result, he asserted, "fascism was neither dead nor alive." On the positive side, Dornberg believed that the West German judiciary had responded adequately to the swastika wave by punishing the perpetrators and considering new laws against Nazi activism; he disagreed with Tetens' warnings about a Nazi resurgence, saying that it was "an exaggeration of the crassest sort" to claim "that the Nazis are back in power."[38] At the same time, he raised doubts about the Federal Republic's political stability, writing that "Germany's independence was granted too fast and its democracy was based upon too shaky a foundation." The worrisome result was that the Germans had "forgotten to come to grips with their history."[39]

Other studies during this phase of the debate explicitly raised the question of a future Fourth Reich. New York-based journalist Paul Meskil's book *Hitler's Heirs* (1961) resembled Tetens' and Dornberg's studies in chronicling the presence of ex-Nazis in the West German state. But he lent his analysis extra rhetorical emphasis in a chapter entitled "The Fourth Reich," which used the term to describe the estimated 10,000 Germans still living in West Germany who "took part in Nazi mass murders" during the Second World War.[40] Like other writers, Meskil detailed the biographies of such figures as Globke, Oberländer, and Heyde, but he went further by connecting them to a worldwide "Nazi underground" that was "busily, quietly, secretly working for a Fourth Reich."[41] Given these international links to unrepentant Nazis abroad, Meskil concluded that the Federal Republic was not to be trusted. The journalist Charles Allen advanced a similar claim in his book, *Heusinger of the Fourth Reich* (1963) (Figure 4.2). Rather than surveying the many ex-Nazis in postwar political service, Allen focused on a single pivotal figure – West Germany's chief of the Bundeswehr and chairman of the NATO military committee, General Adolf Heusinger. Allen's study challenged the US State Department's effort to whitewash the general's "sordid career" in the Third Reich and rehabilitate him for postwar service against the Soviets. Rejecting the "myth" that Heusinger was an apolitical opponent of Hitler, Allen showed that the general had loyally served the Nazi regime and was involved in its worst crimes. As Chief of the General Staff of the Army (*Oberkommando des Heeres*, OKH), Heusinger helped plan Operation Barbarossa, drafted the infamous "Commissar Order" of March 1941, and was fully informed of the crimes of the Einsatzgruppen. After the war, according to Allen, Heusinger sought to revive German militarism and advance the country's national interests by infiltrating NATO.[42] In so doing, he was working to establish "the basis of the Fourth Reich."[43] Allen never clarified the exact nature of

"The German General Staff itself must be utterly destroyed."
General of the Armies, **Dwight D. Eisenhower**

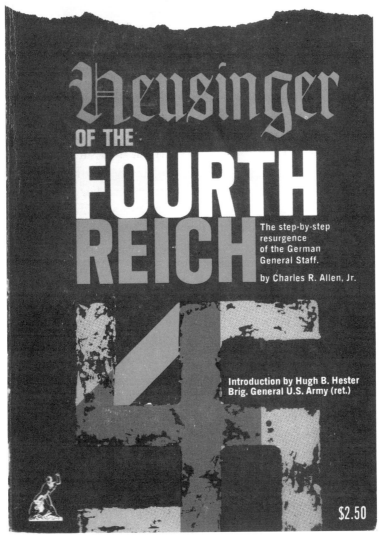

Figure 4.2 In 1963, journalist Charles Allen's book *Heusinger of the Fourth Reich* exposed the Nazi past of West Germany's chief of the *Bundeswehr* and chairman of the NATO military committee, General Adolf Heusinger.

this future state, but in liberally quoting other alarmist critics in his study, such as Tetens, Dornberg, Shirer, and the Society for the Prevention of World War III, he aligned himself with their conclusions that West Germany could not be fully trusted.

The reaction of observers to these books, as well as to current events in Germany, further sustained fears of a Fourth Reich. Commenting on Dornberg's *Schizophrenic Germany* in June of 1961, Whitney Bolton wrote that a recent visit to Berlin had confirmed his suspicion that "the spirit that created the Third Reich was still sufficiently alive to bring about a possible Fourth Reich."[44] Taking a similar position was Clifford E. Carpenter, who, during the Berlin crisis of 1961, warned that as long as the country remained divided there remained the possibility that, one day, "some German [would] ... lead a resurgent Fourth Reich on a global blood spilling to bring Germany together."[45] Around this same time, the Fourth Reich was increasingly employed as a marketing tool. Dornberg's book was prominently advertised in *The New York Times Book Review* in June of 1961 with the attention-grabbing headline, "Will there be a Fourth Reich?"[46] The same was true of Shirer's *The Rise and Fall of the Third Reich*, with a Salt Lake City bookstore telling readers: "Quick, before the FOURTH REICH rises, read 'The Rise and Fall of the Third Reich' – Now in paperback."[47]

East German commentators also expressed fears of a Fourth Reich. In 1959, journalists reacted to the swastika wave by claiming it proved that the Adenauer regime had "never purged itself of fascism like the German Democratic Republic."[48] As the SED politburo member and director of the East German propaganda war against West German renazification, Albert Norden, put it in *Neues Deutschland* in January of 1960, the "regents of the Fourth Reich in Bonn" had cloaked the "skeletons in [West Germany's] closet" with a "brown veil of silence."[49] Not long thereafter, the First Secretary of the communist party, Walter Ulbricht, decried West German militarism, declaring that "the thousand-year Third Reich was not destroyed so that its successor could establish a Fourth Reich."[50] Beyond these statements by high-level government officials, the East German press routinely cited references to the Fourth Reich that appeared in the foreign media.[51] In 1963, it even published a poem by the writer Kurt Stern entitled, "Declaration – To Be Read at Election Rallies," which featured the following lines:

When you [in the west] describe financial power . . . as freedom . . .
When you protect war criminals and executioners
When you allow Jew killers to sit in your offices . . .
When you love atom bombs . . .

Then I say to myself
And I say to you all . . .
That we will survive
Your Fourth Reich
Which so resembles its predecessor.[52]

These references to the Fourth Reich, like those employed by communists outside of East Germany, revealed how the term served political ends during an increasingly tense period of the cold war.[53]

The Renazification Debate: The Apologists

In contrast to the alarmists, more apologetic critics responded soberly to the swastika wave, dismissing fears about the Federal Republic and defending the country's postwar development. This position was advanced in British journalist Terence Prittie's book *Germany Divided* (1960), Christopher Emmet and Norbert Muhlen's study *The Vanishing Swastika* (1961), and conservative American historian William Henry Chamberlin's book *The German Phoenix* (1963).[54] All three volumes addressed the same instances of neo-Nazi and antisemitic activity from the late 1950s, but interpreted their significance more optimistically.[55] Emmet, Muhlen, and Prittie, for instance, acknowledged that the Zind and Nieland affairs were "repulsive" instances of antisemitism, but said they were "untypical" of the German "general public."[56] They made a similar point about the swastika wave, noting that most of the perpetrators were apolitical "juvenile delinquents" who had been widely rebuked.[57] These authors further dismissed the threat of former Nazis. Emmett and Muhlen declared that most "opportunistic" Nazis had adjusted easily to democracy and insisted that "surviving Nazi die-hards" presented "no threat" because they were monitored by the government.[58] Chamberlin joined Emmett and Muhlen in dismissing concerns about the presence of ex-Nazis in Adenauer's cabinet, claiming that they had been nominal party members during the Third Reich and had little influence over postwar policy.[59] On balance, the apologists argued that the West German government had steered an "undeviatingly democratic course" in their policies, had "tried hard to bar the road to resurgent Nazis," and had done their utmost to "atone for the crimes committed by the Nazi government."[60] "Gradually, but decisively," they concluded, "the Swastika is vanishing from West Germany."[61]

The apologists remained frustrated, however, that their opponents outside of West Germany refused to recognize the country's progress. Prittie took issue with the "extreme gloom" that characterized most "book[s] on the Germany of today," dismissing most neo-Nazi activity as stemming from the "lunatic fringe."[62] He added that the Germans deserved "greater credit" than they had received for their admirable response to the swastika wave, concluding that "too much thought on the subject of the Cologne incident would defeat itself."[63] Chamberlin argued that West Germany's postwar renaissance had been distorted by "an anti-German campaign" seeking "to convince Americans that Nazism is a real ... force in Germany today."[64] These claims, the apologists warned, could easily backfire. As the former US land commissioner of Bavaria in 1950–51, George Shuster, wrote in the foreword to Chamberlin's book, any "exaggeration ... of [the Nazi] ... danger" would "strengthen the very elements in Germany whose revival we fear." By "crying 'Wolf!'" he concluded, "we might well prepare the way for a future return of the Nazi werewolves."[65]

The Swastika Wave beyond West Germany

These critics' defense of the Federal Republic gained legitimacy thanks to the spread of the swastika wave to other countries. Several days after the vandalism in Cologne, antisemitic attacks were reported in Western Europe and North America. The hardest-hit country was the United States. Between late December 1959 and the end of February 1960 there were a total of 643 incidents. Throughout every region in the country, from large cities like Los Angeles to small towns like Darien, Connecticut, swastikas were smeared on synagogues, Jewish fraternities, and Hillel houses, as well as on churches, schools, and stores.[66] There were also reports of individual Jews being targeted for harassment and attack. There were even scattered bombings. On the night of January 28, 1960, in Kansas City, Missouri, assailants firebombed the Kehilath Israel synagogue, shattering more than fifty windows.[67] Two months later, a synagogue in Gadsden, Alabama was firebombed, and several congregants shot and injured.[68]

As in West Germany, there was tremendous condemnation of the "swastika epidemic" and heartfelt soul-searching about its causes. President Eisenhower condemned "the virus of bigotry" as a "threat to freedom," while clergy of all faiths emphasized the need to fight hatred and embrace tolerance.[69] One of the most systematic efforts to understand the antisemitic vandalism appeared in 1961, when the Anti-Defamation League published a study by David Caplovitz and Candace Rogers entitled *Swastika 1960*.[70] It reported that a majority of the perpetrators were young males of high school age who were less motivated by virulent antisemitism than immature hooliganism; in many cases, the authors observed, "personality disturbances" were channeled into acts of "random hostility."[71] Yet Caplovitz and Rogers also pointed out that other perpetrators were driven by political motives. A significant number of the apprehended vandals belonged to loosely organized, semi-secretive "neo-Nazi clubs."[72] Led by self-appointed "Boy 'Fuehrers,'" the clubs varied in size, but they were all linked by a penchant for collecting Nazi memorabilia, especially military uniforms, swastika banners, and weapons.[73] Interviews with apprehended perpetrators confirmed that they held strong antisemitic beliefs. Summing up the trend, the *Jewish Advocate* bleakly explained in 1960 that "To be pro-Nazi is 'in'; tolerance is 'out'; . . . anti-Nazism is 'square.'"[74]

Some of the neo-Nazi groups found inspiration in the idea of a Fourth Reich. This was true of the Kansas City perpetrators, whose members belonged to two different branches of a larger "Nordic Fourth Reich" group at two different high schools.[75] The members had attracted attention at their schools for wearing swastikas on their clothing and were later found to have painted the symbol on local synagogues.[76] The group furthermore issued identification cards to its members that read: "By order of Der Fuehrer, ____ is a member of the 4th Reich."[77] This story echoed reports from May of 1959, when a group of high school students in Cleveland were arrested after forming a neo-Nazi group called the "Fourth Reich" that, according to the local press, was planning to "set up a Fourth Reich not in Germany but right here [in Ohio]."[78] Both the Kansas City and Cleveland groups expressed hatred of Jews, communists, and "Negroes," with the Ohio club planning an assassination campaign against various enemies, including President Eisenhower.[79] These reports revealed that the idea of the Fourth Reich had filtered down to the level of popular culture, where it appealed to the rebellious instincts of American teenagers.

The American swastika wave faded relatively swiftly, but the reaction to it revealed a nascent tendency to universalize the Nazi past. Given the fact that certain Americans were displaying the same extremist behavior as certain Germans, observers sensed that the neo-Nazi vandalism did not stem from factors unique to the Federal Republic. Instead, they were rooted in broader forces. The authors of *Swastika 1960*, for instance, suggested that the antisemitic vandalism partly reflected anxieties among Americans about social change in the United States. The study speculated that the postwar migration of Jews into previously homogenous suburban neighborhoods, together with the advancing push for desegregation in the American South, had prompted some American whites to protest the emergence of an increasingly inclusive society by becoming "preoccup[ied] ... with Nazi ideology."[80] The study also pointed to cold war fears, citing a possible connection between the "widespread anxiety among high school youth" about declining "American prestige ... since [the Soviet Union's launching of the space probe] Sputnik I [in 1959]" and the "belief that only a militaristic master-race ideology can withstand it."[81] According to this theory, the tendency of American teenagers to identify with the Fourth Reich reflected deeper feelings of insecurity.

While these analyses universalized the Nazi past in relation to the motives of the perpetrators, others did so in relation to the identities of the victims. Many saw the swastika wave as a threat not only to Jews but other American groups. The African-American press, for example, saw the swastika wave as a manifestation of scapegoating, which could just as easily affect "the Negro" as the Jew. According to the Memphis-based *Tri-State Defender*, hatred directed towards Jews stemmed from the same "racial prejudice ... against the American black man" and was part of a larger "virus that can infect a whole social system, if not checked at the source."[82] In order to counteract it, *The Los Angeles Tribune* recommended that the American authorities remind the public about Nazism's evil by "showing us the six million Jews ... exterminated in [the] camps" and "tell[ing] ... us what would have happened to the 20 million Negroes in the United States."[83] One New York Rabbi agreed, arguing that the swastika was "less a symbol of hatred for one people than … for the forces of freedom [and] justice." The swastika was "as much the enemy of the Christian as the Jew."[84] These comments did not specifically address the notion of a Fourth Reich. But they established a new context for the concept's future development.

Neo-Nazism, the New Left, and the Fourth Reich

By the middle of the 1960s, German and western observers once more began to worry about neo-Nazi political activity in the Federal Republic. The reason was the rise of a new far right-wing political party known as the NPD. Founded in 1964 as an alliance of conservative nationalist and extreme right-wing forces, the NPD grew out of Rudolf von Thadden's DRP, which itself had emerged from the SRP of Fritz Dorls and Otto Ernst Remer. The two wings of the party were originally led by Thadden (Figure 4.3) and conservative nationalist Friedrich Thielen, both of whom sought to unite the Federal Republic's disparate conservative right-wing groups into a single party. Initially, the two worked together on behalf of this common goal; but by 1967, Thadden wrested sole control of the party and became its undisputed leader.[85]

Under his leadership, the NPD straddled the line between extreme conservatism and neo-Nazism. Thadden's experience with the DRP made him sensitive to the possibility of the NPD being banned by the West German courts; as a result, he made sure that the party did not openly avow Nazi principles. He also removed ex-Nazis from the party's leadership to boost its respectability. At the same time, the NPD leader sought to rehabilitate the Third Reich by promoting a sanitized view of the Nazi past.[86] Believing that the shameful burden of the Third Reich had made the Germans a "people without history" and damaged their national identity, Thadden relativized the regime's crimes as a means of restoring Germany's "national dignity."[87] Not only did the NPD's founding manifesto of 1966 reject "the lie of Germany's sole guilt" for the Second World War, party leaders routinely minimized the number of Jews killed in the Holocaust and emphasized German suffering at the hands of the Allies.[88] The party further rejected the continuation of war crimes trials against Nazi perpetrators and the payment of reparations to Israel.[89] Only by freeing themselves from their "chronic status of being indicted" could the German *Volk* end their country's tragic division and achieve true "national self-

Figure 4.3 In 1967, the former Nazi, Adolf von Thadden, became the undisputed leader of the far right National Democratic Party (*Nationaldemokratische Partei Deutschlands*, NPD) (Source: Getty Images).

determination." In pursuing this goal, the NPD opportunistically drew on the era's anti-colonial rhetoric, describing the Germans as one of the "oppressed peoples of the world," who were struggling to emancipate themselves from the cold war domination of "foreign powers."[90] In practice, the party sought to free the Federal Republic from the NATO alliance, secure the return of lost eastern territories, and forge a "reunited independent Germany" within an "independent Europe." At the same time, the NPD expressed a clear anticommunist line, decrying the subjugation of "Middle Germany by the Soviet dictatorship" and condemning the left-wing activism of the West German student movement. Finally, the party sought to protect German cultural values from alien influences, whether foreign immigrants or American popular culture.[91]

In the first several years of its existence, the NPD attracted little attention, but, starting in 1966, it raised concerns after achieving unexpected electoral success. In that year, the party tallied 7.9 and 7.4 percent of the vote in regional elections in Hesse and Bavaria. One year later, the NPD gained 6.9 percent of the vote in Rhineland-Palatinate, 7.0 percent in Lower Saxony, and 8.8 percent in Bremen. The year 1968 represented the party's high-water mark, when it received 9.8 percent of the vote in Baden-Württemberg.[92] In registering these successes, the NPD became the first extreme right-wing party to enter regional parliaments since the SRP in 1952. Like earlier parties, the NPD received much of its support from former Nazi Party members – a fact that mirrored the Nazi backgrounds of a majority of the party's original leaders.[93] But, in a new and disturbing development, the party also appealed to younger Germans, who were seeking new political options in a period of growing upheaval in the Federal Republic.[94]

The NPD's success reflected the era's deepening political polarization. Starting in the mid 1960s, West Germany experienced a minor, but nevertheless perceptible, economic slowdown that, together with mounting budget deficits and uncertainty about revaluing the Deutschemark, raised doubts about the leadership of Adenauer's CDU successor, Ludwig Erhard.[95] The FDP soon pulled out of the CDU-led governing coalition, thereby thrusting the political system into a brief period of paralysis that was only resolved when the Christian Democrats and their new chancellor, Kurt Georg Kiesinger, forged a "grand coalition" with the SPD. This development alienated right-wing Germans, who rejected cooperating with the left-wing opposition. But it also alienated the increasingly radical student members of the New Left. They were shocked by the older socialists' pragmatic alliance with the right, as well as their support for such controversial policies as the Emergency Laws of 1967.[96] They were especially appalled that the SPD establishment had allied with a party whose new leader, Kiesinger, had been a member of the NSDAP. In the period that followed, the New Left intensified its protest against what it saw as the capitalist, imperialist, and "fascist" foundations of the Federal Republic. It also condemned the country's alliance with the US (then at war in Vietnam); celebrated anti-colonial resistance movements in Asia and the Middle East; and rebelled against bourgeois social and cultural norms by embracing the unholy trinity of sex, drugs, and rock and roll. This growing protest wave reached a climax in the mass demonstrations and street violence of the years 1967 and 1968, a traumatic period that only served to deepen the sense of political polarization in the

Federal Republic. With conservative Germans skeptical that the centrist CDU could restore law and order, many turned to the NPD as the only true right-wing alternative.[97]

The NPD's electoral success in the years 1966–69 raised concerns among West German and foreign observers. Within the Federal Republic, intellectuals, journalists, and academics explored the reasons for the party's emergence, debated whether it was neo-Nazi, and argued over whether it should be banned, like the SRP.[98] Many critics drew polemical comparisons between the NPD and NSDAP, pointing out that the abbreviation of the former was the same as the latter once the letters 'S' and 'A' (referring to the Nazi *Sturmabteilung*) were deleted, thereby suggesting that the NPD was merely the Nazis without a paramilitary force.[99] Others noted that Thadden shared a first name with the Nazi Party's infamous founder, calling him "Adolf II" and protesting with slogans like "One Adolf was enough!"[100] Alarmist analyses of the party were also published, the most notable being left-wing journalist Kurt Hirsch's 1967 book, *Kommen Die Nazis Wieder?* (*Are the Nazis Returning?*).[101] In this study, Hirsch methodically exposed the continuities of ideology, personnel, and electoral support between the NSDAP and the NPD. But he particularly blamed the Federal Republic's "bourgeois parties" for promoting the nationalist sentiments that sustained the NPD, likening their actions to those of the Harzburg Front alliance of conservatives and the NSDAP from 1931. Only by recognizing the parallels between past and present, he concluded, would "democratically minded citizens regardless of party" be able to rise up and protect the West German state from "renewed harm."[102]

In the Anglo-American realm, the NPD's rise sparked similar jeremiads. Ivor Montagu's *Germany's New Nazis* (1967), Wellington Long's *The New Nazis of Germany* (1968), and Lord Russell's *Return of the Swastika?* (1969) explained the NPD's emergence against the backdrop of postwar events, such as the failure of denazification, the rise of the SRP, the entry of ex-Nazis into the postwar establishment, and the eruption of the swastika wave.[103] They explained the NPD's principles as a reaction to the crisis of the mid 1960s, especially West Germany's growing social divisions and foreign policy frustrations. All of the authors were pessimistic about West Germany's present, although they remained measured in predicting its future. Montagu said it was "extremely improbable" that the NPD would "rise to master Germany as the Nazi Party did," but warned that the party was making "Nazi ideas" once again "fit for polite society."[104] Long argued that the NPD's fate would depend on its ability to appeal to the "one-quarter of the population who still lack confidence in the Democratic system."[105] Lord Russell was the most downcast, arguing that there was "even more justification" to be worried about Nazi political parties in 1969 than there had been in 1952.[106] Although he denied that Germany's democracy was "about to give way to a new Hitler," the fact that "more and more young people are turning . . . to the new Adolf" revealed that the NPD was effectively exploiting "real nostalgia for the Hitler regime."[107]

All of these developments prompted fears that the NPD's emergence could herald the rise of a Fourth Reich in Germany. For its part, the NPD never mentioned the concept explicitly, which differentiated it from the SRP in the early 1950s. Yet the notion of a revived Reich nonetheless remained associated with the party. Already in the early 1960s, Thadden had been accused of using the NPD's predecessor party, the DRP, to pursue the creation of a new Reich.[108] Such comparisons increased after the NPD's electoral successes of 1966–68. In November of 1966, Canadian journalist Peter Lust argued that the NPD's success in Bavaria raised the prospect that the party would "seize power [in] . . . a Putsch," "reestablish Nazism," and proclaim "the Fourth Reich."[109] In the US, Robert Segal hoped that the NPD's electoral success in 1966, together with the rise of Kiesinger as chancellor, would "shake the complacency out of Germany's best friends" and alert them to the fact that the neo-Nazis were "promoters of the Fourth Reich."[110] In the spring of 1968, the Society for the Prevention of World War III ran an article under the title, "A Fourth Reich for Germany," which outlined the NPD's many links to National Socialism and warned that the party was poised to increase further in strength in the 1969 federal elections.[111] West German observers issued similar warnings. *Die Zeit* nervously wondered whether the NPD's success meant that "a Fourth Reich was in sight."[112] Kurt Hirsch's book *Kommen Die Nazis Wieder?* predicted that the NPD's most prominent members would become "leaders of a Fourth Reich."[113] And in November of 1966, thousands of anti-NPD protesters vocalized similar concerns at a mass demonstration in Munich.[114]

Around this time, the East German press amplified this line of argumentation with a flurry of articles. Some reported with satisfaction that Munich students had protested the NPD by warning about a "Fourth Reich" arising in the Federal Republic.[115] But most articles used the concept to attack what it regarded as the West German government's increasingly nationalistic foreign policy. In October of 1966, *Neues Deutschland* referred to an underground bunker used by West German politicians during NATO emergency drills in the Ahr valley as the "Wolf's Lair of the Fourth Reich," thereby evoking Hitler's East Prussian command headquarters during World War II.[116] Earlier that year, the same newspaper reported that the French communist journal *Combat* had accused West Germany of "setting itself up as a kind of Fourth Reich" by continuing the "Lebensraum" tradition of Joachim von Ribbentrop and laying claim to former eastern territories in the Soviet realm.[117] One year later, *Neue Zeit* reported that the Soviet Press had objected to Chancellor Kiesinger's refusal to accept the finality of the Oder–Neisse line as proof that he was aiming to be the "Führer of all Germans at the helm of a Fourth Reich."[118] In the years 1968–69, finally, the East German media frequently published foreign comparisons of the Federal Republic to the "Fourth Reich" that appeared in the French, Russian, Bulgarian, Indian, and Syrian press.[119]

In the end, all of the warnings proved to be needless. Although the NPD gained seats in seven different state legislatures in West Germany, it was never able to make a national breakthrough. In the Federal elections of 1969, the NPD attained only 4.3 percent of the vote and failed to clear the 5 percent threshold necessary for it to enter the Bundestag. This failure partly reflected the improving economy.[120] But it mostly revealed the West German electorate's general turn to the left. In the elections of 1969, the SPD received the largest percentage of the vote (42.7 percent) and forged a coalition with the FDP, which abandoned the CDU/CSU. For the first time since the creation of the FRG in 1949, power shifted peacefully from the right to the left. The new chancellor, Willy Brandt, became the country's first socialist leader since the Weimar period. This notable milestone lent unprecedented legitimacy to West Germany's young democracy. Indeed, it suggested that the Federal Republic had finally overcome the country's historically tragic *Sonderweg* and become a "normal" western nation.[121] By proving that the country was less vulnerable to right-wing parties than had been feared, the election revealed that the country faced no imminent danger of becoming a Fourth Reich. For the first time in the postwar period, West Germany's historical development did not appear susceptible to counterfactual second-guessing.

Universalizing the Fourth Reich in the United States

Ironically, at the same time that western observers were encouraged by the growing strength of democracy in West Germany, they were starting to worry about its future in the United States. The turmoil of the 1960s hit the US particularly hard. The intensification of the civil rights struggle, the eruption of race riots in American cities, the assassination of Martin Luther King Jr., and the emergence of the Black Nationalist movement exposed the country's ongoing racial divide. The explosion of student protests against the Vietnam war, the demand for women's and gay rights, and the emergence of the counterculture revealed the presence of growing social and cultural divisions. The growing polarization between liberal and conservative Americans eventually produced a sharp turn to the right when voters elected Richard Nixon president in 1968 and then again in 1972. The disastrous course of Nixon's nearly two-term presidency, culminating with the Watergate scandal, soured many Americans on the health of their country's democracy and inspired them to attack it with unprecedented rhetorical ferocity. Not surprisingly, critics frequently drew on the history of the Nazi era and used the idea of the Fourth Reich to indict American, rather than German, realities.

The sense that America might have its own fascist potential first gained plausibility in the early 1960s with the creation of the American Nazi Party (ANP). Founded in 1958 by the notorious antisemite and segregationist, George Lincoln Rockwell, the ANP was always a tiny fringe organization (Figure 4.4). But it received considerable media attention (not to mention government surveillance) for its highly public protests against Jews and Blacks. Believing the Civil Rights Movement was part of a Jewish conspiracy, Rockwell made headlines in 1958 when he picketed in front of the White House with a sign demanding "Save Ike from the Kikes" and later attacked Martin Luther King Jr. as "Martin Luther Coon."[122] Rockwell's racist rabble-rousing sparked violent counter-protests in the early 1960s, and he earned further condemnation in 1965 when he ran for governor of Virginia on a blatantly racist platform that he later called "white power."[123]

Figure 4.4 In 1958, the notorious antisemite and segregationist George Lincoln Rockwell founded the American Nazi Party (ANP) and reintroduced Nazi ideas into the United States. This image portrays Rockwell marching with supporters in 1967 (Source: Getty Images).

Around this time, Rockwell became associated with the possibility of a Fourth Reich. In 1966, a close German confidante of Rockwell in the burgeoning international Nazi movement, the former Hitler Youth member, Wehrmacht veteran, and self-styled "Fuehrer," Bruno Armin Ludtke, was given an eight-month suspended sentence by a court in Frankfurt for "trying to form a Fourth Reich government" in West Germany.[124] That same year, several German-American and German men linked to Ludtke – Reinhold Ruppe, Erich Lindner, and Kurt Reinheimer – were arrested for plotting to kill West German war crimes prosecutor Fritz Bauer and establish a "Fourth Reich."[125] These reports, in addition to continuing cases of vandals in American towns and cities smearing the phrase "The Fourth Reich" on synagogues and other buildings in the years 1966–67, revealed that support for Nazism was not confined to West Germany's NPD, but also existed in the putatively more democratic United States.[126] It revealed that the idea of a new Reich had as much to do with American racism as German antisemitism.

These burgeoning connections help explain why civil rights activists – both Black and white – were among the first to claim that the United States had the potential to become a Fourth Reich. Already in 1964, *Jet* magazine warned that Republican presidential nominee Barry Goldwater's endorsement of "extremism in the cause of liberty" was a "danger ... not only to Negroes but also to Jews," and insisted that "if we do not want a Fourth Reich here, racial and religious minorities must unite at the polls and bury Barry Goldwater's presidential bid."[127] Following the "Bloody Sunday" events in Selma, Alabama in March 1965, one citizen compared George Wallace's supporters to Nazis and anxiously asked, "Are we trying to establish the Fourth Reich [in] my beloved state?"[128] By 1967, worsening racial tensions led Black nationalists to embrace the term to describe the divided nation. In August of that year, H. Rap Brown of the Student Nonviolent Coordinating Committee (SNCC) declared, "You see we recognize America for what it is: the Fourth Reich, and we tell America to be on notice, because if white folks is going to play Nazis, black folks ain't going to play Jews!" (Figure 4.5).[129] The most sustained critique was offered by Max Stanford, a leading member of the Revolutionary Action Movement (RAM), who, while imprisoned in the spring of 1968, wrote a manifesto for "independent Black nationhood," in which he declared:

> Instead of America admitting the truth of injustices done to the African-American ... it has chosen instead to eliminate him ... The Fourth Reich is here ... Armageddon is here, race war is at hand ...
>
> The whole Fourth Reich will ... try to wipe us out when Black Americans rebel against racism.
>
> The Fourth Reich will use the latest ... electronic, biological, and chemical warfare against us. They know if they lose this war their whole empire will crumble ... The Fourth Reich will unleash a more brutal war on us than they're waging against the Vietnamese.[130]

Black journalists commonly echoed these alarmist comments. In 1967, the editor of *Ebony Magazine*, Lerone Bennett, pointed to "the rise of the Radical Right, the deepening despair in the ghetto, [and] the

Figure 4.5 In 1967, H. Rap Brown of the Student Nonviolent Coordinating Committee (SNCC) declared, "You see we recognize America for what it is: the Fourth Reich." On his right is the lawyer William Kunstler, who also accused the US of being a Fourth Reich (Source: Bettmann / Getty Images).

deepening fear in the white community" to conclude that unless "we . . . make revolutionary changes at every level in our lives," America was in danger of becoming "a Fourth Reich."[131] In 1969, The *Philadelphia Tribune* attacked Philadelphia mayor Frank Rizzo's refusal to investigate local cases of police brutality by saying that the city government had "learned their lessons well from the Third Reich" and were "helping to bring on a Fourth Reich" in the city of brotherly love.[132]

Black activists directed particular attention to the role of Richard Nixon in promoting this right-wing trend. In 1970, *The Milwaukee Star* criticized President Nixon's authoritarian tendencies by calling him "'King Dick,' ruler of the Fourth Reich."[133] Such comments multiplied after Nixon's reelection. In a 1973 interview, the writer James Baldwin decried American voters' decision to return "Nixon . . . [to] the White House," declaring that "to keep the nigger in his place, they brought into office law and order, but I call it the Fourth Reich."[134] One year earlier, in his book *No Name in the Street* (1972), the writer expressed his concern about the entire 1960s generation, observing, "I could not help feeling, watching them, that, exactly as the Third Reich had at first to conquer the German opposition before getting around to the Jews ... my republic, which ... I was beginning to think of as the Fourth Reich, would be forced to power under the flower children ... before getting around to the blacks and then the rest of the world."[135] Similar comments appeared well into the mid 1970s, for example, when Lerone Bennett delivered a speech in November of 1975 in which he listed a series of programs intended to "correct ... social wrongs" by warning "there are only two roads ahead of us ... one of becoming a democracy for the first time, the other a fascist fourth reich."[136]

Building upon the efforts of civil rights activists, other leftist critics employed the idea of the Fourth Reich to condemn the Vietnam war. In 1970, the famed lawyer, William Kunstler, argued that, in light of the My Lai massacre and the fact that American jails "are being used as concentration camps [for political prisoners]," the US shared many similarities with Nazi Germany. As he put it, "if you are going to condemn the German people for supporting the Third Reich, then you must condemn yourselves for supporting the Fourth Reich."[137] French communist activist Régis Debray, then imprisoned in Bolivia, expressed his admiration for Charles De Gaulle in 1970 as an inspirational nationalist resistance figure for "every country fighting for national independence against the domination of the 'Fourth Reich' – the empire of the USA – which is more fearful than the Third Reich."[138] In early 1973, Pamala Haynes in *The Philadelphia Tribune* wrote that President Nixon's "murderous bombing [in Vietnam]" constituted "the most vicious war crimes ... since Adolf Hitler bombed ... Rotterdam" and had transformed "racist Amerika" into "the Fourth Reich."[139] Finally, in 1968 Lyndon Johnson was attacked in a biting poster depicting the president seated in a Volkswagen Beetle (originally designed as the "Strength Through Joy Car" by Hitler's German Labor Front in the 1930s) with the caption, "The Rise and Fall of the Fourth Reich" (Figure 4.6).

Critics employed similar terminology to attack Richard Nixon's administration during the Watergate scandal. Already before news of the Watergate break-in surfaced in the spring of 1973, journalists used

The Rise and Fall of The Fourth Reich

Figure 4.6 During the Vietnam war, this poster attacked President Lyndon
B. Johnson by depicting him seated in a Volkswagen Beetle (originally designed as
the "Strength Through Joy Car" by Hitler's German Labor Front in the 1930s) with
the caption, "The Rise and Fall of the Fourth Reich" (Source: International Poster
Corp., *The Rise and Fall of the Fourth Reich*, 1968, from the *Daniel Wolf Collection
of Protest Posters*. Offset lithograph, 29 × 21 in (73.7 × 53.3 cm). Whitney Museum
of American Art, New York; purchased with funds from The American
Contemporary Art Foundation, Inc., Leonard A. Lauder, President 2017.10.202).

Nazi-era references to describe Nixon and his advisers. In 1971,
The Boston Globe observed that "nearly all the ... President's top
White House aides" had "unmistakably Teutonic surnames –
Kissinger, Haldeman, Ehrlichman ... and Schultz" – and were
"known collectively as the ... Fourth Reich."[140] After the Watergate
scandal broke, such observations acquired a more critical edge. In May
of 1973, *The Billings Gazette* referred to "the Fall of the Fourth Reich"
in reference to Nixon's beleaguered administration.[141] Across the
nation, meanwhile, ordinary citizens wrote letters to the editor of their
local newspapers expressing the fear that "America has become the
Fourth Reich and the President is the son of Hitler."[142]

 Finally, conspiracy theorists linked the assassination of
President John F. Kennedy to a larger plot to establish a Fourth Reich
in the US. In the mid 1960s, the famed New Orleans district attorney,

Jim Garrison, expanded upon his well-known rejection of the Warren Commission report by pursuing the theory that the president's murder was part of a larger "Nazi operation," funded by "oil-rich millionaires in Texas," who were opposed to Kennedy's effort to "reach an understanding" with Nikita Khrushchev and Fidel Castro. In 1967, Garrison discussed this theory in an essay bearing the provocative title, "The Rise of the Fourth Reich" or "How to Conceal the Truth about an Assassination without Really Trying."[143] In it, he argued that the American government was seeking to sell the American public an "illusion" about the Kennedy killing and, in the process, was behaving in Nazi-like fashion. As he put it: "The ... illusion ... that we are living in the best of all possible worlds is a favorite strategy of the fascist type of government ... in order to keep people from being restless. And ... you are seeing it applied ... in a number of areas in the government of the United States today."[144] Garrison's claims were echoed by another legendary conspiracy theorist, the California-based radio show host Mae Brussell. After spending years researching Kennedy's assassination, she insisted that a cabal of oil barons, CIA operatives, and anticommunist Nazis associated with the John Birch Society had killed the president because of his "drive to educate Southern blacks and register them to vote." Brussell noted, however, that their actions were part of an even larger plot. As she put it, the killing of other progressive figures in the 1960s, such as "[Robert F.] Kennedy ... Malcolm X, Martin Luther King, labor leaders, judges, entertainers, reporters, authors, students, Black Panthers, Indians, Chicanos and hippies," could all be traced to the US government's postwar recruitment of former Nazi intelligence officers and rocket scientists to help "the ... Southern states ... build ... the Fourth Reich" in the US.[145]

While left-leaning critics made the majority of these comments, right-of-center observers occasionally made them as well. In 1963, an angry Louisiana segregationist sent a letter to the editor of his local newspaper expressing his opposition to the Federal government's decision to send in "30,000 armed soldiers into Mississippi to force the university to accept one Negro," arguing that it reeked of "rank despotism" and suggested that "we are under the Fourth Reich now."[146] In February of 1969, racist whites calling themselves "The Students of the Fourth Reich" sent death threats to members of a Black student group pursuing the creation of a Black Studies Program at Sacramento City College.[147] In 1970, the conservative music producer Sidney

O. Fields produced a propagandistic record album entitled *The Fourth Reich: The Communazis Exposed in Their Own Words: Revolution Today in the USA*, which likened speeches delivered at the Black Panther Party's National Revolutionary Conference for a United Front against Fascism in July of 1969 to Nazi propaganda rallies (Figure 4.7).[148]

Whether these rhetorical attacks hailed from the left or the right, it remains unclear why so many American critics embraced the idea of the Fourth Reich in the 1960s. There is no obvious explanation for the term's sudden ubiquity in popular discourse. No single major figure popularized it. No major cultural work employed it. Instead, the concept seems to have gradually seeped into American discourse via news coverage of events in West Germany during the 1960s. This begs the question, however, of why the concept developed such traction in the United States. In part, the popularity of the Fourth Reich reflected the increasing universalization of the Nazi past in American memory. This development represented the collision of two trends: the era's growing interest in the history of the Third Reich, and its growing concern about contemporary social and political problems. Both trends mutually reinforced one another: the growing knowledge of the Nazi era influenced how people interpreted present-day problems, and the growing concern about present-day problems prompted comparisons to the Nazi past in order to raise awareness about them.

Throughout the 1960s, political discourse in the United States became suffused with references to the Third Reich. President Kennedy justified the United States' cold war fight against Soviet communism by invoking the country's defense of "freedom" against Nazi totalitarianism, while President Johnson cited Europe's appeasement of Hitler in the 1930s to justify America's involvement in Vietnam.[149] Anti-government protesters employed similar analogies.[150] In 1968, the Black Panther Party cited the German government's payment of reparations to Israel to atone for the "genocide" of "6,000,000 Jews" in order to demand compensation for "the American racist ... slaughter of over 50,000,000 black people."[151] At the same time, James Baldwin predicted that an increasingly "fascist" America was poised to set up "concentration camps in California ... New York ... [and] Philadelphia," and warned that if Blacks and whites did not "come together, they're going to end up in the same gas oven."[152] Finally, antiwar activists likened American actions in Vietnam to the Nazis'

Figure 4.7 The photomontage that was featured on the cover of the album *The Fourth Reich: The Communazis Exposed* revealed how right-wing critics sought to portray 1960s left-wing radicalism as "Nazi" in inspiration. Note the peace sign in the letter "o" of "Fourth."

brutal wartime behavior in Europe, with Bertrand Russell comparing "the burning children of Vietnam" with "the gassed Jews of Auschwitz."[153]

The growing presence of the Fourth Reich in American public discourse can be understood as fulfilling the era's need for a rhetorically powerful term of indictment. The concept of a Fourth Reich provided multiple social groups with a concise, polemical signifier to express their fear that the present-day world was headed in a "fascist," if not outright Nazi, direction. The concept's future-oriented character lent heightened urgency to the prospect of a nightmare that had not yet happened – but still might. The Fourth Reich's admonitory character further allowed it to serve as a rallying cry for activists hoping to prevent it from coming into being, in whatever form. Whether the Fourth Reich was applied to the threat of racism, imperialism, or militarism, its versatility and effectiveness in directing attention towards contemporary concerns explains its growing appeal.

In becoming universalized, however, the Fourth Reich began to show signs of rhetorical overstretch. After the concept was extended beyond Germany to the United States, it was applied to still other nations. In 1967, at a Greek Independence Day parade in New York City, protesters attacked Greece's new military dictatorship by carrying signs reading "Greece Must Not Become the Fourth Reich," while, two months later, Greek film star Irene Pappas employed the phrase in calling for a cultural boycott of the country.[154] In Australia in 1970, anti-Apartheid activists protested a women's basketball game between a South African and Australian team by chanting "Smash the Fourth Reich."[155] These uses of the phrase were applied to other dictatorial regimes and thus remained within the limits of rhetorical plausibility. But other uses of the term were more questionable. In 1965, Indiana Republican State Senator Marlin McDaniel blasted the Democratic-run state legislature's reapportionment plan by declaring, "We need a more constructive two party system in Indiana, not a Fourth Reich run by a handful of political bosses from one party."[156] In 1970, a student protester at a mass demonstration in Pennsylvania against college tuition increases was arrested for defacing an American flag with a swastika and the words, "America the Fourth Reich."[157] In 1974, an angry letter to the editor condemned a Florida proposal to permit doctor-assisted suicide for severe cases of mental retardation and Down's Syndrome by warning: "Fellow Floridians, welcome to the Fourth Reich. We have a new leader to decide ... who should live and who may die."[158]

These comments were meant in earnest, but by extending the concept of the Fourth Reich far beyond its original historical context, they adversely affected its meaning. They revealed, first of all, problems of rhetorical usage. In many instances, the phrase "Fourth Reich" was used in passing fashion as a slogan for any number of contemporary evils. Its increasing usage further showed that the phrase was being subjected to the dynamics of "symbolic inflation," in which the excessive use of a symbol leads to its devaluation.[159] Finally, the Fourth Reich was shaped by "Gresham's law of language," a dynamic in which "bad" meanings of words drive "good" meanings out of circulation.[160] In adhering to this pattern, the proliferation of inflated references to the Fourth Reich began to compete with the original ones and devalue the concept altogether.

The logical end point of the Fourth Reich's rapid universalization during this period was its increasing aestheticization. At the same time that the concept was being used as a term of indictment, it was being stripped of its original moral and political content. Throughout the 1960s, the idea of the Fourth Reich came to be associated with a wide range of groups lacking any links to the Nazi era whatsoever. A large number of motorcycle gangs, for instance, adopted the name "The Fourth Reich" to distinguish themselves from their rivals. Press accounts from Michigan, Massachusetts, and Ontario reported on fights between men "wearing leather motorcycle jackets with 'Fourth Reich' written on them" and other gangs, such as "the Violators, the Half-Breeds, and the Highwaymen." Subsequent articles about the ensuing court cases and peacemaking efforts between the rival gangs suggested that few of their members understood the historical meaning behind the term.[161] When the members of a "Fourth Reich" motorcycle gang in Pittsfield, Massachusetts were brought into court in 1969 to face charges after attacking a motorist who had thrown beer cans at them, for instance, their attorney insisted his clients "had no idea . . . what was meant by the Fourth Reich or . . . the Nazi . . . symbols . . . on their leather . . . jackets."[162] These claims may have been disingenuous, but regardless of what the gang members actually knew about the history of Nazi Germany, their embrace of the name "Fourth Reich" was likely driven by aesthetic considerations.

The same was true of other depoliticized uses of the phrase. In March of 1968, a junior high school dance in Mill Hall, Pennsylvania featured a "dance band" called "The Fourth Reich."[163] The same band – or perhaps another by the same name – played a public concert on the downtown square of Jasper, Indiana in May of 1970.[164] In January of 1968 in Ukiah, California, a recreational basketball league featured a game between the "Fourth Reich" and the more conventionally named "Eagles."[165] "The Fourth Reich of Wilmington, Del." was one of many groups participating in the increasingly popular activity of wargaming in 1967.[166] Finally, and most irreverently, the influx of a series of German-themed restaurants in Houston, Texas prompted a local journalist to proclaim that the city was witnessing the invasion of a "culinary Fourth Reich."[167] All of these lighthearted examples suggested a growing willingness to use the concept ironically instead of politically. While it is impossible to know what inspired each individual example, taken together they represented a reaction against the highly hyperbolic uses of the Fourth Reich at the time. In the same way that seriousness invariably inspires satire, the term's inflation inevitably provoked efforts to cut it down to size.

Conclusion

Over the span of a few short years during the turbulent 1960s, the concept of the Fourth Reich underwent a profound evolution. Having faded from view at the end of the previous decade, it returned to prominence with the revival of international attention to West Germany's Nazi past. The eruption of the swastika wave in 1959–60, the sharpening of great-power conflict over Berlin, and the electoral success of the NPD in the years 1966–69 revealed that the Federal Republic had failed to emerge from under the shadow of the Third Reich. At the very same time, however, this newfound attention paradoxically diverted attention away from West Germany. As the Nazi past increasingly became a subject of public interest, it became a benchmark for assessing problems in other countries. Especially in the United States, but elsewhere as well, critics – mostly on the left – reacted to the Civil Rights Movement, the war in Vietnam, the Watergate scandal, and the JFK assassination by invoking the legacy of the Nazi era. Many anxiously began to fear that their own country might be heading down the path towards fascism. To sum up this fear, they invoked the rhetorically powerful concept of a "Fourth Reich." In so doing, they implied that West Germany was far from being the only country whose democratic order faced a Nazi threat. As the prospect of a Fourth Reich was becoming internationalized, its significance was becoming universalized. Precisely as this happened, however, signs of a reaction against it became visible in the nascent efforts to aestheticize the Fourth Reich by stripping it of its moral and political significance. In the 1970s, this development would reach a new level of intensity.

5 "HITLER IN ARGENTINA!": FICTIONALIZING THE FOURTH REICH IN THE LONG 1970S

They were everywhere, thought Johann von Tiebolt, as he walked to the door. Everywhere. *Die Sonnenkinder*. The Children of the Sun . . . .

Thousands. Selected genetically, the . . . families traced back several generations . . . Only the purest were sent out and . . . guided, trained, indoctrinated . . .

Millions [of dollars] funneled judiciously, *politically*. One by one, nations would fall in line, shaped internally by the *Sonnenkinder* . . .

Chile had cost less than twenty-seven million, Panama no more than six. In America, Senate and congressional seats were to be had for a few hundred thousand . . .

The Eastern bloc would be next [and] . . . when the signal came . . . people's collectives everywhere would suddenly realize there was a better way . . .

The Fourth Reich would be born . . . and spread all over the world. The Children of the Sun would be the rightful masters of the globe.[1]

American writer Robert Ludlum's depiction of a neo-Nazi conspiracy pursuing world domination in his bestselling 1978 novel, *The Holcroft Covenant*, illustrates an important development in the postwar evolution of the Fourth Reich. At the same time that the idea was becoming universalized, it was becoming increasingly fictionalized. From the early 1960s to the early 1980s – a period that can be called the "long 1970s" – the topic increasingly found expression in western popular culture. Especially in the United States and Great Britain, the theme of a Nazi return to power figured centrally in dozens of novels, films, television episodes, radio plays, and comic books. These narratives altered the previous image of the Fourth Reich. Instead of portraying it as a threat emanating exclusively from the Federal Republic of Germany, they imagined it as part of an international conspiracy being plotted by a diaspora community of fugitive Nazis in Latin America, the Middle East, and even the United States.

The fictionalization of the Fourth Reich paradoxically reflected the belief that a Nazi comeback no longer represented a real political threat. Tales of an international Nazi network conspiring to return to power were based on genuine fears that began during the Second World War and lasted through the 1960s. By the end of that decade, however, developments in the international political arena – especially in West Germany – diminished western concerns that the Nazi diaspora could actually shape global affairs. As the prospect of an imminent Fourth Reich receded as a political threat, it became a source of entertainment. The literary and cinematic narratives that emerged during the ensuing period portrayed the possibility of a Nazi comeback in diverse ways. Some imagined foreign Nazis plotting a coup in the Federal Republic. Others depicted them seizing power on a global scale. All of them, however, featured familiar villains, including die-hard Nazi Werewolves, militant Wehrmacht generals, fugitive SS men, and unrepentant war criminals, ranging from Martin Bormann to Hitler himself. The authors of these narratives were driven by diverse motives: some were purely escapist; others were more didactic. All of them, though, used the Fourth Reich allegorically to assess the past's relevance to the present. In so doing, their narratives expressed diverging methods of remembering the Nazi era.

The response to the wave of Fourth Reich narratives was equally diverse. The popular reception was enthusiastic. Millions of people embraced the genre and made it a major commercial success. Critics, however, were more divided, praising individual works, while attacking the larger wave for aestheticizing and trivializing the Nazi legacy. By the early 1980s, the proliferation of narratives gradually ebbed and eventually receded. But it helped anchor the Fourth Reich in western popular consciousness.

The Nazi Diaspora: How Real a Threat?

The idea that a Fourth Reich was being planned from abroad dates back to the Second World War. After the course of the conflict turned against the Nazi regime in 1942, American diplomats and journalists became increasingly convinced that its leaders were conspiring to flee to Latin America with the goal of plotting an eventual return to power.[2] One of the main countries of concern was Argentina. As a result of the country's large German immigrant community and its Military Government's wartime neutrality, Argentina was viewed by many American officials as the most likely place to harbor Nazi fugitives; indeed, the first explicit reference to the possibility of a Nazi "Fourth Reich" in Argentina dates to mid 1944.[3] These fears were bolstered in the spring of 1945, when the Anglo-American press published sensationalistic stories of Nazi officials – including Martin Bormann and even Hitler – arriving by submarine in Argentine ports, along with looted assets meant to fund a "worldwide Nazi underground."[4] Convinced of the threat's seriousness, the US State Department published a *Blue Book on Argentina* in February of 1946 warning that "Nazi leaders have combined with Argentina totalitarian groups to create a Nazi-fascist state."[5] The warning ironically achieved the opposite of its intended goal. Several weeks later, Argentine voters, resentful of American meddling, elected General Juan Peron as their country's new president. Peron's ensuing decision to welcome German immigrants to his country, regardless of their backgrounds, caused further anxiety and led American watchdog organizations, such as the Society for the Prevention of World War III, to warn in 1946 that tens of thousands of Nazis "were tinkering away on a Fourth Reich" in Argentina.[6]

Intensifying cold war fears of the Soviet Union in the latter 1940s led to the decline of such rumors, but they resurfaced in the early 1950s with the upsurge of neo-Nazi activity in West Germany.[7] In the US and Great Britain, journalists examined the role of foreign Nazis in aiding the political ambitions of the SRP and Naumann Circle. These suspicions were granted plausibility by the fact that Hans-Ulrich Rudel and Otto Skorzeny regularly traveled between Argentina, Spain, and other lands of the Nazi diaspora.[8] They were further reinforced by the activities of the right-wing, Buenos Aires-based monthly journal, *Der Weg*, which was described by the Society for the Prevention of World War III in 1950 as the "most dangerous Nazi outpost outside the borders of Germany."[9] These trends, finally, dovetailed with journalistic exposés about a burgeoning "Fascist International" stretching from Europe to Latin America.[10] The Australian press, for instance, reported in 1952 that the Nazis had hidden "millions" in plundered loot (including "22 cases of gold teeth 'collected' by ... Eichmann") in the Austrian lake region of Alt-Aussee in order to "prepare the ground for the Fourth Reich."[11] Similar stories appeared in the British and even the Brazilian press, which in 1950 reported about Argentine-based groups "working for the successful return of National Socialism."[12]

Western anxieties about an international Nazi underground also focused on the Middle East. These anxieties reflected the awareness that many Arab countries had been pro-Nazi during World War II and some, such as Egypt, Syria, and Iraq, provided refuge to Nazi fugitives after 1945. Some were notorious war criminals, such as Treblinka commandant Franz Stangl, Eichmann assistant Alois Brunner, gas van technician Walter Rauff, Foreign Ministry official Franz Rademacher, Mauthausen doctor Aribert Heim, and Reich Ministry of Propaganda official Johann von Leers; other individuals had fled the Federal Republic after running afoul of the authorities, such as SRP politician Fritz Rößler and the indicted antisemites Hans Eisele and Ludwig Zind.[13] The cases of these fugitives were highlighted in the early 1950s by American writers like John Dornberg and T. H. Tetens, both of whom detected varying connections between "the Nazi expatriates in the ... Arab countries and the ... neo-Nazi movements in Western Germany."[14] Perhaps the most worrisome were Nazi rocket scientists, who were recruited by Egyptian dictator Gamel Abdel Nasser to help build up the country's military strength.[15] Scattered journalists claimed to see a larger conspiracy in these links.[16] But cold war fears of the Soviet Union left them with few sympathetic listeners.

Concerns about fugitive Nazis spread to a much larger audience, however, after the capture of Adolf Eichmann in 1960. The West German government knew that Eichmann was in Argentina as early as 1952, but the belief that he posed no security threat impeded the effort to apprehend him.[17] Only in the late 1950s did the Israeli government, believing that Eichmann was part of a larger Nazi network helping the Arabs fight the Jewish State, authorize the Mossad to kidnap him and bring him to Jerusalem to stand trial for crimes against the Jewish people.[18] Eichmann's capture revived world interest in the existence of other fugitive Nazis in foreign sanctuaries, such as Bormann, Stangl,

Figure 5.1 In his book *The Murderers among Us* (1967), the Holocaust survivor and Nazi hunter, Simon Wiesenthal, claimed that a secret organization of Nazi fugitives called ODESSA was striving to create a Fourth Reich (Source: Getty Images).

and the Auschwitz doctor, Josef Mengele, and stimulated fears that they might be plotting a return to power.[19] In 1960, the *Daily Express* wrote that "the Nazis in the Argentine ... hope ... that Germany will once again be master of Europe" and were organizing discussions on "the subject ... [of] the Fourth Reich."[20] In 1963, multiple media outlets reported on the Austrian government's dredging of Lake Toplitz for treasure hidden by the Nazis to "fund a Fourth Reich" after the war.[21] That same year, news reports about German scientists working in Egypt to develop missiles for use against Israel led to comments that they were part of a larger plan to create a "Fourth Reich" that would "reunify all Germany and control the world."[22]

    The most important figure to stoke popular interest in the Nazi diaspora was the famed Nazi hunter, Simon Wiesenthal (Figure 5.1). Thanks to his work tracking down fugitive war criminals as an OSS agent and private investigator in the late 1940s and 1950s, Wiesenthal believed that an international conspiracy existed to return the Nazis to power. In his autobiographical book, *The Murderers among Us* (1967), he described how an unnamed former German intelligence operative told him at the Nuremberg Trials about the existence of a secret organization called ODESSA that was linked to "Nazi circles ... [pursuing] a Fourth Reich."[23] An abbreviation of the *Organisation der Ehemaligen SS-Angehörigen* (Organization of Former SS Members), ODESSA was formed, according to Wiesenthal, in 1947 by ex-SS men in order to smuggle former Nazis to Latin America, undermine West German democracy, wage a covert war against Israel, and generally threaten world peace. To finance its activities, ODESSA allegedly drew on state assets and looted Jewish wealth that had been hidden at sites in the Nazi Reich or transferred overseas following a secret conference organized by Martin Bormann and German industrialists on August 10, 1944 in Strasbourg, France.[24] The overall goal, Wiesenthal emphasized, was to use the "hidden funds for the building of a Fourth Reich."[25] This new Reich was part of a broader "world movement" supported by countries in Europe, the Americas, and the Middle East; it was aided by political parties, such as West Germany's NPD and George Lincoln Rockwell's ANP; and it was staffed by fugitive Nazis such as Mengele, Stangl, and Skorzeny. Most sensationally, Wiesenthal asserted that Bormann himself was an active member of the Nazi international, helping to lead it from his hideout "near the frontier of Argentina and Chile."[26]

Thanks in part to Wiesenthal's book, fears of an international Nazi conspiracy during the 1960s increasingly concentrated on Bormann (Figure 5.2). After 1945, the former Reichsleiter was widely believed to have died in Berlin while trying to elude the Red Army, but the failure to find his body fueled postwar suspicions that he might be alive. These suspicions increased following Eichmann's capture.[27] They spiked even further in November of 1972, when Hungarian-American journalist and former military intelligence official Ladislas Farago published a sensational, six-part series of articles in the London-based *Daily Express* claiming, on the basis of Argentine intelligence documents, that Bormann was living under an assumed name in several Latin American countries.[28] Interest peaked several weeks later following the West German authorities' declaration that they had discovered and positively

Figure 5.2 In the late 1960s and early 1970s, Hitler's former secretary and Reichsleiter Martin Bormann was widely rumored to be living in South America and plotting to establish a Fourth Reich (Source: Getty Images).

identified Bormann's remains, which had been dug up as part of a road construction project in West Berlin.

The ensuing attention sparked a wave of journalistic studies, including William Stevenson's *The Bormann Brotherhood* (1973), Farago's *Aftermath: Martin Bormann and the Fourth Reich* (1974), and Erich Erdstein's *Inside the Fourth Reich* (1977).[29] These studies were breathless, first-person accounts of how Bormann and other Nazi fugitives had fled Germany for foreign sanctuaries in order to plot a return to power. Significantly, all of the books highlighted the existence of a Fourth Reich in their analyses, thereby lending the concept new prominence. According to Stevenson, Bormann had begun "to plan for a Fourth Reich" following the German defeat at Stalingrad and, since 1945, had served as the future Reich's "Führer," steering a "brotherhood" of fanatical supporters across vast "Nazi networks in the Mideast and Latin America" as they worked towards the "rebirth of the National Socialist movement."[30] Farago's book-length expansion of his earlier articles was more document-based than Stevenson's and invoked the idea of a Fourth Reich in a more varied fashion. At the outset of his book, he explained that his study sought "to establish how successful Nazis were in reviving Nazism in exile and how much of a threat their amorphous Fourth Reich represented to the world."[31] Farago's frequent use of the term "amorphous" in his ensuing narrative – like his use of the term "nebulous" – to describe the Fourth Reich implied that it was mostly a nascent threat.[32] Although he portrayed the survival of Nazi sentiment throughout Latin America's German immigrant communities as a serious problem, Farago ended his book on a sober, rather than alarmist, note. In the conclusion, he claimed to have conducted a brief, five-minute meeting with the by-now senile Bormann in a Bolivian nursing home and described how the Reichsleiter's retirement from politics had robbed Latin America's Nazi community of its leader and ended its run as "a 'movement' or a 'force.'"[33] By contrast, Erdstein's melodramatic study portrayed the Fourth Reich as a more pressing danger. Written as a spy thriller, *Inside the Fourth Reich* autobiographically detailed Erdstein's experience as an Austrian Jewish refugee who used his wits to emigrate to Latin America, where – according to his own stylized account – he became a Uruguayan intelligence agent, a Brazilian police officer, and, finally, a Nazi hunter. Like Farago, Erdstein claimed to have seen Bormann, but his narrative focused more on the hunt for Josef Mengele, whom he sensationalistically (and erroneously) claimed to have shot to death in 1968. In narrating his adventures hunting Nazis across the frontier regions of Rio del Sul and Marchel Candido Rondon, Erdstein described Bormann and Mengele, along with Franz Stangl, as "plotting a Nazi revolution" that would culminate with "the rise of a Fourth Reich."[34] At the same time, Erdstein questioned the Nazi exiles' plan to "manipulate dictators and control the world" by describing them as "living in a dream world" divorced from reality.[35] That said, his claims, like those of Farago and Stevenson, bolstered the connection between Nazi fugitives and a possible Fourth Reich.

The wave of Nazi-hunting studies received considerable publicity. Not only were they aggressively marketed by publishers and profiled in full-page advertisements in major American newspapers, they sold well and were widely reviewed.[36] Wiesenthal's book was hailed in the American, British, and German media as an "extraordinary" volume written by "the conscience of a forgetful world."[37] By contrast, the monographs that made up the "Bormann Books Boom" received a more mixed response.[38] Anglo-American critics touted Farago's volume as full of "fascinating material" based on "imposing ... sources," yet skeptics – including Wiesenthal himself – called it a "dubious" work with "serious shortcomings."[39] German critics were even more hostile, dismissing the book as entirely "unconvincing."[40] Reviewers of Stevenson's volume described it as "creepy," "chilling," and "exciting," but more than a few found it "hard to accept as factual."[41] Finally, reviewers of Erdstein's book regarded it as intriguing, but some openly wondered whether it was "the real thing or fantasy."[42] These caveats notwithstanding, critics insisted that the books cast needed attention on "a sorry segment of our history" and provided a useful warning against the western world's tendency to "forget and forgive."[43] As one critic put it, the books showed that, regardless of whether individual Nazis were alive or dead, it was clear that "there exists in South America a 'Fourth Reich' of Nazi fugitives . . . financed by Nazi loot."[44] Only by remaining vigilant would history be kept from repeating itself.[45]

Scholars today are skeptical about the existence of a foreign Fourth Reich. Although they acknowledge the existence of fugitive Nazis in Latin America and the Middle East – and have shown how they arrived there from Europe – they reject the idea that ex-Nazis were involved in an international conspiracy to return to power. In his recent study, *Odessa und das Vierte Reich*, for instance, the former West German ambassador to Paraguay, Heinz Schneppen, flatly declared that "all serious evidence speaks against the existence of an SS escape organization by the name of ODESSA," adding "at no time was there ever any real danger . . . of a Fourth Reich."[46] Indeed, according to Ronald Newton, the idea of a Fourth Reich was a "myth" that only existed in "the realm of . . . fantasy."[47] The studies of Schneppen, Newton, and others make a compelling case that the Nazis never wielded significant power in Argentina or anywhere else in Latin America. Of the tens of thousands of German immigrants that left for Argentina after the war, only a small percentage (2–3 percent) were Nazis, and no more than a few dozen were war criminals.[48] Fears to the contrary were the result of wartime deception. The US State Department's wartime concern that Nazis were fleeing Germany for Argentina originated in the American interception of "black propaganda" reports generated by British intelligence officers – including the journalist Sefton Delmer – that were intended to demoralize the German home front by pretending that the Nazi leadership was abandoning ship.[49] Fears of a Nazi exodus to Argentina were also partly based on forged evidence. Some of Wiesenthal and Farago's key claims – about ODESSA, the 1944 Strasbourg conference, and Bormann's survival – were based on fraudulent materials provided by politically biased middlemen and outright hucksters.[50] In reality, the Nazi fugitives who fled to South America were not helped by ODESSA, but by the International Red Cross, the Catholic Church, and private individuals.[51] There never could have been any Strasbourg conference, moreover, as many of the alleged participants were dead or in concentration camps at the time it was ostensibly convened.[52] Finally, there was no conspiracy between Peron and Nazis, as the Argentine dictator had no reason to permit the creation of a Nazi state within his own state.[53]

These ill-founded rumors were believed for many reasons. American officials accepted British propaganda about a Latin American Fourth Reich partly out of sheer gullibility, but also did so deliberately to pursue hemispheric hegemony and limit German and British economic competition.[54] Latin American countries, such as Brazil, nurtured the rumors as a way to limit the power of Argentina.[55] Within Argentina itself, critics of Peron spread stories of his alleged collusion with ex-Nazis in order to discredit him.[56] The concept of a Fourth Reich was also utilized to promote cold war interests: the US hoped to distract attention from the failures of their denazification program; leftists in West Germany wanted to keep people vigilant about the danger of neo-Nazism; and communists in East Germany sought to delegitimize the Federal Republic.[57] Finally, the idea of the Fourth Reich served the interests of ordinary individuals and society at large. Simon Wiesenthal and other journalists employed the idea for personal self-aggrandizement and profit. And the general public gravitated to the topic because of its obsession with conspiracy theories.[58]

Yet, while fears of a Fourth Reich were often exaggerated, they also had a basis in fact. Argentina, for example, had a large cohort of Nazi true believers who sought to revive their movement after the war through journalistic activism. In 1947, the pro-Nazi, Argentine-born German, Eberhard Fritsch, founded the journal *Der Weg* (*The Path*) in Buenos Aires in order to provide ex-Nazi officials, journalists, and intellectuals with a venue in which to reaffirm their ideological principles.[59] In hundreds of essays published until the journal's demise in 1958, its contributors relativized Germany's guilt for the outbreak of World War II, sought scapegoats for the country's military defeat, minimized the regime's crimes against the Jews, rehabilitated its leadership and institutions, and warned against the enduring threats posed by Jews and Bolsheviks. *Der Weg*'s editors sought to win support for their beliefs not only among German readers in Latin America, but in Germany itself, exporting thousands of issues of the journal there.[60] In response, the mainstream German press condemned the journal in strident terms, and Allied officials, fearing that *Der Weg* was part of an Argentine-based "Nazi resistance center," eventually banned it in May of 1949.[61] At the same time, the American and German media attacked the journal for making Argentina a "laboratory for a Fourth Reich."[62]

In fact, the evidence suggests that the editors of *Der Weg* actually pursued such a goal. Fritsch openly romanticized the idea of "a unified, free, and proud Reich," in keeping with the Nazi ideal of the *Volksgemeinschaft*, and explored methods of achieving it from abroad.[63] In the early 1950s, *Der Weg* moved in a more right-wing direction under the influence of the fanatical antisemite Johann von Leers and sought to become more politically active.[64] The journal's editors forged close relations with the SRP and DRP in West Germany, flirted with forming a German "government in exile," and even weighed the possibility of pursuing a coup via "armed revolt once the objective preconditions for success" came into being."[65]

Most significantly, *Der Weg*'s editors sought to realize their political goals by establishing a relationship with Adolf Eichmann (Figure 5.3). As Bettina Stangneth has shown in her book *Eichmann before Jerusalem*, one of the journal's most important contributors was the Dutch Nazi collaborator Willem Sassen, who became acquainted with Eichmann through Fritsch's social circle in the early 1950s and sought to enlist him in the journal's increasingly important project of Holocaust denial. Like Fritsch and Rudel, with whom he was closely connected, Sassen remained a true believer in National Socialism after 1945 and hoped that a "revolution in Germany" might pave the way for a "Nazi Renaissance."[66] He and the other leaders of *Der Weg* hoped that by proving the Holocaust to be a Jewish lie, they would not only be able to rehabilitate Nazism, but also weaken Adenauer's government – then particularly unpopular among right-wing Germans because of his 1952 reparations agreement with Israel – prior to the upcoming 1953 Federal elections.[67] For his part, Eichmann agreed with much of Sassen's agenda. In contrast to Hannah Arendt's later portrayal of him as a faceless, apolitical bureaucrat, Eichmann was an unrepentant Nazi who acted as if the war had not been lost and the Third Reich had never

Figure 5.3 Together with other Nazis associated with the right-wing Argentine journal, *Der Weg*, the former SS officer and war criminal Adolf Eichmann was committed to replacing Adenauer's government with a restored Nazi Reich in the 1950s (Source: Getty Images).

collapsed.[68] More importantly, Eichmann also had political ambitions and pursued "plans for a political overthrow" in West Germany.[69] In the mid 1950s, he drafted a book-length manuscript defending his wartime actions and drew up plans to present his "findings" in the form of an "open letter to Konrad Adenauer."[70] According to Stangneth, Eichmann drafted this defense as part of a larger plan to return to West Germany, be put on trial, receive a mild sentence (then standard practice at the time for former Nazi perpetrators), and, upon release, enter the world of politics and unseat Adenauer, who would be up for reelection in 1957.[71] As matters turned out, Eichmann agreed that same year to sit down with Sassen for what became four months of taped interviews on the subject of the Holocaust. Yet, unfortunately for Sassen (who hoped to use the material for a book), Eichmann was uninterested in denying the Final Solution and instead proudly took credit for his role in it.[72] He flatly declared that "if of the 10.3 million Jews [in Europe] ... we had killed 10.3 million, I would be satisfied [that] ... we had destroyed an enemy."[73] Realizing that this admission doomed his effort to prove the Holocaust a lie, Sassen distanced himself from Eichmann and abandoned the project of rehabilitating Nazism. Adenauer's reelection in 1957 constituted an additional setback for the agenda of Fritsch's Argentine Nazi circle, and within a year *Der Weg* ceased publication altogether.

Despite their ultimate defeat, the activities of the Nazi loyalists surrounding *Der Weg* deserve to be taken seriously. Even though scholars admit that Fritsch and Sassen overestimated their influence and concede that Eichmann's "insane" plans had no chance of succeeding, the fact remains that many Nazis in Argentina dreamt of returning to power.[74] Even though few of them besides Fritsch invoked the idea of a Fourth Reich to describe their plans, foreign concerns about them were far from groundless.[75] Given the knowledge of people in the early 1950s, it was reasonable, Stangneth writes, for them to perceive the "many activities of National Socialists" as part of "a huge, worldwide conspiracy."[76] Although their concerns turned out to be exaggerated, contemporaries had no idea how the future would unfold. For this reason, their vigilant warnings about the dangers of a Fourth Reich were prudent.[77]

This conclusion may seem unobjectionable, but it has surprising counterfactual implications. Knowing what we know today about the plotting taking place in the Nazi diaspora, it might seem easy to conclude that western observers should have acted on their fears and waged a more aggressive campaign against foreign Nazis. Scholars have commonly floated "missed opportunity" counterfactuals bemoaning the failure to bring ex-Nazis like Eichmann to justice. Stangneth and others have argued, for example, that West German's security establishment knew where Eichmann was in 1952 and might have been able to capture him – but chose not to. Had they done so, the Federal Republic might have been able to pursue "a genuine new beginning" after the Third Reich.[78] History could have turned out better than it did in reality.

But is this necessarily true? In order to determine whether this failure should be critiqued or condoned, we need to recall the motives that underpinned it. The reluctance of West German officials to pursue Eichmann in the early 1950s was partly due to their uncertainty about the domestic political consequences of capturing him. In real history, when Eichmann went on trial in Israel, Adenauer desperately sought to minimize what he expected would be the negative consequences for

West Germany's international reputation.[79] In 1960, Germany's democratic order was comparatively stable, but in the early 1950s, it was more vulnerable. Adenauer's government was under attack from right-wing forces domestically, while, in the international arena, reluctance persisted about integrating the country into the western alliance. Had Eichmann been put on trial in West Germany at this time, Adenauer's government might have been destabilized. Right-wing forces would have condemned the chancellor's departure from his commitment to amnesty and integration. Foreign critics in both the west and east would have found new reason not to trust the new democracy. This would have been especially true if Eichmann's testimony exposed embarrassing facts about the Nazi pasts of West German officials. These considerations help explain why West German officials "missed" the "opportunity" to pursue Eichmann.

It may have been for the best. The Federal Republic's democratic development probably benefited from the fact that prominent ex-Nazis remained hidden abroad and were not brought back to West Germany to stand trial. Even if they were busy hatching fanciful plots to return to power and establish a Fourth Reich, they were doing so from a safe and harmless distance. Rather than being a concrete threat, the Nazi diaspora may have served as a safety valve. Like Frederick Jackson Turner's famous frontier thesis – which argued that the ability of Americans to migrate to new lands in the west helped defuse social discontent in the nineteenth-century United States – the Nazi diaspora may have diverted the energies of unrepentant Nazis away from West Germany and protected the country from political destabilization. It may also have been for the best that Eichmann was ignored by the Germans and caught by the Israelis. Simon Wiesenthal himself speculated that if Eichmann had been caught earlier "at the end of the war and tried at Nuremberg, his crimes might now be forgotten," for he would have been merely "another face among the defendants," and the destruction of the Jews would not have received that prominence that it later received.[80] For the sake of Holocaust memory, a belated confrontation with Eichmann – one that highlighted the ongoing threat of other fugitive Nazis and the role of postwar amnesia in allowing them to escape – more effectively underscored the importance of remembrance. The idea of foreign-based Nazis pursuing a Fourth Reich may have largely been a myth, but it was one with a meaningful message.

The Cultural Turn: The Fictional Fourth Reich

During the long 1970s, the myth assumed new prominence in western culture. While novels and films explored the idea of a Fourth Reich during and immediately after World War II, they largely disappeared in the 1950s. A decade later, however, they returned in unprecedented fashion. From the early 1960s to the early 1980s, dozens of novels, films, television programs, and comic books explored the nightmare scenario of a Nazi return to power. They presented their narratives in diverse forms, including war dramas, spy thrillers, detective stories, horror tales, and superhero sagas. Whatever the form, the works consistently portrayed the Fourth Reich as an enduring threat to the entire world. This claim struck a chord among audiences throughout North America and Europe. As was shown by the commercial success of the era's narratives, millions of readers and viewers were attracted to the subject of the Fourth Reich. In the process, it became a mainstay of western popular culture.

Aestheticizing Nazism

The fictionalization of the Fourth Reich reflected the wider aestheticization of the Nazi past in western culture. Starting in the 1960s and lasting until the 1980s, European and North American novels, films, and television programs became obsessed with Hitler and the Third Reich. The representation of the Nazis in these works was not static, but changed over time. The earliest examples, which included André Schwartz-Bart's novel *The Last of the Just* (1959), Leon Uris's novel *Mila 18* (1961), and Stanley Kramer's film *Judgment at Nuremberg* (1961), portrayed the Nazis in strictly moralistic terms as the embodiment of evil. They expressed the upsurge in Holocaust consciousness that accompanied the swastika wave and the revelations of the Eichmann trial. By the end of the decade, however, a new pattern of representation appeared. As Nazis became increasingly familiar figures in mass culture, they became stock villains drained of ethical significance; instead, they were reduced to superficial symbols (black uniforms, swastika armbands, leather jackboots) and generically sociopathic behaviors (sadistic violence and deviant sex). This trend manifested itself in highbrow films, such as Luchino Visconti's *The Damned* (1969) and Liliana Cavani's *The Night Porter* (1973), as

well as in novels like William Styron's *Sophie's Choice* (1979) and
D. M. Thomas's *The White Hotel* (1981).[81] The aestheticization of
Nazism also shaped popular culture. In film, it influenced B-grade
"Nazisploitation" films such as *Ilse – She Wolf of the SS* (1975) and
mainstream movies like *Raiders of the Lost Ark* (1981).[82] In music, it
influenced the Nazi-themed fashions of punk rock bands like the Sex
Pistols, the names of hard rock bands such as KISS, and the song lyrics of
musicians such as David Bowie.[83] Still other works of popular culture
aestheticized the Nazi era by representing it comedically: films and
television programs like *Dr. Strangelove* (1966), *The Producers*
(1969), and *Hogan's Heroes* (1965–71), for instance, played the Nazi
legacy for laughs instead of lessons. These works were highly diverse,
but they signaled a worrisome "fascination" with fascism that identified
more with the perpetrators than the victims.[84] It augured a tendency to
forget the very aspects of the past that needed to be remembered in order
to prevent its recurrence.

These trends dovetailed with the so-called "Hitler Wave."
Beginning in the late 1960s and lasting until the mid 1980s in West
Germany, the United States, and Great Britain, a stream of historical
biographies, films, and novels signaled a spike of popular interest in the
deceased Führer.[85] The wave began in 1969 when Albert Speer – just
released from Spandau prison – published his memoir, *Inside the Third
Reich*. The book's swift rise to bestseller status helped inspire additional
monographs, films, and novels – among them, Joachim Fest's *Hitler*
(1973), Hans-Jürgen Syberberg's *Hitler: A Film from Germany* (1977),
and George Steiner's *The Portage to San Cristóbal of A. H.* (1981) – and
even sparked scandals, such as the one surrounding the publication of
the (forged) Hitler Diaries in 1983.[86] The surging interest in Hitler was
partly a reaction against the simplistic early postwar depiction of the
Führer as a demonic figure and reflected a desire to see him more as
a real human being.[87] It was also a reaction against the era's social-
scientific analyses of fascism that deemphasized the role of personality
in history.[88] The new studies moved beyond examining Hitler's political
policies to studying the ins and outs of his private life – including his
early education, friendships, romantic relationships, artistic interests,
habits, hobbies, and pets. The humanization of Hitler, however,
sparked alarm among many critics, who feared that the tendency to
sensationalize his life and exploit it for commercial gain marginalized
the importance of viewing the Nazi era from an ethical perspective.[89]

The growing fascination with the Nazis also reflected changes in the international political climate. Starting in the early 1970s, the US government's policy of *détente* with the communist world, epitomized by President Nixon's trip to China in 1972, produced a thaw in the cold war. This development had an important impact on western popular culture. As observers noted at the time, the improvement in east–west relations led the "Russian spy [to] fall on hard times in the publishing world" and created a void that needed to be filled with new villains. Before long, the Nazis were enlisted as the enemy that people "loved to hate" and became the focus of an unprecedented "publishing blitzkrieg."[90] This was especially easy as most people no longer feared that the Nazis were going to come back any time soon in West Germany. Although western suspicions about the Federal Republic's susceptibility to Nazi ideas briefly flared with the rise of the NPD in the mid 1960s, they faded following the party's poor showing in the elections of 1969. Further reducing western fears was Chancellor Willy Brandt's foreign policy of *Ostpolitik*, which, by normalizing relations with East Germany and Poland, diminished western anxieties about West German irredentism and shored up the country's postwar democratic reputation.[91] Finally, worries about German neo-Nazism in the 1970s were dampened by the rise of left-wing terrorist groups such as the Red Army Faction (RAF) and the Baader-Meinhof gang, both of which showed that the chief danger facing West Germany no longer came from the right.[92]

Worries about neo-Nazism instead shifted from West Germany to other countries, especially the United States. The publication of exposés by journalists and governmental officials about the presence of mid-level Nazi collaborators living in the US cast attention on the American government's abandonment of denazification for the sake of cold war politics.[93] Around the same time, concerns were sparked by the emergence of neo-Nazi groups related to Rockwell's American Nazi Party, such as the National Socialist White People's Party (1967), the National Socialist Party of America (1970), the National Alliance (1974), and the National Socialist German Workers Party Development and Foreign Organization (1971).[94] The surge in neo-Nazi activity was further visible in the booming market for Nazi memorabilia and paraphernalia, including uniforms, furniture, flags, jewelry, daggers, and other pieces of assorted kitsch.[95] It was also seen in the surging production of neo-Nazi literature, most notably the racist

and antisemitic novel *The Turner Diaries* (1978), by Rockwell's collea-
gue, William L. Pierce, and Holocaust denial literature published by the
California-based Institute for Historical Review, which was founded in
1978.[96] Much of this material alarmingly found its way to West
Germany, thanks to the success of American Nazis in forging links
with their German colleagues.[97]

Representing the Fourth Reich: Plots and Genres

All of these trends shaped the fictionalization of the Fourth
Reich. During the long 1970s, approximately five dozen narratives
appeared in the form of novels, films, television episodes, radio plays,
and comic books. Most were produced in Great Britain and the United
States, although many reached a broader audience after being translated
into other languages, exported to foreign movie theaters, and airing as
syndicated re-runs.[98] The narratives represented different branches of
historical fiction: most were "secret histories" that depicted the conspiratorial (but ultimately unsuccessful) effort of key characters to alter the
course of history; some were "future histories" set in the near future;
others were "alternate histories" that portrayed the alteration of actual
historical events. The narratives borrowed from different literary genres – espionage thrillers, war adventures, conspiracy dramas, murder
mysteries, and horror tales – but they all focused on the conflict between
unrepentant Nazis striving to create a Fourth Reich and anti-Nazi forces
seeking to thwart them. The narratives came in four different versions:
1) political thrillers in which contemporary Nazis worked to seize control of the West German government; 2) adventure tales in which
present-day Nazis wrought international havoc while striving for global
domination; 3) war sagas in which Nazi Werewolves sought to regain
power; and 4) mysteries in which present-day Nazis attempt to reestablish a still-living Adolf Hitler as Germany's dictator. By identifying how
these different narratives portrayed the Fourth Reich, we can better
understand how the concept took shape in popular culture.

Nazi Plans for a West German Coup

One of the era's most popular themes involved fanatical Nazis
trying to seize power in the Federal Republic of Germany. This theme
defined many works in the 1960s. In 1962, British writer Harry

Patterson's novel *The Testament of Caspar Schultz* depicted a British spy attempting to track down the tell-all memoir of a rueful ex-Nazi exposing the existence of a Nazi underground movement in the Federal Republic.[99] In 1966, British writer David Ray's novella *The End of the Fourth Reich* portrayed a Spanish-based Nazi general stealing a British-designed laser to force British, American, and Soviet troops to withdraw from Germany.[100] In the fall of 1967, three episodes of the American television show *Mission Impossible* explored similar scenarios: "The Legacy" depicted the sons of Hitler's "faithful officers" using the Führer's personal fortune of $300 million "to launch the Fourth Reich" in Germany; "The Bank" portrayed an East German financier secretly working to fund a new Nazi Party; and "Echo of Yesterday" featured a West German neo-Nazi working to convince West German voters that "the Nazis of today are no longer gangsters" but the leaders of a respectable political movement. Finally, Herbert Leder's horror movie *The Frozen Dead* (1966) featured a London-based Nazi scientist striving to seize power by reanimating the frozen bodies of 1,500 elite Nazi soldiers hidden in German caves.[101]

Narratives in the 1970s, by contrast, portrayed a West German power grab being launched from the Nazi diaspora. American writer Harris Greene's novel *Canceled Accounts* (1972) featured a Latin American-based ODESSA leader, Richard Reichart, forcing a Jewish Holocaust survivor and Swiss banker to release looted assets in order to fund a Palestinian terrorist campaign against Israel that will help create a "Fourth Reich . . . on the ruins of the present rotten capitalistic German system begun by Adenauer."[102] Irish writer Manning O'Brine's novel *No Earth for Foxes* (1974) portrayed an Austrian neo-Nazi group, "Die Wespe" (The Wasp), trying to hasten the withdrawal of American and Soviet forces from Germany and facilitate the creation of a reunified Reich.[103] American writer William Craig's *The Strasbourg Legacy* (1975) depicted the effort of a Latin American- and Middle Eastern-based Nazi cabal to return to power by assassinating Chancellor Willy Brandt, disabling NATO forces, and proclaiming martial law in response to an engineered Soviet attack (Figure 5.4).[104] Finally, American writer Madelaine Duke's novel *The Bormann Receipt* (1977) portrayed a Latin American mafia headed by Bormann hatching a conspiratorial plan to use funds amassed from the sale of looted Jewish artworks to replace West Germany's "weak and unworkable democracy" with a "Fourth Reich [that] will last a thousand years."[105]

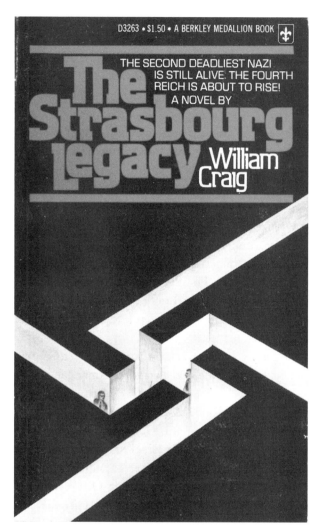

Figure 5.4 William Craig's novel *The Strasbourg Legacy* (1975) depicted the effort of foreign Nazis to assassinate Chancellor Willy Brandt and return to power in West Germany (Source: Random House).

Nazi Plans for World Conquest

A second group of narratives portrayed internationally based Nazis trying to establish a Fourth Reich by sparking global war. British writer Adam Hall's spy thriller *The Quiller Memorandum* (published in 1965 and turned into a film the following year starring George Segal) depicted an Argentine-led, neo-Nazi cabal known as "Phoenix" infiltrating the West German government and attempting to spark an armed conflict between the US and Soviet Union in Berlin by disabling Soviet troops with vials of pneumonic plague and using West Germany's ensuing military advantage over Allied forces to seize the country.[106] A similar scenario was explored around the same time in an episode of the American television show *Voyage to the Bottom of the Sea* entitled "The Last Battle" (1965), which portrayed an SS colonel using a secret tropical island base to launch simultaneous nuclear strikes on the US and Soviet Union, thereby sparking a "nuclear Holocaust" and building "the Fourth Reich ... destined to last one thousand years." British writer Martin Hale's spy thriller *The Fourth Reich* (1965) imagined a Hitler loyalist becoming the Secretary-General of the United Nations and unleashing a wider African war by using UN troops to conquer the Uranium-rich region of Katanga.[107] In 1967, episodes of *Mission Impossible* and *The Man from U.N.C.L.E.* portrayed South American Nazis based in "New Berchtesgaden" and "San Rico" striving to "sow the seeds of Nazism around the world." Most prominently, Frederick Forsyth's novel *The Odessa File* (originally published in 1972 and later made into a film starring Jon Voight) focused on a diabolical plan hatched by a Nazi war criminal – former SS-officer and Riga ghetto chief Eduard Roschmann (operating under the codename "Vulkan") – to supply Egypt with a sophisticated missile guidance system for attacking Israel with plague-laden warheads (Figure 5.5).[108]

Starting in the 1970s, the Nazi threat was increasingly portrayed as emanating from the United States. In November of 1970, an episode of the American television show *Mannix* entitled "To Cage a Seagull" depicted the fanatical head of the American "Party of the Fourth Reich" plotting to "gun down the police and massacre the civil authorities" in "one hundred key American cities" as part of a larger bid for world power. In 1975, American novelist Thomas Gifford's murder mystery *The Wind Chill Factor* chronicled the effort of American Nazis, led by high government officials, to rehabilitate the "virtues of Nazism" from its German "debauchers" and pursue a "worldwide conspiracy ... [to create] a ... Fourth Reich."[109] A similar premise informed writer Ben Stein's novel *The Croesus Conspiracy* (1978), which portrayed a plan of US-based Nazis to engineer the election of one of their pawns, an ambitious California Senator named Travis Bickel, to the presidency, thereby safeguarding the future of the Aryan race.[110] Robert Ludlum's novel *The Holcroft Covenant* (published in 1978 and turned into a film in

Figure 5.5 The film version of Frederick Forsyth's 1972 hit novel, *The Odessa File*, starred Jon Voight trying to thwart a campaign of global terror organized by the ex-SS man and wanted war criminal Eduard Roschmann (Source: Everett Collection, Inc. / Alamy Stock Photo).

Figure 5.6 Robert Ludlum's best-selling novel *The Holcroft Covenant* (1978) depicted foreign-based German sleeper agents pursuing a brutal assassination campaign meant to establish a global Fourth Reich (Source: Harper Collins).

1985) depicted the effort of foreign-based German sleeper agents known as "Sonnenkinder" to secure nearly $1 billion in looted funds and pursue a global assassination campaign meant to establish "the Fourth Reich ... all over the world (Figure 5.6).[111] Andrew Kaplan's novel *Hour of the Assassins* (1980) explored the joint effort of a Peruvian-based ODESSA

leader, Von Schiffen, and American CIA officials to overthrow the governments of Latin America, renew the fight against Soviet communism, and
ensure that "from the backwater of the Third World, the Fourth Reich will
be born!"[112] Mike Pettit's novel *The Axmann Agenda* (1980) explored
how an American-based conspiracy led by a former SS Lebensborn official
seeks to corner "the world's food and water supplies" and pass on the
wealth to a new generation of racially superior children.[113] Finally, in
1982, an episode of the American television show *Greatest American Hero*
portrayed American neo-Nazis proclaiming "Power to the Fourth Reich!"
as they collaborate with Arab nations to prevent an American arms
shipment to Israel.[114]

Besides novels and films, comic books often depicted the
Nazis pursuing a global Fourth Reich. During World War II, Nazi
characters were ubiquitous in American comic books and were consistently portrayed as going down in defeat. Starting in the 1960s,
however, they were depicted as a renewed threat. Leading the charge
to create a Fourth Reich was the classic wartime Marvel villain, Red
Skull.[115] Between 1965 and 1980, the demented Nazi mutant was
featured on many occasions trying to bring the Nazis back to
power.[116] In 1972, for example, issue #148 of *Captain America*
depicted Red Skull attacking the city of Las Vegas and proclaiming
that his organization, Hydra, had "always been a decoy … buying
time for the birth of the Fourth Reich!" (Figure 5.7). In early 1977,
eleven consecutive issues (#17–27) of the Marvel UK comic *Captain
Britain* showed the British superhero trying to prevent Red Skull from
using a "germ bomb" hidden in Big Ben to defeat Britain and establish "the glory of the Fourth Reich." Beyond the Red Skull saga,
other comics portrayed Nazis fomenting global mayhem from Latin
America. In late 1974 and early 1975, issues #23–24 of the comic
Master of Kung Fu portrayed the hero, Shang Chi, trying to prevent
an Amazon-based Nazi racist from using a nuclear warhead to create
a "glorious Fourth Reich." And in 1982, issues #188–89 of
The Brave and the Bold featured Batman trying to keep Latin
American Nazis from "plot[ing] … the rise of a 4th Reich" and
launching "another Holocaust" and with the aid of a stolen "bacteria
serum."

Figure 5.7 In 1972, issue #148 of *Captain America* depicted the infamous villain Red Skull attacking the city of Las Vegas in the effort to forge a Fourth Reich in the United States (Source: Marvel, Comics, © MARVEL).

Werewolf Tales

A third group of narratives depicted Nazi Werewolves laying the foundations for a Fourth Reich. Building on early postwar fears, these tales were mostly set at the end of World War II and featured die-hard Nazi insurgents working with Martin Bormann to ensure a Nazi return to power. Geoff Taylor's novel *Court of Honor* (1966) described a blind German general creating a *Fehme* ("honor") court system at the end of World War II to punish German "collaborators" and make Bormann "the Führer of the new Fourth Reich."[117] In 1976, Jack Higgins (writing under his real name, Harry Patterson) published *The Valhalla Exchange*, which focused on the effort of two elite German SS-officers to implement Bormann's plan of escaping from Berlin through a prisoner exchange with a group of prominent western hostages held at a remote Austrian castle.[118] Ib Melchior's *Sleeper Agent* (1975) depicted an SS-officer, Rudolf Kessler, helping Bormann escape from Germany and create a sleeper cell of Nazi agents in the United States dedicated "to assur[ing] ... the rise of the Fourth Reich."[119] Jack Hunter's *The Tin Cravat* (1981) portrayed a German anti-hero, Bruno Stachel, working with American forces in 1945 to expose the Werewolf campaign as a cover for Bormann's real plan to fund Nazi resistance cells all over the world.[120] Shifting the premise to the later postwar period, John Gardner's novel *The Werewolf Trace* (1977) depicted a Nazi agent (codenamed "Werewolf") masquerading as a present-day Danish émigré businessman named Joseph Gotterson and waiting for the moment to lead right-wing Britons in a fascist take-over of the country.[121] And George Markstein's novel *The Goering Testament* (1978) imagined a conspiracy of aging, but unrepentant, British Nazi sympathizers using Hermann Goering's last will and testa-ment (dictated before his suicide in 1946) to revive a worldwide Nazi movement.[122]

Hitler Lives!

The last category of narratives portrayed radical Nazis using Adolf Hitler himself to create a Fourth Reich. British writer Robert Muller's 1962 television drama (and later stage play) *The Night Conspirators* imagined German elites secretly meeting in a foreign embassy and plotting to use the frail Führer (recently returned from

Icelandic exile) in a bid to seize power. Two years later, an episode of the television show *The Man from U.N.C.L.E.* portrayed a fugitive Nazi scientist endeavoring to bring Hitler's body back from "suspended animation" so that the "bitter young men" of his Fatherland have "someone to lead them."[123] David Bradley's film *They Saved Hitler's Brain* (1963) depicted Hitler living in the South American hideout of Mandoras and planning to take over the world by launching a deadly nerve gas attack.[124] Brad F. Ginter's film *Flesh Feast* (1967) portrayed Hitler undergoing cosmetic surgery as part of a plan to mount a political comeback with shadowy Latin American Nazis. Joseph Kane's film *The Search for the Evil One* (1967) represented the senile Nazi dictator serving as the key to Bormann's plan ("Operation Fourth Reich") to conquer Argentina and then the world. Edwin Fadiman Jr.'s novel *Who Will Watch the Watchers?* (1970) dramatized the effort of a vicious, Paraguayan-based neo-Nazi organization, known as the "Sons of Liberty," to keep Hitler alive and help the "Fourth Reich … rise again."[125] In 1975, an episode of *CBS Radio Mystery Theater*, "The Rise and Fall of the Fourth Reich," depicted a group of Germans nursing an ailing Hitler back to health in Mexico City and convincing him that "the day of the Fourth Reich had dawned."[126] In 1976, an episode of the British television show *The New Avengers*, entitled "The Eagle's Nest," portrayed a group of Nazis in England reviving a cryogenically frozen Führer in order to "conquer again."[127] Finally, Philippe van Rjndt's novel The *Trial of Adolf Hitler* (1978) imagined Hitler being deliberately placed on trial before the world as part of a neo-Nazi effort to transform him into a martyr and establish a clean foundation for a Fourth Reich.[128]

A related subcategory of this scenario imagined Hitler's survival in altered form. Ira Levin's novel *The Boys from Brazil* (published in 1976 and turned into a film starring Gregory Peck and Laurence Olivier in 1977) portrayed the notorious Nazi doctor, Josef Mengele, pursuing a demented scheme to kill the fathers of ninety-four teenage boys who have been artificially cloned from Hitler's genetic material in the effort to create a "pan Aryan" version of the "Fourth Reich" (Figure 5.8).[129] In 1977, an episode of the American television show *Wonder Woman* depicted a cloned version of Hitler in Latin America pursuing a renewed bid for world domination.[130] Ib Melchior's detective thriller *The Watchdogs of Abaddon* (1979) imagined a Los Angeles-based Nazi cell, led by an evil SS-officer, Franz Schindler, scheming to use

Figure 5.8 The movie version of Ira Levin's 1976 novel, *The Boys from Brazil*, portrayed the notorious Nazi doctor, Josef Mengele, trying to establish a Fourth Reich with the help of Hitler clones (Source: Getty Images).

Hitler's mentally retarded grandson, Dolfi (who lives in a bunker in North Hollywood), to manufacture an international crisis in the Middle East, seize global power, and establish a "North American Reich" in the United States.[131] Finally, American writer Timothy B. Benford's novel *Hitler's Daughter* (1983) imagined the Führer's offspring – a Congresswoman named Leora Gordon – eliminating her rivals, getting elected president, and setting out to establish a "Fourth Reich in America."[132]

Patterns of Representation

Generalizing about the era's many narratives is challenging, but broader trends are discernible. Regardless of whether they featured Werewolf resisters, fanatical SS men, fugitive war criminals, or closeted West German politicians, the accounts uniformly depicted the Nazis as evil. They diverged, however, in portraying their opponents: one group of tales depicted the Americans, British, and Israelis as idealistic heroes; a second group portrayed them as craven collaborators. These diverging representations reflected the intentions of their creators. The era's authors were a heterogeneous bunch: many were professional writers who worked in the worlds of literature, film, and television; others were former journalists who moved into the world of popular fiction; still others were amateur writers who worked in other careers. Several things linked them, however: nearly all of them were men; the vast majority of them, moreover, had completed military service during or after the Second World War. In producing their narratives, the authors regularly offered commentaries on historical and present-day topics. They did not do so uniformly, however: one group of authors sought to warn about the persistence of neo-Nazism in present-day West Germany; another group self-critically warned about the survival of fascist trends closer to home. These diverging messages partly reflected the two groups' differing biographies: the first group was generally composed of World War II veterans who triumphalistically sought to validate their wartime role in defeating the Nazis; the second group's members belonged to a younger generation that came of age after 1945 and were more concerned about present-day domestic and international crises. Both groups' narratives were published more or less concurrently, but their differences signaled a nascent shift in the western memory of the Nazi era. Over time, the fictional accounts of the Fourth Reich increasingly universalized and aestheticized the Nazi era.

Tales of Triumph: Nazi Villains, Allied Heroes, and the Enduring German Threat

The first group of narratives clearly underscored Nazism's evil. They did so, first of all, by emphasizing the ideology's enduring power. Most of the works depicted postwar Nazis collectively pursuing their goals in secret organizations, such as ODESSA (featured in *Cancelled Accounts*, *The Bormann Receipt*, and *The Odessa File*), Die Spinne (*The Werewolf Trace*), or fictional organizations like "the Phoenix" and "Die Wespe" (*The Quiller Memorandum* and *No Earth for Foxes*). Many texts portrayed the Nazis as having already infiltrated the West German government: *The Quiller Memorandum* revealed that forty Germans linked to the Phoenix had already found posts in the Federal Republic's bureaucracy, while *The Odessa File* and *The Strasbourg Legacy* depicted Nazis masquerading as legitimate West German politicians. Other works imagined the Nazis quietly biding their time in sleeper cells until the moment arises to seize power. This concept was epitomized by the SS-officer Rudolf Kessler in *Sleeper Agent*, while it found a corollary in Mengele's plan in *The Boys from Brazil* to "activate" his dormant child-Hitlers by murdering their fathers. The Nazis were also portrayed as forging powerful alliances with equally evil collaborators, most typically, hostile Arab terrorists or governments (as seen in *Canceled Accounts*, *The Odessa File*, *The Strasbourg Legacy*, and *The Watchdogs of Abaddon*). Most of the narratives, finally, showed the Nazis liberally using kidnapping, torture, and murder to realize their goals.

The Nazis' evil was further illustrated by their penchant for sadism. Some texts made this clear by using flashbacks to the war years. *No Earth for Foxes* described an SS massacre of Italian civilians outside of Bologna in late 1944 in which one soldier hacks "the fetus of an eight-month baby ... from the mother's body." *The Strasbourg Legacy* depicted the chief villain, the Nazi doctor August Bleemer, planning "medical experiments at Dachau" where prisoners are "injected ... with gas gangrene" and forced "to lie naked in snow-drifts." *The Odessa File* graphically represented SS-officer Eduard Roschmann behaving as the "Devil incarnate" in the Riga ghetto by taunting Jews before shooting them.[133] Other texts, such as Martin

Hale's *The Fourth Reich*, portrayed contemporary acts of torture, with one Nazi thug using a "burning firebrand" to scorch the back of the novel's British protagonist "with erotic deliberation."[134]

The narratives emphasized the Nazis' evil by portraying them as sexually deviant. In *The Watchdogs of Abaddon*, for instance, Hitler's grandson, Dolfi, is the progeny of an incestuous relationship between Hitler's son and daughter, while Hitler himself has "kinky sex" with "various centerfolds."[135] Other texts homophobically portrayed Nazi characters as gay. In *No Earth for Foxes*, a band of Nazi agents are "queers to a man"; in *The Axmann Agenda*, the chief Nazi enforcer, Spade, rapes several male intelligence officers; and in *Canceled Accounts*, SS leader Reichart organizes a prostitute-fueled orgy in Marrakesh featuring gay "sexual aberrations."[136]

Many texts amplified the Nazis' evil by contrasting it with the goodness of their pursuers. Among the many American and British characters, there are admirable military figures: *Sleeper Agent*'s "patriotic ... [and] smart" CIC official, Tom Jaeger; *The Vahalla Exchange*'s indefatigable American general, Hamilton Canning; and *Court of Honor*'s brave British RAF pilot and POW, Tommy Dart.[137] There are also tough American police detectives (Harry Bendicks in *The Watchdogs of Abaddon*) and Israeli intelligence agents (Zvi Harari, who hunts down Reichart in *Canceled Accounts*, and Rudi Ebel, who combats the members of "The Wasp" in *No Earth For Foxes*).

The narratives commonly portrayed Nazi villains failing to achieve their goals and meeting with defeat. To list but a few examples: Reichart is arrested in *Canceled Accounts*; Bleemer is caught and deported to a Soviet POW camp in *The Strasbourg Legacy*; and Schindler, the chief villain in *The Watchdogs of Abaddon*, is killed on a Hollywood movie set. Real historical Nazis also meet with death: Martin Bormann perishes in fiery plane crashes in both *Court of Honor* and *The Tin Cravat*. Many of the deaths are particularly brutal. In *The Boys from Brazil*, Mengele is viciously torn to pieces by a pack of Dobermans unleashed by one of the young Hitler clones, Bobby Wheelock. The most violent death appears in *No Earth for Foxes*, in which a sadistic SS-officer, Kappler, dies in agony after being shot by "a short burst ... obliterating his penis."[138] Finally, Adolf Hitler is killed off in a variety of original ways: by having his unconscious body pushed into the flames of a burning laboratory (*The Man from U.N.C.L.E.*), being devoured by maggots (*Flesh Feast*), incinerated in a burning car (*They Saved Hitler's Brain*), blown up by a land mine *(The Search for the Evil One)*, and riddled with bullets (*The New Avengers*).

The narratives' endings presented the didactic lesson that remembering the Nazis' crimes is the key to justice. In some texts, the protagonists' commitment to hunting down Nazi war criminals reflects traumatic wartime experiences: in *No Earth for Foxes*, the most rabid Nazi hunter, Mills, obsessively tracks down the war criminal Kappler because of the former's desire to avenge SS atrocities he witnessed in Italy. In other tales, characters born after the war decide to hunt down Nazis after learning about their crimes for the first time: in *The Odessa File*, the young West German journalist, Peter Miller, becomes morally committed to locating the whereabouts of SS-officer Roschmann after serendipitously finding the diary of Holocaust survivor Solomon Tauber, which details the officer's crimes. Other texts make the point in reverse by underscoring the danger of forgetting. In *The Watchdogs of Abaddon*, the son of Los Angeles detective Harry Bendicks initially tells his father that the war was "a long time ago" and insists that the Nazi war criminals are mostly "harmless" old men; before long, however, the son realizes the truth of his father's conviction that the Nazi threat remains acute.[139] Unless people remember the past, the texts make clear, they will allow it to be repeated. In *Canceled Accounts*, an Israeli Mossad agent proclaims that the Nazis represent "a future menace to Germany and the world if they ever rise again," for they would produce "another holocaust."[140] Many narratives underscored the need for vigilance, finally, by allowing certain Nazis to evade justice. In *The Valhalla Exchange* and *Sleeper Agent*, Martin Bormann appears to escape to Latin America. In Greene's *Canceled Accounts*, the arrest of ODESSA's leader, Reichart, does not prevent the group's remaining members from reaffirming their commitment to a Fourth Reich. Fighting the Nazis thus remains an ongoing task.

In endorsing remembrance, the narratives reflected contemporary concerns. Many of the works expressed worries about Germany's ongoing susceptibility to Nazi ideas. The rise of the NPD was a major influence on some of the era's works. Some texts mentioned the party explicitly – for example, *The End of the Fourth Reich*, in which the chief villain, General von Klaus, confidently affirms that the NPD "will immediately accept my authority," since, like most Germans, its members want to "follow a man who is going to lead them back to dignity and power."[141] Fears that the NPD's public embrace of democracy masked an enduring commitment to Nazism were also visible in the film version of *The Quiller Memorandum*, where a British intelligence official (Sir Alec Guinness) tells Quiller (George Segal) to be on guard against Nazis because, today, "nobody wears a brown shirt" and they "look like everybody else." The influence of the NPD also probably explains the proliferation of works of television and film in the years 1966–69, including episodes of *Mission Impossible* and *The Man from U.N.C.L.E.* and the films *Flesh Feast* and *The Frozen Dead*.

The commitment to memory exhibited in these narratives reflected the historical experiences and present-day beliefs of their authors. Many of the writers had acquired a keen hatred of Nazism as a result of their service in World War II and remained suspicious of the Germans after 1945. The author of *Court of Honor*, Geoff Taylor (1926–2007), was an Australian bomber pilot for the RAF who was shot down and held as a POW by the Germans until being liberated by the Russians in 1945; in an interview in 1966, he confessed that he needed years to overcome his war experiences and write about them in an "objective" manner, confessing that if had he done so earlier, "the novel would have been a hymn of hate."[142] Similarly, the Irish novelist Manning O'Brine (1913–77) wrote *No Earth for Foxes* by drawing on his experiences as a British military intelligence official who fought the Nazis in occupied Italy, a point he made clear in a prefatory note to the novel, where he admitted that he was willing to be criticized as a "prejudiced man" for warning that the Germans' commitment to Nazism did not die "in the flame of the Berlin bunker."[143] The British writer Martin Hale (1937–2016) was too young to fight against the Nazis, but in writing his novel *The Fourth Reich* he channeled the anti-German views of his father, the war veteran and owner of the *Daily Telegraph*, Lord Hartwell – a fact made clear in his novel's afterword, where Hale insisted that "German methods and ideas are hundreds of years old, and are therefore in danger of reversion to type" in the present.[144] The Danish-American author and Hollywood screenwriter Ib Melchior (1917–2015) served in the US Counterintelligence Corps, participated in the liberation of the Flossenbürg concentration camp, and won a Bronze Star for helping to capture a Werewolf unit in 1945. In *The Watchdogs of Abaddon*, Melchior ended each chapter of his novel with "headlines and news stories" about neo-Nazi activity that were "taken from actual reports in the world press during the late

1970s."[145] In *Sleeper Agent*, Melchior claimed that the idea of secret Nazi agents working abroad was based in "fact" and ominously warned, "Where are they today?" Finally, other authors were refugees from Germany and Austria. The author of *The Night Conspirators*, Robert Muller (1925–98), was a German-Jewish writer who had fled Nazi Germany for England in 1938 and thereafter harbored deep suspicions about his former homeland. The author of *The Bormann Receipt*, Madelaine Duke (1919–96), had no military service to her credit, but she had personal reasons to write about her topic, given the theft of her Viennese Jewish family's art collection by Nazi looters, the murder of her relatives in the camps, and her prolonged postwar struggle to secure restitution from the Austrian government.[146]

Other authors shared suspicions about the Germans, but refrained from generalizing about them. Like other writers, the American novelist Harris Greene (1921–97) had seen time in wartime and postwar Germany as a CIC agent and later as a diplomat, but in writing *Canceled Accounts* he included a virtuous German double agent named Dieter who infiltrates ODESSA on behalf of the Mossad.[147] The author of *The Tin Cravat*, Jack Hunter (1921–2009), worked for American occupation forces in postwar Germany rounding up Nazi Werewolves and playing a leading role in Operation Nursery. Many of his novels, however, featured a "good German" hero, Bruno Stachel, who, despite his wartime service of the Reich, cooperates with US forces.[148] By contrast, some of the writers who included positive representations of the Germans did not fight them in World War II. The famed British journalist and writer Frederick Forsyth (1938–) was too young for wartime military service (although he was an RAF pilot thereafter) and had relatively moderate views of the Germans. Not only did he make the hero of *The Odessa File* a morally upright German journalist, Peter Miller, he depicted the Holocaust survivor Solomon Tauber proclaiming in his diary that "I bear no hatred … toward the German people."[149] Ira Levin (1929–2007) also did not serve in the war (instead, he served in the Army Signal corps in the mid 1950s), but he offered a similar message in *The Boys from Brazil*, whose Simon Wiesenthal-like protagonist, Yakov Lieberman, forswears "vengeance" at the novel's conclusion by destroying the list of ninety-four Hitler clones, thereby preventing a militant Jewish organization from tracking them down and killing them.[150]

Self-Critical Stories: Nazi Villains, Allied Collaborators, and Universal Fascism

The second category of narratives also portrayed the Nazis as evil. Works such as *The Testament of Caspar Schultz*, *The Werewolf Trace*, *Who Will Watch the Watchers?*, *The Wind Chill Factor*, *The Holcroft Covenant*, *The Croesus Conspiracy*, and *The Hour of the Assassins* depicted the Nazis as immensely powerful thanks to their collaborative work in organizations like ODESSA, Die Spinne, and other international networks. These texts also depicted the Nazis as highly sadistic: *The Testament of Caspar Schultz* showed an evil Nazi doctor named Kruger whipping an imprisoned female Israeli agent named Anna Hartmann before killing her, while *The Hour of the Assassins* shows Joseph Mengele torturing the novel's American protagonist, John Caine, by locking him in a stifling Amazonian shed filled with fire ants. The narratives also represented the Nazis as sexually deviant. The scheming, London-based Nazi Johann von Tiebolt has an incestuous sexual relationship with his sister, Gretchen, in *The Holcroft Covenant*; Mengele has sexual relations with his masochistic daughter, Inger, in *The Hour of the Assassins*; and the Munich-based Nazi Gunter Brendel is likened to an "art-loving homosexual" in *The Wind Chill Factor*.[151] All of the texts, moreover, showed the Nazis using murder to achieve their goals.

These texts differed, however, in portraying the Nazis' opponents in unsympathetic terms. This divergence first appeared in British accounts. *The Testament of Caspar Schultz* concluded by revealing that the story's main villain is the British intelligence official, Sir George Harvey, who helps the closet Nazi, Kurt Nagel, destroy the tell-all memoir in order to cover up Harvey's wartime appeasement of Hitler and his identity as the country's designated puppet prime minister following the Nazis' expected defeat of Great Britain. *The Werewolf Trace* portrayed British intelligence agents as doubly incompetent: first, by allowing ex-Nazis to escape justice after 1945; second, by overcompensating for this failure by exaggerating the threat posed by the Danish émigré (and suspected Nazi sleeper agent) living in England, Joseph Gotterson, whom they drive to suicide by sending him subliminal messages that he may be Joseph Goebbels' surviving son, Helmut. *The Goering Testament* portrayed British government officials as "devious" figures willing to sacrifice the lives of ordinary citizens in their effort to uncover a conspiratorial cell of British neo-Nazis.[152]

Finally, issue #22 of the comic book *Captain Britain* portrayed England as a down-and-out country whose population is so demoralized that Red Skull easily recruits Nazi collaborators "right here in *London*."[153]

American accounts offered similar accusations. The chief villain in *The Wind Chill Factor* is the American lawyer and closet Nazi agent Arthur Brenner (codename "Barbarossa"), who, at the novel's conclusion, divulges to the protagonist, John Cooper, that US government officials have long worked with committed Nazis to place "a hand-picked "man ... in the White House" and create a world in which "Washington and the Nazi movement are one..[and] the same."[154] In *The Croesus Conspiracy*, the key villains are the American Secretary of State, Arthur Kosters, and the American plutocrat and Nazi sympathizer Elson Patterson, who engineer the election of a willing pawn, California Senator Travis Bickel, to the presidency and implement a devious Nazi-American plan ("Operation Croesus") to create a "world *Reich*."[155] *The Hour of the Assassins* reveals that the American CIA has helped the ODESSA leader, Von Schiffen, overthrow the Peruvian government and pursue a plan of continental hegemony. The CIA is also the chief villain in Edwin Fadiman Jr.'s *Who Will Watch the Watchers?* for hiding Hitler's survival from the American people, thereby "murdering" their trust in government.[156] In *The Holcroft Covenant*, the CIA is equally untrustworthy, having been infiltrated by sleeper cells of Nazi "Sonnenkinder," who plan to unleash a wave of "killing ... and conflagration in the streets."[157]

In blurring the differences between Nazis and their enemies, the narratives suggested that the putative heroes – whether British or American – had the potential to become fascist villains. The texts thus universalized Nazism's significance. Unlike other tales from the period, they suggested that the capacity towards extreme right-wing thinking was not limited to the Germans, but inherent in all people. This point was driven home by various plot twists involving the identities of the narratives' central characters. Some characters think they know their family histories, only to learn that they have Nazi backgrounds: Noel Holcroft in *The Holcroft Covenant* is told that he is the son of a Nazi financial wizard, Heinrich Clausen, while in *The Wind Chill Factor*, John Cooper learns that his father, Edward, did not actually die while fighting the Nazis in the RAF, but worked as a secret Nazi agent together with his Nazi grandfather, Austin. Other tales revealed that putatively Jewish characters are actually Nazis who have escaped justice by assuming the identities of Holocaust victims. In *The Hour of the Assassins*, the Los Angeles-based, Jewish pornography baron and Holocaust survivor, Karl Wasserman, is secretly the chief villain, Von Schiffen, while in *The Croesus Conspiracy*, the Secretary of State, Arthur Kosters, uses his Jewish background to hide his Nazi identity. The message is clear: anyone can be a Nazi; the Nazis can be anywhere.

In presenting this pessimistic message, the authors of the narratives often critiqued the state of the contemporary world. British writers in the 1960s and 1970s, for example, expressed the era's sense of post-imperial decline by challenging the national myth of the "finest hour." In *The Testament of Caspar Schultz*, Jack Higgins (1929–) challenged the myth's binary portrait of British heroes and German villains by depicting British government officials – most notably, Sir George – as Nazi collaborators, and individual Germans – above all, the heroic Detective Von Kraul – as sympathetic heroes.[158] Higgins's humanized portrayal of the Germans reflected his positive experience as a British soldier in occupied Germany, while his depiction of Sir George collaborating with the Nazis in order to preserve Britain's empire suggested that the author shared the decade's post-imperial skepticism.[159] John Gardner's novel *The Werewolf Trace* also rejected a black-and-white portrait of Germans and Britons. It critically described the British people's postwar fear of the Germans as a byproduct of imperialism, arguing that the country's "pointless colonial rearguard action in Palestine" prevented the British government from fully bringing the Nazis to justice in the late 1940s and sparked an enduring paranoia about "sleeper agents." A similar anti-imperialist message informed the novel's depiction of the British people, whose attraction to the "law and order" message of domestic fascists in the 1970s is rooted in the country's crisis in Northern Ireland ("our small Vietnam").[160]

American narratives alleged that fascism existed in the United States as a means of commenting on the nation's malaise in the era of Vietnam and Watergate. In portraying the US being taken over by Nazis in *The Holcroft Covenant*, Robert Ludlum (1927–2001) articulated his liberal belief that fascist tendencies existed in all modern institutions, ranging from international corporations to intelligence organizations.[161] Sharing this skepticism was Edwin Fadiman Jr. (1925–94), whose indictment of the CIA for covering up Hitler's survival in *Who Will Watch the Watchers?* reflected the era's growing criticism of the intelligence agency.[162] Younger writers expressed a similar sense of disillusionment.

Andrew Kaplan's (1941–) critique of the CIA in *The Hour of the Assassins* reflected his personal experiences as an intelligence official and combat veteran, and were epitomized by his protagonist John Caine's Vietnam flashbacks and belief that that all sides commit atrocities in warfare.[163] It is unknown whether Thomas Gifford (1937–2000) sought to make a specific political point in portraying a fascist takeover of the US in *The Wind Chill Factor*, but his disillusionment with American affairs was visible in the comment, articulated by the novel's protagonist (and the author's alter ego), Cooper, that "everything I believe in has been proven a lie."[164]

American narratives did not only advance liberal, but also offered conservative, perspectives on current events. The scathing indictment of the American political establishment in Ben Stein's *The Croesus Conspiracy* sought to exonerate, rather than indict, the Nixon administration. Written by a former Nixon speechwriter and loyalist, the novel shows President Nixon refusing to cooperate with American Nazi agents, who secretly engineer the Watergate scandal to oust him; moreover, the former president's Watergate misdeeds pale in comparison with the far more violent crimes abetted by the Nazis' handpicked president, (the symbolically named) Travis Bickel.[165] Timothy B. Benford's *Hitler's Daughter* also expressed a conservative message. By showing the Nazi occupation of the White House being led by external forces, it exonerated ordinary Americans of culpability for the novel's dystopian ending, thereby illustrating the author's patriotic leanings.[166]

The Rise and Fall of the Fourth Reich: Popular and Critical Reception

Tales of the Fourth Reich were immensely popular in the 1970s. Many novels became bestsellers, and some were made into successful films. The general public's favorable response, however, was not shared among professional reviewers. While many of the narratives were critically acclaimed, many more were savagely attacked. The divided response reflected the interplay of complex economic and cultural forces. But the causes were less significant than the result: the massive attention received by the fictional Fourth Reich further entrenched the subject in popular consciousness.

Popular Reception

The popularity of the era's narratives was confirmed by their profitability. Among the bestselling books were *The Quiller Memorandum, The Odessa File, The Wind Chill Factor, The Boys from Brazil, The Valhalla Exchange,* and *The Holcroft Covenant.*[167] The fact that these novels were nearly all turned into popular films further reflected their moneymaking ability.[168] Estimating television viewing audiences is difficult, but the Fourth Reich's presence in mainstream American television shows, such as *The Man from U.N.C.L.E., Voyage to the Bottom of the Sea, Mission Impossible, Mannix, The New Avengers, Wonder Woman,* and *Greatest American Hero,* further testified to its popular appeal. The same is suggested by the repeated appearance of the Fourth Reich in American comic books.

The topic's popularity was partly due to economic factors. The production of fictional tales about the Fourth Reich obeyed the forces of supply and demand. On the one hand, the authors and publishers illustrated the influence of Keynesian, "demand side" economic forces, insofar as they produced their narratives in order to satisfy the demands of their audiences; on the other hand, the same producers illustrated the "supply side" forces of "Say's Law," insofar as they stimulated consumer demand by flooding the market with what they hoped people would consume. Once authors, publishing houses, film studios, television companies, and comic-book publishers recognized the Fourth Reich's moneymaking potential, they did their best to sustain it. First, the authors themselves saw the topic of the Fourth Reich as financially promising. The era's biggest names in popular fiction embraced the topic: Jack Higgins, Ira Levin, Frederick Forsyth, Robert Ludlum, John Gardner, and James Patterson. Between them, they had sold tens of millions of books on other subjects, including war (Jack Higgins's *The Eagle Has Landed*), espionage (Frederick Forsyth's *The Day of the Jackal*), and horror (Levin's *Rosemary's Baby*). None of the writers knew much about Nazism before trying their hand at the topic, but the fact that they did so earned their books attention and boosted their chances of success. Publishers also realized that considerable profit could be made with the topic of the Fourth Reich. In 1972, Forsyth received a record £250,000 advance for *The Odessa File* from his British publisher, while, the same year, Ladislas Farago received a six-figure advance from Simon and Schuster to turn his newspaper series about Martin Bormann into a book.[169] Hollywood studios, meanwhile, rushed to secure the film rights to the era's novels and even works of non-fiction.[170]

Publishers and film studios supported the wave with major marketing campaigns. They included large advertisements for their books and films in major newspapers, often employing the phrase "The Fourth Reich" to add an aura of sensationalism. Ads for the film version of *The Boys from Brazil,* for instance, featured the headline: "[They] are the start of the Fourth Reich. If these children survive … will we?"[171] Similar ads were produced for less prominent works, such as Harris Greene's *Canceled Accounts,* which was marketed with the headline: "The last survivors of the Third Reich have already launched the Fourth."[172] Following the success of *The Odessa File* and *The Boys from Brazil,* other texts were marketed with direct reference to the two hit novels. Mike Pettit's *The Axmann Agenda,* for instance, was described by his publisher as "beyond the shocking sheer terror of *The Boys from Brazil,*" while Erich Erdstein's *Inside the Fourth Reich* was promoted with the tag: "The Real Story of The Boys from Brazil." The promotional attention also reached the broadcast media. To promote their books, Wiesenthal, Forsyth, and Ludlum appeared on *The Today Show,* while Erdstein appeared on *The Dick Cavett Show.*[173]

The wave of books on the Fourth Reich was also fueled by deeper cultural and psychological factors. During the 1960s and 1970s, American popular culture was fascinated by evil. Horror tales were especially popular, whether about satanic possession (*The Exorcist*), serial killers (*The Texas Chainsaw Massacre*), the paranormal (*Carrie*), zombies (*Night of the Living Dead*), or psychopaths (*Taxi Driver*). Tales of the Fourth Reich satisfied this interest in evil by featuring Nazi perpetrators committing acts of murder, theft, military aggression, and genocide. Further enhancing these tales' popularity was the fact that they showed the Nazis paying for their crimes with their lives. By routinely depicting the Nazis meeting with violent ends, the narratives served an important psychological function by enabling ordinary people to enjoy a vicarious, fictional form of vengeance against the villains who, in real history, evaded justice for their crimes.

The narratives also exploited the public's prurient interest in sex. The *Hour of the Assassins* described Mengele's daughter, Inger, as having "small pointed breasts" with "nipples erect like tiny daggers."[174] *The Holcroft Covenant*'s femme fatale, Gretchen Beaumont, had "an extraordinary body screaming for . . . invasion and satisfaction."[175] The inclusion of these elements reflected the fact that the narratives were mostly produced by male writers for a male audience. The Fourth Reich was a common theme in men's magazines during this period. The feature story in the March 1962 issue of *Escape to Adventure*, for example, was entitle "Escape from the Torture Dungeon of the Fourth Reich," and shared cover space with an article entitled, "The Sexual Side of Arson."[176] Erich Erdstein's original story about killing Mengele was profiled alongside a scantily clad woman in the German men's magazine *Neue Revue* on January 5, 1969.[177] The cover of the September 1984 issue of *Gallery* magazine featured a photo of a lingerie model and a headline touting an interview with Simon Wiesenthal that read: "The Fourth Reich Lives."[178]

The narratives' popularity also reflected a popular fascination with mystery. The collapse of the Third Reich in 1945 left many unanswered questions: did Hitler and his leading henchmen really die, or did they flee overseas? Was the defeat of the Third Reich permanent, or did the Germans still seek world domination? In the absence of clear answers to these questions, the topic of Nazism remained surrounded by rumors and allegations. Reports about Nazi war criminals being spotted in Latin America, rocket scientists being employed in the Middle East, and treasure being hidden across Europe were a constant presence in the western news media. Fictional tales of the Fourth Reich tapped into this fascination and promised to fill the informational void with dramatic answers.

Finally, the narratives' popularity reflected the era's political mood. In the US, sharpening racial tensions, the ongoing war in Vietnam, the eruption of the Watergate scandal, and the holding of Congressional hearings about covert CIA and FBI missions forced ordinary Americans to confront basic issues of morality. In Britain, the explosion of race riots, the worsening of terrorist violence in Northern Ireland, the onset of economic recession, and the eruption of labor unrest deepened the nation's sense of post-imperial decline. In both countries, the pessimistic mood boosted the popularity of the Fourth Reich narratives. They did so, however, in two different ways: some promoted escapism, while others encouraged self-criticism. The first approach was especially common among older writers and probably resonated most with older readers; both groups had served in the Second World War against the Nazis and often coped with the era's crises by looking back nostalgically to the war years when their countries had experienced their "finest hour" by waging a "good war" against German aggression. Tales of a Fourth Reich allowed these readers to escape into fictional worlds where truth was black and white instead of gray; where the line between villains and heroes was clear rather than murky; and where evil resided abroad rather than at home.[179] The second approach was more commonly advanced by younger authors and probably appealed more to younger audiences. Having grown up in a period of growing instability, this group sought to confront, rather than evade, present-day problems. They entertained the possibility that the Nazis represented an internal, rather than an external, threat and were working within the democratic system to subvert it. In adopting this self-critical stance, this group suggested that Nazism was not restricted to Germany, but remained a universal danger.

Critical Reception

The critical response to the era's narratives was mixed. Certain works were praised while others were panned. On the whole, reviewers responded more favorably to the works that appeared in the first half of the wave (from the mid 1960s to the mid 1970s) than those that appeared closer to its conclusion (from the mid 1970s to the mid 1980s). Reviewers also had more reasons for criticizing the narratives than for praising them. Finally, reviewers did not merely analyze individual works, but explained them as part of a larger cultural phenomenon. In so doing, they set the stage for its collapse.

Many of the era's narratives were reviewed positively by British and American critics. Some won prizes, most notably *The Quiller Memorandum*, which was awarded the best mystery novel published in America in 1965.[180] The novel also received some of the most enthusiastic reviews, with one critic calling it "grippingly readable" and another describing it as "one of the finest espionage novels I have ever read."[181] Other works received equally strong reviews. Forsyth's novel *The Odessa File* was hailed as a "cliffhanger" that was "brilliantly conceived and expertly written."[182] Levin's *The Boys from Brazil* was hailed as a "spellbinder" and "impeccably crafted."[183] John Gardner's *The Werewolf Trace* was described as written "in the best tradition of the British spy thriller."[184] Adam Hall's novel *The Fourth Reich* was commended as "intelligent and entertaining" (and was singled out by Kingsley Amis for being "a bit kinky").[185] Other narratives received more generic praise, including *The Holcroft Covenant* ("packed with action"), *The Strasbourg Legacy* (a "neat idea"), and *The Watchdogs of Abaddon* ("good fun").[186]

Many reviewers praised the narratives for their topicality and plausibility. The film version of *The Quiller Memorandum* was hailed by various reviewers as "ominous" and "timely" in light of the NPD's success in West Germany.[187] *The Watchdogs of Abaddon* was described as especially "credible" thanks to its interspersed news clippings about present-day neo-Nazi activity.[188] Other works were praised as being relevant for contemporary American political life. *Who Will Watch the Watchers?* was hailed for raising the question of whether "those we elect to high office" actually "act in our best interests?"[189] *The Croesus Conspiracy* was singled out for imparting a message that "goes to the very top of our institutions."[190] Other narratives were commended for being broadly believable: *The Odessa File* was praised as "utterly convincing," *The Boys from Brazil* was called "insanely credible," and *The Holcroft Covenant* was described as a "plausible" tale with "an unnerving … result."[191] One reviewer of *The Boys from Brazil* hoped libraries and bookstores would place the volume "on the fiction shelf."[192] Other reviewers praised the accounts for thematizing present-day moral questions. *The Odessa File* was admired for being an effective "study on guilt … and the … value of retribution."[193] *The Trial of Adolf Hitler* was called "thought-provoking" for asking whether any government "can rule without guilt."[194]

In one of the most extended meditations on the wave, Greil Marcus in *Rolling Stone* commended the "Nazi-hunting thrillers" for confronting "an irreducible reality" about Nazism "that no one else is facing." Arguing that "historians and political analysts" had abandoned the dramatic language necessary for describing what was "inexplicable" about Nazism, Marcus asserted that it had "become necessary for thriller writers to claim it." In the process, their narratives articulated the "true fears … that these days can find a voice nowhere else." Novels such as *The Wind Chill Factor*, he declared, effectively depicted "how easily the world the Nazis made could be fitted within our own" by showing that the Third Reich's "destruction of all limits on human action" had persisted into the postwar period.[195]

These positive comments, however, were exceeded by negative ones. In the early 1960s, two works came under particular fire: Robert Muller's television drama *The Night Conspirators* and the film version of Adam Hall's novel *The Quiller Memorandum*. Both sparked political controversy. When it first aired on British television in May of 1962, *The Night Conspirators* received a wave of angry reviews. Many British observers refused to accept the play's central claim that – as one commentator put it – "the German people today ... would willingly accept Hitler again were he still alive."[196] As several reviewers argued, Muller's "hysterical" expression of "hatred" weakened his play's credibility to such an extent that the only people likely to accept it were "anti-fascists [and] Hunno-phobes."[197] No less a figure than the former British High Commissioner for Germany, Sir Ivone Kirkpatrick, observed that the play "was a misrepresentation of the present situation in Germany."[198] The West German media also rejected the television program, dismissing it as full of "clichés."[199] The most notable criticism, however, came from the West German Foreign Ministry, whose London-based diplomats demanded to see the script after fielding complaints from viewers "who were disgusted with the play."[200] The officials acknowledged that "we know some things cannot be forgotten," but, they asked, "why revive bad memories?"[201] The reason for their concern was obvious: in the spring of 1962, the West German government was especially sensitive about foreign views of the Nazi era, which had been revived by the swastika wave, the Berlin crisis, and the Eichmann trial.[202] At the same time, the East German regime was actively using the Nazi era to discredit the Bonn Republic. In fact, East German officials aired *The Night Conspirators* on state television in the fall of 1962, while the government press commended Muller for exposing the fact that the Federal Republic was prepared to welcome back Hitler as the most suitable figure "to help fulfill the dreams of monopoly capitalists, clerics, militarists, and revanchists."[203]

Similar political concerns surrounded the film version of *The Quiller Memorandum*. When it first appeared in England in 1966, the film's focus on neo-Nazism was given immediate topicality by the rise of the NPD (Figure 5.9). Fearing negative political repercussions, the West German film industry's Voluntary Self-Control Board (*Freiwillige Selbstkontrolle*) ordered the American distributor to cut all references to the film's villains being neo-Nazis before it could be released to a West German audience. As a result, the dialogue was

20th Century-Fox Presents Ivan Foxwell's Production
"THE QUILLER MEMORANDUM"
In Panavision® · Color by DeLuxe

Printed in U.S.A.

Figure 5.9 In this scene from the film version of Adam Hall's 1965 novel, *The Quiller Memorandum,* British special agent Quiller (George Segal) finds himself captured by a cell of ex-Nazis, led by "Oktober" (Max von Sydow), who have infiltrated the West German government (Source: Getty Images).

changed so that viewers only heard generic references to "conspirators" and inferred that the villains were communists.[204] The change was widely mocked. *The Times* of London described it as another example of the Germans avoiding "echoes of the past"; the East German press condemned it as evidence of the Bonn Republic's "anticommunist and militaristic" attitude; even the West German newspaper *Die Zeit* criticized the mandated changes, noting that the film's German title, "Danger from the Dark," unintentionally, but accurately, described the domestic trend towards "voluntary" self-censorship.[205]

Following these two political controversies, subsequent narratives were attacked for a variety of literary deficiencies. Critics faulted many texts for problems of writing, style, and character development. *The Boys from Brazil* was called "superjunk" and described as "devoid of grace or wit."[206] *The Odessa File* contained "characters as stiff as cardboard."[207] *The Bormann Receipt* was "confused and amateurish."[208] *The Watchdogs of Abaddon*'s characters were "no more than robots."[209] The most commonly criticized work was Robert Ludlum's *The Holcroft Covenant*. One reviewer described the novel as "perfectly ghastly in [its] ... fortune-cookie characterization," while another noted that its characters came from "the backs of cereal boxes." Some griped that Ludlum's writing was marred by "risible dialogue," while others complained that it was filled with "italics and ellipses" instead of "carefully crafted sentences."[210] While Ludlum was criticized for stylistic flaws, other writers were faulted for including excessive historical material in their narratives. Forsyth was faulted for including so much "tedious detail" in his novel that it read like "an encyclopedia."[211] Jack Hunter, meanwhile, was attacked for inserting obscure "German references" into his tale and pretentiously including an actual "glossary."[212]

Critics also accused the tales of being unoriginal. As early as 1964, one reviewer accused *The Man from U.N.C.L.E.* episode "The Deadly Games Affair" of using "every cliché in the book."[213] Revealingly, only one year later, another observer critiqued the *Voyage to the Bottom of the Sea* episode "The Last Battle" for repeating a theme that "has already been used on 'Man from U.N.C.L.E.'"[214] *The Odessa File*'s plot was merely an "echo of all the B-films made about the Nazis."[215] The film version of *The Quiller Memorandum* was full of clichés.[216] Once again, the most commonly criticized work was *The Holcroft Covenant*. One reviewer mocked Ludlum for his formulaic writing, claiming that he composed his narratives by randomly choosing assorted "scrabble tiles" with key words such as "Nazi war treasure," "CIA," "Buenos Aires," and playing them on a board "whose red and blue squares are marked with violence ... sex ... doublecross ... and so forth." "Fill in the details," the reviewer concluded, "and you have a Ludlum thriller."[217]

Critics also attacked the narratives for their implausibility. The excessive number of characters and subplots contained in *Court of Honor*, according to one observer, prevented the elements from "blend[ing] ... into an effective novel."[218] Another complained that *The Valhalla Exchange*'s "blurry plot doesn't make a whole lot of sense."[219] *The Odessa File*'s narrative was "clumsily ... strung together by a string of unbelievable coincidences."[220] *The Holcroft Covenant*'s penchant for "gratuitous obfuscation," meanwhile, made it so "improbable" that one reviewer exclaimed: "I never believed it nor cared."[221] Similar criticisms were directed towards *The Fourth Reich, The Werewolf Trace, The Strasbourg Legacy, The Croesus Conspiracy,* and the film version of *The Quiller Memorandum.*[222] Other critics doubted the basic plausibility of the Nazis actually plotting a return to power. One skeptical reviewer of *The Quiller Memorandum* wrote that "the modern Nazi organization [seemed to be] . . . so well established" in the West German government that "it is difficult to imagine how these same people ever lost World War II."[223] A reviewer of *The Wind Chill Factor* wanted to know how the Nazis had remained strong enough for the last "30 years" to be "vigorous . . . [enough] to put up a strong threat to the four freedoms, motherhood, and apple pie?"[224] West German reviewers dismissed *The Odessa File*'s claims of an SS conspiracy existing within the Federal Republic as "laughable."[225] Finally, other reviewers complained about the inanity of certain narratives. The film *Search for the Evil One* was entirely dismissed due to its "outlandish absurdities."[226] *The Man from U.N.C.L.E.* episode "The Deadly Games Affair" featured "the most bizarre . . . plotline in many a full moon."[227] Perhaps the most telling criticism was directed at the *Mission Impossible* episode "The Legacy," which one reviewer snarkily described as involving a scheme to "recover Hitler's . . . fortune, and oh mein gosh! Start another reich."[228] This sarcastic comment suggested that the slapdash quality of certain narratives was turning the ostensibly frightening premise of a Nazi Fourth Reich into mere camp.

A decade later, this corrosive trend became more visible. By the late 1970s, critics conceded that the Fourth Reich had become part of a larger literary phenomenon, albeit one that had passed its peak. One observer noted in 1978 that "every month . . . another literary caballero can be seen riding the Swastika to the top of the national best-seller lists."[229] Another wrote that Nazi novels had become a "perpetual motion machine" just "like the Wild West."[230] Still another creatively observed that "the preoccupation of books and movies with Nazi Germany practically constitutes a posthumous Fourth Reich."[231] By the early 1980s, however, critics declared that tales about Nazis "making plans for the Fourth Reich" had become "hackneyed," "tedious," and "done-to-death."[232] In part, these claims reflected the narratives' declining quality. By the turn of the decade, the prospect of a neo-Nazi Fourth Reich had become reduced to a generic scenario. A telling sign was the formulaic utilization of the premise in various adventure book series, including *Nick Carter-Killmaster, Death*

Merchant, Secret Mission, and *James Bond*.[233] In all of these franchises, neo-Nazis served as the convenient villain-of-the-month – as interchangeable as Soviet KGB agents and Arab terrorists. By this point, the Fourth Reich had become victimized by the same economic forces that originally propelled it to prominence. As publishers increasingly saturated the market with titles, they paid less attention to quality, thereby ensuring an eventual decrease in popular demand and a bursting of the bubble they had inflated in the first place.

This dynamic lent credence to critics' damning accusation that the narratives were exploiting the Nazi legacy for entertainment and profit. In 1972, one observer attacked *The Odessa File* by accusing Forsyth of employing "painful, live history in order to spring a few quick thrills."[234] Another said it was "sacrilege to use the ... brutalities of a concentration camp to give a pseudo-serious slant to a spy story."[235] One reviewer of Ira Levin's *The Boys from Brazil* said that the novel "takes certain serious issues," such as "pathological anti-Semitism," and "manipulates them merely for ... entertainment"; in so doing, the novel showed a "lack of respect for evil."[236] Many of the works were accused of prioritizing the profit motive. One observer argued that *The Boys from Brazil* "trades shamelessly on our collective outrage at the Nazi horrors" and sought merely to make "a lot of people a lot of money."[237] The goal of earning a payday from Hollywood was frequently cited by critics as a reason for the novels' poor literary quality. *Court of Honor* was faulted for being pitched to "movie scouts."[238] *The Werewolf Trace* was dismissed as essentially being a "screen treatment."[239] The profit motive also explained the narratives' formulaic character. One observer noted that any ambitious writer merely had to give their detective novel a title like "The Von Richthofen Laundry List" and "you are sure to be signed to a contract."[240] Small wonder, then, that Robert Ludlum was singled out yet again for criticism, being described as having "made more money from Adolf Hitler ... than anyone since Krupp."[241] In offering these observations, critics urged readers to recognize that such authorial opportunism reflected an abdication of moral responsibility to the topic of the Nazi era. In summing up the wave, one critic answered her own rhetorical question – "Do we need another Nazi novel?" – by concluding that the genre's popularity reflected a "need born of the market ... not of the soul."[242]

In light of such comments, the wave of Fourth Reich narratives predictably ebbed by the end of the decade. This development was epitomized by the commercial failure of the film version of *The Holcroft Covenant* in 1985. Despite having a respected director (John Frankenheimer) and a major cast (including Michael Caine), reviews of the film were scathing. One critic calling it a "woeful" film with "lamentable" writing, while another saying its "script … would have disgraced a forties B-picture."²⁴³ Possibly the most revealing criticism faulted the film's lack of "topicality."²⁴⁴ The motion picture was partly victimized by bad timing. When Ludlum's novel first appeared in 1978, the Fourth Reich was at the apex of its popularity; seven years later, however, the topic had lost relevance. Small wonder that one critic wrote that "the prospect of a new Nazi regime is of little concern to today's audiences."²⁴⁵ By this point in time, the international political situation had changed considerably. While the US policy of détente with the Soviet Union in the early 1970s had allowed for the upsurge of fictional Nazis in western culture, the return of cold war tensions less than a decade later made them irrelevant. Thanks to the Soviets' invasion of Afghanistan in 1979, the US boycott of the 1980 Moscow Olympics, and President Ronald Reagan's nuclear saber-rattling, Russians once again loomed large as villains in the American cultural imagination. At a time when Americans were watching films like *The Day After* (1982), *Red Dawn* (1984), and *Invasion: USA* (1985), the prospect of a Fourth Reich had little chance to compete.

Conclusion

The fictional accounts of the Fourth Reich that appeared during the long 1970s signaled a growing split in the memory of the Nazi era. On the one hand, they reflected widespread popular support for remembrance. When the first novels, films, and television programs on the Fourth Reich began to appear in the early 1960s, they expressed lingering western concerns about West Germany's relationship to its Nazi legacy. Influenced by the swastika wave, the Eichmann trial, and the rise of the NPD, the narratives admonished the world not to forget Nazi crimes. They insisted that the Nazis were not merely the vanquished villains of a bygone era but were an enduring threat.

As they proliferated, however, the narratives increasingly reflected the normalization of memory. Many of the works aestheticized the Nazi era. Borrowing the time-honored narrative strategies from different literary genres – including war sagas, espionage tales, murder mysteries, and horror stories – they made abundant use of violence, sex, deception, betrayal, intrigue, and conspiracy. Many of the early tales made these elements integral to their plots, but subsequent ones used them more exploitatively. They increasingly used the Nazis as convenient – indeed, trendy – villains in their otherwise conventional adventures. In so doing, they separated the Nazis from their deeper historical context and transformed them into generic signifiers of villainy. Their function was now to entertain rather than to instruct. This development eventually led to the decline of the fictional Fourth Reich. The more that Nazis proliferated in the era's narratives, the more they became repetitive, derivative, and formulaic. Before long, they had become hackneyed and were eventually abandoned.The era's narratives not only aestheticized, but also universalized, the Nazi legacy. While the early accounts from the 1960s conceived of the Fourth Reich as a threat emanating from Germany, later works imagined the Nazi threat assuming global proportions. Many focused on a Nazi threat emanating from the United States. Tales of Nazis infiltrating the American government served a self-critical function by expressing discontent with the era's crises, whether Watergate or Vietnam. They were the cultural counterpart of the more overtly political claims by left-wing activists that the United States under Johnson and Nixon had embraced fascist principles. Like those political claims, however, the universalization of the Fourth Reich rhetorically inflated the concept, separating it from its historical context and transforming it into an all-purpose, but increasingly meaningless, signifier. This trend continued into the latter part of the 1980s. But before the decade's end, it was interrupted – and ultimately reversed – by unexpected events.

6 RE-GERMANIZING THE FOURTH REICH: FROM REUNIFICATION TO THE REICH CITIZENS' MOVEMENT

> President Bush last week 'reaffirmed' US support for the reunification of Germany . . .
>
> [His] statement . . . should not be underestimated. For it marks a stage in the two great interacting world-historical processes which will . . . dominate the closing decades of our century: the dissolution of the Soviet empire and German reunification . . .
>
> If this view . . . is correct, then German reunification is now inevitable. We are on the road to the Fourth Reich: a pan-German entity, commanding the full allegiance of German nationalists.[1]
>
> Conor Cruise O'Brien, *The Times* (October 31, 1989)

While the concept of the Fourth Reich was increasingly universalized in the 1970s, it became associated once more with Germany in the 1980s. The change was as sudden as it was unexpected. At the beginning of the new decade, few observers in Europe and North America were worried about the Federal Republic of Germany, which they viewed as a reliable member of the western alliance. This relaxed perspective changed quickly, however, with the collapse of the Berlin Wall in the fall of 1989. As was shown by Irish writer Conor Cruise O'Brien's lament in *The Times*, the demise of communism and the prospect of German reunification revived fears of a renewed Reich. These fears were particularly acute in the years immediately following the fusion of the Federal Republic with the German Democratic Republic in October of 1990. Thanks to the resurgence of neo-Nazi activity and Germany's growing influence in the European Union, concerns arose that the country was reverting to its old nationalistic habits. Journalistic essays, academic monographs, and popular works of literature, film, and television further stoked popular fears. Yet by the end of the decade these fears had ebbed; the ability of Helmut Kohl's government to weather the early challenges of reunification and the skill of his successors, SPD Chancellor Gerhard Schroeder (1998–2005) and CDU Chancellor Angela Merkel (2005–), in building upon it boosted popular confidence in the country's stability. The period of calm did not last, however. Following the financial crash of 2008, talk of a Fourth Reich returned. Europeans in different nations claimed that Germany was using the EU as a vehicle for continental hegemony.

These claims were motivated by a mixture of genuine conviction and cynical calculation. On the one hand, the fear that Germany was becoming a new Reich was grounded in real political trends. Following reunification, German right-wing extremists and neo-Nazis – including the Deutsches Kolleg, the NPD, and the Reich Citizens' Movement (*Reichsbürgerbewegung*) – increasingly sought to transform the Federal Republic into a Fourth Reich. Their activities lend credibility to the claims of concerned critics that Germany was moving dangerously to the right. At the same time, however, concerns about a renewed Reich were intentionally exaggerated for ulterior motives. Throughout Europe, politicians and journalists raised the prospect of a Fourth Reich to gain leverage over the Federal Republic in EU affairs and shift populist passions from internal to external targets. While some genuinely sought to make the new Reich a reality, others inflated its imminence for political purposes.

Before the Deluge: The Fourth Reich on the Road to Normality

In the decade prior to German unification, the idea of the Fourth Reich was well on its way to being normalized. The idea continued to be used as a universal signifier of authoritarian intolerance. In the United States, the prominent African-American politician Jesse Jackson often employed the term in his fight against South African Apartheid. When visiting Berlin to mark the fortieth anniversary of the end of World War II in 1985, Jackson told a crowd of 25,000 people that "the same ethical grounds ... that were used ... for rejecting the Third Reich in Germany must be employed to stop the Fourth Reich in South Africa."[2] Jackson invoked the concept repeatedly in the years that followed, as did leading African-American newspapers, which employed it to condemn present-day American racism.[3] President Ronald Reagan's administration was not attacked as a "Fourth Reich" nearly as often as Richard Nixon's had been, but it was not immune. While Reagan was condemned by the left for supporting the Botha regime – on occasion, by Jackson himself – he was also attacked by the far right, for example, by Republican Congressional Candidate Gary Arnold, who in 1982 alleged that the president was cooperating with banker David Rockefeller on economic policies meant to establish a "Fourth Reich" in the US.[4] Outside of the United States, the Fourth Reich was employed by groups eager to raise awareness about other political issues. In 1988, Panamanian newspapers utilized the idea to condemn strongman Manuel Noriega's curtailing of press freedoms.[5] That same year, French-speaking citizens of Quebec employed it to slam Premier Robert Bourassa's proposal for French-only signs outside commercial establishments.[6]

The Fourth Reich also assumed an increasingly normalized presence in western culture. During the 1970s and 1980s, punk rock groups embraced the idea for its edgy connotations, thereby aestheticizing it. In 1979, a Southern California band named itself "The Fourth Reich," while reassuring critics that it did so only for "shock value."[7] Meanwhile, other bands, such as the Dead Kennedys, D.I., and the Lookouts, invoked the concept in song lyrics in order to critique contemporary American life. The Lookouts' 1987 song "Fourth Reich (Nazi Amerika)," for example, echoed left-wing slogans from the 1970s in the following lyrics:

> And now swastikas come in red white and blue
> Fourth Reich Nazi Amerika
> Fascism comes to the USA
> Fourth Reich the night's getting darker
> Too bad a great country had to end this way.[8]

Beyond the realm of music, universalizing tendencies shaped the use of the Fourth Reich in popular art. American cartoonist Garry Trudeau used his comic strip, *Doonesbury*, in 1987 to attack conservative Arizona governor Evan Mecham (who had controversially cancelled Martin Luther King Day as a state holiday in 1986) by portraying the governor appointing an official who was "active in Fourth Reich politics" to state office.[9] In Mexico, meanwhile, the Chilean-born artist Jose Palomo's cartoon strip, *El Cuarto Reich*, criticized the corruption of Latin American governments through a series of characters living under an unnamed dictatorship.[10]

The Fourth Reich also found a place in American sports culture. In 1979, television announcer Beano Cook lightheartedly alluded to the right-wing leanings of NFL football coaches by observing that "if the NFL folded ... all 28 coaches would go to Argentina, find Hitler, and start a Fourth Reich."[11] In 1985, Indianapolis Colt football coach Frank Kush was sarcastically given the "Fourth Reich Award" for expressing his admiration for how Hitler "managed people."[12] That same year, a professional soccer player for the San Diego Sockers described a rival team, the Chicago Sting, "as the Fourth Reich."[13] These examples were scattered. But as with the embrace of the Fourth Reich by motorcycle gangs in the 1970s, the use of the term in American sports reflected its transformation into a generic signifier of toughness.

The process of normalization was best illustrated by the benign application of the term to the Federal Republic of Germany. While the idea of a revived German Reich had been surrounded by an aura of menace during the first three decades of the postwar period, it became less fearsome in the 1980s. This shift was made clear by the publication of American journalist Edwin Hartrich's book, *The Fourth and Richest Reich* (1980).[14] The book's thesis was simple: thanks to the Federal Republic's postwar economic accomplishments, Hartrich noted, "eco-politics has succeeded in achieving for the Germans what geo-politics failed to accomplish in ... Hitler's Dritte Reich."[15] German exports had achieved "unlimited Lebensraum in which to expand" on a far more lasting basis than what "Hitler's millions of soldiers [sought] in their unsuccessful military conquests in Europe, Russia, and Africa." Significantly, many American reviewers endorsed Hartrich's thesis, arguing that the US – then mired in economic recession – could learn a lot from Germany's postwar economic miracle. As David Schoenbrun wrote in *The New York Times,* Hartrich's account should be required reading for Americans who were "watching with dismay our own declining fortunes," since it provided important lessons about "how to regain our position as the economic superpower of the world."[16] The implicit message was clear: no longer was the Fourth Reich a fearsome concept to be avoided. In its latest incarnation – as the prosperous, democratic Federal Republic – it was an admirable model to emulate.

For the remainder of the decade, the idea of the Fourth Reich was rarely applied to West Germany. Compared to the early postwar period, western fears of neo-Nazism remained low in the 1980s. An important reason for this was the rise to power of Helmut Kohl's conservative CDU in 1982. After more than a decade of SPD rule, during which western observers nervously watched West Germany pursue a more independent foreign policy towards the communist east, Kohl's government reaffirmed its commitment to the western alliance. The early 1980s were a period of growing cold war tensions with the Soviet Union, and Kohl's willingness to accept President Ronald Reagan's request to station Pershing II missiles on German soil in 1983 – despite considerable domestic opposition – reassured western observers about Germany's pro-western allegiances. At the same time, Kohl's larger effort to create a new form of national identity by bringing German history out from under the shadow of the Nazi period helped blunt the appeal of the German far right, which remained dormant for most of the decade. The last major party to flirt with success, the NPD, remained stagnant, dropping from 4.3 percent of the vote in 1969 to 0.2 percent of the vote in 1980.[17] New parties, meanwhile, such as Gerhard Frey's Deutsche Volksunion (DVU), which was founded in 1987 on a nationalistic and anti-immigrant platform, and Franz Schönhuber's Republicans (*Republikaner*), which was established in 1983, remained under the 5 percent hurdle in regional elections in the years 1987–90.[18] To be sure, among left-liberals, Kohl's conservative nationalism raised suspicions. But while German leftists – and Soviet government officials – occasionally criticized Kohl by invoking the specter of a "Fourth Reich," the use of the slogan was relatively rare.[19]

German Reunification and Renewed Fears of the Reich: 1989–90

By the turn of the decade, however, the idea of the Fourth Reich suddenly returned to prominence. The revolutionary overthrow of the communist order in Eastern Europe in the years 1989–90 signaled the demise of the East German state and heralded the prospect of German reunification. These dramatic events brought about a major shift in the discursive use of the Fourth Reich by linking the signifier once again to its traditional referent, Germany. Across the western world, critics responded to the possibility of German unity by warning that it might presage the arrival of a new Reich. In so doing, they sparked a fierce debate between those who feared a unified Germany and those who did not. The debate erupted around the time the Berlin Wall was breached in November of 1989 and raged for the better part of a year until the country's eventual unification on October 3, 1990. In this initial period, politicians, journalists, and scholars vigorously debated whether a Fourth Reich would resemble the Third by behaving like an aggressive, Nazi-like state.

The Critics

The first fears were expressed in Great Britain. On October 31, 1989, Conor Cruise O'Brien published a controversial essay in *The Times* of London entitled "Beware, the Reich Is Reviving." Convinced that the Soviet Union's weakness made German reunification only a matter of time, O'Brien declared that "we are on the road to the Fourth Reich" and predicted that German nationalists would begin "cleansing the image of the Third Reich" by pursuing "the rehabilitation of National Socialism ... and Adolf Hitler." Before long, O'Brien feared, "nationalist intellectuals" would describe "the Holocaust ... [as a] courageous ... act," "break ... off relations with Israel," and erect "a statue of Hitler in every German town." His conclusion was as bleak as it was stark: "the Fourth Reich, if it comes, will ... resemble its predecessor."[20] O'Brien's claims predictably attracted immediate attention and initially received considerable support.[21] Articles in the *Daily Express*, the *Guardian*, and other papers echoed the fear that unification would produce a new Reich.[22]

Similar fears were expressed in other countries. In France, a strong majority of French citizens (around 75 percent) feared that German unification would bring about "the revival of some form of Nazism."[23] French government ministers made similar predictions.[24] Yet, in France – as in Britain – many people soberly viewed German unity as inevitable. As the editor of *Politique Etrangère* (*Foreign Affairs*), Dominique Moïsi, wrote in *The New York Times*, "the attempt to preserve a condemned status quo against the potential danger of a 'fourth reich' can only become a self-fulfilling prophecy."[25] Similar fears were articulated in Sweden, Denmark, Italy, and Poland.[26] They were also visible in Israel, where major newspapers declared that a "Fourth Reich in the heart of Europe" would stoke German irredentism and keep many people from "sleeping soundly."[27]

Left-wing critics in West and East Germany made similar comments. In a prominent *Spiegel* essay published in December of 1989, the West German leader of the SPD, Oskar Lafontaine, cautioned against "thoughtless slogans involving reunification" by noting that "the specter of a strong Fourth German Reich horrifies our western neighbors no less than our eastern ones."[28] In East Germany, meanwhile, the official state press furiously reprinted foreign concerns about German unification and published statements by East German political leaders warning about the demise of an independent East Germany. In February 1990, the SED's new successor party, the Party of Democratic Socialism (PDS), opposed the absorption of East Germany into the Federal Republic, declaring "we want neither a Fourth Reich nor a greater Federal Republic."[29] Mass demonstrations that same month in East Berlin linked the threat of a new Reich to the upsurge of "brown violence and fascist ideology."[30] Similar protests lasted into the early fall and were repeated in West German cities, such as Frankfurt, with thousands of demonstrators protesting the looming "Fourth Reich."[31] The most extreme reaction occurred in the summer of 1990, when the Red Army Faction (RAF) terrorist group posted a letter to international news agencies declaring "war on the Fourth Reich."[32]

The most passionate critique in Germany appeared with the German-based Spanish writer Heleno Saña's book *Das vierte Reich: Deutschlands später Sieg (The Fourth Reich: Germany's Late Victory)*.[33] Published in 1990 before the official reunification of the country on October 3, the book anxiously described unification as the first step towards establishing a new Reich. Like O'Brien, Saña feared that the Germans were about to repeat previous mistakes from their history. Calling the "Fourth Reich" a "magic formula" that expressed the German people's "yearning for a new imperialistic era," Saña argued that the dream of a Reich was rooted in "dark passions" that lay "in the depths of [the Germans'] . . . souls."[34] Saña reassured his readers that "the Fourth Reich will not be a crude copy of . . . the Third," insisting that it would eschew "violence and terror."[35] Nevertheless, the new Reich would be driven by the belief that "the Germans have a special destiny to fulfill." As Saña put it:

the Fourth Reich will represent an attempt to expunge the previous failed Reichs from memory and adorn German history with new brilliance ... It will be a Reich dedicated to Germanic hegemony in Europe ... The Fourth Reich will ruthlessly fight anything that blocks its objectives, if need be through ... repression. The expansionistic course of the coming Reich will be ... a repetition of a long-performed ... German tragedy.[36]

The underlying reason for this bleak prediction was the German people's "penchant for excessiveness (*Maßlosigkeit*)."[37] Due to this character flaw, Saña argued, "a unified Germany will not be satisfied to remain a nation state" and would eventually seek a more expansive Reich.[38] Germany's tragic past heralded a bleak future. Because "none of the previous German Reichs ended well," he concluded, "the Fourth Reich has little chance ... of a happy ending, since that which is excessive and irrational must inevitably collapse."[39]

The Defenders

Most Germans, however, rejected any connection between reunification and a Fourth Reich. The West German press widely attacked O'Brien's *Times* editorial in the fall of 1989, none more vehemently than the conservative *FAZ*, which dismissed it as a "hysterical ... prognosis."[40] The paper went so far as to speculate that such "insane views" represented "Anglo-Saxon racism directed against Germans."[41] More moderate German critics published rebuttals in the British press – for example, the editor of *Die Zeit*, Theo Sommer, who wrote in the *Observer* that "what Germans are after is a far cry from [a] 'Fourth Reich.'"[42] Other German journalists, however, realized that foreign concerns could not be ignored. Responding to fears in France, the *FAZ* tried to defuse the aura of menace that surrounded the idea of the Reich, arguing that it "had no fixed historical meaning and was a verbal sheath into which one would pour any kind of content." At the same time, the paper admitted that the idea of the Reich "expressed antipathies" that were "deeply anchored in the consciousness of the French elite."[43] Reviews of Saña's book made a similar point, arguing that the fears expressed in the volume could not be simply dismissed as "unwarranted" attempts to "malign Germany."[44]

Before long, German politicians realized the need to reassure western countries that there were no plans to replace Germany's republic with a Reich. On December 21, 1989, Chancellor Helmut Kohl flatly told foreign journalists in Dresden that "there will be no Fourth Reich. We are not revanchists."[45] In February of 1990, he adopted a less patient tone when he angrily declared that "whoever speaks of a Fourth Reich ... consciously wants to defame the Germans."[46] Nevertheless, on March 7, 1990, Kohl calmly affirmed that a "reunified Germany will be a part of a peaceful Europe."[47] Around the same time, other prominent politicians, such as ex-Chancellor Willy Brandt, proclaimed to the world that "there will be no Fourth Reich."[48] By the summer, Kohl's reassurances to Poland about respecting the inviolability of the country's borders – later confirmed in the treaty signed with Prime Minister Tadeusz Mazowiecki on November 8, 1990 – provided further reassurances. Partly thanks to these official statements, many media observers were placated. Josef Joffe, for instance, felt emboldened to give "one and a half cheers" for unification, writing that "by no stretch of the imagination is the [soon to be unified] Federal Republic ... a precursor of the Fourth Reich." The Federal Republic, he insisted, was a place where "prosperity" reigned, "democracy flourished," and "neo-Nazis [were] on the verge of extinction." Simply put, the country was "part of the Western mainstream."[49]

Many western observers accepted this upbeat verdict as well. This was particularly true of Americans. Although certain journalists were skeptical, diplomats and academics were relatively sanguine about the Federal Republic's future.[50] In a *Spiegel* interview, Deputy Secretary of State Lawrence Eagleburger replied to the question whether "Americans shared the fear of a Fourth Reich" by saying that the United States was "the country where worries about a reunified Germany are the least acute."[51] Historian Gordon Craig agreed, explaining that Americans had few anxieties about a "Fourth Reich," because, unlike the British and French, they "swiftly forgot and forgave" the Germans after 1945.[52] Journalists also made this point. William Tuohy wrote that the "grim specter" of a Fourth Reich was rooted in "outdated stereotypes."[53] Walter Russell Mead agreed, noting that while "the Fourth Reich will be open for business" in a unified Germany, there was little danger of it becoming an extremist state because "fascism is dead."[54] Similar statements were also heard in Britain. In December of 1989, J. P. Stern confidently declared that

O'Brien's anxious vision of a Fourth Reich was destined to remain a "chimera" for the "conceivable future."[55] Lord Weidenfeld wrote that "those who still have a nightmarish vision of a Fourth Reich" should "banish their fears and put their trust in the enduring continuity of the moral standards . . . of Adenauer . . . and in the younger generation of Germans."[56] Finally, a distinguished panel of academic experts convened by Prime Minister Margaret Thatcher in March of 1990 – including Norman Stone, Hugh Trevor-Roper, and Fritz Stern – told the British leader that there were no serious threats to be expected from a unified Germany and "no danger of a Fourth Reich."[57]

The Nazis Return: The Right Revives the Reich

Yet, while the peaceful conclusion of German reunification in October of 1990 seemed to dispel critics' fears of a Fourth Reich, subsequent events revived them. In the first years following reunification, Germany experienced an upsurge of neo-Nazi violence. Unforeseen economic and social problems were responsible. The difficulty of integrating the East German and West German economies led to factory closures and job losses in the east, while it led to higher taxes and inflation in the west. As social disaffection spread throughout the country, growing numbers of Germans embraced right-wing political ideas and lashed out at scapegoats, mostly foreign immigrants and asylum seekers. In 1992, the right-wing *Republikaner*, DVU, and NPD saw modest electoral success, each receiving more than 5 percent of the vote in regional elections.[58] More ominously, neo-Nazi groups and skinhead gangs grew in number. In the years 1991–94, neo-Nazis launched violent attacks against foreign guest workers and asylum seekers in towns such as Hoyersweda, Rostock, Mölln, and Solingen, killing 23 people and injuring dozens more. Right-wing groups also launched antisemitic attacks against Jewish cemeteries and houses of worship.[59]

In the western media, the rise of neo-Nazi violence reanimated fears that a Fourth Reich might once again be a threat in Germany. Following the Rostock attacks in 1992, *The New York Times* described neo-Nazis as pursuing a racially pure "Fourth Reich devoid of Jews, foreigners, and capitalists."[60] That same year, a neo-Nazi attack against the Sachsenhausen concentration camp museum near Berlin led to the eruption of anti-Nazi demonstrations in Frankfurt, Düsseldorf, and

Berlin, with protesters carrying signs reading "No Fourth Reich."[61] One month later, German President Richard von Weizsäcker told 350,000 demonstrators at an anti-Nazi rally in Berlin that it was crucial to defend democracy against neo-Nazis who regard reunification as a "signal for a 'Fourth Reich.'"[62] Demands by ethnic German nationalists in Poland for the return of former German lands were described as being part of the "larger goal of a Fourth Reich."[63] Reports on German women's interest in neo-Nazism prompted articles about "Knitting for the Fourth Reich."[64] Still other articles raised fears that "fascism [was] ... becoming fashionable again."[65]

This press coverage was alarmist, but it was not entirely baseless, as growing numbers of right-wing activists had, in fact, become newly committed to creating a Fourth Reich. Signs of this growing engagement began already in the 1970s and 1980s, when scattered neo-Nazi figures wielded the concept to inspire their followers to explore radical new methods – from mass demonstrations to terrorist attacks – for overthrowing the West German state. This action-oriented policy eventually ended in failure. But a more moderate movement, led by a second group of activists associated with Germany's "New Right," proved more promising. Influenced by the "conservative revolutionaries" of the Weimar era, this movement sought to modernize and lend new intellectual sophistication to right-wing ideas in the effort to make them hegemonic within German society.[66] The leaders of the New Right failed to achieve their goal. But in striving to attain it, they brought the concept of the Fourth Reich to a wider audience.

The Rabble-Rousers: Manfred Roeder and Michael Kühnen

One of the main figures to renew German interest in the Fourth Reich was the right-wing extremist, Manfred Roeder (Figure 6.1). Born in 1929, he was a member of the Hitler Youth generation and had his political worldview profoundly shaped by his experiences in the Nazi school system and the Wehrmacht. After the end of World War II, Roeder maintained his right-wing convictions and refused to make his peace with West German democracy. Although he worked for a time as a lawyer, he became politically radicalized during the late 1960s and transformed into an opponent of what he described as the countercultural era's "moral and cultural decline." Before long, Roeder gravitated to right-wing circles and became active in the burgeoning

Figure 6.1 In the 1970s, Manfred Roeder was one of the first leaders of the German New Right to call for the revival of the German Reich. He popularized the idea that the Federal Republic was illegitimate because the Reich never disappeared in 1945. After turning to terrorism in the 1980s, Roeder later gravitated to the NPD (Source: Getty Images).

Holocaust denial movement. As a result of this activity, he was eventually disbarred and responded by moving further to the right.[67]

During the 1970s, Roeder devoted himself to reviving the German Reich by developing a plan rooted in clear political principles. As he made clear in his self-published underground 1979 manifesto, *Ein Kampf um's Reich* (*Struggle for the Reich*), the first principle was that "the German Reich never disappeared" in 1945, because "the Reich government never resigned."[68] In making this claim, Roeder revived an idea championed by the SRP in the early 1950s. But, in a new move, he justified the idea by citing the West German Federal Supreme Court's 1973 declaration that, according to the *Grundgesetz*, "the German Reich survived the collapse of 1945 and did not disappear as a result of ... Allied occupation."[69] This decision, which sought to clarify the Reich's status in the wake of West Germany's signing of the Basic Treaty (*Grundlagenvertrag*) with East Germany in 1972, clearly described the Federal Republic as the legal successor of the Reich. Roeder rejected this view, however, and advanced a second principle – namely, that the

Republic was illegitimate, a mere "provisional administrative entity of the Allies."[70] These two principles, finally, led Roeder to a third: the need to revive the German Reich.[71] Convinced that the "Reich is unbroken and therefore it will one day reappear in new glory," Roeder quoted the Nazi diaspora leader, Johann von Leers's declaration from the 1950s that "as soon as the Reich returns ... every honorable German will join up with it."[72]

Starting in the mid 1970s, Roeder sought to realize his agenda through a variety of quixotic tactics. In 1975, he contacted and tried to convince Karl Doenitz – the last legal ruler of Nazi Germany in May of 1945 – to publicly affirm that the Reich continued to exist in a legal sense and that he remained its rightful leader. When a bemused Doenitz declined to be recognized as the enduring "President of the German Reich," Roeder tried to revive the Reich himself.[73] In 1975, he formed the Freedom Movement of the German Reich (*Freiheitsbewegung Deutsches Reich*) and theatrically convened a mass demonstration – a "Day of the Immortal Reich" (*"Tag des unvergänglichen Reiches"*) – on May 23 of that year in Flensburg, where the Doenitz government had been disbanded at the end of the war thirty years earlier. This event, which called for "the reestablishment of a free and unoccupied Reich," attracted several hundred adherents and suggested a burgeoning movement.[74] The movement's momentum appeared to increase two years later in 1977, when Roeder convened a second Reichstag in Regensburg, and then again, in 1978, when he dramatically declared himself to be the "Reich Regent" (*Reichsverweser*) and the "spokesman for all Reich-minded citizens." On May 23, he published a new "Appeal" (*Aufruf*) in which he demanded "a reunified, neutral German Reich," free of Allied occupiers, "artificial borders," and "neo-colonial" foreign alliances. Demanding "freedom for all the oppressed peoples of the world," Roeder declared that Germany should be "for the Germans alone."[75]

Despite this increasing activity, however, Roeder's movement failed to catch fire, and by the turn of the decade he abandoned peaceful agitation in favor of violent terrorism. In 1980, he founded the German Action Groups (*Deutsche Aktionsgruppen*), which launched a series of bombings against various targets, including a Jewish school in Hamburg and several shelters for foreign asylum seekers, one of which killed two Vietnamese refugees.[76] As a result of this activity, Roeder was put on trial for terrorist incitement, found guilty, and sent to prison from 1982

Figure 6.2 The neo-Nazi leader Michael Kühnen (middle) formed a variety of right-wing organizations in the 1980s and explicitly called for a Fourth Reich in his 1982 manifesto, *Die zweite Revolution* (*The Second Revolution*) (Source: Getty Images).

to 1990. With this setback, his personal contribution to reviving the Reich was brought to a halt. Although he made his voice heard occasionally in the 1990s, he became overshadowed by a more radical generation of neo-Nazi agitators.[77]

Among them, the most influential was Michael Kühnen (Figure 6.2). Born in 1955, he was much younger than Roeder and quickly became the charismatic new face of the growing West German neo-Nazi movement in the 1980s. After a brief spell associating with the NPD, Kühnen founded a variety of organizations in the late 1970s, the most notable of which was the Action Front of National Socialists (*Aktionsfront Nationaler Sozialisten*, or ANS). Kühnen's group explicitly sought to revive the legacy of the NSDAP and worked with like-minded organizations, such as the American-based NSDAP/AO, which supplied the ANS with propaganda materials. Unlike the NPD and other right-wing parties, Kühnen did not shy away from evoking the NSDAP's propaganda tactics. Influenced by the Hitler wave's fascination with Nazi imagery, Kühnen earned media attention by organizing provocative public appearances, featuring black-clad storm troopers, Nazi-esque flags, and speeches of fidelity to Hitler. More ominously, Kühnen joined with other Nazi groups to pursue small-scale terrorist activity, launching a series of bank robberies and attacks on military bases, which led to his arrest and imprisonment during the years 1979–82.[78]

While in prison, Kühnen mimicked Hitler's example by writing a two-volume political manifesto, entitled *Die Zweite Revolution* (1982).[79] Inspired by the goals of the SA leader, Ernst Röhm (who had strived for a "second revolution" in the years 1933–34), the manifesto presented, among many other things, Kühnen's vision of a future Fourth Reich. Like Roeder, with whom he had interacted in the 1970s, Kühnen believed that Germany's military defeat in the Second World War had "done nothing to alter the legal status" of the German Reich, which he insisted survived after 1945. Because the ensuing Allied occupation was "contrary to international law," there was no escaping the conclusion that "all German postwar governments in the Federal Republic of Germany, the German Democratic Republic, and Austria were and are illegal."[80] Kühnen thus urged "an end to the postwar period" by demanding the "lifting of the ban on the NSDAP," which he wanted to revive as a "freedom movement" devoted to "reestablishing the Reich of the Germans."[81] As he put it:

> We view the Great German Reich as the fulfillment of the German people's centuries-long yearning and know that only a Fourth Reich – the National Socialist people's state (*Volksstaat*) of the future – can guarantee the survival of our people into the next millennium.[82]

While this vision resembled Roeder's, it was more radical in scope. Kühnen argued that the future Reich's goal was to become a world power independent of the US and USSR; in order to achieve it, Germany had to regain its territorial boundaries of September 1, 1939. But to fulfill its great mission of "saving the white race," Germany had to pursue a larger occidental "Reich idea" – embodied in the ancient Roman Empire, the medieval Holy Roman Empire, and the "Third Rome" of the Russian Tsars – by uniting the nations of Western and Eastern Europe together with those of the Islamic world in a grand alliance against "Zionism, capitalism, and communism." The Fourth

Reich was not merely a future German polity, but an inspirational "battle cry" for a German-led coalition committed to asserting the hegemonic power of the white race.[83]

Kühnen had difficulty realizing his political vision. After being released from prison in 1982, he revived the ANS, but, following its ban by the Federal authorities, instructed his followers to infiltrate the neo-Nazi Free German Workers' Party (*Freiheitliche Deutsche Arbeiter Partei*, FAP); two years later, he founded the Community of Like-Minded People of the New Front (*Gesinnungsgemeinschaft der Neuen Front*, or GdNF).[84] This new organization amplified the need for a Fourth Reich, referring to it nearly three dozen times in Kühnen's manifesto, *Lexikon der Neuen Front* (1987).[85] Kühnen's re-arrest and imprisonment from 1984 to 1988 for distributing neo-Nazi propaganda, however, limited his ability to pursue his goals, as did worsening factional infighting with other Nazi groups. Kühnen lost favor after coming out as gay, a revelation that caused a split over the issue of homosexuality within the FAP. In 1989, he reasserted himself and formed another new organization, the German Alternative (*Deutsche Alternative*, or DA), which embraced the slogan "The Fourth Reich is coming."[86] With reunification, Kühnen saw an opportunity to take the DA's neo-Nazi message to the five new states of eastern Germany. But before he could realize its potential, he died of an AIDS-related illness in 1991. The DA was subsequently banned.[87]

The Intellectuals: The *Staatsbriefe* and Deutsches Kolleg

While violent neo-Nazis failed to make progress towards establishing a Fourth Reich, more intellectually minded right-wingers continued to work on its behalf. One of the most active after 1990 was the right-wing academic, and editor of the influential journal *Staatsbriefe*, Hans-Dietrich Sander (Figure 6.3). Born in 1928, Sander oscillated politically in his early life, serving in the Hitler Youth as an adolescent, turning to communism in the 1950s, and then returning to the right in the 1960s. After receiving his Ph.D. in history and becoming a journalist and adjunct university instructor, he gravitated to conservative revolutionary ideas. Around the turn of the decade, he became intrigued with the notion of reviving the Reich, a position he advanced in his book *Der nationale Imperativ: Ideengänge und Werkstücke zur Wiederherstellung Deutschlands*

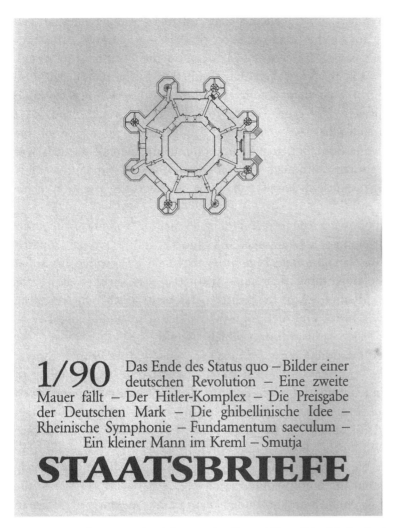

Figure 6.3 In the 1990s, the right-wing intellectual Hans-Dietrich Sander began publication of his influential journal, *Staatsbriefe*, which frequently called for a Fourth Reich. On the cover of the debut issue can be seen a plan of the thirteenth-century Castel del Monte, built by the Hohenstaufen Emperor Frederick II, whom Sander praised in his essay, "The Ghibelline Idea."

(*The National Imperative: Ideas and Components for the Restoration of Germany*).[88] Originally published in 1980, the book argued that the time had finally come for Germans to pursue the "national imperative" of destroying the US–Soviet world order and re-founding their country on a strong nationalistic basis.[89] At this point in time, Sander believed that America's waning international influence under the administration of President Jimmy Carter provided an opening for a renewed focus on the "German question." The key was to "reawaken the slumbering Furor teutonicus" and "restore to the Germans the fighting spirit ... they will need to build a new Reich."[90] Sander hoped that his book would prod West German elites to revive the long "suppressed" discussion of the national question. But, to his disappointment, his call to arms was largely ignored. Although it found a considerable (and predictably negative) response in East Germany, it received little attention in the West.[91]

Following the revolutionary events of 1989–90, however, Sander rebooted his message. In 1990, he published an updated edition of *Der nationale Imperativ*, in which he restated his belief that "the only thing that can satisfy the reawakening desire for German identity" was to create a "Fourth Reich" by restoring Germany's historic borders of 1937.[92] Doing so would give rise to a new Reich constitution, which would inevitably reflect the Germans' "national spirit" (*Volksgeist*) and find its proper "power structure" (*Machtform*); most of all, it would foster a "policy of preserving German interests alone."[93] In the long run, Sander hoped that "the formation of a Fourth Reich" would "mark the death of a United Europe."[94] In the short term, however, he remained cautious. While the book's new preface affirmed that unification between West and East Germany was inevitable, it simultaneously warned that the union would merely create "a larger version of the Federal Republic" and exclude Austria and the historic German lands of the east.[95] Eventually, however, Sander believed that everything would work out: the shortcomings of this liberal form of unification "would become sharpened to such an extent that it would inevitably force the reestablishment of the German Reich."[96]

Around the same time, Sander sought to accelerate this process by establishing a new journal called *Staatsbriefe*. Named after the well-known "letters of state" produced by the medieval Hohenstaufen emperor, Friedrich II, the journal sought to promote a "renaissance of national thinking" and theorize the form of the future German Reich.[97] In the dozen years of the journal's existence (1990–2001), Sander published essays by many right-wing figures – ranging from Michael Kühnen to Léon Degrelle – and addressed a wide range of topics, spanning the history of the Second World War to Holocaust denial.[98] Sander, however, reserved considerable space for himself to revive the neglected "idea of the Reich."

This was the goal of two early articles that he published in 1990–91: "The Ghibelline Idea" and "The Reich as German Political Unity."[99] Drawing on the nineteenth-century German historian Gustav Droysen's identification of the Reich with the agenda of the medieval Ghibelline political faction within the Holy Roman Empire, Sander explained that the "Ghibelline idea" was a form of "authority" (*Oberhoheit*) that "strong peoples" employed to rule over peoples "who fail at self-determination."[100] It was used especially effectively by the Hohenstaufen dynasty to bring the first German Reich to the height of its power in the Middle Ages. Over time, however, the idea of the Reich became corrupted, first by the Hohenzollerns and subsequently the Nazis. Both replaced the idea's universal, metaphysical mission – that of being a "ruling authority" (*Ordnungsmacht*) holding the Antichrist at bay – with a more "territorialist" (*guelfisch*) vision that backfired by forcibly Germanizing the non-German peoples of the east.[101] The result of this corruption, Sander explained, was that "the Reich idea disappeared after 1945."[102] Due to the Allies' "reeducation" program, the German people fell victim to a "mass psychosis" and "denied the Reich's history for the first time in a millennium." The result was the "forgetting," "fear," and "prohibition" of the Reich.[103] The year 1989, however, opened up new possibilities for reclaiming the Reich's original universalistic vision. The collapse of Soviet power raised the tantalizing possibility of "reclaiming" and "recolonizing" the "German East." Sander was convinced that Eastern European Slavs regretted the expulsion of the Germans in 1945 and believed "it would be better if they came back." So long as this sentiment continued to grow, he believed, the "objective conditions for the new creation of the German Reich" would improve.[104] The first challenge was to "recolonize the German west" by reacquainting West Germans with the Reich idea's virtues. Sander was optimistic this was possible. As he buoyantly observed, "The word Reich is being widely discussed … and is once more a topic of fascination." "The Germans need the Reich. Europe needs the Reich. The world needs the Reich." "As Germans, we first must simply want the Reich."[105]

Sander's *Staatsbriefe* influenced other right-wing intellectuals and facilitated the creation of the era's most important organization dedicated to establishing a Fourth Reich, the Deutsches Kolleg (DK).[106] Founded in Berlin in 1994 and led by a group of right-wing activists, including Reinhold Oberlercher, Horst Mahler, and Uwe Meenen, the DK was a "think tank" (*Denkorgan*) and educational institute that sought to "restore the full agency of the ... German Reich" through "theoretical, pedagogical, and programmatic activity."[107] Throughout the decade, the group generated a steady stream of essays, manifestos, and curricular materials, all of which were made available on the group's website in order to inspire the emergence of a new, right-wing "national intelligentsia."[108]

The DK's leaders were mostly former leftists who, like Sander, had moved to the political right. Oberlercher began his career in the late 1960s as a leader of the Socialist German Student Union (SDS) in Hamburg fighting for worker revolution, and received a Ph.D. for a dissertation on pedagogy and philosophy in 1975.[109] By the late 1970s, however, his opposition to West Germany's liberal immigration policies and his resentment of the Soviet Union's opposition to German reunification led him to shift to the right.[110] In the 1980s, he joined a series of extremist organizations and later published articles in New Right journals, such as Armin Mohler's *Criticon* and Sander's *Staatsbriefe*.[111] Horst Mahler was also a former leftist, a trained lawyer who belonged to the SDS, the Extra-Parliamentary Opposition (APO), and, most notoriously, the terrorist Red Army Faction (RAF). After being convicted for various terrorist activities and serving a long prison sentence from 1970 until 1980, he shifted to the right as well. His longstanding desire to redeem the German people's national honor from the shame of the Nazi regime's crimes led him, during the 1990s, to attack what he regarded as the many threats to the country's national identity, including American imperialism, global capitalism, foreign immigration, and the Jewish-led "Holocaust memory cult."[112] By the time he joined the DK later in the decade, he had also entered the orbit of the NPD. For his part, Uwe Meenen did not begin his political career on the left, but was a longtime right-wing nationalist who joined the NPD, rising to the position of district chairman (*Bezirksvorsitzende*) in Lower Franconia and later to the position of state chairman (*Landesvorsitzende*) in Berlin.

Of the three men, Oberlercher was the most active in shaping the DK's agenda (Figure 6.4). Throughout the 1990s, he led the effort to imagine the future Fourth Reich, publishing numerous articles in the

Figure 6.4 Between the 1990s and the turn of the millennium, the right-wing intellectual Reinhold Oberlercher used his think-tank, the Deutsches Kolleg (German College), to advocate for a Fourth Reich (Source: Christian Ditsch).

Staatsbriefe and the DK's website. Some of the articles were philosophical in orientation; others were more programmatic. All of them displayed a flair for the dramatic. Oberlercher histrionically published many documents for a future Reich, including drafts of constitutions, laws, and manifestos exhorting ordinary Germans to overthrow the Federal Republic.

He gave an early view of his agenda in the fall of 1992 in an essay entitled, "The Re-Creation of the German Reich" (*Die Neuschöpfung des deutschen Reiches*).[113] Deeply pessimistic about the early course of unification, he complained in the essay about the "deepening divisions between West and Middle Germany" and predicted that the country faced a bleak future unless radical action was taken. Oberlercher bemoaned the fate of unemployed Germans, whom he described as suffering from the "increasing presence of foreigners (*Verausländerung*) in the labor market"; he further condemned the plight of "poor renters" trapped in "metropolitan foreigner ghettos" and the looming "ethnocide" of the German people, who, having lost their "sovereign rights and currency" to Brussels, had become transformed into a "milkable minority in a continental population conglomerate." Rejecting these trends, Oberlercher called for the "disappearance of the BRD" via the revolt of a "majority of Germans." Such a revolt, he hoped, would lead to the "collapse of the

Europe idea" and its replacement by the "Reich idea." Citing the influence of Sander's *Staatsbriefe*, Oberlercher vowed to move forward by establishing the new Reich's "constitutional principles."

That same year, Oberlercher produced an ambitious "Draft Constitution" (*Reichsverfassungsentwurf*, or RVerfE) for the new Reich.[114] Published in the *Staatsbriefe*, the RVerfE was an aggressively right-wing document that embraced a nationalistic and imperialistic agenda. Article 2 in the section on "People" (*Volk*), for instance, declared that the German people acknowledged "the diversity of all peoples," but insisted on the right to assert their "heritage [and] ... race" and "discriminate against that which is foreign" (*das Fremde*). Article 3, meanwhile, asserted the German people's "right to its traditional Lebensraum in Europe and the integrity of its Vaterland." The RVerfE's overriding concern, however, was the Reich. Mentioned more than 200 times (either as an adjective or noun), the Reich provided the overarching structure for the future state. Oberlercher's constitution envisioned an expanded, *grossdeutsch* Germany, composed of the Federal Republic, Austria, and other Germanic territories, and divided up into dozens of duchies and districts (*Gaue*). It envisioned four main cities: Vienna (the Reich capital), Berlin (the main district, or *Hauptgau*), Zurich (home of the *Reichsbank*), and Rotterdam (home of the main Reich port). The Reich's political system was a non-democratic, neo-feudal arrangement run by elected "counts" and led by a "Supreme Reich leader" (*Reichsoberhaupt*) selected from the ranks of the aristocracy and army. These and many other features served a deeper metaphysical significance; as Oberlerchner concluded, "the ideology of the Reich is the German way of reconnecting man to the realm beyond space and time."[115]

Oberlercher followed up his Draft Constitution one year later with his "Hundred Day Program" (1993).[116] This document was composed of 100 agenda items that were to be implemented by the "national camp" after it "seized power" and declared an "emergency government." The program spanned a range of economic, political, and cultural policies, all of which echoed the agenda of the RVerfE. They included expelling unemployed foreigners, incarcerating homeless people and "asocials," waging war on drug dealers, curtailing press freedoms, and prohibiting pornography. Beyond these punitive policies, the program called for "positively revising Germany's historical image" in

Figure 6.5 The "Fourth Reich" flag, designed by the anti-Nazi German resistance figure Josef Wirmer in 1943–44, features a Nordic Cross together with the black, red, and yellow color scheme of Weimar Germany's flag. The right-wing activist Reinhold Oberlercher appropriated it to serve as the "resistance" flag of his future Fourth Reich and included it in the masthead of the German College (Deutsches Kolleg) website. (Source: Wikimedia Commons).

the international arena and making German "the world's leading cultural language" by "purifying" it of foreign influences. The program also demanded the "reestablishment of the German Reich."

Oberlercher's planning for the Reich extended to its visual symbols. Arguing that the "Fourth Reich requires symbols that are … unmistakably different from those of the previous three Reichs," Oberlercher announced the adoption of a new flag in the late 1990s, declaring that "the Reich flag bears a black cross embedded in gold against a red background."[117] The flag, he explained, dated back to a design from 1943–44 by the conservative anti-Nazi resistance fighter Josef Wirmer, and was the "only known draft for a flag of the Fourth Reich" (Figure 6.5). Even though Oberlercher believed that Wirmer had committed a crime by assisting the German resistance and "was rightly punished with the death penalty," it was acceptable to use his design, for "today, it is a matter of creating a German Reich without Hitler." Since the new flag abandoned the tri-color flag of the Federal Republic, which was rooted in the "French Counterrevolution … of 1789," it constituted a proper new symbol for honoring "the historic era of National Socialism and the heroic saving of the German Reich through the endurance of the German people."

Oberlercher sought to inspire his followers not merely with new symbols, but aggressive rhetoric. In a 1997 essay entitled "The Destruction of Democracy by the Persecution of Patriots" (*Die Zerstörung der Demokratie durch die Verfolgung der Patrioten*),

Oberlercher amplified his effort to establish a new Reich by undermining the legitimacy of the Federal Republic.[118] For too long, he argued, German officials – with Allied collusion – had forced "self-hatred" upon the German people and weakened their sense of patriotism. They had undermined German democracy and turned it into mere "political capitalism." Lacking a patriotic soul, the Federal Republic was spiritually dead. Oberlercher drew the obvious conclusion by echoing the ideas of Roeder, Kühnen, and Sander and asserting that

> the Federal Republic of Germany is the waking coma of the Third Reich. The most famous twelve years of German history are merely the era of the Third Reich's ability to act (*Handlungsfähigkeit*). The period thereafter is its coma, its inability to act .... The Federal Republic must go under so that the Third Reich can finally die and be constructively superseded by the Fourth Reich. Only then will the Reich of the Germans redeem the world and help it blossom.

Oberlercher remained vague about how to revive the Reich, but he hinted at the need for violence. Although he hoped that the German people would "be spared new bloodshed," he vowed to put "the main people responsible" for the "existence of partial states" (*Teilstaaten*) on trial for "high treason" and punish them with the "death penalty."

This strident turn in Oberlercher's thinking became even more radical after Horst Mahler joined the DK in 1998 (Figure 6.6). That year, Mahler convinced Oberlercher and another former leftist-turned-right-winger, Günter Maschke, to collaborate on a manifesto that was published in the *Staatsbriefe*, entitled "Canonical Declaration about the 1968 Movement" (*Kanonische Erklärung zur Bewegung von 1968*).[119] The document made national headlines by controversially reinterpreting the student movement as a "national revolutionary" effort jointly led by the New Right and New Left to bring about Germany's "self-liberation" from Sovietism, Americanism, and capitalism.[120] Mahler and Oberlercher built upon this declaration the following year, in November of 1999, when they published another essay, "Theses on the Reich Governorship" (*Thesen zur Reichsstatthalterschaft*), which repeated the claim that the Reich had survived the end of World War II and was destined to replace the Federal Republic after regaining its agency.[121] Then, in October of 2000, the DK adopted a more violently antisemitic platform, when Mahler,

Figure 6.6 Horst Mahler was the most radical right-wing advocate of a Fourth Reich after German unification, combining his demand for the overthrow of the German government with support for antisemitism and Holocaust denial (Source: Ingo Barth/Ullstein Bild via Getty Images).

Oberlercher, and Meenen published the manifesto "Calling on Those Who Are Decent to Rise up" (*Aufruf zum Aufstand der Anständigen*). This document brazenly called "Judaism a deadly danger for all peoples," described the "two-thousand-year history of the Occident [as] ... the battle against the corrosive (*zersetzenden*) Jewish spirit," and demanded "the banning of the Jewish communities in Germany."[122]

The DK also continued to push for the creation of a Reich. In June of 2002, the group published a "Petition to the German Princes" (*Petition an die deutschen Fürsten*) urging the leaders of twenty-two royal houses, from Anhalt to Württemberg, to "seize power" and "restore the German Reich with its monarchistic-aristocratic constitution."[123] The petition repeated the claim that the three "fragmented Reich regimes" (*Reichszerteilungsregime*) after 1945 – West Germany, East Germany, and Austria – were null and void, and declared that it was time for the German princes to transfer their "imperial authority" (*Reichsgewalt*) to the "German Volk" and convene a "Reich assembly" (*Reichsversammlung*). Led by a Reich Governor (*Reichsstatthalter*) from the Hohenzollern family, the assembly would employ all means – even martial law – to pursue the "revival of the German Reich as a strong centralized European power." In pursuing this goal, the "German Reich would bring an end to the horrible interregnum era and support the emergence of a lasting peaceful order in Central Europe."

Also in 2002, the DK published an extensive series of draft "laws" governing different aspects of life in the Reich. Focusing on nearly a dozen areas, including society, economics, culture, and art, the laws elaborated upon the draft constitution and featured official-sounding names and abbreviations – for instance, the Social Order Law (*Sozialordnungsgesetz*, or SozOG) and Labor Service Law (*Arbeitsdienstgesetz*, or WirtOG) – that mimicked existing Federal laws and lent the future Reich the veneer of authenticity. None of these outward trappings, however, could disguise the laws' right-wing thrust. Among other things, the laws prohibited Judaism (a "mono-theistic cult") and made "discrimination" official state policy, describing it as the "differentiation of good from evil, ugliness from beauty ... and the foreign and the indigenous."[124]

Despite this programmatic activity, the DK increasingly succumbed to factional infighting and began to stagnate after the turn of the millennium. The first sign of trouble came in 1999, when Sander broke with Oberlercher.[125] One year earlier, Sander had run afoul of the German authorities after publishing texts by the Holocaust denier Germar Rudolf, and was sentenced to eight months in jail for hate speech (*Volksverhetzung*).[126] Probably because of this brush with the law, Sander moved to disassociate himself from the DK's increasingly antisemitic turn following Mahler's arrival.[127] By this point, Sander had begun to have misgivings about the DK's "kabbalistic view of the Reich" and its "fetishization of the law and constitution."[128] The DK further fractured when Oberlercher split with Mahler. After 2000, Mahler's behavior became more extreme, as he aggressively embraced Holocaust denial, openly supported Al Qaeda's 9/11 attacks on the US, and defended the NPD from an attempted ban by the Federal authorities.[129] In 2004, Mahler's extremism brought difficulties to Oberlercher when the two men, together with Meenen, were tried for hate speech in conjunction with their 2000 manifesto, "A Call to Those Who Have Remained Decent." At the trial, Mahler repeated the DK's claims that the German Reich continued to exist and that the BRD lacked any legitimacy. But he mostly used the trial to spread his anti-semitic views to the courtroom audience (much of which was made up of neo-Nazis) and stylize himself into a martyr.[130] As this particular emphasis ran counter to Oberlercher's broader agenda, the two men eventually parted ways.[131] As a result, the DK lost much of its activist energy.

The Populists: The NPD and the Reich Citizens' Movement

Other right-wing groups, however, continued to pursue the goal of a Fourth Reich. One was the NPD. Since its swift rise to prominence in the late 1960s, the party had stagnated, being eclipsed by the DVU and Republicans. Following unification and especially after the turn of the millennium, however, the party gained new traction. After 1996, the NPD's new leader, Udo Voigt, sought to turn it into a more "action-oriented" party committed to winning "the battle of the street" by organizing large public demonstrations and gaining attention for its agenda.[132] In the process, the NPD explicitly embraced the Reich idea.[133] Starting in the late 1990s, the party identified Germany's "unification in a Reich" as its highest goal, declaring that the future state would have a strongly "centralized government" and pursue the larger needs of the "national people's community" (*Volksgemeinschaft*).[134] This turn towards the Reich may have reflected the NPD's growing connections with the DK – especially Meenen and Mahler.[135] The DK's influence may explain why Voigt subsequently echoed some of the group's key ideas: in 2004, for example, he called the Federal Republic an illegitimate "vassal state" with "no legitimate constitution" and said that the NPD sought to "dismantle the BRD" through "revolutionary action."[136] Whatever the origins of the party's turn to the Reich, the NPD's embrace of the concept did not hurt, and may have helped, its electoral fortunes; in the regional elections of 2004, the party received 9.2 percent of the vote in Saxony.[137] This success concerned many German journalists and led some to describe the party as pursuing "a Fourth Reich based on the model of the Third."[138]

Despite supporting the idea, however, the NPD failed to do much to bring it to reality. Factional strife was to blame. Two years after Mahler's departure from the party in 2003, several NPD Party leaders in Saxony resigned, citing their opposition to what they explicitly called Voigt's prioritization of a "Fourth Reich" over advocating for the needs of economically suffering Saxons.[139] Around the same time, the leaders of the Republicans cited the NPD's commitment to a new Reich as the reason they refused to work with the party.[140] In the ensuing national elections of 2005, the NPD received only 1.8 percent of the vote; two years later, the German media reported that the party's leaders were deemphasizing the concept of a future Reich in favor of a more anticapitalist message.[141] Subsequent financial difficulties caused further problems for the party, as did the ongoing efforts of the Federal authorities to ban it.[142]

Nevertheless, the dream of a Reich did not die, but found support in the new Reich Citizens' Movement (*Reichsbürgerbewegung*, or RBB). This grassroots movement dated back to the 1980s when a variety of small splinter groups, such as the "Commissar's Reich Government" (KRR), formed with the goal of reviving the Reich.[143] Little was heard from the movement during the 1990s, but after the turn of the millennium, it gained new momentum, thanks to the efforts of Horst Mahler. After leaving the DK and NPD, Mahler worked to spread the belief that the German Reich continued to exist.[144] In February of 2003, he formed the Circle of Reich Citizens (*Freundenkreis von Reichsbürgern*) in the Lower Saxon town of Verden and drafted a manifesto declaring that Holocaust denial would help spark an "uprising of the German people" and enable "the German Reich to arise again."[145] In 2006, Mahler continued to pursue this goal by creating the Folkish Reich Movement (*Völkische Reichsbewegung*) and publishing a programmatic text entitled "Honor, Truth, Homeland" (*Ehre Wahrheit Heimat*). In this document, which presented nearly three dozen pages' worth of draft laws and political principles, Mahler invoked the concept of the Reich more than eighty times and singled it out as the sole legal basis for the German state.[146] "It is the will of the German people," he wrote, "to be constituted through the Führer principle as a Volksstaat and reemerge as the German Reich."[147] Mahler added that the "revived German Reich" would collaborate with other "European powers" to protect "the white man's continent" against "attacks by alien forces" and serve as "the deterrent of evil." By "reanimating the German Reich and restoring its agency . . . freedom and peace would finally come to the Germans and all European peoples."[148]

The RBB comprised many groups besides Mahler's, but his efforts helped radicalize the movement. For years, the RBB was viewed by the Federal authorities as a group of eccentric, but harmless, cranks. After 2010, however, the movement gained increasing national attention when its adherents began to carry out acts of civil disobedience. Across Germany, self-proclaimed "Reich citizens" refused to pay fines for parking tickets, overdue taxes, and other infractions, claiming that the Federal Republic lacked the authority to enact or enforce laws. Citing longstanding right-wing claims, members of the RBB argued that the Reich had never surrendered in 1945, but had merely agreed to a cease-fire. The postwar Federal Republic was thus an artificial "corporation" (GmbH) created by the Allies in order to administer German territory. A unified Germany was equally illegal.[149] Believing that the Reich survived in a dormant condition within the Federal Republic, the RBB sought to make the state once more "capable of action" (*handlungsfähig*) by claiming the authority to act on its behalf. The movement's members declared that they would obey all ensuing decrees from the state as expressions of the legitimate Reich government. To lend reality to this fantasy, the RBB began to sell phony "Reich" documents, such as personal identification cards, driver's licenses, and vehicle registration stickers; they also levied judicial judgments from the "Reich" Judiciary and carried out "arrests" via self-created police forces (*Deutsche Polizeihilfswerk*, DPHW).[150] They even perpetrated acts of violence against state officials. In 2016, in four specialized operations, state police officers were shot in Bavaria (one was killed) while conducting a raid on the home of a RBB activist. Ever since, the Federal authorities have viewed the RBB as a right-wing terrorist threat.[151] If it is true that the movement boasts some 12,000 members, the RBB represents a notable number compared with the size of previous neo-Nazi groups.[152]

Today, the fate of the Reich idea in Germany remains hazy. On the one hand, many of its most important leaders have been neutralized. Kühnen's death in 1991 and the subsequent deaths of Roeder (2014) and Sander (2017) removed some of the Reich's main supporters from the German political scene. Mahler was sentenced to ten years in prison in 2009 and currently remains incarcerated.[153] NPD leaders Voigt and Meenen were found guilty of hate speech in 2012, and their party remains vulnerable to a potential ban from the Federal authorities.[154] On the other hand, the Reich idea has found new

Figure 6.7 In recent years, right-wing Germans, such as the anti-immigrant and anti-Muslim organization Patriotic Europeans Against the Islamization of the West (*Patriotische Europäer gegen die Islamierung des Abendlandes*, or PEGIDA), have flown the "Fourth Reich" flag designed in 1943–44 by the anti-Nazi resistance figure Josef Wirmer, to protest the policies of Chancellor Angela Merkel (Source: Getty Images).

supporters on the political right.[155] The Alternative for Germany Party (*Alternative für Deutschland*, or AfD), has welcomed members of the Reich Citizens' Movement (RBB) and hinted that it views the Federal Republic as illegitimate.[156] Meanwhile, supporters of the anti-immigrant and anti-Muslim organization Patriotic Europeans Against the Islamisation of the West (*Patriotische Europäer gegen die Islamierung des Abendlandes*, or PEGIDA) have been seen at mass demonstrations waving the Fourth Reich flag designed by Josef Wirmer and promoted by the DK (Figure 6.7). The Reich idea has also seeped into mainstream German culture thanks to its embrace by right-wing journalists, celebrities, and self-appointed politicians.[157] These trends show that the idea of a new Reich remains an aspirational goal for the far right. Having proven its capacity to serve as rallying cry and recruiting tool, it retains the potential to serve as a mobilizing force.

A New Life for the Fourth Reich: Cultural Fears of Nazism

The growing concern after 1989 that New Right and neo-Nazi groups were striving to establish a Fourth Reich also found expression in western culture. Between 1990 and the turn of the millennium, the theme of a revived German Reich was prominently articulated in a new wave of novels, films, and television shows. Compared with the proliferation of narratives in the long 1970s, the wave of the 1990s was smaller, but it resembled its predecessor in many ways. The narratives featured gratuitous violence, abundant sex, and clunky writing, but they were updated to fit the post-cold war world. The motives of the narratives' writers varied. Some of them had published notable books during the original boom and hoped to repeat their previous success. Others were newcomers hoping to partake in another Nazi literary revival. Predictably, the texts met with a mixed response.

Most of the narratives focused on secret Nazi plots to turn a unified Germany into a Fourth Reich. Two were sequels. Thomas Gifford's 1994 novel, *The First Sacrifice*, continued where his 1976 novel, *The Wind Chill Factor*, left off by featuring its protagonist, John Cooper, working to prevent a powerful Nazi billionaire, Wolf Koller, from realizing a plan (known as "SPARTAKUS") to dominate Europe through a German–Russian alliance. Robert Ludlum's 1995 novel, *Apocalypse Watch*, continued the narrative of his 1978 bestseller, *The Holcroft Covenant*, by depicting American intelligence agents trying to thwart a revived campaign of the nefarious *Sonnenkinder* – this time, organized in a group called the *Bruderschaft* – to wreak global havoc by poisoning the water supply of various countries in Western Europe and North America. Also back for another swing was Jack Higgins, whose 1993 novel, *Thunder Point*, portrayed British government agents battling present-day Nazi sympathizers searching in the Caribbean for the wreck of a Martin Bormann-commanded Nazi submarine containing incriminating documents listing the names of wartime British and American Nazi sympathizers. The new literary wave also witnessed the arrival of new literary talent. Allan Folsom's novel *The Day after Tomorrow* (1994) described an American doctor trying to thwart a neo-Nazi effort – led by group known as "The Organization" – to "revive the Third Reich" by using cryogenic surgical techniques to create a master race. And Glenn Meade's 1997 novel, *Brandenburg*, portrayed a cell of Latin American and German neo-Nazis pursuing a chilling plan, known as the "Brandenburg Testament," to use smuggled nuclear weapons to depose the existing German government and establish "a new and prosperous and powerful Reich."[158]

Some of the tales borrowed key plot points from the "Hitler Lives!" genre. Ludlum's novel, *Apocalypse Watch*, featured a surprise ending in which the novel's protagonist, Drew Latham, exposes the fact that the *Bruderschaft*'s goal of sowing global chaos is being steered from a rural French chateau, whose main inhabitant is none other than a "bedridden" Adolf Hitler.[159] Folsom's *The Day after Tomorrow* culminates when the novel's protagonist, Doctor Paul Osborne, dispatches the "Organization's" icy villain, Von Bolden, by forcing him off a glacier and into a crevasse at the Jungfraujoch in Switzerland. As he catapults downward into the abyss, Von Bolden loses control of a secret box he has been carrying and spills out its contents – "the severed, deepfrozen head of Adolf Hitler."[160] In this, the novel's final sentence, Folsom reveals that the "Organization's" cryogenic experiments have all along been intended to create a suitable body for the revived Führer of a Fourth Reich. Finally, Glenn Meade's *Brandenburg* borrowed a page from Ib Melchior's novel *The Watchdogs of Abaddon* by featuring a heretofore unknown son of Adolf Hitler and Geli Raubal leading a neo-Nazi effort to realize his deceased father's political vision.

The authors of these tales were driven by different motives. Some hoped for financial gain. Ludlum, Gifford, and Higgins had already achieved bestseller status for their novels of the 1970s and likely hoped that the interest in a unified Germany promised renewed commercial success. Newcomers also sought to capitalize on the demand for tales about Nazis. Alan Folsom was the most successful, receiving the largest advance ever for a first novel – $2 million.[161] The authors were also morally committed to fighting neo-Nazism. In an "author's note" at the outset of *The First Sacrifice*, Gifford declared that "events in the new, reunified Germany were sufficiently disturbing to warrant revisiting the characters" of his previous novel. Folsom, meanwhile, explained that he wrote *The Day after Tomorrow* because "memories [of the Nazi era] were fading" and "I really felt we can't reemphasize what happened enough."[162] Ludlum noted that he wrote *The Apocalypse Watch* after encountering neo-Nazis in the streets of Munich, declaring "I wrote the book with anger ... and the hope of changing people's minds."[163]

The authors, however, did not only portray Nazism solely as a German problem but emphasized its universal dimensions. Gifford's novel showed American intelligence agents secretly aiding Hans Koller's bid to revive Nazism in order to keep Germany's government too distracted to dominate Europe. Ludlum's tale depicted the

Bruderschaft successfully inserting Nazi moles into the American government and sparking a McCarthy-style witch-hunt. Higgins's novel, finally, portrayed British officials suppressing knowledge of wartime collaboration with the Nazis, with the prime minister himself, aware that a close relative is implicated in the documents, burning them in his fireplace. The American and British governments, in short, displayed immoral – if not quasi-Nazi – tendencies of their own.

Many of the narratives were a commercial and critical success. Ludlum's *Apocalypse Watch*, Folsom's *The Day after Tomorrow*, Gifford's *The First Sacrifice*, and Meade's *Brandenburg* all achieved bestseller status or had print runs in the six figures.[164] They also received positive reviews. Folsom's novel was called "hugely entertaining" and "an "exceptional thriller."[165] Ludlum's book was praised as "bloody great fun."[166] Gifford's *The First Sacrifice* was described as a "terrific read" and "horrifyingly plausible."[167] *Brandenburg* was hailed as "fast, sly, and slick."[168] And *Thunder Point* was "immensely entertaining" and a "rollicking adventure."[169] Some of the novels were sufficiently popular to be given the Hollywood treatment, with *Apocalypse Watch* and *Thunder Point* being turned into made-for-television films.[170]

The narratives were nevertheless criticized for a variety of aesthetic and thematic shortcomings. Ludlum's novel – the last of his career – was called "250 pages longer" than it needed to be and labeled a "major disappointment."[171] Gifford's "melodramatic" tale was described as "veer[ing] ... into improbability."[172] *Brandenburg* was as "muddled as an unmade bed."[173] Higgins's novel was "not his best" and had "little depth."[174] The made-for-television films of Ludlum's and Higgins's novels, moreover, received mediocre reviews.[175] The most significant criticism focused on Folsom's *The Day after Tomorrow*. Like other authors, Folsom was accused of imitating Ludlum's "humdrum" writing and producing "relentless exposition" without deeper philosophical insights.[176] At the thematic level, his tale was regarded as superannuated. One reviewer called the "Hitler-lives" premise "tired, shrill, and overextended."[177] Another dismissed the "'Hitler's back!' premise" entirely, declaring that Folsom belonged in a "pop culture wax museum" for producing "a pulpy tombstone for the Age of Intrigue, when career-track white males ... coveted the role of playboy freedom fighters."[178] For their part, German critics were angered by the news that *The Day after Tomorrow* was to be turned into a film; in 1997, the *Frankfurter*

Allgemeine Zeitung's culture critic, Frank Schirrmacher, said he was nauseated by the fact that the book's popularity reflected the "collective unconscious" of Anglo-American readers.[179] Taken together, these comments suggested that the era's narratives had lost whatever originality and relevance they had enjoyed a generation earlier.

This impression was reinforced, finally, by the appearance of scattered narratives in the 1990s that satirized the premise of a Fourth Reich. These works aestheticized the Nazi legacy by prioritizing laughs over lessons, thereby revealing how the passage of time could turn tragedy into comedy. In a brief scene in the hit 1991 film *L.A. Story*, a Los Angeles weatherman played by Steve Martin asks out a young woman played by Sarah Jessica Parker to an exclusive restaurant, and, before he can pay for the bill, has to schedule an interview with a financial adviser at a local branch of the "Fourth Reich Bank of Hamburg."[180] In 1990, *Spy Magazine* made sporadic references to a mock "serialized novel" spoofing the world's rich and famous called *1999: Casinos of the Fourth Reich.*[181] Several years later, the legendary tabloid, the *Weekly World News,* published a series of sensationalistic articles that employed the Fourth Reich as a concept to sow mock terror in readers: one uncovered a "Secret German Plot to Start World War III" and establish a "Fourth Reich" that would "annex California" and force "blonde females to serve the German occupiers as 'breeders,'" while another proclaimed that a "Nazi Army" lay "Frozen in Antarctic Ice" and was plotting to "launch a sinister Fourth Reich and take over the world!"[182] These works were relatively exceptional for the decade, but they revealed how the frightfulness of a Nazi return to power could be tempered with time.

A German Trojan Horse? The European Union as the Fourth Reich

Concerns about a Fourth Reich did not merely focus on the possibility of Germany experiencing a Nazi revival but dominating Europe through the European Union. As far back as the 1970s, fears that Germany could establish an economic "Fourth Reich" were sporadically voiced in various European countries.[183] But they spiked in the years 1989–90, before ebbing during the remainder of the decade. After the turn of the millennium, they returned once again, especially following the financial crisis of 2008. Germany's role in shaping the EU's response to the crisis – particularly, its demand for painful austerity measures – left many European countries feeling resentful about their loss of autonomy and sparked a populist backlash. Critics in Greece, Italy, and other nations voiced their resentment by accusing the Federal Republic of trying to create a new Reich. In so doing, they employed the concept rhetorically to express their discontent with European integration.

Post-Unification Fears in the 1990s

European fears of German economic domination surfaced immediately after the collapse of the Berlin Wall in 1989. In London, *The Times* articulated British anxieties in a November 12 editorial, arguing that the unavoidability of German reunification would lead to "the emergence of a Fourth German Reich as Europe's economic superpower." Fearing that the Soviet Union would only permit reunification in exchange for "German neutrality," *The Times* feared that such a deal would "mean the end of NATO" and leave Germany as "the locomotive" for "rebuilding ... the newly-free market economies of Eastern Europe." The looming question thus emerged: "Where does that leave Britain?"[184] One week later, *The Times* bleakly answered its own question when it declared that Britain was probably fated to "playing a poor second to a Fourth Reich."[185] French observers shared similar concerns. In December of 1989, a poll revealed that three-quarters of French citizens feared German unification would bring about "economic domination" and a "Fourth Reich."[186] In Greece, meanwhile, a radical left-wing terrorist organization, "November 17," accused the Federal Republic in 1990 of being a "Fourth Reich" that sought to use "economic violence" to "buy up Greece."[187]

Fears of Germany's economic dominance were also linked to concerns about the country's foreign policy ambitions. These concerns surfaced in the early 1990s during the Yugoslav Civil War. Following Slovenia and Croatia's declarations of independence from the Yugoslav Federation in 1991, Serbian politicians and journalists repeatedly attacked Helmut Kohl's government as a predatory "Fourth Reich" for diplomatically supporting the break-away states. This rhetorical offensive coincided with the tendency of all sides in the Yugoslav conflict to revive suppressed memories from World War II. Serbs frequently invoked the wartime crimes committed against them by the Croatian Ustasha (which murdered around 600,000 Serbs in the early 1940s) in order to accuse Croatian President Franjo Tudjman's nationalist regime of pursuing a renewed Neo-fascist agenda against them.[188] Citing the fact that Nazi Germany supported Croatia as a puppet state during World War II, Serbs in the early 1990s claimed that Germany's recognition of Croatia was part of a plot to extend German influence into the Balkan peninsula.[189] They added that Germany's acquiescence in the face of Slovenian and Croatian aggression amounted to a new "Munich conference" and accused the Kohl government of pursuing a "Fourth Reich" from the "Baltic to the Adriatic Sea."[190] In Germany, the reaction was predictably split; Marxist groups endorsed Serbian claims that a "Fourth Reich wanted to dominate the Balkans," while German officials rejected the charges as tendentious rhetoric.[191] Soon enough, their suspicions were proven right. As the civil war shifted into Bosnia in 1992, the Serbian government changed its propaganda strategy, abandoning references to the Fourth Reich in favor of claims that Bosnian forces were the spearhead of a Muslim incursion backed by Turkey and Iran.[192] This shift revealed the instrumental motives behind the anti-German attacks.[193]

As the 1990s wore on, new economic difficulties for the Federal Republic reduced European fears of German hegemony. In 1991, French anxieties about German economic power declined when the value of the Deutschemark dropped relative to the French franc.[194] Even critical British observers adopted a more nuanced tone. In 1995, the *Guardian*'s Martin Walker dismissed the fears of British skeptics who worried that "the emerging Europe will be a German-led Fourth Reich" by saying it was "thumpingly wrong to assume that the Fourth Reich will echo the Third."[195] Two years later, Niall Ferguson cited Germany's ongoing economic problems as "good news" for Britain, concluding that a unified Germany was less like "a fourth reich – rich and strong" than "Weimar Mark II – overdrawn and weak."[196] To be sure, scattered British conservatives continued to employ the Fourth Reich as a rhetorical weapon – for instance, using it in 1996 to attack Germany for leading an EU embargo of British beef due to fears of mad cow disease – but they did so less frequently than at the beginning of the decade.

The more relaxed climate was epitomized by the appearance of British journalist Brian Reading's book, *The Fourth Reich*.[197]

Published in 1995, the volume offered a detailed history of the Federal Republic's economic success and an assessment of the country's economic future. Despite the book's sensationalistic title, Reading was optimistic about the unified Germany's prospects. Unlike British believers in the German *Sonderweg*, Reading saw German history as far from deviant. He praised the first Reich, the Holy Roman Empire, for protecting "Western European civilization from barbarian assault from the east"; he described the second Reich as "no worse" than France or Britain; and he said that the "blot" of the Third Reich had been neutralized thanks to the "exemplary" development of the Federal Republic.[198] For Reading, Germany had learned the right lessons from its history. Noting that "the Second and Third Reichs" had taught the country to recognize the perils of "economic nationalism" and "centralized power," he argued that it was the task of "Kohl's Fourth Reich ... to teach Europe a lesson in democracy" and help "keep [it] open and free."[199] The Federal Republic, he believed, was crucial for ensuring European support for free trade and accelerating the process of European integration. It was important for Britain to recognize this reality. Germany's growing drift away from France represented an opportunity for Britain to forge closer ties with Germany and steer Europe in a liberal, free-market direction. As he put it, British policy should "no longer be driven by fears of German hegemony."[200] Instead, "German hegemony should be ... welcomed."[201] The positive reception of the book in the Anglo-American press made clear that, for growing numbers of people, the Fourth Reich had been de-fanged.[202]

For the remainder of the decade and into the first years of the new millennium, Germany was rarely attacked as an economic hegemon. The country's international reputation, in fact, steadily improved. In 2005, the dedication of the Memorial to the Murdered Jews of Europe in Berlin brought Germany international praise for its efforts to come to terms with the Nazi past. The subsequent election of the country's first female chancellor, Angela Merkel, brought the country further admiration for its progressive politics. And the successful hosting of the World Cup soccer championship in 2006 solidified the country's reputation as a respected and even popular nation.[203]

The Financial Crash and the Fourth Reich

Germany's popularity, however, did not last. The world financial crash of 2008 swiftly revived European fears of a Fourth Reich.
The crash's origins lay in a complicated array of global economic forces,
but Germany played a leading role in formulating Europe's response to
it. Around the turn of the millennium, foreign investment from wealthy
northern European countries, such as Germany, France, and Britain,
steered massive capital flows into the developing economies on the
continent's periphery – especially Greece, Ireland, Portugal, Spain, and
Italy. While these countries welcomed the investment, it eventually led
to increased inflation, swelling trade and budget deficits, expanding
sovereign debt, and surging unemployment. The severe recession caused
tremendous social misery and sparked a political crisis for the countries'
governments, all of which struggled to formulate a response. Since they
had sacrificed their national currencies years earlier by joining the
Eurozone, they could not adopt the traditional strategy of currency
devaluation to lighten their debts. EU officials, led by the German-
backed European Central Bank and the International Monetary Fund
(IMF), offered substantial bailouts to Greece and other countries in the
years 2010–14, but insisted that they first reduce their debt by accepting
an austerity program of budget cuts, tax increases, and constitutionally
fixed debt limits. German officials justified this approach by citing the
need to restore investor confidence in the indebted nations, but they also
wanted to ensure that German banks – which were on the hook for
massive loans – would be repaid in full. German officials further pointed
out that austerity measures undertaken by the Schroeder government
between 1998 and 2005 had revived the German economy. And they
cited the "moral hazard" argument that forgiving the debts would
reward irresponsible behavior.[204] Whatever the underlying reasons,
the imposition of austerity worsened the economic crisis and caused
a furious backlash in Greece, Italy, and elsewhere. Populist parties
emerged on both the left and right, and expressed their anger about
their countries' loss of sovereignty. Some ended up leading new governments – for example, Syriza in Greece in 2015 – and threatened to reject
the bailout's terms or leave the Eurozone altogether. In order to amplify
their grievances, they accused Germany and the EU of acting like an
oppressive Fourth Reich.

Figure 6.8 Starting in 2012, Greek demonstrators protested German austerity policies with slogans evoking the Nazi past. In this May 2017 protest in Athens, protesters held up a sign that read, "Third Reich – Tanks; Fourth Reich – Banks" (Source: Getty Images).

The Greeks were among the most active in advancing this claim. When Angela Merkel visited Athens in 2012 for austerity talks, she was met with thousands of protesters, some of whom carried signs proclaiming "No to the Fourth Reich" (Figure 6.8).[205] In other demonstrations, protesters angrily waved placards with Nazified versions of the blue-and-yellow EU flag.[206] In 2012, 77 percent of Greeks polled agreed with the statement that "Germany's policies were serving the creation of a Fourth Reich."[207] One year later, conservative politician Panos Kammenos struck a defiant nationalist tone in declaring, "We are Greeks ... We defeated [the Germans] in the [Second World] war. We will also beat them in the Fourth Reich that they are attempting to push through."[208] These strident claims were meant to have maximum rhetorical effect, but they also touched on deeper historical memories. Since the early nineteenth century, many Greeks had regarded themselves as the victims of a colonial relationship with Germany, especially during the Second World War, when the Nazis brutally occupied Greece, looted hundreds of millions of dollars' worth of assets, and killed approximately 300,000 of its citizens.[209] Although West Germany paid limited reparations in 1960, they were far below what the Greeks expected.[210] Greeks were further exasperated by the fact that while Germany had been bailed out four separate times in the twentieth century by generous creditors, the country refused to forgive Greece's own debt.[211] When the left-wing Syriza coalition won control over the Greek government in January of 2015, therefore, Prime Minster Alex Tsipras sought to leverage historical memories to his advantage. In his first day in office, he evoked the communist left's wartime resistance against the Nazis by paying tribute to the 200 Greeks massacred by Nazi forces in the Athens suburb of Kaisairani in retaliation for the killing of a German general in 1944. One month later, in February, Tsipras claimed that austerity was causing a "social Holocaust." And in March, he demanded Germany pay overdue war reparations.[212]

Similar critiques were voiced in Italy. In the summer of 2012, anti-German sentiment grew after Prime Minister Mario Monti failed to gain Merkel's support for lower borrowing costs in the bond market. At the same time, Monti was facing pressure from the former prime minister, Silvio Berlusconi, who was hinting at a political comeback and claiming that Italy could survive outside of the Eurozone.[213] To rally domestic support, the major newspaper *Il Giornale,* which was run by Berlusconi's brother, Paolo, published a controversial article in August of 2012 that featured the headline "Quarto Reich" and a photograph of Merkel giving a semi-fascist salute.[214] The article went on to declare:

> since yesterday, Italy . . . is no longer in Europe but in the Fourth Reich. In the first Reich, the German sovereign also boasted the title of Emperor of Rome, and it is well known how the other two German [Reichs] subjugated European states: two world wars and millions of deaths are clearly not enough to appease the Germans' hegemonic ambitions. Now they are returning, this time, not with guns but with the Euro.[215]

Two years later, in 2014, two journalists from *Il Giornale,* Vittorio Feltri and Gennaro Sangiuliano, published a book entitled *The Fourth Reich: How Germany Has Subjugated Europe.* It continued the newspaper's polemical assault from 2012, declaring that the Euro resembled the German "tank divisions of yore," in the sense that the currency sought to place European territory under German rule – this time economically instead of militarily.[216]

British observers also participated in the discursive assault. In the summer of 2011, the conservative newspaper, the *Daily Mail*, published an article by Simon Heffer entitled "The Fourth Reich: How Germany Is Using the Financial Crisis to Conquer Europe."[217] Drawing on historical analogies, he argued that accepting "fiscal union" on the part of indebted nations "would entail a loss of sovereignty not seen in those countries since many were under the jackboot of the Third Reich 70 years ago." "Where Hitler failed by military means to conquer Europe," Heffer declared, "modern Germans are succeeding through trade and financial discipline. Welcome to the Fourth Reich."[218] Around the same time, the author of *The Odessa File* and conservative Eurosceptic, Frederick Forsyth, agreed that the first €100-billion bailout deal for Greece amounted to "the founding charter of the Fourth German Reich," as it gave Germany control over the economy of its "client states."[219] In November of 2011, the *Daily Mail* weighed in again on the issue, this time in a humorous vein, by publishing a parody of Mel Brooks' immortal song, "Springtime for Hitler," from the film *The Producers*. Written by journalist Richard Littlejohn, the song included the following lyrics:

> Springtime for Merkel and Germany,
> Meltdown for Ireland and Greece,
> We're marching forward to bankruptcy
> Watching the death of democracy . . .
> Springtime for Merkel and Germany,
> We're building a new Fourth Reich,
> This shouldn't come as a mystery,
> Not if you study your history.[220]

Similar accusations in other nations underscored the instrumental motives behind attacking Germany as a Fourth Reich. In Liechtenstein, Prince Hans-Adam II sparked controversy in 2008 for saying that his country was "waiting for better relations [with Germany] . . . since in the past two hundred years we have survived three German Reichs and I am hopeful we will survive a Fourth as well." While the prince dismissed claims he was insulting the present-day Federal Republic, the press revealed that he was seeking to shift attention away from a German government investigation of Liechtenstein banks that were allegedly hiding funds deposited by German tax evaders.[221] Several years later, in 2013, in Cyprus, the country's communist party (AKEL) printed a story in its press organ, *Gnomi*, with the headline "Invasion by the Fourth Reich," together with a photomontage of Merkel's head superimposed upon the body of a gun-wielding Turkish soldier stepping on the map of Cyprus.[222] In doing so, the party hoped to discredit its Christian Democratic rival (DISY), which was supported by Merkel. Eastern European countries also partook of the trend. In 2016, Poland's nationalistic, pro-government journal, *Gazeta Polska,* responded to German efforts to hasten European integration following England's Brexit vote to leave the EU by publishing a cover story entitled "Will There Be a Fourth Reich?" along with a swastika violently tearing through the EU flag.[223] Around the same time, Russian media sites, such as Pravda Report, RT, and Novorussia Today, echoed Russian governmental officials' attacks against the "Fourth Reich . . . [of] Bundesführer . . . Angela Merkel."[224]

The widespread claim that the German-run EU was becoming a Fourth Reich had several causes. It served, first of all, as a convenient means for European politicians to deflect popular anger away from their countries' internal problems and onto foreign sources. The claim also had a deeper psychological power, due to its ability to channel traumatic historical memories. As Catherine MacMillan has argued, "the Fourth Reich discourse" was marked by "Gothic" literary features – such as the "uncanny," the "return of the repressed," and the "monstrous" – that expressed genuine concerns that Germany was poised to revert to its old, ostensibly buried, habits of domination. The voicing of concerns about the Fourth Reich thus served "as a warning to Germany to stay within [the] limits . . . of democracy, the rule of law, and [the] respect for human rights on which the EU is based."[225]

Whatever its underlying motives, the charge that Germany was preparing to establish a Fourth Reich prompted a swift German backlash. Some observers sought to discredit the accusation with empirical arguments. In 2013, sociologist Ulrich Beck said it was "absurd" to call Merkel's government "a Fourth Reich," pointing out that Germany's reluctance to participate in military action in Libya proved that "Merkel was not striving to create a military power."[226] Others responded to the claims by impugning the motives of those advancing them. Writing in *Junge Freiheit* in 2012, conservative scholar Karlheinz Weissmann observed that foreign critics were aware that "Germany could be easily blackmailed" by invoking its "Nazi past" and did so for opportunistic reasons.[227] Three years later, Dirk Schümer argued that the purveyors of "German hatred" deliberately exploited "Germany's guilt complex," knowing that attacking the country was more effective than attacking other creditor nations, such as Finland and the Netherlands, that were less beholden to the "ghosts of the past."[228] Other observers warned that such baseless charges weakened European unity by stoking the fires of nationalism. The *FAZ* confronted Greek opposition leader Alex Tsipras in 2013 with the fact that Syriza's house newspaper, *Avgi*, knowingly trafficked in "Nazi comparisons" to Merkel's government in order to curry favor with right-wing nationalist parties.[229] Meanwhile, German reviewers attacked Feltri and Sangiuliano's book for "damaging sympathy, goodwill and understanding" between Italy and Germany.[230]

Other German critics offered more unconventional responses to the rhetorical attacks. Some replied with sarcastic equanimity. In 2011, for instance, *Die Welt* responded to the *Daily Mail*'s frequent invocation of the Fourth Reich by wryly noting that Germans "could be happy that [the paper] remained content to make Hitler comparisons" and did not go even further and "accuse us of causing cancer."[231] Others used their attackers' rhetorical assaults against them. Writing about the bailout in the weekend magazine of *Die Zeit* in 2015, Harald Martenstein advised Chancellor Merkel to behave less predictably and reply to accusations of imperial aspirations by saying, "Well, actually the idea of a Fourth Reich might not be so bad after all. Let's discuss it further." That, he asserted, "would confuse" Germany's critics and keep them off balance.[232] *Der Spiegel* took this approach one step further in March of 2015 by running a major cover story, entitled "The Fourth Reich," that featured a present-day photograph of Merkel clumsily attached with scotch tape to an archival photo of a group of Wehrmacht officers on the Athenian Acropolis in 1941. The magazine received criticism for the cover, but the editors responded that they were satirizing, not endorsing, the view that Germany was an aggressive, Nazi-like aggressor in European affairs. As they opined: "The only people who will misunderstand [the cover] are those who want to misunderstand it."[233]

Other European commentators joined the German defense. In November of 2011, *The Sunday Times* rejected the idea that Germany was a Fourth Reich, insisting that the only way the country could assume a "hegemonic ... position in Europe" was by actually "underwriting ... the debts of other countries" – precisely what it had thus far refused to do.[234] Around the same time, historian Richard Evans accused the *Daily Mail*'s Simon Heffer of "Germanophobia" and mocked his claims about a future Reich as "ignorant and hysterical."[235] Other British journalists attacked the *Daily Mail* for leading the discursive assault against Germany, exclaiming that the paper had written about the Fourth Reich "so often ... that we must be on our Seventh or 10th Reich by now."[236] In 2015, *The Irish Times* urged a return to discursive sobriety, arguing that the historically charged rhetoric only reinforced stubbornness on both sides and concluding: "Berlin will only act if the verbal Molotov cocktails stop flying in its direction. Accusations ... that Berlin is pursuing a Fourth Reich are a disgrace to the victims of Nazi crimes and hurtful for ordinary Germans."[237] Finally, in the US, Fareed Zakaria called Sangiuliano and Feltri's book "shameful" for "stok[ing] ... old hatreds that have no basis in today's world," and concluded that "modern Germany is the most powerful example ... that people can change ... and that ... redemption is possible."[238]

Conclusion

In the years since German unification, the idea of the Fourth Reich has fluctuated dramatically both in its usage and meaning. The idea has waxed and waned in keeping with broader historical trends, being invoked in times of crisis and fading in times of stability. The Fourth Reich was the focus of intense attention in two specific periods. The first was the years 1989–94, when the prospect of German unification and the eruption of neo-Nazism prompted fears that Germany was reviving the Reich. These concerns faded in the second half of the 1990s and the early years of the new millennium. But they resurfaced in a second period after 2008, following the eruption of the worldwide financial crisis. In both periods, talk about a looming Fourth Reich exploded, albeit in different ways. The meaning of the Reich oscillated between two visions: that of a neo-Nazi state in keeping with Hitler's Third Reich; and that of an economic superpower using the EU to impose a hegemonic order on Europe. Although those who used the Fourth Reich had a specific meaning in mind, both meanings were inevitably implied each time the term was invoked. Its symbolic flexibility contributed mightily to its rhetorical utility.

CONCLUSION

Dear Mr. So-Called President:

So let me explain to you how this works.

You were elected as chief executive of the United States . . . [albeit] with a minority of the popular vote and a little help from your friend . . . Vladimir Putin.

And this does entitle you to certain things . . .

But . . . your election does not entitle you . . . to do whatever pops into your furry orange head . . . should it run afoul of the Constitution.

You and other members of the Fourth Reich seem to be having diffi-culty understanding this.[1]

> Leonard Pitts, Jr., *The Miami Herald*, February 14, 2017

Despite referring mostly to the unified Germany in the last generation, the idea of the Fourth Reich has recently become the Federal Republic's latest export to America. The comment above by Pulitzer Prize-winning columnist, Leonard Pitts, Jr., reveals that grow-ing numbers of critics believe that Donald Trump's election as president of the United States signals the arrival of fascism in America. The claim reveals that the Fourth Reich has remained a potent slogan up to the present day. It also reflects the concept's ongoing universalization. None of this should come as a surprise, given the long postwar history of the Fourth Reich. Since it emerged more than three-quarters of a century ago, the concept has thrived as a metaphorical slogan connoting present or future peril. What it refers to specifically, however, has varied considerably over time. By surveying its status today and recapping its postwar development, we can better predict how it may develop in the years to come.

The Fourth Reich Today

The Fourth Reich is currently experiencing a new phase of normalization. Thanks to the tumultuous political upheaval throughout the western world, the concept is becoming increasingly universalized. The election of Donald Trump, the many unending conflicts in the Middle East, and the continuing crisis of the European Union have made the prospect of a future Reich highly relevant. The Fourth Reich also continues to be aestheticized. In novels, films, comic books, and tabloid newspapers, the concept has retained its ability to garner attention and spark controversy. As a result of these trends, the concept's meaning is expanding far beyond its original referent.

The election of Donald Trump on November 9, 2016 sparked a proliferation of references to the Fourth Reich in the United States. As in the 1960s, left-liberal and African-American critics led the charge. In late 2016, the famed actor and left-wing activist Harry Belafonte responded to Trump's election by beginning a lecture at New York City's Riverside Church with the mock salutation "Welcome to the Fourth Reich."[2] Around the same time, journalist Stacey Patton argued that Trump was "Building a Fourth Reich" by "align[ing] ... himself with neo-Nazis and white supremacists."[3] Subsequent newspaper editorials and letters to the editor warned about Trump's "emerging Fourth Reich."[4] Social media posts on Twitter, Tumblr, and Pinterest nervously asked whether "the Republican administration [is] the Fourth Reich?"[5] Protest groups, such as Anonymous, vowed to fight "any proposed Fourth Reich by the fascist Donald Trump."[6] And journalists defiantly declared that "our fourth estate will prevent the imposition of the Fourth Reich."[7]

The widespread embrace of the concept confirms its enduring rhetorical utility as a mobilizing slogan. Brandishing the phrase "Fourth Reich" as a headline in a news article or scrawling it on a protest sign helps activists draw attention to their broader agendas. This universalizing function has long been one of the chief forces that have inflated the Fourth Reich's meaning. But it has had the negative effect of eroding the Nazi era's historical specificity in collective memory. In most of the examples noted above, activists have made little effort to explain how the prospect of an impending "Reich" relates to President Trump's right-wing political agenda. This is predictable, perhaps, given the ephemerality and superficiality of Internet tweets and posts. Yet the same pattern has also been visible in more in-depth analyses. In 2016, British journalist Nafeez Ahmed published a four-part essay for the web journal *Medium* entitled "The Return of the Reich," the final part of which was called "A Fourth Reich Is Rising across Europe – with Ties to Donald Trump and Vladimir Putin."[8] The article persuasively traced the connections between right-wing groups in Europe and far-right foreign policy analysts associated with the Trump administration.[9] In his article's conclusion, however, Ahmed never elaborated upon his assertion that "the end goal" of the various parties is "the gradual return of the Reich by stealth … in … multiple European democracies." More importantly, he never actually defined the "Reich," explained how it might be established, or outlined what its impact could be on contemporary life. In other words, Ahmed followed the tradition of using the term merely as a metaphorical slogan for a broader threat.

Given the polemical thrust of such claims, conservative critics have predictably decried them as baseless hyperbole. In early February of 2017, journalist Bernard Goldberg wrote that the "doomsday scenario … that the United States of America will become the Fourth Reich with … Trump playing the role of you know who" was "more than a tad paranoid."[10] Around the same time, *Wall Street Journal* reporter William McGurn condemned the liberal belief that "anyone not relentlessly emoting against the 45th president is helping him build the new Reich."[11] Right-wing polemicist Ann Coulter took a similar position in an essay entitled "Pundits and the Fourth Reich" by challenging what she regarded as ill-founded Hitler comparisons by liberal journalists.[12] Finally, conservative columnist Christine Flowers sought to expose the folly of such claims, noting, "If we really lived in the Fourth Reich, those wack jobs [protesting] at the airport last week … would have been rounded up and thrown in jail … [instead of] sitting happily in their homes."[13]

These objections have some legitimacy, but they ignore the fact that members of the far right continue to be inspired by the dream of a Fourth Reich. In August of 2017, a Black church in Dumfries, Maryland was vandalized with racist signs, including one that read "the Fourth Reich."[14] In May of 2017, a Facebook page called "Alt-Reich" was shut down after one of its members was arrested for murdering an African-American student at the University of Maryland.[15] Around the same time, a Florida teenager was arrested for murdering two of his roommates for belonging to a neo-Nazi group that was allegedly planning a "Fourth Reich."[16] Web users on far-right websites such as Stormfront, meanwhile, have participated in discussion threads on the possibility of a "Fourth Reich Here in America," with an especially long thread being sparked in 2016 by the declaration, "Donald Trump Is Just the Opening Act. Yes, We Will Live to See a Fourth Reich."[17] The concept thus remains a potential rallying cry not only for opponents, but supporters, of the far right.

The idea of the Fourth Reich has also figured in debates about the Middle East. Critics of Israel employed the concept to attack the country during its military conflicts with Hezbollah in Lebanon in 2006 and with Hamas in Gaza in 2009. In May of 2006, Amir Abdul Malik Ali, a Black Muslim imam from a radical Oakland-based mosque, delivered a talk at the University of California at Irvine, sponsored by the campus branch of Students for Justice in Palestine, called "Israel: The Fourth Reich," which sparked controversy for alleging Jewish control of the media and predicting Israel's imminent defeat by Muslim "martyrs."[18] Later that same year, the *Canadian Arab News* drew parallels between the "Zionist (Fourth) Reich and the Nazi Third Reich" by describing Israel as an "apartheid or *Herrenvolk* ('master race')" state.[19] In 2009, the war in Gaza sparked numerous street protests in which demonstrators held up signs with the slogan "Israel: The Fourth Reich." Similar claims were voiced by Arab-American news outlets.[20] More recently, rap songs have attacked Israel as a Fourth Reich, and likeminded claims have appeared on Twitter and in the comments section of the anti-Zionist website Mondoweiss.[21]

Not surprisingly, conservative supporters of Israel responded by employing the idea of the Fourth Reich to attack the country's Muslim and Arab adversaries. In May of 2006, false reports that Iran was planning to have its Jewish citizens wear yellow badges prompted *The New York Daily News* to run a banner headline screaming

"The Fourth Reich."[22] In 2009, Christian Zionist supporters of Israel attacked some of the countries participating in the second United Nations World Conference Against Racism in South Africa (Durban II) as members of a "Fourth Reich."[23] In 2015, meanwhile, the eminent Indian writer V. S. Naipaul attacked the Sunni Muslim terrorist organization ISIS by claiming it was "dedicated to a contemporary Holocaust" and could easily "abandon the label of Caliphate and call itself the Fourth Reich."[24]

References to the Fourth Reich have also surfaced in the ongoing debate about the European Union. While debt-ridden European nations in Southern Europe employed the slogan against Germany after the financial crash of 2008, nationalistic Eastern European governments have increasingly employed it as part of a larger campaign to weaken the EU. Leading the charge was Vladimir Putin's Russia. In response to the EU's imposition of sanctions against Russia in 2014 for its intervention in Eastern Ukraine and annexation of Crimea, *Pravda Report* published an article entitled "The Boys from Brussels," which evoked Ira Levin's novel *The Boys from Brazil*, and argued that "the real Nazis" were not to be found in Latin America, but in a "Fourth Reich" headquartered "in the offices of the European Commission in Brussels."[25] Other Russian sites accused Ukrainian nationalists of building up a "Fourth Reich" opposed to Russia.[26] Some even accused the United States of "creat[ing a] ... Fourth Reich to destroy Russia" by supporting Ukraine and expanding NATO eastward.[27] Taken together with similar claims voiced by commentators in Poland and Hungary, such hyperbole was part of a concerted effort by authoritarian nationalist regimes to undermine the cause of European unity.[28]

In addition to being universalized, the Fourth Reich continues to be aestheticized. Novelists keep coming back to the topic to mine its dramatic potential. Journalist Adam Lebor's 2009 novel, *The Budapest Protocol*, portrayed unrepentant Nazis using the EU as a vehicle for asserting German economic dominance over smaller Eastern European nations.[29] At the other end of the literary spectrum, various "on demand" novels have eagerly exploited the concept with sensationalistic titles, such as *4th Reich of Antarctica: Secrets of South America* (2012), *Treasures of the Fourth Reich: A Novel of Suspense* (2012), and *The Fourth Reich – Head of the Snake* (2016).[30] The same trend is visible in recent films, whether the mainstream production *Beyond*

Valkyrie: Dawn of the Fourth Reich (2016), which portrays SS men trying to revive the Reich from Argentina, or the low-budget movie *Dead Walkers: Rise of the Fourth Reich* (2013), which consummated the long-awaited marriage between Nazis and zombies. Comic books have also returned to the Fourth Reich, with DC comics gathering a team of supervillains – including Captain Nazi, Baroness Blitzkrieg, and Baron Gestapo – under the name "The Fourth Reich" to battle the Justice Society in a series of issues in the years 2006–10.[31] Finally, the Fourth Reich continues to be played for laughs. In 2014, the satirical film *Iron Sky* portrayed a band of fanatical, moon-based Nazis attempting to establish a Fourth Reich by launching an interstellar attack on Earth.[32] The term has even been satirized in song parodies, as with comedian Stephen Colbert's 2017 spoof of R.E.M.'s 1987 hit, "It's the End of the World," featuring the line: "vitriolic, xenophobic, troll spite, Fourth Reich."[33]

These normalizing trends reveal several things about the idea of the Fourth Reich. Its widespread use by political activists, journalists, novelists, and filmmakers reflects its versatility as a political and cultural signifier. Its embrace by activists on both the left and the right confirms that it is politically ecumenical. The term's renewed resonance confirms that its popularity swells in periods of political instability. And the term's polemical power reveals that its significance is as much rhetorical as historical.

The Fourth Reich Yesterday: Between German Threat and Global Peril

These traits are all rooted in the Fourth Reich's long history. When it first came into being in the 1930s, the concept of the Fourth Reich referred exclusively to Germany and its political future. It maintained much of that orientation in the decades that followed. Yet even in a solely German context, the Fourth Reich has evolved considerably in its use and meaning: it has been employed by people in Germany as well as abroad; it has been embraced by political movements on the left and the right; and it has expressed the dueling emotions of fantasy and fear. As it has evolved, however, the Fourth Reich has not remained confined to Germany. It has become normalized into a symbol of global peril.

The Fourth Reich as German Threat

During the years of the Nazi dictatorship, a diverse range of people in and outside of Germany embraced the idea of the Fourth Reich. They included exiled socialists, émigré Jews, renegade left-wing Nazis, conservative monarchists, mutinous Wehrmacht officers, and radical university students. The members of these groups embraced starkly different political views, but they all used the Fourth Reich to express their hopes for a post-Nazi world. For a time, western observers outside of Germany shared this optimistic perspective and viewed the Fourth Reich as a neutral, if not positive, designation for the future nation. Yet, during the second half of World War II and the years after its conclusion, the prospect of a new Reich assumed more ominous significance as the harbinger of a Nazi revival.

This development reflected the repeated efforts of right-wing extremists in postwar Germany to realize their fantasy of creating a Fourth Reich. They first began during the occupation era, with the effort of insurgent groups – including the Werewolf movement, the Hitler Youth conspiracy, and the Deutsche Revolution – to overturn Allied rule. In the 1950s, the pursuit of a new Reich found political articulation with the rise of the SRP and the infiltration of the FDP by the members of Werner Naumann's Gauleiter Circle. Around the same time – albeit a world away – the same goal was being quixotically pursued by Latin American Nazis associated with the Argentine Nazi journal, *Der Weg*, and the fugitive war criminal Adolf Eichmann. In the 1960s, the NPD flirted with the idea of the Reich, while in the 1970s and 1980s, it was given full-throated endorsement by neo-Nazi terrorists, such as Manfred Roeder and Michael Kühnen. In the years following German unification in 1990, New Right intellectuals affiliated with the *Staatsbriefe* and the Deutsches Kolleg, such as Hans Dietrich Sander, Reinhold Oberlercher, and Horst Mahler, sought to give the Reich a more sophisticated theoretical grounding. And more recently, populist movements such as the Reich Citizens' Movement and PEGIDA have incorporated symbols relating to the Fourth Reich into their propaganda activities.

The efforts of these groups to realize the dream of a revived Reich, however, have been effectively opposed by groups who regard it as a nightmare. Already in the last years of World War II, western journalists invoked the prospect of a Fourth Reich to ensure that the

Allies did not lose the peace and permit a Nazi return to power. The term continued to be utilized after the war, especially when Allied occupation forces undertook efforts to squelch Nazi resistance movements with Operation Nursery and Operation Selection Board in the years 1946–47. In the 1950s, fears of a Fourth Reich helped ensure the banning of the SRP and the suppression of the Naumann conspiracy in Operation Terminus. They further prompted German and western observers to monitor neo-Nazi terrorist groups from the 1960s to the 1980s. Finally, after German unification in 1990, international concerns that a unified Germany might become a Fourth Reich helped push Helmut Kohl's government to restrain neo-Nazi radicals. Today, the term encourages people to remain vigilant about the danger of right-wing radicalism.

As the longtime object of competing fantasies and fears, the Fourth Reich has played an important, if heretofore unacknowledged, role in postwar German history. For the most part, scholars have dismissed the idea of the Fourth Reich as a sensationalistic myth. But this is true only in the strictest sense of the term. The Fourth Reich is undeniably mythic insofar as it has never come into existence. But that very fact ironically proves its value. The Fourth Reich's existence in the realm of the possible has prevented it from entering the realm of the real. If it is a myth, it has been a necessary one. The role of the Fourth Reich in postwar German history underscores the probationary power of memory. The frequent postwar invocation of the term by concerned western observers has reminded Germans that the world has not forgotten the events of the Nazi era and will continue to hold the country's leaders responsible for preventing their recurrence.

Viewed purely in retrospect, of course, the idea of the Fourth Reich has distorted the real danger posed by postwar Nazis and fostered an atmosphere of alarmism. After all, the Nazis never made good on their postwar goals. But the fears expressed by the term were mostly genuine. Moreover, they were never groundless. While Germany's postwar democratization today looks inevitable, it was never a certainty. Nazi forces in the early years of the Federal Republic were committed to challenging the country's democratic order. Although they all failed, it is possible that if circumstances had been slightly different, they might have come closer to succeeding. It was vital, therefore, that the defenders of democracy had the ability to counteract this prospect by summoning the specter of a Fourth Reich. In a sense, the specter functioned like a rhetorical insurance policy, as a mobilizing slogan that could be held in reserve until it was needed to combat threatening political trends. The policy paid off. Every time foreign observers voiced concern about a revived Reich, they pressured the German authorities to act decisively against it. In so doing, they helped ensure that the Federal Republic's right-wing enemies never realized their antidemocratic goals. Without the fear of a Fourth Reich, postwar German history might not have turned out as successfully as it did.

The Fourth Reich as Global Peril

The idea of the Fourth Reich did not merely warn about the revival of Nazism in Germany, however, but elsewhere as well. As the concept became more publicized, it became more universalized. Beginning in the turbulent 1960s, the term was embraced by various groups hoping to highlight the emergence of problems beyond Germany. The Fourth Reich was first applied to dangers facing the United States in the late 1950s and early 1960s, especially the threat of domestic Nazism, which became a concern following the eruption of the swastika wave and rise of the American Nazi Party. A few years later, left-leaning students and African-American civil rights activists embraced the concept to attack racial injustice, the US war in Vietnam, and the Watergate crimes of the Nixon administration. As the term gained increasing prominence, activists in other parts of the world embraced it in the 1970s and 1980s, whether to criticize autocratically ruled Greece, Apartheid South Africa, or various juntas in Latin America. Since the 1990s, and especially since the turn of the millennium, the Fourth Reich has been employed by left-wing and right-wing populists to attack transnational institutions, such as the European Union.

Unlike the case of Germany, however, the effectiveness of these polemical attacks is open to question. While they have directed attention to present-day concerns, they have just as often inspired ridicule. These attacks have often been advanced without convincing empirical support. Most of the activists who have employed the Fourth Reich as a rhetorical cudgel have failed to explain how it illuminates present-day problems, whether racism, authoritarianism, or economic injustice. The term implies that these forces are somehow "Nazi" in nature, but, without further evidence, it loses credibility. Reduced to a metaphorical slogan, the concept suffers from semiotic vagueness. As a result, it is rarely taken seriously by anyone but convinced activists. Instead of inspiring vigilance, the term prompts defensiveness and deepens polarization. The universalization of the Fourth Reich has thus arguably impeded rather than promoted historical understanding.

The same can be said about the Fourth Reich's aestheticization. As early as the 1940s, the prospect of the Nazis returning to power in a new Reich found cultural expression in works of fiction and film. These narratives continued to appear during the years of the occupation before fading during the 1950s. Following the reawakening of western interest in the Nazi past in the 1960s, however, the Fourth Reich was dramatically transformed into a cultural trope, inspiring a massive wave of novels, short stories, films, television broadcasts, and comic books that lasted well into the 1980s. A second, if smaller, wave erupted in the mid 1990s, expressing renewed western worries about a unified Germany's potential rightwing turn. Scattered narratives have continued to appear since the turn of the millennium.

The impact of these works has been mixed. On the one hand, they have spread popular awareness of the Fourth Reich and made the concept into an instantly recognizable signifier of global peril. On the other hand, they have transformed it into a pop culture cliché. Having been featured in countless cultural works, the Fourth Reich has become one of many iconic, albeit exhausted, symbols of Nazi evil. It has exploited the Nazi past for the sake of entertainment, used it for commercial profit, played it for laughs, and eroded its moral power. In all of these ways, the Fourth Reich has become increasingly subjected to the forces of normalization. No wonder that scholars, journalists, and other observers have long argued that the topic merits little serious attention.

As this study has shown, however, the Fourth Reich has a rich history that cannot be easily dismissed. It is true that the topic resists simple understanding, but its complexity adds to its intrigue. At its core, the history of the Fourth Reich is the story of an ontological paradox. It has never come into being, but it has never disappeared. It draws on memories of a traumatic past, but expresses fears of an unknown future. Its meaning is both particular and universal. It is immanent to, yet ultimately transcends, German history. It symbolizes our world's ultimate nightmare. But it is a nightmare that – until now – has been averted. Thus far, the Fourth Reich has remained restricted to the realm of myth rather than the realm of reality.

The Fourth Reich Tomorrow

Whether or not it will continue to be so remains to be seen. If the past is prologue, then the history of the Fourth Reich provides a sense of its future evolution. From the vantage point of today, the story of the Fourth Reich has been a fortunate one. It is the story of a nightmare averted. But it could still foretell a disaster to come.

Paradoxically, the failure of the Fourth Reich to come into existence confirms its success as a concept. Whether metaphorically conceived as an insurance policy, a prophylactic, or a self-fulfilling prophecy in reverse, its ability to inspire popular vigilance about, and prevent the possibility of, a Nazi return to power underscores its value. And yet the Fourth Reich has brought with it adverse consequences that suggest it may have outlasted its usefulness. Thanks to its rhetorical inflation, it has become a phrase that is just as likely to alienate people as convince them about the dangers of right-wing political radicalism. The more that the signifier has become separated from its original referent, the more its meaning has become diluted and its significance effaced. No one can legislate ideas out of existence, of course, and so it would be futile to demand that the Fourth Reich be forcibly retired as a concept. But prompting people to think more critically about the term, as this book does, may convince them to treat it more responsibly in the future.

This is especially important given the likelihood that the Fourth Reich will remain with us for some time to come. If the concept's history teaches us anything, it is that the Fourth Reich has preserved a striking capacity to inspire allegiance. For more than a thousand years, the concept of the Reich has retained an uncanny power to survive the turbulent, and often destructive, course of historical events. In every era, it has inspired countless people in Germany with its promise of messianic redemption. Whether conceived in a religious or secular sense, the mystical idea of a "realm," "kingdom," or "empire" has helped mobilize and unite millions of Germans in eras of crisis. Since World War II, the concept has been surrounded with taboos thanks to the disastrous outcome of the Nazis' attempt to realize their thousand-year Reich. But it would be naive to think that these taboos will remain in place forever. In times of turmoil, people look back to eras when their country used to be "great." The Federal Republic has fortunately been spared the kind of crises that might lead people beyond the extremist political fringe to flirt with a new Reich. But should such a crisis arise, opportunistic intellectuals, writers, and politicians may exploit the Reich idea for their own purposes. Should the German masses be sufficiently desperate, there is no reason to think they would abstain from seeing a renewed Reich as the answer to their problems.

The only way to mute the siren call of the Fourth Reich is to know its full history. Although it is increasingly difficult in our present-day world of fake "facts" and deliberate disinformation to forge a consensus about historical truth, we have no alternative but to pursue it. Without knowing the Fourth Reich's origins and evolution, we will be unable to shape its future development. Only by understanding its historic appeal can we prevent its future realization.

ACKNOWLEDGMENTS

In conducting research for this book, I benefited from the help of various friends, colleagues, archivists, and librarians. All of them deserve thanks. At the National Archives in Maryland, I am grateful to Paul Brown and Eric Van Slander for helping me find relevant records pertaining to postwar US Military Government agencies in occupied Germany. I would also like to thank the staff at the Institut für Zeitgeschichte in Munich, the Bavarian State Library, the New York Public Library, and the libraries at Harvard University, the Jewish Theological Seminary, and the University of California at Los Angeles for assistance locating other relevant materials. Academic friends and colleagues Richard Steigmann-Gall, Janet Ward, Thomas Pegelow Kaplan, Alon Confino, and Jonathan Wiesen participated in conference panels where I presented material from the book. At Cambridge University Press, I would like to thank my longtime editor, Michael Watson, for his unfailingly helpful feedback, Christopher Jackson for his meticulous copyediting, and Lisa Carter and Julie Hrischeva for helping with the book's production and design. Thanks also go to my agent, Andrew Stuart, for representing me and my work in the ever-changing publishing world. I am grateful to my father, Alvin H. Rosenfeld, for reading the manuscript and providing astute comments. Finally, heartfelt thanks go to my wife, Erika, and children, Julia and Benjamin, for providing me with endless reasons for wanting to knock off work early.

NOTES

Preface

1. "Arson Believed Certain Bloomington Center," *Jewish Post* (Indianapolis), September 13, 1983, p. 14.
2. "Fire at I.U. Fraternity Declared Arson; 1 Dead," *The Indianapolis Star*, October 22, 1984.
3. "Former Student Arrested in Fraternity House Fire," *The New York Times*, October 23, 1984.
4. The group responsible was the white supremacist group the Covenant, the Sword, and the Arm of the Lord (CSA), which was linked to the Aryan Brotherhood and perpetrated multiple terrorist attacks across America in the early 1980s. The FBI suppressed the group following a siege of its rural Arkansas compound in the spring of 1985. Jessica Eve Stern, "The Covenant, the Sword, and the Arm of the Lord (1985)," in Jonathan B. Tucker, ed., *Toxic Terror: Assessing Terrorist Use of Chemical and Biological Weapons* (Cambridge, MA, 2000), pp. 151–52.
5. Otto Friedrich, *Before the Deluge: A Portrait of Berlin in the 1920s* (New York, 1995), p. xxi.

Introduction

1. Erwin Lessner, *Phantom Victory: A Fictional History of the Fourth Reich, 1945–1960* (New York, 1944), pp. 180–81.
2. Hugh Trevor-Roper, *History and Imagination* (Oxford, 1980), pp. 15, 16, 21.
3. Duncan Gardham, "MI5 Files: Nazis Planned 'Fourth Reich' in Post-War Europe," *Telegraph*, April 4, 2011. "Dawn of the Fourth Reich," *The Toronto Star*, April 11, 2015.
4. Michael Miller, "Antifa: Guardians against Fascism or Lawless Thrill-Seekers?" *The Washington Post*, September 14, 2017.
5. Jim Marrs, *The Rise of the Fourth Reich: The Secret Societies That Threaten to Take over America* (Solon, OH, 2008), and Glen Yeadon, *The Nazi Hydra in America: Suppressed History of a Century – Wall Street and the Rise of the Fourth Reich*

(Joshua Tree, CA, 2008). One of the earliest such studies was Des Griffin's *Fourth Reich of the Rich* (Clackamas, OR, 1976).

6. Carlos Collado Seidel, *Angst vor dem "Vierten Reich": Die Allierten und die Ausschaltung des deutschen Einflusses in Spanien, 1944–1958* (Paderborn, 2001), Ronald Newton, "The United States, the German-Argentines, and the Myth of the Fourth Reich, 1943–47," *The Hispanic American Historical Review*, 1, February 1984, 81–103, Heinz Schneppen, *Odessa und das Vierte Reich: Mythen der Zeitgeschichte* (Berlin, 2007), Scott Selby, *The Axmann Conspiracy: The Nazi Plan for a Fourth Reich and How the U.S. Army Defeated* It (New York, 2012), Daniel Stahl, *Nazi-Jagd: Südamerikas Diktaturen und die Ahndung von NS-Verbrechern* (Göttingen, 2013), pp. 27–28.

7. Mary Fulbrook, *A History of Germany 1918–2014: The Divided Nation* (Chichester, UK, 2014), p. 122.

8. Magnus Linklater, Isabel Hilton, and Neal Ascherson, *The Nazi Legacy: Klaus Barbie and the International Fascist Connection* (New York, 1985), p. 135.

9. Scholars have not merely under-theorized the term, but have erred in the opposite direction by providing overly detailed, ideal-typical definitions of the Fourth Reich. In his magnum opus, *Beyond Eagle and Swastika*, for example, K. P. Tauber argued that "the creation of a Fourth Reich ... [entailed] the establishment of political homogeneity, social unity, and national power through essentially conservative-authoritarian, nonrevolutionary means." K. P. Tauber, *Beyond Eagle and Swastika* (Middletown, CT, 1967), p. 882.

10. Richard Evans, *The Third Reich at War* (New York, 2009), p. 764.

11. Roger Griffin, *The Nature of Fascism* (New York, 1996), p. xii.

12. Dieter Dettke, *The Spirit of the Berlin Republic* (New York, 2003), p. 3.

13. Put differently, understanding the Fourth Reich is partly a question of understanding its discursive features. On the interdisciplinary field of discourse analysis, see Deborah Tannen, Heidi E. Hamilton, and Deborah Schiffrin, eds., *The Handbook of Discourse Analysis* (Oxford, 2015), especially: Laurel J. Brinton, "Historical Discourse Analysis" (pp. 222–43), Teun A. van Dijk, "Critical Discourse Analysis" (pp. 466–85), and John Wilson, "Political Discourse" (pp. 775–94).

14. To employ semiotic terminology, the Fourth Reich is a signifier that refers to a set of diverse meanings (the "signified") that further relate to some external reality (the "referent"). It communicates denotative as well as connotative meaning, the former through description, the latter through suggestion.

15. Robert E. Denton, "The Rhetorical Functions of Slogans: Classifications and Characteristics," *Communication Quarterly*, spring, 1980, 10–18.

16. See Klaus Naumann's essay, "Selbstanerkennung: Nach 40 Jahren Bundesrepublik: Anstöße zur Bewältigung einer 'Erfolgsgeschichte,'" *Blätter*, 9, 1988, 1046–60. Axel Schildt, *Ankunft im Westen: Ein Essay zur Erfolgsgeschichte der Bundesrepublik* (Frankfurt, 1999). Scholars taking this position include Harold Zink, *The United States in Germany* (Princeton, 1957), Fritz René Allemann, *Bonn ist nicht Weimar* (Cologne, 1956), Ralf Dahrendorf, *Society and Democracy in Germany* (London, 1965), Hans-Peter Schwarz, *Die Ära Adenauer: Gründerjahre der Republik, 1949–1957* (Stuttgart, 1981), Christoph Kleßmann, *Die doppelte Staatsgründung: Deutsche Geschichte, 1945–1955* (Bonn, 1991), Edgar Wolfrum, *Die geglückte Demokratie: Geschichte der Bundesrepublik Deutschland von ihren Anfängern bis zur Gegenwart* (Munich, 2007), Heinrich August Winkler, *Germany: The Long Road West: Volume II, 1933–1990* (New

York, 2007), Konrad Jarausch and Michael Geyer, *Shattered Past: Reconstructing German Histories* (Princeton, 2009).

17. Thomas Hertfelder, "'Modell Deutschland' – Erfolgsgeschichte oder Illusion?" in Thomas Hertfelder and Andreas Rödder, eds., *Modell Deutschland – Erfolgsgeschichte oder Illusion?* (Göttingen, 2007), p. 9.

18. Thomas Hertfelder, "Ein Meistererzählung der Demokratie? Die großen Ausstellungshäuser des Bundes," in Thomas Hertfelder, Ulrich Lappenküper, and Jürgen Lillteicher, eds., *Erinnern an Demokratie in Deutschland: Demokratiegeschichte in Museen und Erinnerungsstätten der Bundesrepublik* (Göttingen, 2016), pp. 167–68.

19. Konrad Jarausch, *After Hitler: Recivilizing Germans, 1945–1995* (New York, 2006), pp. 13–17; Hertfelder, "'Modell Deutschland,'" 15. Peter Pulzer, *German Politics, 1945–1995* (Oxford, 1995), p. 71.

20. Jarausch, "The Federal Republic at Sixty," *German Politics and Society*, March 2010, 10. See Hertfelder, "'Modell Deutschland,'" 15.

21. In his book *The German Problem Transformed: Institutions, Politics, and Foreign Policy, 1945–1995* (Ann Arbor, 1999), Thomas Banchoff called western integration "inevitable" (p. 46).

22. Richard Ned Lebow, *Forbidden Fruit* (Princeton, NJ, 2010), pp. 8–12.

23. Ruth Wittlinger and Steffi Boothroyd, "A 'Usable' Past at Last? The Politics of the Past in United Germany," *German Studies Review*, October 2010, 494–99. See also: www.bundespraesident.de/SharedDocs/Reden/DE/Horst-Koehler/Reden/2005/05/20050508_Rede.html

24. On backshadowing, see Michael André Bernstein, *Foregone Conclusions: Against Apocalyptic History* (Berkeley, 1994) and Gary Saul Morson, *Narrative and Freedom: The Shadows of Time* (New Haven, 1994).

25. See Peter Novick, *That Noble Dream: The "Objectivity Question" and the American Historical Profession* (Cambridge, UK, 1989).

26. Sonja Levsen and Cornelius Torp, "Die Bundesrepublik und der Vergleich," in Sonja Levsen and Cornelius Torp, eds., *Wo liegt die Bundesrepublik? Vergleichende Perspektiven auf die Westdeutsche Geschichte* (Göttingen, 2016), p. 13.

27. Andreas Rödder, "Das 'Modell Deutschland' zwischen Erfolgsgeschichte und Verfallsdiagnose," *Vierteljahrshefte für Zeitgeschichte*, 3, 2006, 345–63. On the need to challenge myths, see Hannah Schissler, *The Miracle Years: A Cultural History of West Germany, 1949–1968* (Princeton, 2000), p. 3, and Michael Schwarz, *Vertriebene und 'Umsiedlerpolitik'* (Munich, 2004), p. 3. On the "dark sides" of the country's postwar "success story," see Hertfelder, "'Modell Deutschland,'" 18. Hans Günter Hockerts has written that the "success story" narrative overly emphasizes "the smooth and clear, neglecting losses, detours, and resistance." Hans Günter Hockerts, ed., *Koordinaten deutscher Geschichte in der Epoche des Ost-West Konflikts* (Munich, 2004), p. ix.

28. Jarausch, *After Hitler*, p. vi. Dirk Moses, *German Intellectuals and the Nazi Past* (Cambridge, UK, 2007), p. 6.

29. Philipp Gassert has described "westernization" as an overly "whiggish" term for West Germany's democratization. Philip Gassert, "The Specter of Americanization: Western Europe in the American Century," in *The Oxford Handbook of Postwar European History* (Oxford, 2012), p. 194. Maria Höhn has criticized the inevitability of "modernization" in *GIs and Fräuleins: The German–American Encounter in 1950s West Germany* (Chapel Hill, NC, 2002), p. 228. Michael Hughes questioned the inevitability of democratization in *Shouldering the Burdens of Defeat:*

West Germany and the Reconstruction of Social Justice (Chapel Hill, NC, 1999), p. 150. Peter Graf Kielmansegg, *Lange Schatten: Vom Umgang der Deutschen mit der nationalsozialistischen Vergangenheit* (Berlin, 1989), p. 10.

30. Kristian Buchna, *Nationale Sammlung an Rhein und Ruhr: Friedrich Middelhauve und die nordrheinwestfälische FDP 1945–1953* (Munich, 2010), p. 10.

31. Peter Bowler, *Darwin Deleted: Imagining a World without Darwin* (Chicago, 2013); Richard Ned Lebow, *Archduke Franz Ferdinand Lives! A World without World War I* (New York, 2014); Jeffrey Gurock, *The Holocaust Averted: An Alternate History of American Jewry, 1938–1967* (New Brunswick, 2015).

32. J. H. Elliott's *Empires of the Atlantic World: Britain and Spain in America, 1492–1830* (New Haven, 2006) concludes by asking what if Henry VII had financed Christopher Columbus's first voyage (p. 411). Anthony Pagden's *The Enlightenment: And Why It Still Matters* (New York, 2013) ends by examining what would have happened had the Enlightenment never occurred (pp. 408–15); Steven Kotkin's *Stalin: Volume I, Paradoxes of Power, 1878–1928* (New York, 2014) ends with the coda, "If Stalin Had Died" (pp. 724–39).

33. Gavriel D. Rosenfeld, "The Ways We Wonder 'What If?' Towards a Typology of Historical Counterfactuals," *The Journal of the Philosophy of History*, 3, 2016, 382–411.

34. Richard Ned Lebow, "Counterfactuals, History and Fiction," *Historical Social Research*, 2, 2009, 57. Lebow, *Forbidden Fruit*, p. 40.

35. John Lewis Gaddis, *The Landscape of History: How Historians Map the Past* (Oxford, 2004), p. 102.

36. Fritz Ringer, "Max Weber on Causal Analysis, Interpretation, and Comparison," *History and Theory*, May 2002, 168.

37. Philip E. Tetlock, Richard Ned Lebow, and Geoffrey Parker, eds., *Unmaking the West: "What-If?" Scenarios That Rewrite World History* (Ann Arbor, MI, 2006), pp. 17–18, 25; Roland Wenzlhuemer, "Counterfactual Thinking as Scientific Method," *Historical Social Research*, 2, 2009, 49.

38. John Stuart Mill, *On Liberty* (London, 1864), p. 33.

39. The influential "Whig interpretation of history," for example, emerged during Great Britain's nineteenth-century rise to global dominance, but declined with the empire's collapse after 1945. Richard Evans, *Cosmopolitan Islanders: British Historians and the European Continent* (Cambridge, UK, 2009), pp. 30–31.

40. Azar Gat, *Victorious and Vulnerable: Why Democracy Won in the Twentieth Century and How It Is Still Imperiled* (Lanham, MD, 2010), pp. 5–7.

41. Ibid., p. ix.

42. Hans-Peter Schwarz, "Die ausgebliebene Katastrophe: Eine Problemskizze zur Geschichte der Bundesrepublik," in Hermann Rudolph, ed., *Den Staat denken: Theodor Eschenburg zum Fünfundachtzigsten* (Stuttgart, 1989), p. 151. Schwarz wrote that the Federal Republic's postwar history was defined by people trying to "evade catastrophe" in every area of life. Ironically, Schwarz dismissed the utility of counterfactuals, writing "there is little historiographical glory to be attained in getting bogged down in the unanswerable question, 'what would have happened if?'" Ibid., p. 167.

43. Klaus Naumann, "Die neunziger Jahre, ein nervöses Jahrzehnt am Ende der Nachkriegszeit," in Ursula Heukenkamp, ed., *Schuld und Sühne? Deutsche Kriegserlebnis und Kriegsdeutung in deutschen Medien der Nachkriegszeit (1945–1961)* (Amsterdam, 2001), p. 801.

44. Yemima Ben-Menahem, "Historical Necessity and Contingency," in Aviezer Tucker, ed., *A Companion to the Philosophy of History and Historiography* (Chichester, 2009), pp. 110–30.

45. Winkler, *Germany*, p. 587. Similarly, Richard von Weizsäcker observed in 1992 that "the first German Republic failed … not because there were too many Nazis … but because for too long there were too few democrats." Quoted in: Kevin McAleer, *Dueling: The Cult of Honor in Fin-de-Siècle Germany* (Princeton, 2014), p. 208.

46. For example, A. J. Nicholls's book *The Bonn Republic: West German Democracy 1945–1990* (New York, 1997) devotes little attention to the postwar efforts of ex- and neo-Nazis to challenge West German democracy, relegating the Socialist Reich Party (SRP) to little more than a footnote (p. 92) and granting the National Democratic Party (NPD) less than a page.

47. Allemann, *Bonn ist nicht Weimar*, p. 295; Gerhard Ritter, *The German Problem: Basic Questions of German Political Life, Past and Present* (1965), p. 204. To be sure, more liberal-minded scholars in this period remained cautious – for example, Karl Dietrich Bracher, who focused a good deal on the "survival of National Socialist thinking and myths" in the Federal Republic. Karl Dietrich Bracher, *The German Dictatorship: The Origins, Structure and Effects of National Socialism* (New York, 1970), pp. 478, 500–01.

48. Jeffrey Herf, "Multiple Restorations: German Political Traditions and the Interpretation of Nazism, 1945–1946," *Central European History*, 26, 1, 1993, 53; Kielmansegg, *Lange Schatten*, p. 11; Dennis Bark and David Gress, *A History of West Germany: From Shadow to Substance, 1945–1963* (Oxford, 1989), p. xii. For other examples, see Jarausch, *After Hitler*, pp. 62, 54; Rand Lewis, *The Neo-Nazis and German Unification* (Westport, CT, 1996), p. 14; Dieter Dettke, *The Spirit of the Berlin Republic*, p. 3.

49. Martin Kitchen, *A History of Modern Germany* (Malden, MA, 2006), p. 343; Wolfrum, *Die geglückte Demokratie*, p. 171.

50. See Corey Robin, *Fear: The History of a Political Idea* (New York, 2004); Adam Zamoyski, *Phantom Terror: Political Paranoia and the Creation of the Modern State, 1789–1848* (New York, 2015).

51. Naumann, "Die neunziger Jahre," 801; see also Schwarz, who writes that scholars "must take seriously" the "fears" that surround postwar German history. Schwarz, "Die ausgebliebene Katastrophe," 158–59.

52. See Christian Schletter, *Grabgesang der Demokratie: Die Debatten über das Scheitern der bundesdeutschen Demokratie von 1965 bis 1985* (Göttingen, 2015), pp. 9–11, 361–63. Ian Connor, "The Radicalization That Never Was? Refugees in the German Federal Republic," in Frank Biess, Mark Roseman, and Hanna Schissler, *Conflict, Catastrophe, and Continuity: Essays on Modern German History* (New York, 2007), pp. 221–36.

53. Among the more important works on the subject of *Vergangenheitsbewältigung* are: Charles Maier, *The Unmasterable Past: History, Holocaust, and German National Identity* (Cambridge, MA, 1988); Jeffrey Herf, *Divided Memory: The Nazi Past in the Two Germanys* (Cambridge, MA, 1997); Ulrich Brochhagen, *Nach Nürnberg: Vergangenheitsbewältigung und Westintegration in der Ära Adenauer* (Hamburg, 1994); Manfred Kittel, *Die Legende von der zweiten Schuld: Vergangenheitsbewältigung in der Ära Adenauer* (Berlin, 1993); Helmut Dubiel, *Niemand ist frei von der Geschichte* (Munich, 1999); Bill Niven, *Facing the Nazi Past: United Germany and the Legacy of the Third Reich* (London, 2002).

54. Produced by Jordan Peele, *The Hunt* "follows a diverse band of Nazi Hunters living in 1977 New York City … [who] have discovered that hundreds of … Nazi officials

are ... conspiring to create a Fourth Reich in the U.S." "Jordan Peele-Produced Nazi Hunting Drama Ordered to Series at Amazon," *Variety*, May 17, 2018.

Between Fantasy and Nightmare: Inventing the Fourth Reich in the Third Reich

1. Georg Bernhard, "Entwurf einer Verfassung für das 'Vierte Reich,' Januar/Februar 1936," in Ursula Langkau-Alex, ed., *Dritter Band: Dokumente zur Geschichte des Ausschusses zur Vorbereitung einer deutschen Volksfront* (Berlin, 2005), p. 26.
2. Barnet Nover, "The End of Adolf Hitler," *The Washington Post*, May 3, 1945, p. 6.
3. Dieter Gunst, "Hitler wollte kein 'Drittes Reich,'" *Geschichte, Politik, und ihre Didaktik*, 17, 1989, 303–04.
4. For a discussion, see Claus-Ekkehard Bärsch, *Die politische Religion des Nationalsozialismus* (Munich, 1998), pp. 46–49; David Redles, "Nazi End Times: The Third Reich as Millennial Reich," in Karolyn Kinane and Michael Ryan, eds., *End of Days: Essays on the Apocalypse from Antiquity to Modernity* (Jefferson, NC, 2009), pp. 173–74.
5. Thomas Flanagan, "The Third Reich: Origins of a Millenarian Symbol," *Journal of European Ideas*, 3, 1987, 285. See also Claudia Schmitz-Berning, *Vokabular des Nationalsozialismus* (Berlin, 1998), p. 156.
6. Nicolas Sollohub, "Forerunners of the Third Reich," *The Contemporary Review*, July 1, 1939, p. 57.
7. Generally, see Jost Hermand, *Old Dreams of a New Reich: Volkish Utopias and National Socialism* (Bloomington, IN, 1992). Exceptions include Johannes Schlaf's novel, *Das dritte Reich* (1899) and Hermann Burte's novel, *Wiltfieber, der ewige Deutsche* (1912). Bärsch, *Die politische Religion des Nationalsozialismus*, pp. 48–49; Flanagan, "The Third Reich," 286–87.
8. Hermand, *Old Dreams of a New Reich*, pp. 49–58.
9. In an essay entitled "Kriegsrede" that was published in the *Altonaer Nachrichten/ Hamburger neueste Nachrichten* on February 4, 1916, Richard Dehmel wrote on of the need for the "third Reich of wholeness, of which the apostles of peace dreamed." See also German writer Ernst Krieck's 1917 book, *Die deutsche Staatsidee*. Redles, "Nazi End Times," 183; Flanagan, "The Third Reich," 287–88.
10. Fritz Stern, *The Politics of Cultural Despair: A Study in the Rise of the Germanic Ideology* (Berkeley, 1961), chapter 14.
11. Ibid., p. 259.
12. Ibid., p. 262.
13. Hermand, *Old Dreams of a New Reich*, p. 83; see also Stern, *The Politics of Cultural Despair*, pp. 253–65.
14. Bärsch, *Die politische Religion des Nationalsozialismus*, pp. 52–91. Bärsch believes that Eckart probably got the phrase from the playwright Henrik Ibsen, who wrote of the Third Reich in his 1873 play, *Emperor and Galilean*. Eckart was familiar with Ibsen's work, having translated his play, *Peer Gynt*. Bärsch, *Die politische Religion des Nationalsozialismus*, p. 55.
15. Bärsch, *Die politische Religion des Nationalsozialismus*, p. 56.
16. Stern, *The Politics of Cultural Despair*, pp. 265, 237; Flanagan, "The Third Reich," 284, 293, 12n; Bärsch, *Die politische Religion des Nationalsozialismus*, pp. 49–57; Redles, "Nazi End Times," 181.
17. "The New Order in Germany," *The Times* (London), November 10, 1928, p. 11. See also Hermand, *Old Dreams of a New Reich*, p. 74.

18. "Das dritte Reich," *Börsen-Halle* (Hamburg), March 21, 1926. "Verbündete Prügelhelden," *Berliner Volkszeitung*, August 18, 1930, p. 1.

19. The *völkisch* writer Hermann Wirth employed the idea of the Third Reich in his utopian blood-and-soil novel, *Aufgang der Menschheit* (1928). Hermand, *Old Dreams of a New Reich*, p. 191. The poet Stefan George was known for calling for a "New Reich" headed by a "Führer." Hermand, *Old Dreams of a New Reich*, pp. 47–48.

20. Bärsch, *Die politische Religion des Nationalsozialismus*, p. 114; Alfred Rosenberg, *The Myth of the Twentieth Century* (Ostara, 2000), p. 318; Hermand, *Old Dreams of a New Reich*, p. 148.

21. Adolf Hitler, *Mein Kampf* (Boston, 1971), p. 437.

22. In 1926, German university students called for the creation of a "Third Reich, the great German Reich of the future." Siegfried Scharfe, "Politische Schulung der Studentenschaft," *Hamburger Nachrichten*, February 26, 1926.

23. Gunst makes this argument in his essay "Hitler wollte kein 'Drittes Reich,'" 303–04.

24. The first appearance of the phrase in the *New York Times* was "Berlin Acts to Curb Extremist Parties," *The New York Times*, July 4, 1930, p. 6. See also "Reich Cabinet Stays," September 17, 1930, p. 1 and "Conquest of Russia One Aim of Hitler," September 29, 1930, p. 11.

25. In 1926, Gregor Strasser called for a "Third Reich of national freedom and social justice!" Cited in Detlef Mühlberger, *Hitler's Voice: The Völkische Beobachter, 1920–1933: Volume II, Nazi Ideology and Propaganda* (Bern, 2004), p. 136. Other examples from 1927 to 1928 are cited in ibid., pp. 271, 339, 354. In *Der Angriff*, the phrase was invoked by Otto Baugert in his story, "Hans Sturms Erwachen," *Der Angriff*, April 16, 1928, whose titular character is described as a "soldier for the Third Reich." Cited in Russell Lemons, *Goebbels and der Angriff* (Lexington, KY, 1994), pp. 93, 153n.

26. Karl Kaufmann invoked the Third Reich in a speech in early 1931. See "Reichsgründungstag in Hamburg und Altona," *Hamburger Nachrichten*, January 19, 1931, p. 5. Wilhelm Kube delivered a talk in Altona entitled "Hitler's Path to the Third Reich," *Hamburger Nachrichten*, February 10, 1932, p. 4; Julius Streicher invoked it in a speech in 1927, Redles, "Nazi End Times," 181.

27. On party members' use of the phrase, see: "Vor dem Strafrichter," *Hamburger Anzeiger*, April 14, 1932; "Schüsse auf Polizeibeamte," *Hamburgischer Correspondent und neue hamburgische Börsen-Halle*, November 16, 1932.

28. See David Redles, *Hitler's Millennial Reich: Apocalyptic Belief and the Search for Salvation* (New York, 2005) for the recollections of ordinary party members, pp. 98–100.

29. "Wen sollst du wählen?" *Hamburger Anzeiger*, August 28, 1930, p. 1.

30. See poster collection at Landesarchiv Baden-Württemberg: Staatsarchiv Freiburg, at www.dhm.de/lemo/bestand/objekt/plakat-spd-193233.html

31. "'Das dritte Reich' vor Gericht," *Börsen-Halle* (Hamburg), March 9, 1931. The same year, a satirical film produced by the Social Democratic Party, entitled *Into the Third Reich,* was banned by Germany's Film Review Office after the Interior Ministry and Foreign Ministry said the film could damage the country's international reputation. "Das Kino als Parteikampfarena," *Hamburger Anzeiger*, January 30, 1931, p. 1.

32. "Luftkampf über dem Berliner Luftgarten," *Hamburger Anzeiger*, April 23, 1932, p. 1.

33. Hitler is quoted using the phrase in the *New York Times* article, "Hitler Would Scrap Versailles Treaty and Use Guillotine," September 26, 1930, p. 1.

34. Alfred Rosenberg, "Der Grundstein zum Dritten Reich," *Der Völkischer Beobachter*, January 31, 1933, pp. 1–2.

35. The concept of the Third Reich also found literary endorsements. See, for example, Wilhelm Höper, *Die drei Reiche: Von der Kaiserkrone zum Hakenkreuz* (Breslau, 1934).

36. Max Domarus, *Hitler: Speeches and Proclamations, 1932–1945, The Chronicle of a Dictatorship* (Wauconda, IL, 1990). After 1933, the Nazis increasingly referred to the Weimar Republic as the "Zwischenreich" (or "in-between Reich"), between the second and third Reichs. Schmitz-Berning, *Vokabular des Nationalsozialismus*, p. 710.

37. Domarus, *Hitler*, pp. 321–22.

38. Ibid., pp. 542, 718.

39. Ibid., p. 863. Hitler further praised German women for having "given the Third Reich their children." Ibid., p. 874.

40. In a speech delivered to the townspeople of Reichenberg in the Sudetenland on December 2, 1938, Hitler declared that "it is necessary to render complete the birth certificate of the Greater German Reich!" Ibid., p. 1259.

41. Schmitz-Berning, *Vokabular des Nationalsozialismus*, pp. 159–60. Christian Zentner and Friedemann Bedürftig, *Das Grosse Lexikon des Dritten Reiches* (Munich, 1985), p. 135.

42. Karl Lorenz, *Methodenlehre und Philosophie des Rechts in Geschichte und Gegenwart* (Berlin, 2010), p. 114.

43. Reinhard Bollmus, *Das Amt Rosenberg und seine Gegner: Studien zum Machtkampf im nationalsozialistischen System* (Munich, 2006), p. 236. See also Schmitz-Berning, *Vokabular des Nationalsozialismus*, pp. 159–60.

44. The phrase still appeared in the years 1939–41 but disappeared thereafter. See, for example, "Das Dritte Reich militärisch unbesiegbar," *Deutsches Nachrichtenbüro*, October 16, 1939, and "Eine Idee hat uns besiegt," *Altonaer Nachrichten*, May 6, 1941. The main search engine of the European Library records 1,825 hits for the phrase "dritte reich" in German language newspapers in the years 1930–39 and only 46 in the years 1940–49.

45. Cornelia Berning, *Vom 'Abstammungsnachweis' zum 'Zuchtwart': Vokabular des Nationalsozialismus* (Berlin, 1964), p. 57.

46. Generally, see Mariano Delgado, Klaus Koch, and Edgar Marsch, eds., *Europa, Tausendjähriges Reich und Neue Welt: Zwei Jahrtausende Geschichte und Utopie in der Rezeption des Danielbuches* (Freiburg, Switzerland, 2003).

47. Jürgen Ebach, *Neue Schrift-Stücke: Biblische Passagen* (Gütersloh, 2012), pp. 35–39.

48. The Byzantines and Russians also claimed the Roman imperial legacy and argued that their empires represented the "Third Rome." Ibid., p. 38.

49. It was at this time that the "four kingdom theory" (*Vier-Reiche-Lehre*) came into being. Franz Brendle, *Das konfessionelle Zeitalter* (Berlin, 2015), p. 12. Luther argued that because Daniel's prophecy could not be wrong in implying that the Holy Roman Empire was the last Reich, it would not fall to the Turkish assault. Wolfgang E. J. Weber, "... oder Daniel würde zum Lügner, das ist nicht möglich: Zur Deutung des Traums des Nebukadnezar im frühneuzeitlichen Reich," in Peer Schmidt and Gregor Weber, eds., *Traum und res publica: Traumkulturen und*

Deutungen sozialer Wirklichkeiten in Europa von Renaissance und Barock (Berlin, 2008), pp. 209–10.

50. Napoleon's dissolution of the Holy Roman Empire in 1806 was a particularly traumatic event that led conservative Germans to anticipate the imminent arrival of the end of days. Stefan Bodo Würffel, "Reichs-Traum und Reichs-Trauma: Danielmotive in deutscher Sicht," in Delgado, et al., eds., *Europa, Tausendjähriges Reich und Neue Welt*, 407–11. See also Klaus Koch, "Europabewusstsein und Danielrezeption zwischen 1648 und 1848," in Delgado, et al., eds., *Europa, Tausendjähriges Reich und Neue Welt*, 326–84.

51. Johannes Friedrich Hoffmann, *Antiochus IV. Epiphanes, König von Syrien: Ein beitrag zur allgemeinen und insbesondere israelitischen Geschichte, mit einem Anhange über Antiochus im Buche Daniel* (Leipzig, 1873), p. 85. For references in the press, see "Gedanken über Daniel, 7. Cap. 19. Vers.," *Grazer Volksblatt*, February 15, 1871. "Atlantis," *Hamburgischer Correspondent und neue hamburgische Börsen-Halle*, March 1, 1922.

52. Kurt van Emsen, *Adolf Hitler und die Kommenden* (Leipzig, 1932).

53. Strünckman supported the German Life Reform, physical culture, and youth movements. Mohler, *Die konservative Revolution in Deutschland*, p. 450. Bernd Wedemeyer-Kolwe, *"Der neue Mensch": Körperkultur im Kaiserreich und in der Weimarer Republik* (Würzburg, 2004), p. 173. Florentine Fritzen, *Gesünder leben: Die Lebensreformbewegung im 20. Jahrhundert* (Stuttgart, 2006), pp. 61–62.

54. Van Emsen, *Adolf Hitler und die Kommenden*, p. 8.

55. Ibid., p. 12.

56. Ibid., pp. 95, 13–14, 99, 133.

57. Ibid., pp. 125–26, 151. Van Emsen argued that the Nazi Party should be "aided to victory." Ibid., p. 100.

58. Ibid., p. 11.

59. Ibid., pp. 99, 21.

60. Ibid., p. 130.

61. Ibid., p. 131.

62. Ibid., p. 43.

63. Ibid., p. 134.

64. Ibid., pp. 102, 138, 118.

65. Ibid., p. 15.

66. Ibid., pp. 102, 138, 118.

67. Kevin Starr, *The Dream Endures: California Enters the 1940s* (New York, 1997), p. 374. This view appeared as early as 1935, in E. J. Passant's review of *After Hitler's Fall* in *International Affairs*, May–June 1935, p. 425, and "A German's Hope for Germany," *The Courier-Journal* (Losuiville, KY), April 7, 1935.

68. Hubertus zu Loewenstein, *After Hitler's Fall: Germany's Coming Reich* (London, 1934), p. xxvi.

69. Ibid., p. 12.

70. Ibid., p. 20.

71. Ibid., pp. 24–27.

72. Ibid., pp. 39, 42.

73. Cited in Walter F. Peterson, *The German Left-Liberal Press in Exile: Georg Bernhard and the Circle of Émigré Journalists around the Pariser Tageblatt-Pariser Tageszeitung, 1933–1940* (Ph.D. Dissertation, State University of New York at Buffalo, 1982), p. 200.

74. Ibid., pp. 219, 178.

75. Ibid., p. 286.

76. Ibid., pp. 367, 294.
77. Georg Bernhard, "Entwurf einer Verfassung für das 'Vierte Reich,' Januar/Februar 1936," in Ursula Langkau-Alex, ed., *Dritter Band: Dokumente zur Geschichte des Ausschusses zur Vorbereitung einer deutschen Volksfront* (Berlin, 2005), pp. 25–33.
78. Ibid., p. 25.
79. Ibid., p. 26.
80. The communist faction rejected the constitution's principles. Milorad M. Drachkovitch and Branko Lazitch, *The Comintern: Historical Highlights, Essays, Recollections, Documents* (Palo Alto, 1966), pp. 131–32.
81. W. F. Peterson, *The German Left-Liberal Press in Exile*, p. 299.
82. Peterson writes that "the majority of those who joined the staff of the *Pariser Tageblatt* were Jewish," while 80 percent of the German refugees in France were Jewish. Ibid., pp. 100, 181.
83. Between 100,000 and 150,000 German-Jewish refugees arrived in the US between 1933 and 1940. Approximately 20,000 of them settled in Washington Heights. Steve Lowenstein, *Frankfurt on the Hudson: The German Jewish Community of Washington Heights, 1933–1983, Its Structure and Culture* (Detroit, 1989), pp. 22, 68.
84. Valerie Popp, *Aber hier war alles anders...: Amerikabilder der deutschsprachigen Exilliteratur nach 1939 in den USA* (Würzburg, 2008), p. 58. Gerhard Jelinek, *Nachrichten aus dem 4. Reich* (Salzburg, 2008), p. 18. Claudia Appelius, "Die schönste Stadt der Welt": Deutsch-jüdische Flüchtlinge in New York *(Essen, 2003), p. 11.*
85. Ernest Stock, "Washington Heights' 'Fourth Reich': The German Émigrés' New Home," *Commentary*, June 1951, pp. 581–88. See "Refugee Jews Living in New York's 'Fourth Reich' Panic-Stricken over Fate of Relatives," *The Wisconsin Jewish Chronicle*, November 18, 1938, p. 1.
86. Another nickname was "Frankfurt on the Hudson." Appelius, *"Die schönste Stadt der Welt,"* p. 11.
87. Hans-Jochen Gamm, *Der Flüsterwitz im Dritten Reich* (Munich, 1963), p. 121.
88. "Hitler's Fall Near, Vladeck Declares," *The New York Times*, October 5, 1935, p. 7.
89. "Eine Klubrevue aus dem Jahre 1956," *Aufbau*, January 6, 1936, p. 10.
90. "Wie wir hören," *Aufbau*, August 1, 1939, p. 7.
91. Charles Shulman, *Europe's Conscience in Decline* (Chicago, 1939), p. 27. See also "Hitler's Ten Plagues," *The Wisconsin Jewish Chronicle*, July 13, 1934.
92. Ben Mordecai, "I Think as I Please," *Jewish Advocate*, March 8, 1940, p. 4.
93. Martin Panzer, "Democracy's Revenge," *The Jewish Exponent*, May 2, 1941, p. 1.
94. By James Donohoe, *Hitler's Conservative Opponents in Bavaria: 1930–1945* (Leiden, Netherlands, 1961), pp. 15, 20–21. Broadly, see Jeffrey Herf, *Reactionary Modernism: Technology, Culture, and Politics in Weimar and the Third Reich* (Cambridge, UK, 1984), especially chapter 2.
95. Otto Strasser, *Hitler and I* (Boston, 1940); Douglas Reed, *Nemesis? The Story of Otto Strasser and the Black Front* (Boston, 1940).
96. Reed, *Nemesis?* p. 28.
97. Ibid., p. 29.
98. Ibid., pp. 225, 223, 228.
99. Ibid., see chapter 11 and postscript. Reed's discussion of Strasser's antisemitism makes it clear that the journalist himself subscribed to a virulent form of Jew-hatred. Reed said "the view is coming now to be more and more widely accepted

... that Jews are an alien community, with a fiercely anti-Gentile religion ... [with] religious laws far more rabid than Hitler's anti-Jewish laws, which are but a pallid inversion of them." Ibid., p. 273.

100. Strasser elaborated upon this vision in numerous essays, pamphlets, and books. But he always stressed the importance of the revised Bamberg platform of the NSDAP from 1925, which took the party in a more left-wing direction, and his subsequent book, published after his break with Hitler in 1930, *The Structure of German Socialism*.

101. Strasser, *Hitler and I*, p. 27.

102. Ibid., pp. 207–08, 215.

103. Ibid., pp. 224, 228, 230.

104. See Hans Bauer, "Ohne Kragen ins Dritte Reich!" *Hamburger Anzeiger*, October 25, 1930, p. 7.

105. "Bausteine für das Vierte Reich gefällig?" *Das Schwarze Korps*, June 19, 1935, p. 16.

106. Ralph Thompson, review of *Nemesis?* June 27, 1940, p. 21; short untitled article about Strasser in *Life*, December 4, 1939. Many other articles made the same connection. *The Montreal Gazette* referred to "Strasser's blue-print for the Fourth Reich." Donald MacDonald, "Strasser's Life and Work," *Montreal Gazette*, October 3, 1941. *Kirkus Reviews* referred to Strasser as a "candidate for leadership of the Fourth Reich": *Kirkus Reviews*, August 21, 1940. See also "Leader of the Fourth Reich," *The Wellington Times* (New Zealand), February 1, 1940, p. 4. *The Christian Science Monitor* reported that Strasser "strives at substituting his 'Fourth Reich' for Hitler's Third Reich": *The Christian Science Monitor*, April 10, 1943, p. WM5. *The New Statesman and Nation* called Strasser the "prophet of the Fourth Reich": "The Strasser Brothers," *New Statesman and Nation*, March 30, 1940, p. 438. See also R. M. W. Kempner, review of *Hitler and I* and *Nemesis?* in *Annals of the American Academy of Political and Science*, March 1941, pp. 223–24.

107. Cited in Yale University's Avalon Project: *Nuremberg Trial Proceedings, Volume IX*. http://avalon.law.yale.edu/subject_menus/imtproc_v9menu.asp

108. "Goering Nipped Hitler–Strasser Plot, Paris Told," *The New York Herald Tribune*, July 6, 1934, p. 1.

109. Shepard Stone, "Why Dr. Rauschning was a Nazi," *The New York Times*, September 14, 1941, p. BR9.

110. Hermann Rauschning, *The Conservative Revolution* (New York, 1941), p. 116. See also "Hope for Future of Europe," *The Advertiser* (Adelaide, Australia), February 14, 1942, p. 12.

111. "Germany Will Try Three for Treason Today; Announcement Made to Decry 'Conspiracy,'" *The New York Times*, January 3, 1939, p. 1.

112. "A Prophet of the Fourth Reich?" *Free Europe*, December 3, 1943, pp. 191–92.

113. "Mystisches Österreich," *Vossische Zeitung*, September 13, 1933, p. 1.

114. "The Habsburgs: Vitriolic Attack in Nazi Newspaper," *Manchester Guardian*, March 2, 1937, p. 14. Goebbels himself was lampooned in Germany as transforming himself into the aristocratic "Count von Goebbels" in a future, noble-dominated "Fourth Reich." See "The Spread of Underground Humor in Germany," *The St. Louis Post-Dispatch*, May 5, 1935, p. 69.

115. See Bernhard Vollmer, *Volksopposition im Polizeistaat: Gestapo- und Regierungsberichte, 1934–1936* (Stuttgart, 1957), p. 259. Manuel Becker and Christoph Studet, *Der Umgang des Dritten Reiches mit den Feinden des Regimes* (Berlin, 2010), p. 68.

116. "Nazi Extremism," *The West Australian* (Perth, Australia), August 10, 1935, p. 19.

117. "Hitler's Weak Spot," *The Chronicle* (Adelaide, Australia), February 8, 1940, p. 47. Relatedly, some articles even predicted a return to power of the Junkers in a Fourth Reich. The hope that Hitler might have to yield to German conservatives was expressed in 1935 when Karl Brandt in *Foreign Affairs* declared that the Night of the Long Knives "might indeed be called the birthday of the Fourth Reich" because it paved the way for a Nazi "retreat in practically every sphere of political life" and set the stage for a Junker restoration. Karl Brandt, "Junkers to the Fore Again," *Foreign Affairs*, October 1, 1935, pp. 129, 134.

118. "Report on Munich Bomb Plot," *Press and Journal* (Aberdeen, Scotland), November 14, 1939, p. 6. Supporting this position was Dorothy Thompson, "The Revolutionary Weapon," *The Daily Boston Globe*, November 17, 1939, p. 20. Several years later, in 1942, *The Boston Globe* opined, "When Hitler perishes with the regime he created, Goering wants to rise triumphantly from the ashes to rule the Fourth Reich": "Goering Planning to Seek Peace with Us through Big Business via France," *The Boston Globe*, August 17, 1942, p. 3. During the war, *The Hartford Courant* speculated that former Reichsbank Director Hjalmar Schacht was "planning [a] Fourth Reich." See "Dr. Schacht Germany's Big Puzzle," *The Hartford Courant*, December 13, 1942, p. B5.

119. See Joachim Scholtyseck, *Robert Bosch und der liberale Widerstand gegen Hitler 1933 bis 1945* (Munich, 1999), pp. 394–96, and p. 670, 571n.

120. Stefan Noethen, "Pläne für das Vierte Reich: Der Widerstandskreis im Kölner Kettelerhaus 1941–1944," *Geschichte in Köln*, 39, 1996, 62–64.

121. *The New York Times* described the future state as "Field Marshal General Erwin von Witzleben's Fourth Reich." "Hitler Has Pledge from Brauchitsch," *The New York Times*, August 20, 1944, p. 14. Hans Peters of the Kreisau Circle referred to Goerdeler in the same terms. Quoted in Agostino von Hassell and Sigrid MacRae, *Alliance of Enemies: The Untold Story of the Secret American and German Collaboration to End World War II* (New York, 2006), p. 197. Ruth Andreas-Friedrich reported that "Goerdeler . . . [is] traveling around the country, distributing posts in the Fourth Reich," p. 141.

122. Gabriel A. Almond, "The German Resistance Movement," *A Current History*, May 1, 1946, p. 419.

123. Hans Bernd Gisevius, *Bis zum bitteren Ende: Vom Reichstagsbrand bis zum 20. Juli 1944*, Volume II (Hamburg, 1959), p. 326.

124. "The weapon of the joke," according to Gamm, "is the last free game (letzte freie Spiel des Individuums) of the individual that the state cannot subject to 'coordination.'" Gamm, *Der Flüsterwitz im Dritten Reich*, p. 173.

125. Klemperer, *I Will Bear Witness: A Diary of the Nazi Years, 1933–1941* (New York, 1998), p. 399. An earlier reference to the joke appeared in the October 1938 issue of *Das wahre Deutschland*, a Catholic Center Party affiliated newspaper. Cited in Günter Buchstab, Brigitte Kaff, and Hans-Otto Kleinmann, eds., *Verfolgung und Widerstand, 1933–1945: Christliche Demokraten gegen Hitler* (Düsseldorf, 1986), p. 109.

126. Ruth Andreas-Friedrich, *Berlin Underground: 1938–1945* (New York, 1947), p. 65.

127. Andreas-Friedrich further recounted how, in the spring of 1944, a Jewish acquaintance requested a new identity card at a government office after a bombing raid and was told by a desk clerk, "We'll check our records later" – a remark that prompted the man's companion to cheerfully think to himself: "Later – in the Fourth Reich." In March of 1945, Andreas-Friedrich learned that governmental authorities had

discovered "a satirical poem about Hitler . . . [in] the Fourth Reich" in the handbag of a Jewish acquaintance. Ibid., pp. 120, 220.

128. Arthur Dix, "'Wirtschaftsfrieden' der Völker," *Hamburger Nachrichten,* December 29, 1934.

129. "Kube in Altona," *Altonaer Nachrichten,* March 5, 1936.

130. "Hitler's Shopkeeper Supporters Now Disillusioned," *Derby Evening Telegraph* (England), January 9, 1940, p. 2.

131. Institut für Zeitgeschichte, ED 474/216. Document: "In Name des Deutschen Volkes in der Strafsache gegen den Studenten der Chemie, Hans-Konrad Leipelt" (1944).

132. "Das Bild der Lage," *Znaimer Tagblatt,* August 26/27, 1944, p. 1. See also "Roosevelts wahre Nachkriegsziele," *Znaimer Tagblatt,* August 4, 1944, p. 2.

133. "Ein vergeblicher Sturmlauf," *Neue Warte am Inn,* July 12, 1944, p. 3.

134. "'Decent End of Nazism is Held Unlikely," *The Hartford Courant,* March 26, 1944, p. C6; "Zapp, Mackensen, and Prince Seized," *The New York Times,* April 16, 1945, p. 14.

135. Michaela Hoenicke Moore, *Know Your Enemy: The American Debate on Nazism, 1933–1945* (Cambridge, UK, 2010).

136. Quoted in "Czech Seizure Shocks German-Americans," *The Winnipeg Tribune,* March 29, 1939, p. 13.

137. "The Fourth Reich," *The New Leader,* April 27, 1940, p. 3. See also "After Hitler," *The New Leader,* May 11, 1940, p. 5.

138. Heinrich Mann, "Outlook on the Fourth Reich," in Will Schaber, ed., *Thinker versus Junker* (New York, 1941), p. 272. Harry Levin, *Memories of the Moderns* (New York, 1982), p. 71.

139. "Goethe in Hollywood," *The New Yorker,* December 20, 1941, p. 22.

140. See R. D. Charques, "German Socialist Plea," *Times Literary Supplement,* December 4, 1943.

141. R. G. Waldeck, *Meet Mr. Blank: The Leader of Tomorrow's Germans* (New York, 1943), pp. 173, 171, 162.

142. Dorothy Thompson, "After Hitler, What?" *The Boston Globe,* March 13, 1939, p. 12.

143. Wallace Deuel, "The 'Other' Germany," *The New York Times,* January 30, 1944, p. BR4.

144. Christof Mauch and Jeremiah Riemer, *The Shadow War against Hitler: The Covert Operations of America's Wartime Secret Intelligence Service* (New York, 2002), pp. 151, 160–61.

145. Curt Riess, *The Nazis Go Underground* (New York, 1944), pp. 185, 82. Riess also published op-eds on the topic, including "The Nazis Dig in for World War III," *The New York Times,* August 6, 1944, p. SM9, and "The Fourth Reich Casts a Shadow," *Esquire,* February 1944, pp. 49, 131–32.

146. Riess, *The Nazis Go Underground,* pp. 7, 96, 142.

147. Ibid., pp. 185–86.

148. Ibid., pp. 43, 91–92, 189.

149. Gordon Young, "Mein Zweiter Kampf," reprinted in *The Sunday Times* (Perth, Australia), August 8, 1944.

150. Vincent Church, "Danger," *Daily Mail* (London), June 29, 1944, p. 2.

151. Maxwell Macartney and J. H. Freeman, *Times Literary Supplement,* October 21, 1944, p. 506.

152. Barnet Nover, "How Shall Germany Be Dealt with?" *The Washington Post,* September 26, 1944, p. 6. In April of 1945, the State Department provided official

confirmation of this suspicion in announcing that "German leaders were planning for conquest of the world through a third world war" by "exporting capital and sending highly skilled German technicians to areas of safety so that they could be used another day by Germany." "Assert Nazis Map New War in Detail," *The New York Times*, April 8, 1945, p. 19.

153. Jürgen Heideking and Christof Mauch, *American Intelligence and the German Resistance to Hitler* (Boulder, CO, 1996), p. 9. See also appendix for Deuel Memorandum to Donovan, p. 250.

154. Robert Vansittart, "How Hitler Made the Grade," *The Shepparton Advertiser* (Australia), February 2, 1945, p. 6.

155. Lessner, *Phantom Victory*, p. 78.

156. Ibid., p. 128.

157. Ibid., p. 149.

158. Ibid., p. 166.

159. Ibid., p. 181.

160. Ibid., pp. 177, 193.

161. Ibid., p. 227.

162. See the back book-jacket of *Phantom Victory*.

163. Ibid., p. 227.

164. Charles Rolo, "A Preview of Chaos," *The New York Times*, November 12, 1944, p. BR30. Bernard De Voto, review of *Phantom Victory*, *The New York Herald Tribune*, October 10, 1944, p. 19. Rolo added that Lessner's "damning indictment" of the Germans enjoyed extra credibility because he "fought on Germany's side in the First World War."

165. E. S. P., "Nazis after the War," *The Christian Science Monitor*, October 28, 1944, p. 18; Herbert Kupferberg, review of *Phantom Victory*, *The New York Herald Tribune*, October 15, 1944, p. E8.

166. T. E. M., "Fourth Reich Grim Warning," *The Hartford Courant*, November 5, 1944, p. SM13; *The Washington Post* noted that *Phantom Victory* had "a greater impact than any other book ... to date [about] the dangers [of] ... a 'soft peace.'"

167. "Phantom Victory," *Life Magazine*, May 14, 1945. The profile featured eight paintings by the Russian-born American artist Vera Bock, depicting various scenes from the novel accompanied by descriptive captions. Based on the favorable letters to the editor from ordinary readers, *Life*'s profile struck a nerve in its audience. "Letters to the Editor," *Life Magazine*, June 4, 1945, p. 7.

From Werewolves to Democrats: The Fourth Reich under Allied Occupation

1. Alfred Werner, "The Junker Plot to Kill Hitler: The Dying Gesture of a Class," *Commentary*, January 1, 1947, p. 42.

2. Lynn W. Landrum, "Price of Peace," *The Dallas Morning News*, June 27, 1947.

3. See Hans Dieter Schlosser, *"Es wird zwei Deutschlands geben": Zeitgeschichte und Sprache in Nachkriegsdeutschland 1945–1949* (Frankfurt, 2005), pp. 26–30.

4. "Reich Will Be Years under Allied Control," *The Examiner* (Launceston, Tasmania), May 10, 1945, p. 1. See also "Fourth Reich Will Be a Smaller, Quieter Place," *The Stars and Stripes*, May 8, 1945, p. 2.

5. "British and U.S. Take Over in Berlin To-Day," *Courier and Advertiser* (Dundee, Scotland), July 12, 1945, p. 3.

6. "Fourth Reich," *Time*, September 10, 1945, p. 40.

7. "The Fourth Reich," *The Palestine Post*, July 20, 1945, p. 4; Joachim Josten, "Germany's Capital," *The Washington Post*, February 21, 1947, p. 9.

8. "A Plan for Germany," *The Courier-Mail* (Brisbane, Australia), September 9, 1946, p. 2.

9. Drew Middleton, "Big 4 Have Four Plans for Remaking Germany," *The New York Times*, March 23, 1947, p. E4.

10. "At Last, Victory," *The Cleveland Plain-Dealer*, May 8, 1945, p. 8. See also Jay Franklin, "We the People," *The Cleveland Plain-Dealer*, May 11, 1945, p. 24.

11. "The Problem of Germany," *The New York Times*, May 21, 1945, p. 18.

12. Anthony Eden, "Issues Empire Statesmen Must Face," *The Sydney Morning Herald*, March 20, 1946, p. 2.

13. Sefton Delmer, "There's a Revolution Going on in Europe," *The News* (Adelaide), March 25, 1946, p. 2.

14. "United Europe Envisaged," *The New York Times*, June 1, 1946, p. 11.

15. Erich Koch-Weser, *Hitler and Beyond: A German Testament* (New York, 1945), p. 187.

16. "Bodies of German Leaders Cremated," *The Irish Times*, October 18, 1946, p. 1.

17. "Nazi Hangings to be Filmed," *The Sunday Times* (Perth, Australia), October 13, 1946, p. 2; "Still Doodling," *The Glasgow Herald*, October 14, 1946, p. 4. "Hess Assumes Goering's Role," *The Trenton Evening Times*, October 21, 1946, p. 1.

18. Friedrich Gaupp, *Deutsche Fälschung der abendländischen Reichsidee* (Berne, 1946).

19. Ibid., p. 8.

20. Ibid., p. 10.

21. Ibid., p. 10.

22. Ibid., pp. 32–33, 73.

23. Ibid., p. 11.

24. Ibid., pp. 85–86.

25. Ibid., p. 13.

26. Ibid., p. 11.

27. Ibid., p. 13.

28. Ibid., p. 13.

29. Ibid., p. 9.

30. Ibid., p. 14.

31. Ibid., p. 90.

32. Ibid., p. 9.

33. Dolf Sternberger, *Dreizehn politische Radio Reden* (Heidelberg, 1947), p. 9.

34. Ibid., p. 9.

35. Ibid., p. 9.

36. Ibid., pp. 10, 12.

37. Ibid., p. 13.

38. Ibid., pp. 17–18.

39. Drew Middleton, "Germans Return to Nationalism," *The New York Times*, February 25, 1946, p. 3. C. L. Sulzberger, "Educators Stress Needs in Germany," *The New York Times,* April 1, 1946, p. 5.

40. "Anti-Ally Slogans Spread in U.S. Zone of Germany," *The New York Times*, May 19, 1947, p. 14. Sudeten German expellees shared the view that the Fifth Reich would be better than the Fourth. See "Czechoslovakia Recovering Fast," *St. Louis Post-Dispatch,* May 5, 1946.

41. "What Is Germany Thinking?" *Le Courrier Australien*, November 28, 1947, pp. 1, 3.

42. Perry Biddiscombe, *Werwolf!: The History of the National Socialist Guerrilla Movement, 1944–1946* (Toronto, 1998). Perry Biddiscombe, *The Last Nazis: Werewolf Guerilla Resistance in Europe, 1944–1947* (Stroud, UK, 2006).

43. Biddiscombe describes the movement's failure, but points out that it was more significant than acknowledged by previous scholars. See also Gerhard Rempel, *Hitler's Children: The Hitler Youth and the SS* (Chapel Hill, NC, 1990), which acknowledges the fanaticism of the Werewolves' often very young members (pp. 244–50). More definitive in asserting the Werewolves' failure is Volker Koop's book, *Himmlers letztes Aufgebot* (Cologne, 2008), which argues that the movement never had any popular support (pp. 119, 244). See also Christina von Hodenberg, "Of German Fräuleins, Nazi Werewolves, and Iraqi Insurgents: The American Fascination with Hitler's Last Foray," *Central European History*, 41, 2008, pp. 75, 81; Tauber, *Beyond Eagle and Swastika*, p. 23; Rodney G. Minott, *The Fortress That Never Was: The Myth of Hitler's Bavarian Stronghold* (New York, 1964); Frederick Taylor, *Exorcising Hitler: The Occupation and Denazification of Germany* (New York, 2011), chapter 2; Antony Beevor, *The Fall of Berlin 1945* (New York, 2002), p. 175; Stephen Fritz, *Endkampf: Soldiers, Civilians, and the Death of the Third Reich* (Lexington, KY, 2004), pp. 221–22.

44. Biddiscombe, *The Last Nazis*, p. 10; Biddiscombe, *Werwolf!*, p. 7; Koop, *Himmlers letztes Aufgebot*, p. 265. Biddiscombe was also influenced by "everyday history" (*Alltagsgeschichte*) to show how persisting resistance against the Allies challenges the myth of German passivity in defeat. Biddiscombe, *Werwolf!*, p. 3.

45. Biddiscombe discusses this phenomenon in "Donald and Me: The Iraq War and the 'Werwolf' Analogy," *International Journal*, summer, 2004, 669–80. See also David B. MacDonald, *Thinking History, Fighting Evil: Neoconservatives and the Perils of Analogy in American Politics* (Lanham, MD, 2009), pp. 138–44.

46. Colin Fernandez, "Killer Sausages: How the Nazis Plotted to Fight Back after Losing the War," *Daily Mail* (London), April 4, 2011. Duncan Gardham, "MI5 files: Nazis Plotted to Kill Allied Troops with Coffee," *Telegraph*, April 4, 2011.

47. Biddiscombe, *The Last Nazis*, p. 23.

48. Koop, *Himmlers letztes Aufgebot*, pp. 72, 172, 183.

49. Ibid., pp. 47–48; Biddiscombe, *The Last Nazis*, pp. 40, 48.

50. Koop, *Himmlers letztes Aufgebot*, p. 41.

51. Ibid., p. 54, Biddiscombe, *The Last Nazis*, pp. 11–16. Fritz, *Endkampf*, pp. 195–96.

52. Koop, *Himmlers letztes Aufgebot*, p. 55.

53. Biddiscombe, *The Last Nazis*, pp. 13–15.

54. Koop, *Himmlers letztes Aufgebot*, pp. 188–89.

55. See, for example, the headline of the newspaper *Front und Heimat* from April 1945, "Werwolf, Attack!" www.dhm.de/lemo/kapitel/zweiter-weltkrieg/kriegsverlauf/werwolf; Koop, *Himmlers letztes Aufgebot*, pp. 107–08.

56. Biddiscombe, *The Last Nazis*, pp. 63–87.

57. Biddiscombe says that nearly fifty American soldiers were killed. Biddiscombe, "Donald and Me," 672.

58. Koop, *Himmlers letztes Aufgebot*, p. 159.

59. Biddiscombe in *The Last Nazis* mentions the case of the mayor of Kirchlegen: *The Last Nazis*, p. 135.

60. Ibid., p. 172.

61. Ibid., p. 8. Biddiscombe estimates between "3,000–5,500 dead." Ibid., p. 276.

62. The first reports about Werewolves include: "Nazi Force for Last Stand," *The Times* (London), October 20, 1944, p. 4; "Nazis Plan Underground Fight," *The*

Sydney Morning Herald, August 29, 1944, p. 2; "Nazis Preparing to 'Go Underground' When Germany is Occupied," *Townsville Daily Bulletin* (Queensland, Australia), February 10, 1945, p. 3.

63. "Hitler Orders Party Men to Quit State Jobs," *The Chicago Daily Tribune*, April 8, 1945, p. 2.
64. Koop, *Himmlers letztes Aufgebot*, pp. 62, 77; "Near the End," *The New York Times*, April 29, 1945, p. E1. "Battle of Germany," *The New York Times*, April 8, 1945, p. 52; "Spreading German Disaster," *The New York Times*, April 9, 1945, p. 18.
65. Harlowe Hoyt, "Germany's Werewolves Follow Same Old Pattern," *The Cleveland Plain-Dealer*, April 24, 1945, p. 6.
66. "Clear-Cut Reich Surrender Is Doubted by Eisenhower," *The New York Times*, April 6, 1945, p. 1.
67. Dwight D. Eisenhower, *Crusade in Europe* (Baltimore, 1997), p. 397.
68. "Werewolves," *The Washington Post*, April 5, 1945, p. 6; "Himmler Warns of 'Werewolves' War on Victors," *The Los Angeles Times*, April 7, 1945, p. 4; "Current Events," *Evening Telegraph and Post* (England), April 3, 1945, p. 2.
69. "Hitler's Last Failure," *The New York Times*, April 10, 1945, "Reich Army Rebels," *The New York Times*, April 29, 1945, p. 1.
70. "Nazi Werewolves Fail to Terrify Any But Germans," *Springfield Daily Republican*, April 10, 1945, p. 13. "First of 'Werewolves' Prove to Be Boys of 15," *The Sunday Oregonian*, April 18, 1945, p. 2.
71. "Goebbels Berlin's Pet 'Hate': Germans Jeer His 'Werewolf,'" *The Atlanta Constitution*, April 11, 1945, p. 1.
72. "Werewolves Can't Huff," *Sunday Mail* (Brisbane, Australia), April 8, 1945, p. 1.
73. "Murders Blamed on 'Werewolves,'" *The Baltimore Sun*, April 3, 1945, p. 1.
74. Drew Middleton, "Nazi Die-Hards Man Their 'National Redoubt,'" *The New York Times*, April 8, 1945, p. 54.
75. Wes Gallagher, "Nazi Werewolf Effect Called 'Flop' Thus Far," *The Los Angeles Times*, April 10, 1945, p. 2.
76. "First of 'Werewolves' Prove to Be Boys of 15," *The Sunday Oregonian*, April 18, 1945, p. 2.
77. Biddiscombe, *The Last Nazis*, p. 56.
78. Koop, *Himmlers letztes Aufgebot*, p. 248.
79. Ibid., p. 76.
80. Letter from US Ambassador to France (Caffery) to Secretary of State, May 1, 1945, in *Foreign Relations of the United States, Diplomatic Papers, 1945: European Advisory Commission, Austria, Germany*, Volume III (Washington, DC, 1945), p. 938.
81. Memorandum from Brewster Morris, July 16, 1945, in ibid., p. 952.
82. Telegram from the Minister in Sweden (Johnson) to Secretary of State, April 11, 1945, in ibid., pp. 753–54.
83. Biddiscombe, *The Last Nazis*, p. 173.
84. "Werewolves Busy in British Zone," *Courier and Advertiser* (Dundee, Scotland), July 7, 1945, p. 3. Biddiscombe, *The Last Nazis*, p. 204. Koop, *Himmlers letztes Aufgebot*, pp. 180–82. On the killings of Czech policemen and German antifascists, see Petr Blahus, "Werwölfe 1945," *Reflex*, 17, April 22, 2004. www.zukunft-braucht-erinnerung.de/werwoelfe-1945
85. "In the Bavarian Redoubt," *The Times* (London), May 28, 1945, p. 3. "14 Youths Boast 'Werewolf' Ties," *The Alexandria Times-Picayune* (Alexandria, Indiana), July

13, 1945, p. 3. "'Werewolves' Arrested," *Daily Mail* (Hull, UK), August 20, 1946, p. 4; "Nazi-Geheimorganisation in Trutnow," *Berliner Zeitung*, October 6, 1945, p. 3.

86. "Nazi Underground Is at Work – With Rumors," *The News* (Adelaide, Australia), September 20, 1945, p. 2; "Sinister Nazi Movement Uncovered by Allies," *The Mercury* (Hobart, Tasmania), July 17, 1945, p. 2.

87. *Prevent World War III*, October 1945. Calls for vigilance persisted into the spring of 1946. See also "British Expect Trouble in Germany," *Daily Mail* (Hull, UK), March 11, 1946.

88. Koop, *Himmlers letztes Aufgebot*, p. 244.

89. Ibid., p. 7.

90. Ibid., p. 30.

91. Ibid., pp. 89-90.

92. Ibid., p. 119.

93. Biddiscombe, *Werwolf!*, p. 277.

94. Koop says the Werewolves mostly killed fellow Germans instead of Allied troops. Koop, *Himmlers letztes Aufgebot*, p. 61.

95. Similarly, David Donald has speculated that Confederate soldiers could have easily fought a prolonged underground resistance campaign against Northern occupation forces after 1865, but chose not to. David Donald, *Liberty and Union* (Boston, 1978), pp. 173–75.

96. Koop, *Himmlers letztes Aufgebot*, p. 244.

97. Biddiscombe, *The Last Nazis*, p. 8.

98. Koop, *Himmlers letztes Aufgebot*, pp. 17, 81; Biddiscombe, *The Last Nazis*, p. 201.

99. Koop, *Himmlers letztes Aufgebot*, pp. 208–25. Biddiscombe, *Werwolf!*, pp. 268–70. Biddiscombe, *The Last Nazis*, pp. 248–50.

100. British General Bernard Montgomery observed that "Germans . . . were willing to carry out whatever orders were issued to them [by the Allies after 1945], their chief fear being that they might be handed over to the Russians." David MacDonald, *Thinking History, Fighting Evil*, p. 144.

101. For a comparison of the American occupations of Germany and Iraq, see Thomas W. Maulucci, Jr., "Comparing the American Occupations of Germany and Iraq," *Yale Journal of International Affairs*, winter, 2008, pp. 120–28.

102. Another key factor was Iraqi society's ethno-religious heterogeneity and resulting sectarianism – both of which were not factors in Germany's occupation after 1945. MacDonald, *Thinking History, Fighting Evil*, p. 143.

103. Norman Davies, *Rising '44: The Battle for Warsaw* (New York, 2004), p. 417.

104. John Lewis Gaddis, *The Cold War: A New History* (New York, 2005), p. 14.

105. Michael Bess, *Choices under Fire: Moral Dimensions of World War II* (New York, 2008), p. 172.

106. The Soviets also could have taken Germany by themselves if Winston Churchill had won support for his original plan in 1942 to open up a second front against the Nazis by attacking the "soft underbelly" of the Balkans instead of invading Normandy. This plan was partly motivated by Churchill's desire to keep Stalin from imposing communist control over southeastern Europe, but it was opposed by Roosevelt and Eisenhower and rejected at the Casablanca conference in January 1943. See Dwight D. Eisenhower, *Crusade in Europe* (Baltimore, 1997), pp. 281–84. Had the decision gone the other way (enabled, say, by FDR dying earlier and being replaced by a more pliant Harry S. Truman), the western Allies might have seized the Balkans, thereby keeping them from falling under Soviet control, but at

the price of enabling the Red Army to capture Germany all the way to the Rhine. See Gerhard Weinberg, "Who Won World War II and How?" in Walter L. Hixson, ed., *The American Experience in World War II*, Volume XII (New York, 2003), pp. 7–8.

107. Jacques Pauwels, *The Myth of the Good War: America in the Second World War* (Toronto, 2002), pp. 104, 88. Churchill scotched this plan after the disastrous assault on Dieppe, known as Operation Jubilee, in August of 1942.

108. Caleb Carr, "VE Day – November 11, 1944," in Robert Cowley, ed., *What If? 2: Eminent Historians Imagine What Might Have Been* (New York, 2001), pp. 333–43.

109. www.bbc.co.uk/history/worldwars/wwtwo/battle_arnhem_01.shtml

110. Biddiscombe, *The Last Nazis*, p. 252.

111. www.dhm.de/lemo/biografie/arthur-axmann

112. Biddiscombe, *Werwolf!*, p. 77.

113. Koop, *Himmlers letzte Aufgebot*, p. 252.

114. "Operation Nursery," March 16, 1946. Folder "3rd Army G-2 Operation Nursery 380.4, Third United States Army, G-2 Section, Decimal Files 1944–1947, RG 338, NA."

115. Ibid.

116. Scott Selby, *The Axmann Conspiracy: The Nazi Plan for a Fourth Reich and How the U.S. Army Defeated It* (New York, 2012), p. 150.

117. Ibid., pp. 151, 219. "Attempt to Revive Nazism Crushed," *The Times* (London), April 1, 1946, p. 3.

118. Selby, *The Axmann Conspiracy*, p. 219.

119. Koop, *Himmlers letzte Aufgebot*, p. 253.

120. The rift was between Heidemann in the south and Willi Lohel and Kurt Budaeus in north Germany. The latter were more inclined than the former to use violence against the Allies and wanted to merge groups. Selby, *The Axmann Conspiracy*, pp. 180, 190–91.

121. "Operation Nursery," March 16, 1946.

122. "200 Towns Raided in Hunt for Nazis," *The New York Times*, April 1, 1946, p. 5; "Nazis Battle Allied Troops," *Detroit Free Press*, March 31, 1946; "Raids Smash Plot to Re-Nazify Germany," *The Cincinnati Enquirer*, March 31, 1946, p. 1.

123. "Underground Raid Holds 183 Germans," *The New York Times*, April 2, 1946, p. 2.

124. Cited in "Underground Nazi Movement Smashed," *The Canberra Times* (Australia), April 1, 1946, p. 1. See also "Yanks Smash Nazi Plot," *The Boston Globe*, March 31, 1946, p. D1.

125. "Stateside Editorials Point Up the Lesson of 'Operation Nursery,'" *Weekly Information Bulletin*, May 1946, pp. 21–22. See also "Repeat Performance?" *The Boston Globe*, April 1, 1946, p. 10.

126. "Nazis Are Still Fighting Like Cornered Dingoes," *The World's News* (Sydney), May 4, 1946, p. 3.

127. "Patrioten?" *Passauer Neue Presse*, April 2, 1946, p. 1; "How Could It Happen?" *Weekly Information Bulletin*, April 1946, p. 15.

128. "Hoegner und die Reaktion," *Neue Zeit*, April 24, 1946, p. 1.

129. The conspiracy finds no mention in important studies such as: James F. Tent, *Mission on the Rhine: Reeducation and Denazification in American-Occupied Germany* (Chicago, 1982); John Gimbel, *The American Occupation of Germany: Politics and the Military, 1945–1949* (Palo Alto, 1968); Edward Peterson, *The American Occupation of Germany: Retreat to Victory* (Detroit,

1977); Earl Frederick Ziemke, *The U.S. Army in the Occupation of Germany: 1944–1946* (Washington, DC, 1975); Eugene Davidson, *The Death and Life of Germany* (New York, 1959); Zink, *The United States in Germany*; Terence Prittie, *Germany Divided: The Legacy of the Nazi Era* (New York, 1960).

130. "Artur Axmann, 83, a Top Nazi Who Headed the Hitler Youth," *The New York Times*, November 7, 1996, p. D27. "Obituary: Artur Axmann: In the Bunker with Hitler," *Guardian*, November 6, 1996, p. 15; "Hitler treu bis zur letzten Minute," *TAZ*, November 4, 1996.

131. Selby, *The Axmann Conspiracy*; for a much briefer mention, see Fritz, *Endkampf*, p. 219.

132. This prediction from the *Guardian* is cited in *Weekly Information Bulletin*, September 1945, p. 24.

133. In the British zone, there was a shortfall of 600,000 tons of grain. F. Taylor, *Exorcising Hitler*, p. 205. Davidson, *The Death and Life of Germany*, p. 135.

134. "British to Quell Hamburg Rioting," *The New York Times*, March 24, 1946, p. 11. "Shots Deter Mob in Hamburg Riot," *The New York Times*, March 22, 1946, p. 4.

135. Zink, *The United States in Germany*, pp. 298–300.

136. "Nazis Charged with Making Human Sausages," *The Daily Advertiser* (New South Wales, Australia), December 5, 1946, p. 1. "Policemen Went into Sausages," *The Scone Advocate* (New South Wales, Australia), December 6, 1948, p. 2. A total of thirty-one persons belonging to the group of "Nazi cannibals" were arrested, all of whom belonged to a larger "Nazi underground movement."

137. "Nazi Revival Fails," *The New York Times*, April 1, 1946, p. 20.

138. Alan Barth, "Rule or Ruin in Germany," *The New Republic*, June 24, 1946, p. 897.

139. "Nazism Scotched – Not Killed," *The Sydney Morning Herald*, April 2, 1946, p. 2.

140. Ibid., p. 2.

141. See, for example, "End of the German Era," *Courier and Advertiser* (Dundee, Scotland), April 5, 1945, p. 2. Tania Long, "They Long for a New Fuehrer," *The New York Times*, December 9, 1945, p. 89. "Reich Girls Want Return of Nazism," *The New York Times*, October 22, 1945, p. 3.

142. "Nazi Virus Thrives in American Zone," *The New York Times*, April 22, 1946, p. 1.

143. "The Shape of Things," *The Nation*, May 4, 1946, p. 521.

144. "New Bomb Hurled in Stuttgart Area," *The New York Times*, October 29, 1946, p. 12; "55 Germans Taken in Stuttgart Raids," *The New York Times*, October 22, 1946, p. 8.

145. "Rumblings in Germany," *The Boston Globe*, October 23, 1946, p. 16.

146. "Schacht Trial Bomb Target," *The Trenton Evening Times*, October 21, 1946, p. 1. "Bombs at Nazi Record Rooms," *Press and Journal* (Aberdeen, Scotland), October 21, 1946, p. 1. "3 Bombs Set Off in Germany," *The Wilkes Barre Record*, October 21, 1946.

147. "Bomben auf Spruchkammern," *Der Spiegel*, January 11, 1947, p. 5.

148. "More Bombings Are Expected in Germany," *The Hope Star* (Arkansas), October 21, 1946, p. 2.

149. Fritz, *Endkampf*, p. 220; "Bomb Exploded in Denazification Court," *Dunkirk Evening Observer*, January 8, 1947, p. 4.

150. Biddiscombe, *The Last Nazis*, p. 214; "Öhringen," *Neues Deutschland*, March 26, 1947, p. 1; "Anti-Nazi in Stuttgart Shot by 2 Gunmen," *Santa Cruz Sentinel*, March 23, 1947, p. 1.

151. "75,000 at Stuttgart Strike in Protest against Bombings," *The Boston Globe*, October 23, 1946, p. 6.

152. Arthur D. Kahn, *Experiment in Occupation: Witness to the Turnabout: Anti-Nazi War to Cold War, 1944–1946* (University Park, PA, 2004), p. 179.

153. "Bombenattentat in Nürnberg," *Neues Deutschland*, January 9, 1947, p. 1.

154. Zitzmann later became a member of the Socialist Reich Party (SRP). Rempel, *Hitler's Children*, p. 251.

155. "Bomben auf Spruchkammern," *Der Spiegel*, January 11, 1947, p. 5. "He Planned to Succeed Hitler," *Press and Journal* (Aberdeen, Scotland), January 16, 1947, p. 1. "Wahnwitziges Komplott," *Berliner Zeitung*, January 15, 1947, p. 2.

156. "Kabus-Geschwister Scholl," *Passauer Neue Presse*, February 28, 1947, p. 3.

157. "'Fourth Reich' Boss Due to Be Hanged," *The Alexandria Times-Picayune* (Alexandria, Indiana), February 21, 1946, p. 3. See also "U.S. Swoop on Nazis," *Courier Advertiser* (Dundee, Scotland), November 21, 1946, p. 2.

158. See Perry Biddiscombe, "Operation Selection Board: The Growth and Suppression of the Neo-Nazi 'Deutsche Revolution' 1945–47," *Intelligence and National Security*, 1, 1996, 59–77.

159. Tom Bower, *Klaus Barbie: The "Butcher of Lyons"* (New York, 1984), p. 124.

160. Biddiscombe, "Operation Selection Board," 61. "Right-Wing Movements Curtailed by Operation Selection Board," July 15, 1947, p. 6. Operation Selection Board File. 114. NA.

161. Biddiscombe, "Operation Selection Board," 65.

162. "Right-Wing Movements Curtailed by Operation Selection Board," July 15, 1947, pp. 2, 10. Operation Selection Board File. 114. NA.

163. "Round-Up Thwarts Budding Nazi Plot for War on Soviet," *The New York Times*, February 24, 1947, p. 1.

164. Biddiscombe, "Operation Selection Board," 66–67.

165. Ibid., pp. 69–70. See "The Comeback of the Nazis," *The Boston Globe*, January 28, 1947, p. 14.

166. Biddiscombe, "Operation Selection Board," pp. 70–71.

167. A total of 89 persons were arrested in the British zone and 44 in the American zone, for a total of 133. "Appendix B: Summary of Arrests and Disposal," no date, Operation Selection Board File. 114. NA.

168. Guy Walters, *Hunting Evil: The Nazi War Criminals Who Escaped and the Quest to Bring Them to Justice* (New York, 2010), pp. 210–14.

169. "Sudden Swoop by Allies Smashes Nazi Plot," *Press and Journal* (Aberdeen, Scotland), February 24, 1947, p. 1.

170. "Blow at Nazi Coup Ends," *The New York Times*, February 26, 1947; "The Nazi Underground," *The New York Times*, February 24, 1947. "Biggest Nazi Round-Up Made Since Hitler Died," *The Telegraph* (Brisbane, Australia), February 24, 1947.

171. "Nazi Plan to Use Disease Germs as World Plot," *The Canberra Times* (Australia), March 3, 1947, p. 1.

172. "Round-Up Thwarts Budding Nazi Plot for War on Soviet," *The New York Times*, February 24, 1947, p. 1, "Allies Crack Germ-War Plot," *The Democrat and Chronicle* (Rochester, NY), February 24, 1947, p. 1. While Rosenberg and Eisman had bacteriological experience, they were not part of the Deutsche Revolution and were simply arrested as part of the larger sweep. Biddiscombe, "Operation Selection Board," p. 76, 16n.

173. "Biggest Nazi Round-Up Made Since Hitler Died," *The Telegraph* (Brisbane, Australia), February 24, 1947; "Nazi Germ Threat To Britain," *The Courier-Mail* (Brisbane, Australia), February 25, 1947, p. 1.

174. "High Nazis Held in Germ Warfare Plot," *The Boston Globe*, February 24, 1947, p. 1; see also "Leaders in Nazi Plot Arrested, Army Says," *The Stars and Stripes*, February 25, 1947, p. 1.

175. See "Bazillen," *Der Spiegel*, March 1, 1947, p. 2.

176. "Memorandum for the Officer in Charge," Frank J. Buttenhoff, March 17, 1947. Document entitled "Subject: Operation Selection Board," signed by John R. Himmelright, March 13, 1947. Operation Selection Board File. 114. NA. CIC officials were surprised by the indifferent German reaction to the conspiracy's existence and believed it reflected their preoccupation with the "current fuel and food crisis." Officials speculated that "had this operation taken place during the summer months, when people have fewer domestic worries, it probably would have roused greater reaction." "Memorandum for the Officer in Charge," signed by Edwin Eich, March 13, 1947. Operation Selection Board File. 114. NA.

177. "Naziverschwörer," *Tribüne*, February 25, 1947. Operation Selection Board File.

178. "Die Grossen hängen," *Neues Deutschland*, February 25, 1947, p. 2. See also "Späte Erkenntnis," *Neues Deutschland*, February 6, 1947, p. 2, and "Ein ernstes Alarmsignal," *Tägliche Rundschau*, February 26, 1947.

179. This holds true for all the studies mentioned in note 130. An exception is Stephen Fritz's *Endkampf*, which alludes to Operation Selection Board, but does not mention it by name; ibid., pp. 220–21. Most of the attention has appeared in the journalistic literature on Klaus Barbie. See Magnus Linklater, Isabel Hilton, and Neal Ascherson, *The Nazi Legacy: Klaus Barbie and the International Fascist Connection* (New York, 1985), p. 143. Brendan Murphy, *The Butcher of Lyon: The Story of Infamous Nazi Klaus Barbie* (New York, 1983), pp. 225–27. Bower, *Klaus Barbie*, pp. 128–29. Stephen Dorril, *MI6: Inside the Covert World of Her Majesty's Secret Intelligence Service* (New York, 2000), p. 109. Wellington Long, *The New Nazis of Germany* (Philadelphia, 1968), p. 41.

180. "Right-Wing Movements Curtailed by Operation Selection Board," July 15, 1947. "High Nazis Held in German Warfare Plot," *The Boston Globe*, February 24, 1947, p. 1.

181. "Razzia gegen Nazis," *Kasseler Zeitung*, February 24, 1947.

182. "Biggest Nazi Round-Up Made Since Hitler Died," *The Telegraph* (Brisbane, Australia), February 24, 1947, p. 1.

183. Biddiscombe, "Operation Selection Board," 74.

184. Allan A. Ryan, Jr., *Klaus Barbie and the United States Government: A Report to the Attorney General of the United States* (Washington, DC, August 1983), pp. 35–37, 60. By April of 1947, CIC agent Robert S. Taylor had enlisted Barbie to conduct intelligence work against the French and Soviets. He was arrested in December of 1947, but only to be interrogated about the activities of fellow SS men; ibid., p. 39. Barbie later went to Bolivia and maintained close ties with other ex-Nazis. Murphy, *The Butcher of Lyon*, pp. 293, 270, 276.

185. Murphy, *The Butcher of Lyon*, p. 228.

186. Erhard Dabringhaus, *Klaus Barbie: The Shocking Story of How the U.S. Used This Nazi War Criminal as an Intelligence Agent. A First-Hand Account* (Washington, DC, 1984), p. 132.

187. Dorril, *MI6*, p. 110.

188. As Biddiscombe concludes: "it was . . . fortunate that the occupying powers were on hand to guide Germany through its transitional period," for they "successfully

laid the groundwork for a democratic Germany" by helping to "suffocate the remains of . . . [the] the National Socialist movement." Biddiscombe, "Operation Selection Board," 75.

189. "The Nazi Underground," *The New York Times*, February 24, 1947, p. 18.

190. Hugh R. Trevor-Roper, "The Danger of a Neo-Nazism," *The New York Times*, July 27, 1947.

191. See also Delbert Clark, "Economic Crisis First in the German Picture," *The New York Times*, April 6, 1947, p. E4; Delbert Clark, "Quarrels among Allies Wreck Aims in Germany," *The New York Times*, September 7, 1947, p. E5; "Germans Still Clinging to Nazism," *Derby Evening Telegraph*, March 25, 1947, p. 1.

192. Tauber, *Beyond Eagle and Swastika*, p. 35.

193. Zink, *The United States in Germany*, p. 299.

194. Geoffrey Cocks, "Hollywood über Alles: Seeing the Nazis in American Movies," *Film & History*, 45.1, summer, 2015, 42.

195. Welles also had a didactic streak and a keen interest in public education. Jennifer Lynde Barker, *The Aesthetics of Antifascist Film: Radical Projection* (New York, 2013), p. 114.

196. Joseph McBride, *Whatever Happened to Orson Welles? A Portrait of an Independent Career* (Lexington, KY, 2006), p. 88. Welles said that it was good "to get the public to look at any footage of a concentration camp." Gene D. Phillips, *Out of the Shadows: Expanding the Canon of Classic Film Noir* (Lanham, MD, 2012), p. 204.

197. Rashna Wadia Richards, *Cinematic Flashes: Cinephilia and Classical Hollywood* (Bloomington, IN, 2013), p. 150. "Disturbing Aliens, Some from Space," *The New York Times*, October 27, 2013, p. 13. Welles said on his radio show "that even though Hitler had been defeated in Europe he was succeeding in America." Cocks, "Hollywood über Alles," 44; Barker, *The Aesthetics of Antifascist Film*, p. 113.

198. For reviews, see "'Cornered' Absorbing Melodrama," *The Los Angeles Times*, March 1, 1946, p. A2, and Bosley Crowther, "The Screen in Review," *The New York Times*, December 26, 1945.

199. See Patrick McGilligan, *Alfred Hitchcock: A Life in Darkness and Light* (New York, 2003), pp. 158–59, 361–75. That said, both Hitchcock and Ben Hecht (who wrote the film's screenplay) were steadfast anti-Nazis. Matthew H. Bernstein, "Unrecognizable Origins: 'The Song of the Dragon' and *Notorious*," in R. Barton Palmer and David Boyd, eds., *Hitchcock at the Source: The Auteur as Adapter* (Albany, 2011), p. 140.

200. Review of *The Stranger* in *Variety Movie Reviews*, January 1, 1946; *Time*, review of *The Stranger*, June 17, 1946. For other positive reviews, see *The Boston Globe*, July 19, 1946, p. 8; "Orson Does It Twice as Welles," *Daily Mail* (London), August 23, 1946, p. 2; "The Cinema," *Spectator*, September 6, 1946, p. 239. See also the review in *Time*, June 17, 1946, which described the Germans planning "World War III." Even critical reviews reflected a prevailing suspicion of the Germans. In taking Welles to task for failing to create a compelling "illusion of . . . [a] depraved . . . Nazi," *The New York Times* implied that *The Stranger* did not make his villain sufficiently frightening. Bosley Crowther, review of *The Stranger* in *The New York Times*, July 11, 1946, p. 18.

201. For reviews of *Snowbound*, see "At the Symphony," *The New York Times*, February 21, 1949, p. 20. Richard Coe, "'Snowbound' Gets Lost in the Alps," *The Washington Post*, April 4, 1949, p. 12. For reviews of *Counterblast*, see Stephen Guy, *After Victory: Projections of the Second World War and Its Aftermath in British Feature Films, 1946–1950* (Ph.D. Dissertation, Queen

Mary, University of London, 2002), pp. 142–43. See, in addition to the *Washington Post* review, the reviews in *The Irish Times*, July 26, 1948, and *The New York Times*, February 21, 1949, p. 20.

202. Guy, *After Victory*, pp. 142–43.

203. Review of *Berlin Express*, *Variety Movie Reviews*, January 1, 1948. See also *The New York Times*, May 21, 1948, p. 19; Philip Scheuer, "Granet Makes Picture in Berlin Despite Reds," *The Los Angeles Times*, April 18, 1948, p. C1; review of *Berlin Express* in *The Hartford Courant*, July 22, 1948, p. 16; review of *Berlin Express* in *The Boston Globe*, May 7, 1948, p. 22.

204. Bosley Crowther, "The Screen," *The New York Times*, March 15, 1946, p. 27. Marjory Adams, "New Films," *The Boston Globe*, May 9, 1946, p. 14.

205. See Bosley Crowther, "The Screen in Review," *The New York Times*, August 16, 1946, p. 29. Also Bosley Crowther, "Love Conquers All," *The New York Times*, August 25, 1946, p. 49.

206. In addition to *Berlin Express*, sympathetic cinematic portrayals of ordinary Germans appeared in *Foreign Affair* (1948) and *The Big Lift* (1950). Emily Rosenberg, "'Foreign Affairs' after World War II: Connecting Sexual and International Politics," *Diplomatic History*, January 1994, 59–70.

207. Paul Mittag, "Formalistische Justiz," *Berliner Zeitung*, February 19, 1947, p. 6.

208. "Kampfprogramm für ein 4. Reich," *Neues Deutschland*, April 4, 1947, p. 1.

209. "Russian Talk Adds to Berlin Tension," *The New York Times*, September 12, 1948, p. 2.

210. Leon Dennen, "National Bolshevism in Germany," *The New Leader*, April 27, 1946, p. 29.

211. Drew Middleton, "Soviet Concessions on Berlin Held Possible," *The New York Times*, April 20, 1947, p. E3. Lord Vansittart, "Russia's Plan for Germany Would Mean the Ruin of Britain and France," *The Shepparton Advertiser* (Australia), March 16, 1947, p. 11.

212. E. L. Woodward, "Europe is Worth Saving and Can Be Saved," *The New York Times*, July 13, 1947, p. 107.

213. "West Germany and the French," *Southern Cross* (Adelaide, Australia), June 25, 1948, p. 3.

214. The phrase originated in the Berlin magazine *Sie*. Cited in "Der Marsch in die rote Diktatur," *Mittelbayerische Zeitung*, November 12, 1949.

215. Victor Klemperer, *The Lesser Evil: The Diaries of Victor Klemperer, 1945–1959* (London, 2003), p. 19.

216. Victor Klemperer, *The Language of the Third Reich: LTI, Lingua Tertii Imperii: A Philologist's Notebook* (London, 2000), p. 14.

217. Klemperer, *The Lesser Evil*, pp. 54, 40.

218. Ibid., p. 68.

219. Eberhard Pikart and Wolfram Werner, eds., *Das Parlamentarische Rat, 1948–1949*, Volume V (Boppard, 1993), pp. 169–70.

220. Wolfram Werner, *Das Parlamentarische Rat, 1948–1949*, Volume IX (Munich, 1996), p. 200. In doing so, Seebohm cited the importance of preserving "continuity" with prior German traditions.

221. Ibid., p. 182.

222. Ibid., p. 445.

223. Ibid., p. 437.

224. Ibid., p. 445. After May 8, 1945, the government of the Third Reich ceased to exist, but, according to international law, the concept of the Reich remained in existence in a kind of legal limbo. The Allies never annexed or abolished Germany and

expected to revive it once a unified government was established. East–west disagreements prevented this from happening, however. West German courts later ruled that the FRG was not the successor of German Reich, as it was only a *part* of the old Germany. The Reich thus remained in existence. Bark and Gress, *A History of West Germany*, pp. 58–59.

225. "Name for West Germany: Reich, Republic, Bund?" *The New York Herald Tribune*, October 16, 1948, p. 2.

226. "De Gaulle fordert allgemeine Wahlen," *Die Passauer Neue Presse*, April 20, 1948, p. 1. By 1949, France viewed the creation of the FRG as "the birth of the Fourth Reich" and argued it had to be integrated into community of nations and not succumb to nationalism. *Evening Telegraph and Post* (Dundee, Scotland), May 9, 1949, p. 1.

227. "A Blow in the Face," *Daily Mail* (London), November 12, 1948.

228. Polyzoides, "Strassbourg Talks Guide U.S. Policy," *The Los Angeles Times*, August 21, 1949, p. 17.

229. Ibid., p. 17.

230. "New German Policy," *The Hartford Courant*, November 22, 1949, p. 16.

231. "The Fourth Reich," *Westralian Worker* (Perth, Australia), August 26, 1949, p. 2.

232. Tauber, *Beyond Eagle and Swastika*, pp. 62–71. The party was also known as the DRP.

233. Ibid., pp. 89–90. Some 38 percent of Lower Saxony's population was made up of expellees, refugees, and evacuees.

234. Ibid., pp. 71–75, 99. The party ran on a platform of opposing denazification and striving for "a German Reich under the colors black-white-red."

235. Ibid., pp. 104–05.

236. "Unrest in Germany: Germans Are at It Again, Says Clay," *Press and Journal* (Aberdeen, Scotland), January 11, 1949, p. 1.

237. Milton Friedman, "Capital Spotlight," *The Wisconsin Jewish Chronicle*, August 26, 1949, p. 7.

238. Douglas Willkie, "As I See It," *The Advertiser* (Adelaide, Australia), August 29, 1949, p. 2; "Little Hitlers in Sheep's Clothing," *Daily Mail* (London), February 17, 1949, p. 4.

239. Otto Strasser, *Deutschlands Erneuerung* (Buenos Aires, 1946), pp. 172–74.

240. Ibid., pp. 148–51.

241. Strasser did not use the phrase "Fourth Reich" in his manifesto, but, by referring to the "era of the axe" (*Beilzeit*) and "the era of healing" (*Heilzeit*), he may have revealed the influence of Karl Strünckman, who had used the same phrase in his prediction of a coming Fourth Reich back in 1932. (See p. 31 of the present study.) Significantly, Strünckman and his wife were both affiliated with the dissident socialist wing of Strasser's postwar movement (known as the *Sammlung zur Tat*, SzT) and explicitly sought the creation of a "Christian Communist Fourth Reich" after the war. Tauber, *Beyond Eagle and Swastika*, pp. 112–114. The group got 14 percent of the vote in the American part of Baden-Württemberg.

242. Strasser, *Deutschlands Erneuerung*, pp. 24–25, 76. All the new leadership positions in the future Germany began with the word "Reich." Ibid., p. 80.

243. "Black Front Rises in Reich," *The Los Angeles Times*, January 11, 1949, p. 9. "Strasser Seeks Passport," *The New York Times,* January 11, 1949, p. 7. See also "Extreme Rightists Gain in Germany," *The New York Times*, November 17, 1949, p. 2.

244. "The Fourth Reich?" *The News* (Adelaide, Australia), January 12, 1949, p. 2.

245. "Germans Reviving Nationalist Ideas," *The New York Times*, February 15, 1949, p. 10.
246. "New German President," *Courier and Advertiser* (Dundee, Scotland), September 13, 1949, p. 2.
247. *Sozialdemokratischer Pressedienst*, Hanover, November 5, 1948, p. 7.
248. "Der drohende Zeigefinger," *Berliner Zeitung*, January 11, 1949, p. 2.
249. "Memorandum for the Officer in Charge, Subject: Otto Strasser," signed by J. Thomas Dale, March 25, 1948. Strasser file. NND007017.
250. Ibid.
251. Ibid. See also "Memorandum for the Officer in Charge, Subject: Otto Strasser," signed by Ernest Baer, May 24, 1948. Strasser file. NND007017.
252. Drew Middleton, "British Fear Rightist Groups in Germany Plan to Combine," *The New York Times*, December 12, 1949, p. 1.
253. Tauber, *Beyond Eagle and Swastika*, p. 112.
254. "British Won't Allow Strasser to Enter Their Zone of Reich," *The Chicago Daily Tribune*, September 20, 1949, p. 7.

The Fourth Reich Turns Right: Renazifying Germany in the 1950s

1. "Das 'vierte Reich' der SRP," *Mittelbayerische Zeitung*, February 25, 1950, p. 1.
2. One of the few studies on renazification is Norbert Frei's "Vergangenheitsbewältigung or 'Renazification'? The American Perspective on Germany's Confrontation with the Nazi Past in the Early Years of the Adenauer Era," in Michael Ermarth, ed., *America and the Shaping of German Society, 1945–1955* (New York, 1993), pp. 47–59.
3. K. P. Tauber was one of the first scholars to problematize the term "renazification." See Tauber, *Beyond Eagle and Swastika*, pp. 881–83. Juliane Wetzel argues that "the political system of the Federal Republic was ... never really endangered by right-wing extremist parties," in her "Der parteipolitische Rechtsextremismus," in Wolfgang Kowalsky and Wolfgang Schroeder, eds., *Rechtsextremismus: Einführung und Forschungsbilanz* (Opladen, 1994), p. 99.
4. The treaty was signed on May 26, 1952, but only went into effect on May 5, 1955, after delays caused by the failure to ratify the European Defense Community (EDC) treaty (and the ensuing decision to allow the FRG to join NATO instead).
5. "The Road to Disaster," *Prevent World War III*, May–August 1949, p. 1. Earlier mentions of renazification can be found in "Hitler's Ex-Enemy Turns to Defense of 'Little Nazis,'" *The Abilene Reporter-News*, March 24, 1948; "U.S. Policy in Germany Called 'Renazification,'" *The Wisconsin Jewish Chronicle*, November 26, 1948, p. 1.
6. Drew Middleton, "Hitler Aides Ruling Bavaria; Germans Cool to Democracy," *The New York Times*, November 30, 1949, p. 1; Drew Middleton, *The Renazification of Germany* (New York, 1949).
7. "Renazification," *The New York Times*, December 2, 1949, p. 28.
8. Delbert Clark, *Again the Goose Step* (New York, 1949), p. 296.
9. The *Daily Express* was the largest newspaper in the world, with a daily circulation of 4.4 million in 1954. "Illustrierte Schreckenskammer," *Der Spiegel*, January 6, 1954, p. 24. See also Karen Bayer, *"How Dead Is Hitler?" Der Britische Starreporter Sefton Delmer und die Deutschen* (Mainz, 2008).
10. Sefton Delmer, "Can Germany Harm Us?" *Daily Express*, September 12, 1949.
11. William Shirer, "Germany Is Marching Again," *See Magazine*, May 1950, p. 10.

12. "Nothing to Worry About?" *Prevent World War III*, June–August 1950, p. 1.
13. Moses Miller, *Nazis Preferred: The Renazification of Western Germany* (New York, 1950); West Side Committee against Renazification of Germany, *Shadow of the Swastika: German Rearmament & Renazification. The Road to World War III* (1950); Anglo-Jewish Association, *Germany's New Nazis* (1951).
14. Carolus, "The Road to Hell," *The Nation*, April 29, 1950, pp. 394–95; Louis Harap, "Renazification Versus the People," *Jewish Life*, July 1950, pp. 8–11.
15. The American Jewish Committee devoted an entire section to the problem of "renazification" in its yearbook coverage of the year 1950–51, *The American Jewish Year Book*, 1952, pp. 438–40. See also "Nazis Returning to Power Says Anti-Defamation League," *The Brooklyn Daily Eagle*, May 21, 1950.
16. "Die Gefahren der Renazifizierung," *Mittelbayerishe Zeitung*, June 3, 1948. "Gegen Renazifizierung der Presse," *Passauer Neue Presse*, August 30, 1949; "Regierungspräsident gegen Renazifizierung," *Passauer Neue Presse*, June 11, 1948; "'Braunes Haus' in München," *Berliner Zeitung*, October 8, 1949, p. 2.
17. Quoted in Manfred Görtemaker, *Thomas Mann und die Politik* (Frankfurt, 2005), p. 227.
18. Eugen Kogon, *The Theory and Practice of Hell* (New York, 1964), p. 319.
19. Deutscher Bundestag – 40. Sitzung, February 23, 1950, p. 1330. http://dip21.bundestag.de/dip21/btp/01/01040.pdf
20. Alvarez Del Vayo, "Germany: Cold War Victor?" *The Nation*, April 1, 1950, p. 295; see also Alvarez Del Vayo, "The Eternal Dr. Schacht," *The Nation*, February 18, 1950, p. 157.
21. Ernest S. Pisko, "This World . . . , *The Christian Science Monitor*, January 31, 1950, p. 7.
22. Anglo-Jewish Association, *Germany's New Nazis*, p. 71.
23. Brian Connell, "Muddle as Bonn Rulers Meet," *Daily Mail* (London), September 8, 1949, p. 1.
24. "A Fourth Reich," *The Dallas Morning News*, December 10, 1949.
25. Daniel E. Rogers, *Politics after Hitler: The Western Allies and the German Party System* (New York, 1995), p. 21. The refugee lobbying organization known as the League of German Expellees and Those Deprived of Rights (BHE) was founded in January of 1950 and received more than 24 percent of the vote in Schleswig-Holstein that same year. Richard Stöss, *Die extreme Rechte in der Bundesrepublik: Entwicklung – Ursachen – Gegenmaßnahmen* (Opladen, 1989), p. 88.
26. "Neo-Nazi Parties of Today," *Prevent World War III*, March–April 1950, pp. 20–21.
27. Tauber, *Beyond Eagle and Swastika*, p. 743.
28. Norbert Frei, *Adenauer's Germany and the Nazi Past: The Politics of Amnesty and Integration* (New York, 2002), chapter 10, especially pp. 237–40. Hedler said the Nazis could have used "other methods" to get rid of the Jews besides gassings. Two-thirds of the court's members were ex-Nazis.
29. For other newspaper coverage, see Antony Terry, "Will German Dilemma End in New Hitler?" *Press and Journal* (Aberdeen, Scotland), March 29, 1950.
30. "Das 'Vierte Reich' marschiert," *Neue Zeit*, February 24, 1950, p. 1.
31. Norbert Muhlen, "In the Backwash of the Great Crime," *Commentary*, February 1952, p. 110.
32. "German Nationalism High Again on Day Hitler Took Full Rule," *The Anniston Star* (Anniston, AL), January 30, 1950, p. 1; "New German Party Pledges 4th

Reich," *The Boston Globe,* January 23, 1950, p. 2; "A Führer Sets Them Singing," *Daily Mail* (London), January 23, 1950, p. 1. See also Tauber, *Beyond Eagle and Swastika,* p. 743, for Richter's support of the Reich while still a member of the DRP.

33. "Franz Richter: The New Adolf Hitler?" *Daily Mail* (London), March 4, 1950, p. 4.

34. *Information Bulletin,* March 1952.

35. Anne Freemantle, "Was It Better under Hitler?" *The New Republic,* December 29, 1952, p. 15.

36. Henning Hansen, *Die Sozialistische Reichspartei (SRP): Aufstieg und Scheitern einer rechtsextremen Partei* (Düsseldorf, 2007), p. 78; Otto Busch and Peter Furth, *Rechtsradikalismus im Nachkriegsdeutschland: Studien über die Sozialistische Reichspartei (SRP)* (Berlin, 1957), p. 23; Tauber, *Beyond Eagle and Swastika,* p. 692.

37. Busch and Furth, *Rechtsradikalismus im Nachkriegsdeutschland,* p. 18. Dorls controversially described the gas chambers as one of the "revolutionary methods" of the Nazi era. Quoted in William J. Collins, "Otto Remer: The New Nazi Threat," *Jewish Advocate,* June 21, 1951, p. 1. On Dorls, see also Leonard J. Schweitzer, "Hitler's Would-Be Heirs," *The Reporter,* December 25, 1951, pp. 31–32.

38. Remer originally supported the July 20 plotters, but opportunistically switched sides after being confronted by Joseph Goebbels, who arranged to have Remer speak to Hitler by telephone to prove the Führer was still alive. Tauber, *Beyond Eagle and Swastika,* p. 87.

39. Hansen, *Die Sozialistische Reichspartei,* pp. 52–53; Busch and Furth, *Rechtsradikalismus im Nachkriegsdeutschland,* p. 20; Tauber, *Beyond Eagle and Swastika,* p. 692.

40. Tauber, *Beyond Eagle and Swastika,* pp. 119–32. Martin A. Lee, *The Beast Reawakens: Fascism's Resurgence from Hitler's Spymasters to Today* (Boston, 1997), pp. 76–77.

41. *Germany's New Nazis,* p. 26. Hansen, *Die Sozialistische Reichspartei,* p. 178; Peter Dudek and Hans-Gerhard Jaschke, *Entstehung und Entwicklung des Rechtsextremismus in der Bunderepublik: Zur Tradition einer besonderen politischen Kultur* (Opladen, 1984), p. 67.

42. "Die gleiche Blutgruppe?" *FAZ,* March 7, 1952, p. 2.

43. *Information Bulletin,* September 6, 1949, p. 4; "Schickt deutsche Maurer," *Der Spiegel,* May 2, 1951.

44. Ibid.

45. Busch and Furth, *Rechtsradikalismus im Nachkriegsdeutschland,* pp. 33–44.

46. Hansen, *Die Sozialistische Reichspartei,* p. 117.

47. Ibid., p. 123. "Otto Remer: The New Nazi Threat," *Jewish Advocate,* June 21, 1951, p. 1; Don Doane, "Reich Party Frankly Wants a Dictator," *The Washington Post,* December 23, 1951, p. B3.

48. Anne Freemantle, "Was It Better under Hitler?" *The New Republic,* December 29, 1952, p. 14.

49. Hansen, *Die Sozialistische Reichspartei,* p. 120.

50. "Trial of Nazi Accents Voluntary Reeducation," *The Christian Science Monitor,* April 17, 1952, p. 13.

51. "Are the Nazis Coming Back?" *Picture Post,* June 16, 1951.

52. Hansen, *Die Sozialistische Reichspartei,* pp. 117, 130.

53. As historians Otto Busch and Peter Furth have written, "the SRP viewed the 'Reich' as the German people's time-honored existential reality, the mythical source of its missionary consciousness." Busch and Furth, *Rechtsradikalismus im Nachkriegsdeutschland*, p. 296.

54. The Anglo-Jewish Association, *Germany's New Nazis*, p. 24; Hansen, *Die Sozialistische Reichspartei*, p. 124.

55. See the Aktionsprogramm der SRP (1949), in Uwe Backes and Eckhard Jesse, *Politischer Extremismus in der Bundesrepublik Deutschland*, Volume III (Cologne, 1989), pp. 87–89.

56. Busch and Furth, *Rechtsradikalismus im Nachkriegsdeutschland*, pp. 24, 295–96; Günter J. Trittel, "Die Sozialistische Reichspartei als Niedersächsische Regionalpartei," in Bernd Weisbrod, ed., *Rechtsradikalismus in der politischen Kultur der Nachkriegszeit: Die verzögerte Normalisierung in Niedersachsen* (Hanover, 1995), p. 74.

57. Frei, *Adenauer's Germany*, p. 254; Busch and Furth, *Rechtsradikalismus im Nachkriegsdeutschland*, pp. 298–99.

58. In the mid 1950s, the Federal Supreme Court endorsed the idea that, with the end of the war, the Reich had not been abolished, but had been merely "suspended" and rendered "unable to act" (*handlungsunfähig*), since the Allies never agreed on a peace treaty and simply replaced the defeated Nazi government with two newly created, but "provisional," postwar states. In 1955, the West German Press and Information Office declared that "the Federal Republic is the legitimate form of the German Reich." Allemann, *Bonn ist nicht Weimar*, p. 17.

59. "Das 'Vierte Reich' marschiert," *Neue Zeit*, February 24, 1950, p. 1. See also "Das 'Vierte Reich,'" *Hamburger Abendblatt*, February 21, 1950, which refers to Heimhardt delivering a talk in Luckau in which he proclaimed the intention "to create the Fourth Reich."

60. Cited in Heiko Buschke, *Deutsche Presse, Rechtsextremismus und nationalsozialistische Vergangenheit in der Ära Adenauer* (Frankfurt, 2003), p. 161. "Nazis Find New Fuhrer," *The Advertiser* (Adelaide, Australia), May 8, 1951, p. 3.

61. "Saalschlachten wie einst," *Neue Zeit*, February 7, 1950, p. 2. "Remer in Aktion," *Aufbau*, September 15, 1950. "Tumult um Remer," *FAZ*, January 12, 1950, p. 4.

62. "Tumult um Remer," *FAZ*, January 12, 1950, p. 4.

63. The Anglo-Jewish Association, *Germany's New Nazis*, p. 33; Tauber, *Beyond Eagle and Swastika*, p. 693.

64. Hansen, *Die Sozialistische Reichspartei*, pp. 196–203; Beate Baldow, *Episode oder Gefahr? Die Naumann-Affäre* (Ph.D. Dissertation, Freie Universität Berlin, 2012), pp. 105–06.

65. "Geheim ins Reich," *Der Spiegel*, March 18, 2013.

66. Bernd Weisbrod, "Einleitung," in Weisbrod, ed., *Rechtsradikalismus in der politischen Kultur der Nachkriegszeit*, p. 9. David Johst, "Nur allerbeste Nazis," *Die Zeit*, March 29, 2012.

67. Heiko Buschke, "Die Sozialistische Reichspartei im Raum Lüneburg 1949–1952," in Weisbrod, ed., *Rechtsradikalismus in der politischen Kultur der Nachkriegszeit*, 91.

68. In reality, the SRP probably had around 10,000 members. Hansen, *Die Sozialistische Reichspartei*, p. 59; Steffen Kailitz, *Politischer Extremismus in der Bundesrepublik Deutschland: Eine Einführung* (Wiesbaden, 2004), p. 32; Tauber, *Beyond Eagle and Swastika*, p. 698.

69. Trittel, "Die Sozialistische Reichspartei als Niedersächsische Regionalpartei," p. 83; Hansen, *Die Sozialistische Reichspartei*, p. 64.

70. Hansen, *Die Sozialistische Reichspartei*, p. 173; David Johst, "Nur allerbeste Nazis," *Die Zeit*, March 29, 2012.

71. Jaschke and Dudek, *Entstehung und Entwicklung des Rechtsextremismus in der Bunderepublik*, p. 65.

72. Hansen, *Die Sozialistische Reichspartei*, pp. 29, 86; Weisbrod, "Einleitung," 12.

73. The Anglo-Jewish Association, *Germany's New Nazis*, p. 15. Hansen, *Die Sozialistische Reichspartei*, p. 173.

74. Hansen, *Die Sozialistische Reichspartei*, p. 68.

75. Ibid., p. 81.

76. Buschke, "Die Sozialistische Reichspartei im Raum Lüneburg 1949–1952," pp. 99–100.

77. Drew Middleton, "Neo-Nazism: 'A Cloud Like a Man's Hand,'" *The New York Times*, July 1, 1951, p. 115.

78. Don Doane, "Otto Remer Wants to Be New Hitler," *The Abilene Reporter-News*, March 26, 1952, p. 3B; Richard Hanser, "Is He Germany's New Hitler?" *The St. Louis Post-Dispatch*, November 4, 1951. "The New Hitler?" *Prevent World War III*, November–December 1949, p. 21.

79. Richard Hanser, "He Hopes to Be Tomorrow's Führer," *The Reader's Digest*, December 1951, p. 120.

80. Sefton Delmer, "Is a New Hitler Rising?" *Daily Express*, July 6, 1951. Sefton Delmer, "I Heard Remer Echo That Nazi Style," *Daily Express*, July 10, 1951.

81. "Are the Nazis Coming Back?" *Picture Post*, June 16, 1951.

82. William Stevenson, "General Remer – A New Hitler?" *The Seattle Times*, February 3, 1952.

83. William Attwood and Seymour Freidin, "The Nazis March Again," *Collier's*, November 25, 1950, p. 23.

84. John LaFarge, "Reconstructing a Divided Germany," *America*, July 28, 1951, p. 417.

85. "West German Unions Rebuff Communists But Warn against Any Growth of Nazism," *The New York Times*, June 23, 1951, p. 3.

86. "Das 'Vierte Reich' marschiert," *Neue Zeit*, February 24, 1950, p. 1.

87. Frei, *Adenauer's Germany*, p. 263.

88. Kailitz, *Politischer Extremismus in der Bundesrepublik Deutschland*, p. 33; Hansen, *Die Sozialistische Reichspartei*, p. 179.

89. See the collection of SPD leaflets published to counter the SRP at http://archiv2.fes.de/vtrech.FAU?sid=129062E3&dm=4&RO_ZEILE_1=remer

90. "'Das wär' bei Hitler nicht passiert ...,'" *Die Zeit*, May 3, 1951.

91. See "The Radical Right," *Information Bulletin*, September 1951, pp. 65–68.

92. "McCloy Warns of Neo-Nazis," *The New York Times*, February 28, 1952, p. 8; John J. McCloy, "Germany's Future," *Information Bulletin*, January 1952, pp. 7–9. Frei, *Adenauer's Germany*, p. 260.

93. Hansen, *Die Sozialistische Reichspartei*, pp. 205–08.

94. Frei, *Adenauer's Germany*, p. 400, 51n.

95. Hansen, *Die Sozialistische Reichspartei*, pp. 179, 204n, p. 225.

96. "Schickt deutsche Maurer," *Der Spiegel*, May 2, 1951, p. 8.

97. Rand C. Lewis, *A Nazi Legacy: Right-Wing Extremism in Postwar Germany* (New York, 1991), p. 44.

98. The SRP was declared hostile to the state (*staatsfeindlich*) on September 19, 1950. The *Reichsfront* was banned in 1951. Remer was banned from speaking in 1951. Tauber, *Beyond Eagle and Swastika*, p. 710.

99. Remer was first subjected to speaking bans at the regional level in February of 1950. Frei, *Adenauer's Germany*, pp. 252, 267. In March of 1952, he was put on trial in Brunswick and later found guilty of slandering the July 20 resistance group as traitors.

100. Trittel, "Die Sozialistische Reichspartei als Niedersächsische Regionalpartei," 69; Frei, *Adenauer's Germany*, p. 274.

101. Dorls actually dissolved the SRP right before September 12, 1952.

102. Tauber, *Beyond Eagle and Swastika*, pp. 714–25. Dorls fled to Spain to avoid arrest, while Remer fled to Egypt in order to avoid serving jail time for his second defamation conviction. Remer remained active in right-wing circles and later became a Holocaust denier.

103. Hansen, *Die Sozialistische Reichspartei*, p. 275. "Nazi Threat of Comeback Is Exploded," *The Hartford Courant*, September 13, 1952.

104. Kommunistiche Partei Deutschlands, *Viertes Reich fällt aus: Das Urteil des Bundes-Verfassungsgerichtes über die SRP* (Hilden, 1952).

105. Hansen, *Die Sozialistische Reichspartei*, pp. 274–75.

106. "Das Ende der SRP," *Die Zeit*, September 18, 1952.

107. Hugh Trevor-Roper, "The Germans Reappraise the War," *Foreign Affairs*, January 1953, 233. Frei, *Adenauer's Germany*, p. 276; Allemann, *Bonn ist nicht Wiemar*, p. 294.

108. Baldow, *Episode oder Gefahr?*, pp. 17–23.

109. See Werner Naumann, "The Time to Decide" (from April 1945), at the Calvin College propaganda archive. http://research.calvin.edu/german-propaganda-archive/naumann1.htm

110. Günter Trittel, *"Man kann ein Ideal nicht verraten ... " Werner Naumann – NS-Ideologie und politische Praxis in der frühen Bundesrepublik* (Göttingen, 2013), pp. 72–90.

111. Baldow, *Episode oder Gefahr?*, p. 25; Trittel, *"Man kann ein Ideal nicht verraten ...,"* p. 81.

112. Baldow, *Episode oder Gefahr?*, pp. 39–55; Tauber, *Beyond Eagle and Swastika*, pp. 119–32.

113. Baldow, *Episode oder Gefahr?*, p. 83.

114. Ibid., pp. 2–3, 85; Tauber, *Beyond Eagle and Swastika*, pp. 133–35. See also "Naumann-Kreis," no date, p. 10. In the papers of Leo Freiherr Geyr von Schweppenburg, ED 91, Bd. 1–54, at Institut für Zeitgeschichte, Munich.

115. Baldow, *Episode oder Gefahr?*, pp. 29, 33–34, 57–58, 82.

116. Ibid., p. 28.

117. Trittel, *"Man kann ein Ideal nicht verraten ...,"* p. 7.

118. Tauber, *Beyond Eagle and Swastika*, p. 38.

119. This comes from a treatise written by Naumann in 1951. Baldow, *Episode oder Gefahr?*, pp. 25–26, 92–94, 111–12, Trittel, *"Man kann ein Ideal nicht verraten ...,"* p. 134.

120. Trittel, *"Man kann ein Ideal nicht verraten ...,"* p. 130.

121. Trittel rejects the idea that Naumann wanted to take over, or seize power through, the FDP, arguing that the FDP pursued Naumann instead. Trittel, *"Man kann ein Ideal nicht verraten ...,"* pp. 13, 136–37 177n, 156–59, 162–63. Most scholars, however, see Naumann as an active plotter. See Baldow, *Episode oder Gefahr?*

pp. 93–96; Alistair Horne, *Return to Power: A Report on the New Germany* (New York, 1956), p. 169; Tauber, *Beyond Eagle and Swastika*, pp. 135–39.

122. Trittel, *"Man kann ein Ideal nicht verraten ...,"* p. 130.
123. Ibid., pp. 128, 133.
124. Ibid., p. 148.
125. Ibid., pp. 128, 134.
126. Baldow, *Episode oder Gefahr?*, p. 30.
127. Buchna, *Nationale Sammlung an Rhein und Ruhr*, p. 217.
128. Baldow, *Episode oder Gefahr?*, p. 148; Buchna, *Nationale Sammlung an Rhein und Ruhr*, p. 220.
129. Frei, *Adenauer's Germany*, pp. 289–90; Baldow, *Episode oder Gefahr?*, p. 32.
130. Baldow, *Episode oder Gefahr?*, p. 33.
131. Best was the highest-ranking former RSHA official alive in Germany and knew Achenbach and Six from the war years.
132. Diewerge was one of the major figures who forged the contacts between the FDP and Naumann, who had been his superior at the Propaganda Ministry.
133. Susanna Schrafstetter, "Siegfried Zoglmann, His Circle of Writers, and the Naumann Affair," in David A. Messenger and Katrin Paehler, eds., *A Nazi Past: Recasting German Identity in Postwar Europe* (Lexington, KY, 2015), p. 118. Zoglmann helped edit FDP's journals, *Die Deutsche Zukunft* and *Die Plattform*, both of which featured apologetic, pro-Nazi articles by Grimm and Diewerge. Baldow, *Episode oder Gefahr?*, pp. 136–38.
134. Frei, *Adenauer's Germany*, p. 280; Schrafstetter, "Siegfried Zoglmann," 122–26.
135. See the text of the document in Peter Juling, *Programmatische Entwicklung der FDP 1946 bis 1969: Einführungn und Dokumente* (Meisenheim am Glan,1977), pp. 120–24.
136. Ibid.
137. Trittel, *"Man kann ein Ideal nicht verraten ...,"* pp. 164–65; Baldow, *Episode oder Gefahr?*, pp. 154–58.
138. Baldow, *Episode oder Gefahr?*, pp. 96–97, 160–69, 193–95. Trittel, *"Man kann ein Ideal nicht verraten ..."* pp. 169–72. Naumann originally believed he would not go into public political life before 1957. Trittel, *"Man kann ein Ideal nicht verraten ..., "* p. 148.
139. Ibid., p. 185.
140. Tauber, *Beyond Eagle and Swastika*, p. 895.
141. "British Arrest Seven Nazi Ringleaders," *The Times* (London), January 16, 1953; Baldow, *Episode oder Gefahr?*, p. 205.
142. "Naumann-Kreis," no date, p. 17. In the papers of Leo Freiherr Geyr von Schweppenburg, ED 91, Bd. 1–54, at Institut für Zeitgeschichte, Munich.
143. "New Nazi Specter in Western Germany," *The New York Herald Tribune*, January 25, 1953.
144. "7 Ex-Nazis Seized by British for Plot," *The New York Times*, January 16, 1953, p. 1; "Nazism Hangs On," *The New York Times*, January 19, 1953, p. 22.
145. "Echo from the Bunker," *Daily Mail* (London), January 16, 1953, p. 4; "The Web Spun by Naumann," *The Times* (London), May 6, 1953, p. 7.
146. Baldow, *Episode oder Gefahr?*, p. 233.
147. "The Re-Nazification of Germany," *Prevent World War III*, summer, 1953, p. 31.
148. "Germans Threaten Allied Forces' Security," reprinted in *The Examiner* (Launceton, Tasmania), March 10, 1953, p. 2.
149. "British Break Up Nazi Plot to Seize Power in Germany," *The Jerusalem Post*, January 16, 1953, p. 1.

150. "British Nab 7 Nazis, Charge Plot to Create '4th Reich,'" *The Cleveland Plain-Dealer*, January 16, 1953. "Seventh Nazi Seized in Communist-Backed Plot," *The Los Angeles Times*, January 16, 1953, p. 2. "7 Ex-Nazis Jailed for Plotting Coup," *The Boston Globe*, January 16, 1953, p. 13.

151. The British press reported that members of the German Free Corps were planning a Fourth Reich when they were arrested in early February of 1953. "Nazi Leaders Are Hunted by Night," *Daily Express*, February 11, 1953. The demand for a "new Reich" was also advanced by war veterans associated with General Hermann Ramcke: *Daily Mail* (London), January 23, 1953. Reports about the crushing of another Nazi coup, this time by the Freikorps Deutschland, appeared in *The New York Times*, February 11, 1953. Three days after the Naumann arrests, a HICOG poll seemed to confirm growing support among Germans for neo-Nazism. According to the results, 41 percent of Germans thought that there had been "more good than bad" in the Third Reich, while 35 percent said the reverse; only 4 percent said that the German people bore any blame for the Nazi era; finally, 24 percent affirmed that they would support a new National Socialist movement. Drew Middleton, "Rise in Neo-Nazism Is Shown by Survey in West Germany," *The New York Times*, January 18, 1953, p. 1.

152. See Baldow, *Episode oder Gefahr?*, pp. 215–22; "Mit Nau-Nau Argumenten," *Der Spiegel*, March 11, 1953, p. 19. For a general listing of claims, see "Nau-Nau," *Der Spiegel*, January 21, 1953, p. 6.

153. Trittel, *"Man kann ein Ideal nicht verraten …,"* p. 197.

154. "Nau-Nau," *Der Spiegel*, January 21, 1953, p. 8. In the US, *The Wall Street Journal* questioned the seriousness of the Nazi threat in "Nazi Revival," February 26, 1953, p. 8.

155. "Nau-Nau," *Der Spiegel*, January 21, 1953, p. 6; "Zum Totenschädel verzerrt," *Der Spiegel*, March 11, 1953, p. 6.

156. Baldow, *Episode oder Gefahr?*, pp. 222–24; Trittel, *"Man kann ein Ideal nicht verraten …,"* pp. 204, 263.

157. Trittel, *"Man kann ein Ideal nicht verraten …,"* p. 207. Dehler noted that the Naumann Circle's goal was "to seize power after the forthcoming elections." "The Re-Nazification of Germany," *Prevent World War III*, summer, 1953, p. 31.

158. Baldow, *Episode oder Gefahr?*, p. 225; Frei, *Adenauer's Germany*, p. 288.

159. Baldow, *Episode oder Gefahr?*, p. 242.

160. Ibid., p. 298.

161. "Naumann, a New Hitler?" *The Corpus Christi Caller*, August 24, 1953. "Ex-Nazi Reviving Hitler Technique," *The New York Times*, August 17, 1953, p. 6.

162. Trittel, *"Man kann ein Ideal nicht verraten …,"* p. 260.

163. Baldow, *Episode oder Gefahr?* pp. 298, 283; Trittel, *"Man kann ein Ideal nicht verraten …,"* pp. 264–70. "Rotten Eggs Hurled at Naumann in Kiel," *The New York Times*, August 21, 1953, p. 2. "Naumann Out of German Politics Under Ruling That He Is a Nazi," *The New York Times*, August 25, 1953, p. 1.

164. Baldow, *Episode oder Gefahr?*, p. 273.

165. Tauber, *Beyond Eagle and Swastika*, pp. 803–07. The FDP went from 11.9 to 9.5 percent, the DP from 4.0 to 3.3 percent, and the DRP from 1.8 to 1.1 percent. The BHE achieved merely a less-than-expected 5.9 percent of the vote. Only 34 percent of expellees voted for the party. Baldow, *Episode oder Gefahr?*, p. 287.

166. Tauber, *Beyond Eagle and Swastika*, p. 811. Wolfrum, *Die geglückte Demokratie*, pp. 128–29.

167. Tauber, *Beyond Eagle and Swastika*, pp. 806–07.

168. Baldow, *Episode oder Gefahr?*, pp. 298–301. After being absolved of seeking to "reestablish a National socialist Führer state" in December of 1954, the FDP co-conspirators came away comparatively unscathed. Middelhauve, claiming total innocence, stayed in office. Achenbach was mildly demoted but, in 1957, became a Bundestag representative, along with Zoglmann. Frei, *Adenauer's Germany*, pp. 289–90.

169. T. H. Tetens, *Germany Plots with the Kremlin* (New York, 1953).

170. Ibid., p. 6.

171. Ibid., pp. viii–ix.

172. Ibid., p. 95.

173. Ibid., p. 94.

174. Ibid., p. 158.

175. Ibid., p. 159.

176. Ibid., p. 179.

177. Ibid., p. viii.

178. Hans Habe, *Our Love Affair with Germany* (New York, 1953).

179. Ibid., p. 27.

180. Ibid., pp. 233, 165.

181. Ibid., pp. 61, 66.

182. Ibid., pp. 71–72.

183. Ibid., pp. 236–37.

184. Ibid., pp. 242–43.

185. While some reviewers found Tetens' book "timely," others argued that its "alarmist tone" did "more harm than good." See the reviews of Tetens by Louis Snyder in *The American Historical Review*, July 1953, pp. 963–64; by Koppel Pinson in *Jewish Social Studies*, April 1954, pp. 182–86; and by Elizabeth Wiskemann in *International Affairs*, April 1954, pp. 235–36. Habe's book, meanwhile, was described as being marred by "personal pique" (Pinson, p. 184); see also Richard F. Schier's review in *The Western Political Quarterly Review*, June 1954, pp. 264–65.

186. Norbert Muhlen, *The Return of Germany* (1953). Norbert Muhlen, "Is There a West German Menace?" *Commentary*, June 1953.

187. Muhlen, *The Return of Germany*, pp. 50–52.

188. Ibid., p. 69.

189. Ibid., pp. 4–5.

190. Ibid., pp. 12, 7.

191. See also Norbert Muhlen, "German Anti-Americanism: East and West Zones," *Commentary*, February 1953, p. 130.

192. Muhlen, "Is There a West German Menace?" *Commentary*, June 1953.

193. Peter Schmid, "The Germans' Present Conservatism: Its Roots," *Commentary*, November 1953, pp. 422–23.

194. Herbert Lüthy, "Behind Reawakened German Nationalism," *Commentary*, February 1, 1952, p. 116.

195. Richard Lowenthal, "The New Nazi Round-up," *The New Leader*, February 23, 1953, p. 36.

196. Horne, *Return to Power*, p. 165.

197. Bayer, "*How Dead Is Hitler?*". Reprinted in *Prevent World War III*, summer, 1954, pp. 24–28.

198. Bayer, "*How Dead Is Hitler?*", pp. 205–17.

199. "Schwarze Propaganda," *Der Spiegel*, September 8, 1954, pp. 16–22.

200. Lord Russell, *The Scourge of the Swastika* (London, 1954), p. 1.

201. Horne, *Return to Power*, pp. 41–45, 182, and chapter 9.
202. Jacques Soustelle, "France and Europe," *Foreign Affairs*, July 1952, p. 547.
203. Lewis Namier, *Avenues of History* (London, 1952), pp. 94, 98.
204. Frederick Schuman, "The Tortured German Psyche," *The Nation*, January 8, 1955, pp. 34–35.
205. Anthony Terry, "Germans Unhappy over New Fourth Reich," *The Pittsburgh Press*, January 15, 1955, p. 9.
206. Louis Mitelberg, Walter Heynowski, and Hans Picard, *Das Vierte Reich* (Berlin, 1955).
207. The East German propaganda campaign was led by the Socialist Unity (SED) Party member Albert Norden. See Michael F. Scholz, "Active Measures and Disinformation as Part of East Germany's Propaganda War, 1953–1972," in Kristie Macrakis, Thomas Wegener Friis, and Helmut Müller-Enbergs, eds., *East German Foreign Intelligence: Myth, Reality and Controversy* (New York, 2010), p. 114.
208. The cartoons originally appeared in the French communist journal *L'Humanité*.
209. Norbert Frei has described these fears as "overdrawn" and "frequently trumped up." Frei, *Adenauer's Germany*, pp. 52, 59. Wetzel says overreaction was not a useful strategy, "Der parteipolitische Rechtsextremismus," 99.
210. Norbert Frei asserts that "the political amnestying and social reintergration of the army of 'fellow travelers' was as necessary as it was unavoidable," *Adenauer's Germany*, pp. xiv, 310. Ulrich Herbert writes that "Adenauer's policy towards former Nazis was validated": Ulrich Herbert, *Best:Biographische Studien über Radikalismus, Weltanschauung und Vernunft, 1903–1989* (Bonn, 1996), p. 474. Wilfried Loth and Bernd-A. Rusinek write that "out of Nazis emerged democrats, although without exploring their responsibility for Nazism," in Wilfried Loth and Bernd-A. Rusinek, "Einleitung," in Wilfried Loth and Bernd-A. Rusinek, eds., *Verwandlungspolitik: NS-Eliten in der westdeutschen Nachkriegsgesellschaft* (Frankfurt, 1998), p. 8. Richard Stöss wrote, "The political integration of postwar right-wing extremism … contributed crucially to the enormous stability of the Federal Republic": Stöss, *Die extreme Rechte in der Bundesrepublik*, p. 94. Jeff Olick, *In the House of the Hangman: The Agonies of German Defeat, 1943–1949* (Chicago, 2005), pp. 9–10. Klaus Epstein argued that the "policy of 'domesticating' ex-Nazis through kindness must … be considered a political success," in Pinson and Epstein, *Modern Germany*, p. 580.
211. Klaus Dietmar Henke, "Die Grenzen der politischen Säuberung in Deutschland nach 1945," in Ludolf Herbst, ed., *Westdeutschland 1945–1955: Unterwerfung, Kontrolle, Integration* (Munich, 1986), pp. 132–33.
212. Adenauer said denazification had brought "great misfortune to Germany" and complained about the endless "sniffing around for Nazis" (*Naziriecherei*). Quoted in Georg von Bönisch, "Amnesie und Amnestie," *Der Spiegel*, February 21, 2006, pp. 112–18. See also "Böse Erinnerungen," *Der Spiegel*, April 4, 1956, p. 18.
213. Adenauer realized that around 10 percent of the voters in the 1949 Bundestag elections displayed the potential to vote for extreme right-wing parties. Because the CDU only received 31 percent of the vote in 1949, and his bloc of coalition partners only got a total of 46 percent, he understood that it was crucial to win over any voters who might support a party to the right of the CDU. Stöss, *Die extreme Rechte in der Bundesrepublik*, pp. 86–88.
214. In 1949, the first amnesty law (*Straffreiheitsgesetz*) was passed, which pardoned, and restored voting rights to, approximately 800,000 persons who had been given

light sentences of between six months and one year for crimes committed before 1949. Two years later, in 1951, the "131 Law" was passed, which granted pensions to approximately 160,000 Nazi-era civil servants who had been dismissed after 1945 and allowed them to return to work (this even included some Gestapo personnel). In 1954, the second amnesty law (*zweite Straffreiheitsgesetz*) pardoned crimes committed at the end of the Second World War. Frei, *Adenauer's Germany*, chapters 2–4; see also Dominik Geppert, *Die Ära Adenauer* (Darmstadt, 2002), pp. 74–77.

215. Adenauer's amnesty policy was part of a "double strategy" of ignoring the Nazi past of private individuals while condemning Nazism in the public sphere. Helmut König, "Das Erbe der Diktatur: Der Nationalsozialismus im politischen Bewusstsein der Bundesrepublik," *Leviathan*, 2, 1996, 169–70.

216. Herbert, *Best*, pp. 473–76.

217. Frei, *Adenauer's Germany*, p. 310; Tauber, *Beyond Eagle and Swastika*, pp. 809–13; Herbert, *Best*, pp. 474–75. Herbert, "Rückkehr in die Bürgerlichkeit: NS-Eliten in der Bundesrepublik," in Weisbrod, ed., *Rechtsradikalismus in der politischen Kultur der Nachkriegszeit*, pp. 157–73.

218. Hermann Lübbe, "Der Nationalsozialismus im politischen Bewusstsein der Gegenwart," in Martin Broszat, ed., *Deutschlands Weg in die Diktatur* (Berlin, 1983), pp. 333–34.

219. Hermann Lübbe, *Hermann Lübbe im Gespräch* (Munich, 2010), p. 158.

220. Christian Meier, *Das Gebot zu vergessen und die Unabweisbarkeit des Erinnerns: Vom öffentlichen Umgang mit schlimmer Vergangenheit* (Munich, 2010), p. 62. See the interview with Götz Aly, "Vereiste Vergangenheit," *Die Zeit*, March 14, 2013. Dirk Moses refers to the "functionally necessary silence" and argued that it "would have been impossible to integrate the largely Nazified population into the new order" if a radical attempt at "an antifascist revolution" had been pursued after the war. Moses, *German Intellectuals and the Nazi Past*, pp. 69, 73. Ulrich Herbert has argued that "without the former Nazi leadership groups in the administration, the constitution of the new state would … have been impossible." Ulrich Herbert, "NS-Eliten in der Bundesrepublik," in Loth and Rusinek, eds., *Verwandlungspolitik: NS-Eliten in der westdeutschen Nachkriegsgesellschaft*, p. 114.

221. Norbert Frei, "Das Problem der NS-Vergangenheit in der Ära Adenauer," in Weisbrod, ed., *Rechtsradikalismus in der politischen Kultur der Nachkriegszeit*, pp. 26–31.

222. Thomas Schmid, "Der Streit der alten Männer," *Die Welt*, December 5, 1998.

223. Wolfrum, *Die geglückte Demokratie*, p. 171.

224. Lübbe resisted making explicit counterfactual claims. He came close when he speculated that "a German-led [denazification] program might have been better" than the Allied one, but he insisted that "any alternatives remain imaginary history." Lübbe, *Hermann Lübbe im Gespräch*, p. 375.

225. Ralf Beste, Georg Bönisch, Thomas Darnstaedt, Jan Friedmann, Michael Fröhlingsdorf and Klaus Wiegrefe, "From Dictatorship to Democracy: The Role Ex-Nazis Played in Early West Germany," *Der Spiegel*, March 6, 2012.

226. Cited in Joachim Perels, *Das juristische Erbe des Dritten Reiches* (Frankfurt, 1999), p. 125.

227. Helmut Schmidt and Fritz Stern, *Unser Jahrhundert: Ein Gespräch* (Munich, 2010), p. 250.

228. Epstein in Pinson, *Modern Germany*, p. 580.

229. Rudolf Augstein, "Konrad Adenauer und seine Epoche," *Der Spiegel*, 41, 1963, p. 99.
230. Hansen, *Die Sozialistische Reichspartei*, p. 300.
231. Baldow, *Episode oder Gefahr?*, p. 7. Baldow also quotes Theo Rütten making this point in his book *Der deutsche Liberalismus 1945 bis 1955*. Baldow, *Episode oder Gefahr?*, p. 309.
232. Ibid., pp. 305–06.
233. Trittel calls the Naumann affair the "most serious renazification project in the history of the Federal Republic." Trittel, '*Man kann ein Ideal nicht verraten . . .,*' p. 306. Walters says the Naumann affair has been "severely underestimated." More generally, William Hagen has written that if the Allies had not presided over postwar Germany, the country "would perhaps have fallen into . . . civil strife." William W. Hagen, *German History in Modern Times: Four Lives of the Nation* (Cambridge, MA, 2012), p. 360.
234. Ivone Kirkpatrick, *The Inner Circle: Memoirs of Ivone Kirkpatrick* (New York, 1959), pp. 252–53.
235. Tauber, *Beyond Eagle and Swastika*, p. 146. Similarly, Terence Prittie speculated in 1960 that "had the Naumann group captured forty members of the Bundestag and then held one of the major parties to ransom, it would have had a unique chance of creating its planned national rally out of the millions of ex-Nazis . . . who had still not come to terms with democracy." Prittie, *Germany Divided*, p. 326.
236. Frei, *Adenauer's Germany*, p. 233. Die Zeit said it's an "open question" whether the SRP would have planted roots elsewhere in Germany if it had existed longer. David Johst, "Nur allerbeste Nazis," *Die Zeit*, March 29, 2012.
237. Frei, *Adenauer's Germany*, p. 306. Frei added that "without such direct Allied control, the past-political boundaries would have been even more amorphous," ibid. Kielmansegg has written that "the physical presence of the Allies prevented things that would have made a democratic new beginning more difficult." Kielmansegg, *Lange Schatten*, p. 10.
238. Buchna, *Nationale Sammlung an Rhein und Ruhr*, pp. 222–23. By intervening when they did, the British prevented Naumann from waiting until 1957 to pursue his plans and forced him to act before he was ready. Trittel, "*Man kann ein Ideal nicht verraten . . .,* " pp. 304–05. If they had waited, Naumann would have been able to develop his plans further. Tauber adds that Naumann could have infiltrated the BHE and gotten Kraft to sign up for his plan if he had not been arrested, *Beyond Eagle and Swastika*, p. 145.
239. Herbert, *Best*, p. 462.
240. Trittel, "*Man kann ein Ideal nicht verraten . . .,* " p. 8.
241. Stöss, *Die extreme Rechte in der Bundesrepublik*, p. 94.
242. This was the title of Ernst Nolte's controversial 1986 essay in the *Frankfurter Allgemeine Zeitung* that helped spark the Historians' Debate (*Historikerstreit*) about the singularity of the Third Reich.
243. In 1950, Arendt wondered whether a "bloody . . . uprising" might have been possible, "against all of whose who were . . . representatives of the Nazi regime." Quoted in König, "Das Erbe der Diktatur," 166. In 1950, Walter Dirks condemned the "restorationist" mood in West Germany and in 1967 wrote, "I can imagine another Germany" that would have emerged without the "obstacle" of Adenauer. See Dirks's article, "Der restaurative Charakter der Epoche," *Frankfurter Hefte*, 9, 1950, 942–55.
244. Wehler made this observation in "Podiumsdiskussion zum Thema des Abschlußvortrages," in Broszat, ed., *Deutschlands Weg in die Diktatur*, p. 359.

245. Wilfried Loth, "Verschweigen und Überwinden: Versuch einer Bilanz," in Loth and Rusinek, eds., *Verwandlungspolitik: NS-Eliten in der westdeutschen Nachkriegsgesellschaft*, pp. 357–59.

246. Kielmannsegg, *Lange Schatten*, pp. 39–41.

247. Pinson and Epstein, *Modern Germany*, p. 580.

248. Jeffrey Herf, "The Holocaust and the Competition of Memories in Germany, 1945–1949," in Dan Michman, ed., *Remembering the Holocaust in Germany, 1945–2000: German Strategies and Jewish Responses* (New York, 2002), pp. 15–16.

249. Jason Dawsey, "The Antinomies of German Memory," *H-German*, September 2009. www.h-net.org/reviews/showpdf.php?id=25045

250. Peter Merseburger, "Ein deutscher Sozialdemokrat," *The European Circle*, November 8, 2010. See also Edgar Wolfrum, *Geschichte als Waffe: Vom Kaiserreich bis zur Wiedervereinigung* (Göttingen, 2001), p. 107.

251. Ulrich Herbert, "NS-Eliten in der Bundesrepublik," 94–95; Kielmansegg, *Lange Schatten*, p. 20.

252. Marc von Miquel, *Ahnden oder amnestieren?: Westdeutsche Justiz und Vergangenheitspolitik in den sechziger Jahren* (Göttingen, 2004), pp. 28, 66–68. "Germany's FBI Examines Its Nazi Roots," *Der Spiegel*, October 1, 2007; "A German Ministry's Criminal Past," *The Wall Street Journal*, October 26, 2010; Klaus Wiegrefe, "The Nazi Criminals Who Became German Spooks," *Der Spiegel*, February 16, 2011; "Mitarbeiter mit braunen Flecken," *TAZ*, January 29, 2015.

253. Sven Felix Kellerhoff, "Wie viele Nazis arbeiteten für Adenauers Polizei?" *Die Welt*, February 29, 2012. See also "Nazis zählen reicht nicht," *Die Zeit*, February 25, 2016.

254. Ulrich Brochhagen shows the steep decline in the number of Nazis convicted for criminal offenses between 1945 and 1958. Brochhagen, *Nach Nürnberg*, p. 165.

255. Klaus Wiegrefe, "Triumph der Gerechtigkeit," *Der Spiegel*, March 28, 2011, pp. 37–43; Georg Bönisch and Klaus Wiegrefe, "From Nazi Criminal to Postwar Spy," *Der Spiegel International*, January 20, 2011.

256. Lutz Hachmeister, "Mein Führer, es ist ein Wunder!" *TAZ*, December 27, 1996, pp. 11–13. Hachmeister argues that Rudolf Augstein hired the ex-SS-officers Horst Mahnke und Georg Wolff because of the insider knowledge they could provide for stories about the Nazi past. See also "Eine Handvoll Nazis," *Der Spiegel*, September 22, 2012, and also "The Role Ex-Nazis Played in Early West Germany," *Der Spiegel*, March 6, 2012.

257. Herbert, "Rückkehr in die Bürgerlichkeit," 157–73.

258. See Dirk van Laak's discussion of the cases of former DAF official Otto Wetzel and constitutional scholar Theodor Maunz in "'Nach dem Sturm schlägt man auf die Barometer ein ...' Rechtsintellektuelle Reaktionen auf das Ende des 'Dritten Reiches,'" *WerkstattGeschichte*, 17, 1997, 36–37.

259. Kielmansegg has deterministically argued that "the Bonn democracy was never endangered by the fact that its civil servants retained sympathies for ... any alternative to democracy." Kielmansegg, *Lange Schatten*, pp. 41–42. Herbert argues that few major Nazis went into postwar politics because it would have been a step down for them in status (compared with what they had enjoyed in the Third Reich) and might have jeopardized their postwar economic opportunities. Herbert, "NS-Eliten in der Bundesrepublik," 106–15.

260. Tauber, *Beyond Eagle and Swastika*, p. 810; Winkler, *Germany*, p. 148; Kielmansegg, *Lange Schatten*, p. 12.

261. Van Laak, "Nach dem Sturm," 40.

262. Kleßmann, *Die doppelte Staatsgründung*, pp. 223–26. Wolfrum, *Die geglückte Demokratie*, p. 51; Adam Tooze, "Reassessing the Moral Economy of Post-War Reconstruction: The Terms of the West German Settlement in 1952," *Past and Present*, 2011, 53–54.

263. Wolfrum, *Die geglückte Demokratie*, p. 78.

264. Ibid., p. 80; Herbert Giersch, et al., *The Fading Miracle: Four Decades of Market Economy in Germany* (Cambridge, UK, 1992), pp. 62–65. Winkler, *Germany*, p. 148; Gert-Joachim Glaeßner, *Politik in Deutschland* (Wiesbaden, 2006), p. 90. Kitchen, *A History of Modern Germany*, pp. 330–31.

265. See Tooze, "Reassessing the Moral Economy of Post-War Reconstruction," 56–60; Wolfrum, *Die geglückte Demokratie*, pp. 80–81.

266. Lawrence S. Kaplan has counterfactually speculated that if the US had not approved the NATO treaty in 1949 and returned to a more isolationist foreign policy, Germany might have moved in the direction of a neo-Nazi "Fourth Reich." Kaplan's point of divergence involves the US Senate potentially rejecting article 5 of the treaty (obligating member states to collective defense). This appears to be a far-fetched scenario, however, given the fact that the Senate eventually ratified the treaty by a wide margin, 82–13, in July of 1949. See Lawrence S. Kaplan, "NATO after Forty-Five Years: A Counterfactual History," in S. Victor Papacosma and Mary Ann Heiss, eds., *NATO in the Post-Cold War Era: Does It Have a Future?* (New York, 1995), pp. 5–6, 12–14.

267. L. C. B. Seaman, *Post-Victorian Britain 1902–1951* (London, 1966), p. 385. See also chapter 6 ("Korean War Alternatives") of Jennifer Milliken's book, *The Social Construction of the Korean War: Conflict Possibilities* (Manchester, UK, 2001). Arthur Mitchell, *Understanding the Korean War: The Participants, the Tactics, and the Course* (Jefferson, NC, 2013), p. 236. Benjamin David Baker, "What if the Kuomintang Had Won the Chinese Civil War?" *The Diplomat*, December 24, 2015.

268. Tooze argues that the US pressured Germany to finalize a deal with the Jewish state in exchange for debt reduction, but German officials like Fritz Schäffer wanted to prioritize domestic spending on refugees and only agreed to Adenauer's compromise plan under immense pressure. Tooze, "Reassessing the Moral Economy of Post-War Reconstruction," 61. In the end, Germany reduced its pre-1933 and post-1945 foreign debt from 30 billion to 14 billion DM. This did not include the Nazi-era debt of more than 20 billion RM. Germany was shielded from any claims for reparations for Nazi-era forced-labor policies until a final peace treaty was signed between the Allies and a unified Germany. West Germany thus received very lenient treatment. Tooze, "Reassessing the Moral Economy of Post-War Reconstruction," 56, 60.

269. Tooze, "Reassessing the Moral Economy of Post-War Reconstruction," 68–69.

270. Michael Hughes, *Shouldering the Burdens of Defeat*, 1999; Hagen, *German History in Modern Times*, pp. 360–65. The law aimed to compensate expellees for the loss of some 300 billion DM of private assets. In the end, the law only provided partial compensation (roughly half the total amount). Görtemaker, *Geschichte der Bundesrepublik Deutschland*, p. 171.

271. Ulrich Herbert has argued that "without the economic miracle the integration of the refugees ... would have been impossible." At the same time, he has hypothesized that "without [the] vast influx of refugees ... an enormous labor shortage would have developed in the 1950s," adding that "without the additional labor they provided, the economic miracle itself would have been an impossibility."

Ulrich Herbert, *A History of Foreign Labor in Germany* (Ann Arbor, 1990), p. 195.

272. Görtemaker writes that the only "alternative" to the *Lastenausgleich* was the "violent realization of the expellees' demand to return to their homes," which "would have sowed new enmity and made it impossible to arrive at a lasting solution for the German and European problem." Görtemaker, *Geschichte der Bundesrepublik Deutschland*, p. 172; see also Hughes, *Shouldering the Burdens of Defeat*, p. 194.

273. Rudolf Augstein, "Konrad Adenauer und seine Epoche," *Der Spiegel*, 41, 1963, p. 87.

274. Most expellees were reluctant to return to the east once they realized how dramatically their hometowns had been transfigured by communist rule. But this was true only after the *Lastenausgleich* gave expellees a secure foundation and enabled them to take solace in an imaginary "Heimat of memory" rather than their actual homes. See Andrew Demshuk, *The Lost German East: Forced Migration and the Politics of Memory, 1945–1970* (New York, 2012), pp. 60–61, 77, 120.

275. "Trial of Nazi Accents Voluntary Reeducation," *The Christian Science Monitor*, April 17, 1952, p. 13.

276. Trittel, "*Man kann ein Ideal nicht verraten ...,* " p. 256. See also "Ex-Nazi Reviving Hitler Technique," *The New York Times*, August 17, 1953, p. 6.

277. Theodor W. Adorno, "What Does Coming to Terms with the Past Mean?" in Geoffrey Hartman, ed., *Bitburg in Moral and Political Perspective* (Bloomington, IN, 1986), p. 121.

278. In 1952, 21 percent of West Germans believed that Germany would have won the war if there had not been a resistance movement, while 45 percent believed the war was lost anyway. Kittel, *Die Legende von der zweiten Schuld*, p. 224.

279. This scenario was outlined by Richard Lowenthal in his essay, "The New Nazi Round-Up," *The New Leader*, February 23, 1953, p. 11.

280. Many have invoked the premise without bothering to show how it might have happened. See Banchoff, *The German Problem Transformed*, p. 46. Edgar Wolfrum, *Geschichte als Waffe: Vom Kaiserreich bis zur Wiedervereinigung* (Göttingen, 2001), p. 107. Lewis Joachim Edinger, *Kurt Schumacher: A Study in Personality and Political Behavior* (Palo Alto, 1965), p. 142.

281. Edinger, *Kurt Schumacher*, p. 206; Wolfrum, *Die geglückte Demokratie*, pp. 47–48; Ina Brandes, "Kurt Schumacher: Der Kandidat aus Weimar," in Daniela Forkmann and Saskia Richter, eds., *Gescheiterte Kanzler-Kandidaten: Von Kurt Schumacher bis Edmund Stoiber* (Wiesbaden, 2007), p. 36.

282. Of the total 402 votes needed, his own vote gave him the 202nd, which was one more than half.

283. Von Thomas Rieke, "Erinnerung an den 'Kanzlermacher,'" *Mittelbayerische Zeitung,* May 23, 2013. www.mittelbayerische.de/region/regensburg-stadt-nachrichten/erinnerung-an-den-kanzlermacher-21179-art918696.html

284. Görtemaker, *Geschichte der Bundesrepublik Deutschland*, pp. 99–100.

285. David Childs and Jeffrey Johnson, *West Germany: Politics and Society* (New York, 1981), p. 204.

286. Wolfrum, *Die geglückte Demokratie*, p. 49. "Eine Stimme mehr? Das reicht!" *Der Tagesspiegel*, August 23, 2009. www.tagesspiegel.de/meinung/kommentare/konrad-adenauer-eine-stimme-mehr-das-reicht/1585880.html

287. Geppert, *Die Ära Adenauer*, p. 31. Wolfrum, *Die geglückte Demokratie*, p. 50.

288. Geppert, *Die Ära Adenauer*, p. 31. Brandes, "Kurt Schumacher," 42.

289. Schwarz continues: "The bourgeois coalition could have collapsed if the Western Treaties had not been completed [or] if the Korean War and accompanying Korea boom had not happened." Schwarz's remarks appear in "Podiumdiskussion: Kurt Schumacher – Mensch und Staatsmann," sponsored by the Friedrich Ebert Stiftung, September 1999, pp. 169–71.

290. Tooze, "Reassessing the Moral Economy of Post-War Reconstruction," 49.

291. See Christopher Simpson, *Blowback: America's Recruitment of Nazis and Its Effects on the Cold War* (New York, 1988), pp. 146–48. Deborah Kisatsky, *The United States and the European Right, 1945–1955* (Columbus, OH, 2005), chapter 3. "Hitlers Werewolf sollte wiedererstehen," *Aufwärts* (Cologne), March 19, 1953.

292. "Podiumdiskussion: Kurt Schumacher – Mensch und Staatsmann," sponsored by the Friedrich Ebert Stiftung, September 1999, p. 169.

293. See Barnard A. Cook, *Europe since 1945: An Encyclopedia*, Volume I (New York, 2001). Cook writes, "if there had been federal elections in 1950, the government probably would have fallen," ibid., p. 467.

294. Herf, *Divided Memory*, pp. 242–52; Kittel, *Die Legende von der zweiten Schuld*, p. 80.

295. See Herf, *Divided Memory*, esp. pp. 267–80.

296. See Jürgen Weber, *Germany, 1945–1990: A Parallel History* (Budapest, 2004), p. 44. As a result, doubt can be cast on A. J. Nicholls's claim that "had Schumacher's SPD been in office in 1950, the continued exclusion of former collaborators in the Third Reich might have been continued," thereby making them "irrevocably opposed to the new regime." Nicholls, *The Bonn Republic*, p. 110.

297. Frank M. Buscher, "Kurt Schumacher, German Social Democracy and the Punishment of Nazi Crimes," *Holocaust and Genocide Studies*, 3, 1990, 262.

298. Ibid., p. 265. Edinger, *Kurt Schumacher*, pp. 90–92. Herf, *Divided Memory*, pp. 278–79.

299. Edinger, *Kurt Schumacher*, p. 90.

300. Even Herf notes this. Herf, *Divided Memory*, p. 295.

301. Brandes, "Kurt Schumacher," 39–40.

302. The East German press already reflected on the counterfactual possibilities of this offer in the article "Was wäre, wenn . . .," *Neues Deutschland*, May 22, 1952, p. 4. For the literature, see Ruud van Dijk, "The 1952 Stalin Note Debate: Myth of Missed Opportunity for German Unification?" *Working Paper No. 14, Woodrow Wilson International Center for Scholars* May 1996. Görtemaker, *Geschichte der Bundesrepublik Deutschland*, pp. 305–10. See also Winkler, *Germany*, pp. 137–41.

303. Winkler, *Germany*, p. 138; see also "Podiumdiskussion: Kurt Schumacher – Mensch und Staatsmann," sponsored by the Friedrich Ebert Stiftung, September 1999. Augstein considers the possibility that reunification might have occurred had Adenauer not been chancellor.

304. Herbert Lüthy, "Behind Reawakened German Nationalism," *Commentary*, February 1, 1952, p. 120.

305. Geppert, *Die Ära Adenauer*, pp. 52–54; Wolfrum, *Die geglückte Demokratie*, pp. 115–21.

306. Banchoff, *The German Problem Transformed*, pp. 46–49.

307. Lothar Kettenacker briefly reflects on what would have happened if the June 17 rebellion had succeeded in overthrowing the East German regime in *Germany 1989: In the Aftermath of the Cold War* (New York, 2009), p. 41.

From Germany to the United States: Universalizing the Fourth Reich in the Turbulent 1960s

1. "Marsch gegen Neofaschismus," *Neues Deutschland*, November 19, 1966, p. 1.
2. John H. Bracey, Jr., August Meier, and Elliott Rudwick, eds., *Black Nationalism in America* (Indianapolis, 1970), p. 514.
3. James Bryant Conant, *Germany and Freedom: A Personal Appraisal* (Cambridge, MA, 1958), pp. 13, 33.
4. Drew Middleton, "Geneva Mood: Less 'Spirit,' More Realism," *The New York Times*, October 30, 1955, p. E3.
5. William Henry Chamberlin, "Adenauer's Fourth Reich," *The Saturday Review*, November 19, 1960, p. 27.
6. "Goings On About Town: Motion Pictures," *The New Yorker*, February 20, 1960; see also the neutral reference to "the citizens of the Fourth Reich" in an article about the spread of Berlitz language schools in West Germany. Mel Heimer, "My New York," *The Kane Republican*, May 12, 1958.
7. In an article in *Der Spiegel*, German diplomat Otto Bräutigam declared that he once feared his diary falling "into the wrong hands during the Third Reich, but not in the Fourth Reich": "Es gab Gänsebraten," *Der Spiegel*, March 21, 1956, p. 23. See also Federal Press Minister Felix von Eckhardt's comment about wanting to write a sequel to a film he helped write in the Third Reich – *Die Entlassung* (1942) – "in the Fourth Reich": "Die heilgraue Eminenz," *Der Spiegel*, February 6, 1957.
8. "Brecht Scene Brought Up to Date," *The Times* (London), December 16, 1959, p. 9; "Commie Berthold Brecht Sacred Cow Even in Café of 'Free City of Berlin,'" *Variety*, December 30, 1959.
9. In 1962, the *Passauer Neue Presse* declared that East Germany's communist leader, Walter Ulbricht, was "dreaming of being the creator of a Fourth Reich … under communist auspices." "Ulbrichts 'Nationalkongreß,'" *Passauer Neue Presse*, June 5, 1962, pp. 1–2. Similarly, David S. Collier and Kurt Glaser's book, *Berlin and the Future of Eastern Europe* (Chicago, 1963), referred to "Ulbricht's Fourth Reich" as a "totalitarian" government (p. 17).
10. Roger Morgan, *The United States and West Germany, 1945–1973: A Study in Alliance Politics* (London, 1974), pp. 115, 75–97. See also Wolfram Hanrieder, *Germany, America, Europe: Forty Years of German Foreign Policy* (New Haven, 1989), pp. 164–72.
11. Shida Kiani, "Zum politischen Umgang mit dem Antisemitismus in der Bundesrepublik: Die Schmierwelle im Winter 1959/1960," in Stephan Alexander Glienke, Volker Paulmann, and Joachim Perels, eds., *Erfolgsgeschichte Bundesrepublik? Die Nachkriegsgesellschaft im langen Schatten des Nationalsozialismus* (Göttingen, 2008), pp. 115–45.
12. "Vandals Desecrate Synagogue Opened by Adenauer in Cologne," *The New York Times*, December 26, 1959, p. 1.
13. Kiani, "Zum politischen Umgang," 116. See also "Cologne Vandals Defiant in Court," *The New York Times*, February 6, 1960, p. 5.
14. "Wieder mehrere antisemitische Übergriffe," *FAZ*, January 2, 1960, p. 3; "Das Kabinett befaßt sich mit den antisemitischen Übergriffen," *FAZ*, January 4, 1960, p. 1. "Nach der Synagogenschändung," *FAZ*, December 31, 1959, p. 5. Church in Gelsenkirchen. "Hakenkreuzschmierereien," *FAZ*, April 13, 1961.

15. "West Germans Fight Anti-Semitism," *The Chicago Daily Tribune*, December 31, 1959, p. 3.

16. Kiani, "Zum politischen Umgang," 118.

17. "Synagogue Arson Foiled in Bavaria," *The New York Times*, January 20, 1960, p. 15.

18. John Dornberg, *Schizophrenic Germany* (New York, 1961), p. 102.

19. "Hakenkreuze vor der Hamburger Synagoge," *FAZ*, April 22, 1961, p. 3.

20. "The Swastika Syndrome," *The Washington Post*, January 14, 1960, p. A22.

21. "Neo-Nazi Outrages," *The New York Times*, December 31, 1959, p. 20.

22. "Britons Protest Anti-Semitic Acts: Jewish War Veterans Lead London Throng in March on Bonn's Embassy," *The New York Times*, January 18, 1960, p. 8.

23. Ulrich Brochhagen, *Nach Nürnberg: Vergangenheitsbewältigung und Westintegration in der Ära Adenauer* (Berlin, 1999), p. 295.

24. The fact that Germany was "fat and prosperous" boded well for the country's future, according to "Nazis in High Office at Issue in Germany," *The New York Times*, January 24, 1960, p. 1.

25. "British Press Attacks Germans," *The Chicago Daily Tribune*, January 4, 1960, p. B4. Drew Pearson, "Nazism Revival Laid Partly to U.S.," *The Washington Post*, January 13, 1960, p. D11.

26. Critics focused on media reports that West German history textbooks only devoted one paragraph to the Nazis' persecution of the Jews. "German Students Get Swastika Truth," *The Salt Lake Tribune*, January 18, 1960, p. 30.

27. "Ghost of Nazism Still Haunts Bonn," cited in *The Washington Post*, January 23, 1960, p. A10.

28. Kiani, "Zum politischen Umgang," 130–34; "Adenauer verurteilt die antsemitische Schmierereien," *FAZ* January 6, 1960, p. 4.

29. "Das Kabinett befaßt sich mit den antisemitischen Übergriffen," *FAZ*, January 4, 1960, p. 1.

30. Only 12 percent of Germans believed the swastika wave was the result of unrepentant old Nazis. Kiani, "Zum politischen Umgang," 136.

31. Ibid., p. 135. Manfred Kittel, "Peripatie der Vergangenheitsbewältigung: Die Hakenkreuzschmierereien 1959/60 und das bundesdeutsche Verhältnis zum Nationalsozialismus," *Historisch-Politische Mitteilungen*, 1, 1994, 56.

32. "Berliners Decry Ex-Nazis' Power," *The New York Times*, January 19, 1960, p. 7; "35,000 in Berlin Parade Denounce Hate Wave," *The Washington Post*, January 9, 1960, p. A4.

33. In light of the growing pressure, Adenauer accepted the resignation of Oberländer in 1960. Kiani, "Zum politischen Umgang," 139. "Spread of Anti-Semitism Indicates W. German Youth in Vacuum of Ideals," *The Washington Post*, January 7, 1960, p. A5.

34. William L. Shirer, *The Rise and Fall of the Third Reich* (New York, 1960).

35. Gavriel D. Rosenfeld, "The Reception of William L. Shirer's *The Rise and Fall of the Third Reich* in the United States and West Germany, 1960–1962," *Journal of Contemporary History*, January 1994, 95–129.

36. T. H. Tetens, *The New Germany and the Old Nazis* (New York, 1961), pp. 84, 82, 86.

37. Ibid., pp. 256, 254.

38. Dornberg, *Schizophrenic Germany*, p. 288.

39. Ibid., p. 287.

40. Paul Meskil, *Hitler's Heirs* (New York, 1961), p. 112.

41. Ibid., p. 8.

42. Charles Allen, *Heusinger of the Fourth Reich* (New York, 1963), p. 222.
43. Ibid., p. 34.
44. Whitney Bolton, "Glancing Sideways," *The Cumberland Evening Times* (Maryland), June 15, 1961.
45. C. E. Carpenter, "A Miscalculation by K, and Lights Go Out," *The Democrat and Chronicle* (Rochester, NY), August 17, 1961.
46. *The New York Times*, June 4, 1961, p. BR20.
47. *The Salt Lake Tribune*, May 21, 1962.
48. "Nazis schänden die Kölner Synagoge," *Berliner Zeitung*, December 28, 1959, p. 1; "Die Kölner Hakenkreuze," *Neues Deutschland*, December 28, 1959, p. 2; "Die Antworten," *Berliner Zeitung*, December 29, 1959, p. 1.
49. "Ihre Saat geht auf," *Neues Deutschland*, January 6, 1960, p. 2. Albert Norden condemned Theodor Oberländer for supporting the "imperialist policies of the Fourth Reich," and drew links between the "Gestapo heads from the Third Reich and the regents of the Fourth Reich." Albert Norden, "In Urlaub? Vor Gericht!" *Neues Deutschland*, April 13, 1960, p. 1; "Revanchisten-Allianz gegen Entspannung," *Neues Deutschland*, December 7, 1963, p. 3; Norden referred to the Springer publishing company as the "Fourth Reich's war press trust." "Nazi-Journaille beherrscht Bonns Presse," *Neue Zeit*, March 17, 1962, p. 1.
50. "Deutschlands Weg zum Friedensvertrag," *Berliner Zeitung*, July 7, 1961, p. 3.
51. "Gedanken eines Engländers zur Deutschlandfrage," *Neues Deutschland*, August 10, 1961, p. 7; "Das vierte Reich ist im Entstehen begriffen," *Neue Zeit*, November 8, 1961, p. 2. "Pressespiegel, 'La Tribune des Nations,'" *Berliner Zeitung*, November 21, 1961, p. 12; "Holländer müssen Westirian räumen," *Berliner Zeitung*, August 17, 1962, p. 5; "Ein Buch warnt vor Bonn," *Neues Deutschland*, March 27, 1963, p. 5.
52. Kurt Stern, "Erklärung," *Neues Deutschland*, October 13, 1963, p. 4.
53. In 1960, Thomas Harlan, the son of the Nazi filmmaker, Veit Harlan, received support from the Polish government for a massive study to be entitled *The Fourth Reich*, which sought to trace the biographies of 17,000 Nazi perpetrators and reveal their importance in the postwar Federal Republic. The study was funded by the Polish communist party and the Italian communist publisher Giangiacomo Feltrinelli, but was never completed, due to a power rivalry within the Polish communist party. Pierre Stephan, *Thomas Harlan: Das Gesicht deines Feindes: Ein deutsches Leben* (Berlin, 2007), pp. 105–37; "Thomas Harlan von Warschau aus," *FAZ*, January 18, 1960, p. 4; Jonas Engelmann, "Sauvater, du Land, du Un, du Tier," *Jungle World*, 7, February 18, 2010. Stephan, *Thomas Harlan*, pp. 125–31, 136–37.
54. Prittie, *Germany Divided*; Christopher Emmet and Norbert Muhlen, *The Vanishing Swastika: Facts and Figures on Nazism in West Germany* (Chicago, 1961); William Henry Chamberlin, *The German Phoenix* (New York, 1963). See also Chamberlin's apologetic essay "Jews in Germany," *The Wall Street Journal*, January 13, 1960, p. 12.
55. Emmet and Muhlen, *The Vanishing Swastika*.
56. Ibid., pp. 19–20. Prittie, *Germany Divided*, pp. 259, 257. See also Chamberlin, *The German Phoenix*, pp. 267–69.
57. Emmet and Muhlen, *The Vanishing Swastika*, pp. 8, 47; Prittie, *Germany Divided*, pp. 331–35; Chamberlin, *The German Phoenix*, pp. 220–21.
58. Emmet and Muhlen, *The Vanishing Swastika*, p. 21.
59. Ibid., pp. 30–38; Chamberlin, *The German Phoenix*, p. 224.

60. Emmet and Muhlen, *The Vanishing Swastika*, p. 3.
61. Ibid., p. 54.
62. Prittie discussed the country's enduring Nazi tendencies, taking note of the activities of the SRP, DRP, and Naumann Circle. Prittie, *Germany Divided*, pp. 354, 303.
63. Ibid., pp. 331–35.
64. Chamberlin, *The German Phoenix*, pp. 234, 7.
65. Ibid., p. ix.
66. "Swastika Smeared in 13 U.S. Cities," *The Washington Post*, January 10, 1960, p. D19.
67. "Bomb Blast at Temple," *The Kansas City Times*, January 28, 1960, p. 1.
68. "Jews in Gadsden Reassured," *Jewish Telegraphic Agency*, March 28, 1960.
69. "President Scores 'Virus Of Bigotry,'" *The New York Times*, January 13, 1960, p. 1.
70. David Caplovitz and Candace Rogers, *Swastika 1960: The Epidemic of Anti-Semitic Vandalism in America* (New York, 1961).
71. Ibid., p. 33.
72. Ibid., p. 36.
73. "Boy 'Fuehrers,'" *The Washington Post*, January 17, 1960, p. A8.
74. Milton Friedman, "Nazism in American Schools," *Jewish Advocate*, February 11, 1960, p. A2.
75. "Neo-Nazis Reported in Kansas City Schools," *Bridgeport Post*, February 1, 1960.
76. "On in Bombing Probe," *The Kansas City Times*, January 30, 1960, p. 1.
77. "Neo-Nazi Youth Party in U.S. Schools," *The Age* (Melbourne, Australia), February 1, 1960, p. 4.
78. "Nazi Activities of Boys Stirs Debate on Studies," *The Hartford Courant*, May 26, 1959, p. 1A. "'4th Reich' Plot Confessed by Ohio High School Boys," *The New York Tribune*, May 26, 1959, p. 8.
79. "Youthful Nazis Idealize Bitter Period of World," *The Kansas City Times*, January 30, 1960, pp. 1, 5.
80. Caplovitz and Rogers, *Swastika 1960*, p. 51.
81. Ibid., p. 41.
82. "Negroes and Jews Face Bias," *Tri-State Defender* (Memphis, TN), January 23, 1960, p. 7.
83. Leon Carter Smith, "Young Ideas," *The Los Angeles Tribune*, January 15, 1960, p. 14.
84. "Rabbi Scorns Swastika," *The New York Times*, January 26, 1960, p. 24.
85. John David Nagle, *The National Democratic Party: Right Radicalism in the Federal Republic of Germany* (Berkeley, 1970), pp. 33–34, 52–57.
86. Ibid., pp. 84, 93.
87. See the party platform of 1967 in Ivor Montagu, *Germany's New Nazis* (London, 1967), pp. 130–31.
88. Nagle, *The National Democratic Party*, pp. 77–79.
89. Montagu, *Germany's New Nazis*, pp. 130–31.
90. "Programm der NPD," www.hdg.de/lemo/bestand/objekt/druckgut-flugblatt-npd-kurier.html
91. Montagu, *Germany's New Nazis*, pp. 24, 127, 128; Nagle, *The National Democratic Party*, pp. 88–92.
92. Nagle, *The National Democratic Party*, chapter 3.
93. Two-thirds of the leadership had belonged to the NSDAP: Montagu, *Germany's New Nazis*, pp. 49–51; Nagle, *The National Democratic Party*, p. 34.

94. Between 14 and 18 percent of German voters were thought to be potential NPD voters. Dietrich Strothmann, "Das Gespenst der NPD," *Die Zeit*, 19, 1968. Nagle, *The National Democratic Party*, pp. 133–34.

95. The unemployment rate rose over 3 percent in March of 1967. Nagle, *The National Democratic Party*, p. 50.

96. Stöss, *Die extreme Rechte in der Bundesrepublik*, pp. 97–121; Montagu, *Germany's New Nazis*, pp. 59–62.

97. Nagle, *The National Democratic Party*, p. 66.

98. See Karl Dietrich Bracher, "Democracy and Right Wing Extremism in West Germany," *Current History*, May 1, 1968, 281–87.

99. Dietrich Strothmann, "Die Nationalen probten den Aufstand," *Die Zeit*, 26, 1966.

100. "Close-Up: Von Thadden Boss of the Reich's Reborn Right," *Life Magazine*, July 19, 1968, p. 37.

101. Kurt Hirsch, *Kommen Die Nazis Wieder? Gefahren für die Bundesrepublik* (Munich, 1967).

102. Ibid., pp. 37–97, 115–51, 178–79.

103. Montagu, *Germany's New Nazis*.

104. Ibid., pp. 82–83. He also blamed Kiesinger for helping "to whitewash the NPD" and revive German nationalism.

105. Long, *The New Nazis of Germany*, p. 247.

106. Lord Russell, *Return of the Swastika?* (New York, 1969), p. 28.

107. Ibid., pp. 103–04, vii–viii.

108. George Vine wrote that Thadden was committed to "whitewashing" the Nazis' crimes against the Jews because "the unsightly rubble of the Third Reich [must be] removed in readiness for erection of the new myths on which the Fourth Reich will be built." George Vine, "Fanatical Nazis Seek to Destroy the Truths about Hitler's Germany," *The Age* (Melbourne, Australia), February 3, 1960, p. 8. The *Montreal Gazette* wrote that the DRP demanded "the creation of a 'fourth Reich' and the unification of all German-speaking areas … in Europe." Brian Horton, "Nazi Underground Discounted," *The Montreal Gazette*, March 30, 1961.

109. Peter Lust, "Sees History Repeating Itself in Germany," *The Canadian Jewish Chronicle*, November 25, 1966.

110. Robert E. Segal, *The Wisconsin Jewish Chronicle*, December 23, 1966. See also Nino Lo Bello, "Specter of Horror: Neo-Nazis Arise," *Philadelphia Inquirer*, February 26, 1967.

111. "A Fourth Reich for Germany?" *Prevent World War III*, 71, winter/spring, 1968, pp. 10–12.

112. Dietrich Strothmann, "Das Gespenst der NPD," *Die Zeit*, May 10, 1968.

113. Hirsch, *Kommen die Nazis wieder?*, p. 38.

114. "Students Fight the Extremists in Munich," *Guardian*, November 18, 1966; "Munich Clashes over Right-Wing Rally," *The Times* (London), November 19, 1966, p. 1.

115. "Marsch gegen Neofaschismus," *Neues Deutschland*, November 19, 1966, p. 1.

116. "Sechs drängende Fragen," *Neues Deutschland*, October 23, 1966, p. 1.

117. "'Combat': Bonn gebärdet sich as 'Viertes Reich,'" *Neues Deutschland*, February 12, 1966, p. 1.

118. "Kiesingers 'Geheimnis,'" *Neue Zeit*, September 17, 1967, p. 2.

119. "Ein neuer 'Rat der Götter' entsteht in Westdeutschland," *Berliner Zeitung*, June 5, 1968; "Bonn schuf 'viertes Reich,'" *Neues Deutschland*, February 1, 1968; "Prawda: Wölfe bleiben Wölfe," *Neues Deutschland*, July 28, 1968, p. 7; "Strauß giert nach der Atombombe," *Neues Deutschland*, January 17, 1969, p. 7; "Kurs auf das 'vierte

Reich,'" *Neue Zeit*, January 30, 1969, p. 3; "Polen warnt Bonn," *Neue Zeit*, February 13, 1969, p. 1.

120. Nagle, *The National Democratic Party*, p. 201.

121. See Jarausch, *After Hitler*, pp. 99–185.

122. Frederick J. Simonelli, *American Fuehrer: George Lincoln Rockwell and the American Nazi Party* (Urbana, IL, 1999), pp. 27, 75.

123. Ibid., pp. 98–101; "Washington Crowd Attacks Rockwell," *The New York Times*, July 4, 1960, p. 28; "American Nazi Stoned in Boston," *The New York Times*, January 16, 1961, p. 22.

124. "Neo-Nazi's Fourth Reich Plan Dropped," *The Pittsburgh Post-Gazette*, January 15, 1966, p. 3. See Frederick J. Simonelli, "The World Union of National Socialists and Postwar Transatlantic Nazi Revival," in Jeffrey Kaplan and Tore Bjørgo, eds., *Nation and Race: The Developing Euro-American Racist Subculture* (Boston, 1998), pp. 37–42. See also Simonelli, *American Fuehrer*, pp. 82–95; "Plot to Set Up 'Fourth Reich,'" *The Canberra Times* (Australia), November 9, 1966, p. 5.

125. "'Schuhgrösse neun reicht im allgemeinen," *Der Spiegel*, November 14, 1966, pp. 80–82. "West Germany Accuses 2 of Neo-Nazi Murder Plot," *The New York Times*, September 25, 1966, p. 13.

126. "Swastika Charge," *The News-Herald* (Franklin, PA), October 25, 1966, p. 24. "Police Investigating Two Building Defacings," *The Journal News* (White Plains, NY), June 22, 1966, p. 25; "Seek Solution to Wave of Vandalism in Dubuque," *The Des Moines Register*, July 3, 1967.

127. "*Jet* Editorial Comment," *Jet*, July 30, 1964, p. 10. A *New York Times* profile of the town of Philadelphia, Mississippi, where three civil rights activists were murdered in 1964, elicited a response from one reader who criticized the town as the "Fourth Reich." "Civilized?" *The New York Times*, January 24, 1965, p. SM6.

128. Cited in Aniko Bodroghkozy, *Equal Time: Television and the Civil Rights Movement* (Urbana, IL, 2012), p. 142.

129. Cited in Judith Trotsky, "Generations of Silence," *Harper's*, October 1, 1973, p. 44. See also "Protesters Plan 'Attack' on Pentagon," *Newsday*, August 29, 1967, p. 3; "4th Reich," *Independent* (Long Beach), August 9, 1967, p. 2.

130. Cited in Bracey, Meier, and Rudwick, *Black Nationalism in America*, pp. 513–17. After changing his name to Muhammad Ahmed, Stanford in December of 1972 warned that the US government was pursuing a plan to make "America Nazi Germany – the Fourth reich – by putting militant blacks in concentration camps." "The Ahmed Case," *The Oakland Post*, December 3, 1972.

131. Lerone Bennett, "What Do You Say?" *Negro Digest*, March 1967, p. 76.

132. Timothy S. Lewis, "Press 'Cop-Out' Helping to Bring on Fourth Reich," *The Philadelphia Tribune*, June 3, 1969, p. 9.

133. "The Fourth Reich," *The Milwaukee Star*, May 2, 1970.

134. Fred L. Standley and Louis H. Pratt, eds., *Conversations with James Baldwin* (Jackson, MS, 1989), p. 145.

135. James Baldwin, *No Name in the Street* (New York, 1972), p. 184. Baldwin referred to the US as the "Fourth Reich" as early as 1968, at a rally in East Harlem marking the third anniversary of the assassination of Malcolm X. "Negroes Urged at I. S. 201 to Arm for 'Self-Defense,'" *The New York Times*, February 22, 1968, p. 1.

136. "Editor Points Social Wrongs, Urges Billions for Jobs Program," *The Journal News* (Hamilton, OH), November 19, 1975, p. 86.

137. "Kunstler Calls U.S. 4th Reich," *The Troy Record*, May 20, 1970, p. 34.

138. "Famous Last Words?" *Guardian*, December 7, 1970, p. 15.

139. Pamala Haynes, "Right On!" *The Philadelphia Tribune*, January 16, 1973, p. 9.

140. "What's Your Origin?" *The Boston Globe*, September 12, 1971, p. E10.

141. "Friday Finishers," *The Billings Gazette*, May 11, 1973.

142. "Fourth Reich," *The Fresno Bee*, October 13, 1973, p. 11; "'Dictatorship' Symptoms," *The Courier-Journal* (Louisville, KY), January 30, 1973, p. 14. See also "Suggests New Title," *The Des Moines Register*, July 7, 1973, p. 10; "Maximum John," *The Lowell Sun* (Lowell, MA), March 5, 1975, p. 11.

143. Gerald Posner, *Case Closed: Lee Harvey Oswald and the Assassination of JFK* (New York, 2003), p. 440. Jim Garrison, "The Rise of the Fourth Reich," *The Los Angeles Free Press*, December 22, 1967, p. 3.

144. Ibid. Garrison's critique resembled the discourse coming from the far left, but he advanced it from more of a libertarian perspective. Although formally a Democrat, Garrison shifted his political allegiances in the late 1960s, pointing out in a famous *Playboy* interview that he had begun to identify with a "libertarian sense of conservatism." http://22november1963.org.uk/jim-garrison-political-views

145. See Alex Constantine, ed., *The Essential Mae Brussell: Investigations of Fascism in America* (Port Townsend, WA, 2014), pp. 11–12, 5.

146. "Mr. Hyde Fourth Reich," *Monroe Morning* (LA), June 2, 1963.

147. "BSU Leader Says: Administration Betrayed BSU," *The Sacramento Observer*, February 27, 1969.

148. A representative clip features a recording of cheering masses from Nazi Germany, with the narrator intoning: "These are the voices of the third Reich, the socialist party of Germany." A short clip of a Black Panther speech then follows, with the narrator saying: "these are voices of today's Fourth Reich, the socialist communist Nazis of America, the communazis."

149. Etheridge, *Enemies to Allies: Cold War Germany and American Memory* (Lexington, KY, 2016), pp. 167–68.

150. Civil rights activists and Black nationalists invoked Nazi comparisons already in the 1930s and 1940s. Thomas Sugrue, "Hillburn, Hattiesburg, and Hitler: Wartime Activists Think Globally and Act Locally," in Kevin M. Kruse and Stephen Tuck, eds., *Fog of War: The Second World War and the Civil Rights Movement* (New York, 2012), pp. 90–91. See also Chris Vials, *Haunted By Hitler: Liberals, the Left, and the Fight against Fascism in the United States* (Amherst, MA, 2014), chapter 6.

151. Bracey, Meier, and Rudwick, *Black Nationalism in America*, p. 532.

152. Fred L. Standley and Louis H. Pratt, eds., *Conversations with James Baldwin* (Jackson, MS, 1989), 96, 140. The outspoken Black nationalist Milton Henry told *Esquire Magazine* in 1969 that he had urged "every black home [to] have a gun for self-defense against the possibility of a Treblinka." Bracey, Meier, and Rudwick, *Black Nationalism in America*, p. 523.

153. John Duffett, *Against the Crime of Silence: Proceedings of the International War Crimes Tribunal* (New York, 1970), p. 51. In 1972, Swedish Prime Minister Olof Palme compared the bombing of Hanoi to the Nazi "outrages [of] Guernica, Oradour, Lidice, and Treblinka." Similar claims were expressed by SDS leader Mark Rudd and religious activists Daniel Berrigan and Abraham Joshua Heschel. See Walter L. Hixson, *The United States and the Vietnam War / 3 Leadership and Diplomacy in the Vietnam War* (New York, 2000), p. 441; Melvin Small, *Antiwarriors: The Vietnam War and the Battle for America's Hearts and Minds* (Wilmington, DE, 2002), p. 105. Betty Friedan's *Feminine Mystique* (1963) described suburban women being confined in "comfortable concentration camps."

154. "Parade and a Protest Mark Greek Independence Day Here," *The New York Times*, May 22, 1967, p. 3; "Irene Pappas Asks Boycott of Greece's 'Fourth Reich,'" *The New York Times*, July 20, 1967 p. 2.

155. "Arrests, Batons in Park Battle," *The Age* (Melbourne, Australia), June 4, 1970, p. 1.

156. "Democrats Propose New State Reapportionment Plan," *The Alexandria Times-Picayune* (Alexandria, Indiana), October 5, 1965, p. 1.

157. "5,000 Pa. Students Rally to Protest Tuition Hikes," *Bucks Co. Courier Times* (PA), October 16, 1970, p. 14.

158. "Mongoloid Death Plan Deplored," *Florida Today* (Cocoa, FL), May 31, 1974, p. 8A.

159. See Orrin E. Klapp, *Inflation of Symbols: Loss of Values in American Culture* (New Brunswick, NJ, 1991), pp. 1–5.

160. Gresham's Law describes how "bad" (as in "inflated and debased") money drives out good money from the market. References to "Gresham's law of language" appear in Klapp, *Inflation of Symbols*, p. 18.

161. "Cowboy–Longhair Fight Brings Killings," *Detroit Free Press*, November 23, 1970; "26 Charged after Motorbike Gangs Clash," *The Ottawa Journal*, June 4, 1968, p. 5; "Police and Cyclists Hold Peace Talks," *Detroit Free Press*, April 2, 1967, p. 8.

162. This claim was greeted with skepticism by the presiding judge. "Judge Orders Disbanding of 'Fourth Reich' Group," *The Berkshire Eagle*, September 10, 1969, p. 1.

163. "Pantherama at BEN March 15, 16," *The Express* (Lock Haven, PA), March 14, 1968, p. 8.

164. See advertisement in *The Herald* (Jasper, IN), May 25, 1970, p. 5.

165. "Boys, Girls Open Rec Cage Loops Thursday," *Ukiah Daily Journal*, January 9, 1968, p. 2.

166. "Armchair Generals," *The Boston Globe*, September 24, 1967, p. C4.

167. "German 'Invaders' Link Chain," *The Port Arthur News* (Port Arthur, TX), September 1, 1974, p. 15.

"Hitler in Argentina!": Fictionalizing the Fourth Reich in the Long 1970s

1. Robert Ludlum, *The Holcroft Covenant* (New York, 1978), pp. 179–80.

2. Ronald Newton argues that State Department officials developed these fears by 1942: "The United States, the German-Argentines, and the Myth of the Fourth Reich, 1943–47," 92. See also Stahl, *Nazi-Jagd*, pp. 27–28.

3. Heinz Schneppen, *Odessa und das Vierte Reich: Mythen der Zeitgeschichte* (Berlin, 2007), p. 111; Newton, "The United States, the German-Argentines, and the Myth of the Fourth Reich, 1943–47," 96.

4. Newton, "The United States, the German-Argentines, and the Myth of the Fourth Reich, 1943–47," 97. "Hitler Is Reported Alive," *The New York Times*, July 17, 1945, p. 14; "Hitler and Eva Braun Reported on Nazi Submarine Reaching Argentina," *The Coshocton Tribune* (Ohio), July 17, 1945, p. 6. "Argentines Deny Nazi's Arrival," *The New York Times*, February 20, 1945, p. 10.

5. US Department of State, *Blue Book on Argentina: Consultation among the American Republics with Respect to the Argentine Situation* (New York, 1946), p. 1.

6. Quoted in Gerald Steinacher, *Nazis on the Run: How Hitler's Henchmen Fled Justice* (Oxford, 2011), p. 220.

7. Newton, "The United States, the German-Argentines, and the Myth of the Fourth Reich, 1943–47," 100. "Nazi Activity in Argentina Told," *The Des Moines Register*, June 15, 1947, p. 10.

8. See T. H. Tetens' book, *Germany Plots with the Kremlin* (New York, 1953). For the role of Spain in Allied fears, see Seidel, *Angst vor dem "Vierten Reich."*

9. "'Der Weg' – Mouthpiece of Pan-Germanism," *Prevent World War III*, summer, 1950, p. 21.

10. On fears of a "Nazi International," see Leon Poliakov, "Launching the New Fascist International," *Commentary*, November 1952; J. Alvarez Del Vayo, "Rebirth of the Nazi International," *The Nation*, April 5, 1952, pp. 318–20; J. Alvarez Del Vayo, "Argentina, Nazi Paradise," *The Nation*, January 1950; "Fascists Clinging to Hope of Coming Back to Power," *The New York Times*, May 29, 1951, p. 8.

11. "Hitler's Hidden Millions Finance Nazi Comeback," *The Worker* (Brisbane, Australia), July 28, 1952, p. 11.

12. The Brazilian article is cited in Daniel Kosthorst and Michael Feldkamp, *Akten zur Auswärtigen Politik der Bundesrepublik* (Munich, 1997), p. 85, 9n. See also "Persistence of Neo-Nazism," *Manchester Guardian*, April 2, 1956, p. 5.

13. Stangl fled Germany for Syria and later went to Brazil. See Gitta Sereny, *Into That Darkness: From Mercy Killing to Mass Murder, a Study of Franz Stangl, the Commandant of Treblinka* (New York, 1974). On Heim, who fled West Germany for Egypt in 1962, see Nicholas Kulish and Souad Mekhennet, *The Eternal Nazi: From Mauthausen to Cairo, the Relentless Pursuit of SS Doctor Aribert Heim* (New York, 2014). Von Leers left Argentina for Egypt in 1956, converted to Islam, and changed his name to Omar Amin. Martin Finkenberger, "Johann von Leers und die 'fascistische Internationale' der fünfziger und sechziger Jahre in Argentinien und Ägypten," *Zeitschrift für Geschichtswissenschaft*, 6, 2011, 522–43. Fritz Rößler fled to Egypt in 1957 and took on the name Achmed Fritz Rößler; *Der Spiegel*, November 6, 1957, p. 64; Eisele and Zind fled to Egypt in 1958.

14. Dornberg, *Schizophrenic Germany*, p. 62.

15. Ray Alan, "Nazis in the Near East," *The New Republic*, December 14, 1953, pp. 8–11.

16. See, for example, *Prevent World War III*, 41, p. 13.

17. Stahl, *Nazi-Jagd*, p. 112.

18. Ben Gurion made this point, as did Mossad chief Isser Harel, and West German prosecutor Fritz Bauer. Ibid., pp. 118–20.

19. "Israeli Agents on Trail of Hitler Deputy," *The Salt Lake Tribune*, May 27, 1960, p. 51.

20. Reprinted in *The El Paso Herald*, October 13, 1960. "Runaway Nazis Are Working for a Revival," *Daily Express*, October 5, 1960.

21. Flora Lewis, "Lake Probed for Rumored Nazi Hoard," *The Los Angeles Times*, November 17, 1963, p. L3; "Das Geheimnis des Toplitzsees," *Berliner Zeitung*, November 5, 1963, p. 5.

22. "'Fourth Reich' Employs Egypt as Lab for War," *Detroit Free Press*, June 14, 1963.

23. Simon Wiesenthal, *The Murderers among Us* (New York, 1967), p. 80. In 1961, Wiesenthal published the German-language book *Ich jagte Eichmann: Tatsachenbericht* (Gütersloh, 1961).

24. Wiesenthal, *The Murderers among Us*, pp. 86–95.

25. Ibid., p. 87.

26. Ibid., pp. 184–87, 332.

27. In 1965, the West German authorities excavated the area around West Berlin's Invalidenstrasse in the attempt to find Bormann's remains, without any luck. See "Verschwörung am Wendekreis des Steinbocks," *Der Spiegel*, 43, 1968, pp. 54–55. "Bormann Arrest Is Sought by Bonn," *The New York Times*, July 5, 1967, p. 15.

28. "British Paper Reports Bormann Alive," *The New York Times*, November 25, 1972, p. 10. Farago relied on documents allegedly given him by Argentine secret police agents that showed Bormann was living as Ricardo Bauer.

29. William Stevenson, *The Bormann Brotherhood* (New York, 1973), Ladislas Farago, *Aftermath: Martin Bormann and the Fourth Reich* (New York, 1974), and Erich Erdstein's *Inside the Fourth Reich* (New York, 1977). See also Paul Manning's *Martin Bormann: Nazi in Exile* (Secaucus, NJ, 1981), which claimed that Hitler told Bormann in 1944 to "'bury your treasure … for you will need it to begin a Fourth Reich'" (p. 29).

30. Stevenson, *The Bormann Brotherhood*, pp. 66, 64, 97.

31. Farago, *Aftermath*, p. 71.

32. Ibid., pp. 167, 307.

33. Ibid., p. 404.

34. Erdstein, *Inside the Fourth Reich*, pp. 133, 136. Erdstein had already begun to refer to the Fourth Reich in 1968. See "'Fourth Reich' Reported in Brazil," *The Christian Science Monitor*, May 22, 1968, p. 6.

35. Erdstein, *Inside the Fourth Reich*, pp. 172, 181.

36. See the full-page ad for Stevenson's book in *The New York Times*, May 6, 1973, p. 462.

37. Richard Shepard, review of *The Murderers among Us*, in *The New York Times*, April 12, 1967, p. 45. Harriett Woods, "In Persistent Pursuit of the Nazi Criminals," *The St. Louis Post-Dispatch*, May 28, 1967. Wiesenthal's book was excerpted in *Der Spiegel*, August 14, 1967, pp. 60–63.

38. "Bormann Books Boom," *Detroit Free Press*, December 6, 1972, p. 60.

39. The positive reviews included Terence Prittie, "The Ramifications of Nazism," *The New York Times*, November 10, 1974, p. 410; "The Vatican and the Nazis," *Commentary*, April 1, 1975, p. 82. Robert Payne, "Bormann – Wanted, Dead or Alive," *The Chicago Tribune*, November 10, 1974, p. F6. More critical were: Eric Pace, "Accuracy of Recent Reports on Bormann Challenged," *The New York Times*, December 10, 1972, p. 2; Margaret Manning, "A Dubious Resurrection of Bormann Mystery," *The Boston Globe*, November 21, 1974, p. A19; Hal Burton, "Alive in Argentina?" *Newsday*, November 7, 1974, p. 7A; Herbert D. Andrews, "Did Bormann Make It?" *The Baltimore Sun*, November 24, 1974, p. D7; Heinrich Fraenkel, "57 Varieties of Bormann," *TLS*, September 26, 1975, p. 1106.

40. "Ich bin tot," *Der Spiegel*, February 2, 1969, p. 150.

41. Review of *The Bormann Brotherhood*, in *The Arizona Republic*, April 21, 1974, p. 185. Bill Shelton, review of *The Bormann Brotherhood*, in *The Independent* (Long Beach, CA), July 12, 1973, p. 81; Sylvia Sachs, "Nazis Still at Top He Says," *The Pittsburgh Press*, February 17, 1974, p. 143. W. Emerson Wilson, "Hitler Described as Just a Stooge," *The Morning News* (Wilmington, DE), May 29, 1973, p. 30.

42. Nicholas Knezevich, "Is 'Fourth Reich' Real or Fantasy?" *The Pittsburgh Press*, June 8, 1978. See also I. J. Blynn, "Mystery Man's Claim: 'I Killed Mengele,'" *The Jewish Exponent*, March 24, 1978, p. 4 and Agnes F. Peterson, review of *Inside the*

Fourth Reich, in *The Library Journal*, March 1, 1978. Later scholars cast doubt on Erdstein's credibility, pointing out that he fled Latin America for Canada not because he was endangered by vengeful Nazis but because he was "passing bad checks." Gerald Posner, *Mengele: The Complete Story* (New York, 1986), p. 218.

43. Bill Shelton, review of *The Bormann Brotherhood, The Independent* (Long Beach, CA), July 12, 1973, p. 81. The West German SPD agreed on the need for vigilance. See "Existiert wirklich ein 'Viertes Reich?'" *Sozialdemokratischer-Pressedienst*, November 12, 1975, pp. 7–9.

44. Robert Kirsch, "Ladislas Farago and the Fourth Reich," *The Los Angeles Times*, November 4, 1974, p. E9.

45. Abraham S. Hyman, "Post-Holocaust Puzzles," *The Jerusalem Post*, January 10, 1975, p. A12; C. L. Grant, "Bormann Myths Still Alive," *The Atlanta Constitution*, June 3, 1973, p. 12C; James J. Devaney, "Flawed Premise," *The Hartford Courant*, January 20, 1975, p. 13.

46. Schneppen, *Odessa und das Vierte Reich*, pp. 22, 112.

47. Newton, "The United States, the German-Argentines, and the Myth of the Fourth Reich, 1943–47," 83.

48. Ibid., 84; Schneppen, *Odessa und das Vierte Reich*, pp. 121, 208.

49. Newton, "The United States, the German-Argentines, and the Myth of the Fourth Reich, 1943–47," 83, 98.

50. Wiesenthal received much of his information in the mid 1950s from an anti-Peron Argentine diplomat named Silvio Santander, who had been deceived by a duplicitous spy, Heinrich Jürges, who worked for the American Military Government in Germany and passed along fabricated information to the US authorities. Schneppen, *Odessa und das Vierte Reich*, pp. 91–106. Newton, "The United States, the German-Argentines, and the Myth of the Fourth Reich, 1943–47," 97. Schneppen says that reports of the Strasbourg conference first surfaced in a November 1944 document given to the Supreme Headquarters Allied Expeditionary Force (SHAEF) by an alleged French informer. Schneppen, *Odessa und das Vierte Reich*, p. 77. On doubts about Farago's claims, see "Tolle Geschichte," *Der Spiegel*, 50, 1972, pp. 87–91; "Verdammtes Ding," *Der Spiegel*, 52, 1972, pp. 73–74.

51. Schneppen, *Odessa und das Vierte Reich*, pp. 41–70, 307.

52. Ibid., pp. 74–87.

53. Ibid., p. 107.

54. Newton, "The United States, the German-Argentines, and the Myth of the Fourth Reich, 1943–47," 82.

55. Stanley E. Hilton, "The United States and Argentina in Brazil's Wartime Foreign Policy, 1939–1945," in Guido Di Tella and D. Cameron Watt, eds., *Argentina between the Great Powers, 1939–1946* (Pittsburgh, 1990), p. 176.

56. This was especially true in the early 1970s, when Peron was mulling over a return to Argentina. "Tolle Geschichte," *Der Spiegel*, 50, 1972, p. 91.

57. See H.-Georg Lützenkirchen, "Keine Angst vor Odessa." http://literaturkritik.de/public/rezension.php?rez_id=11078; Schneppen, *Odessa und das Vierte Reich*, pp. 216–17.

58. Schneppen, *Odessa und das Vierte Reich*, pp. 216–17.

59. Holger Meding, *Der Weg: Eine deutsche Emigrantenzeitschrift in Buenos Aires, 1947-1957* (Berlin, 1997). Fritsch's Dürer-Verlag publishing house was the nerve center of a large circle of Nazi exiles. Ibid., pp. 110–20. See also Finkenberger, "Johann von Leers und die 'faschistische Internationale,'" 534.

60. The journal's circulation rose to 25,000 monthly copies. Finkenberger, "Johann von Leers und die 'faschistische Internationale,'" 534.

61. Meding, *Der Weg*, p. 117.

62. This was the claim made by T. H. Tetens, as cited in the article "German Plotters in Argentina?" *The Des Moines Register*, January 16, 1950; see also "German Dreams of World Domination Still Live in Hearts of Exiled Nazis," *The Salt Lake Tribune*, December 1, 1949, p. 7. The *Neue Zeitung* attacked Fritsch as "the up-and-coming man of the Fourth Reich." Meding, *Der Weg*, p. 117.

63. Meding, *Der Weg*, p. 109.

64. Leers fled West Germany for Argentina in 1950. Finkenberger, "Johann von Leers und die 'faschistische Internationale,'" 529.

65. Meding, *Der Weg*, pp. 126–28, 82.

66. Bettina Stangneth, *Eichmann before Jerusalem* (New York, 2014), pp. 134, 114.

67. Ibid., p. 143.

68. Ibid., pp. 89, 78.

69. Ibid., p. xxi.

70. Ibid., p. 212.

71. Ibid., pp. 213–14.

72. Ibid., p. 143

73. Ibid., p. 304.

74. Ibid., pp. 114–17, 214; see also Nikolaus Barbian, *Auswärtige Kulturpolitik und "Auslandsdeutsche" in Latinamerica, 1949–1973* (Wiesbaden, 2013), pp. 279–80.

75. Stangneth, *Eichmann before Jerusalem*, p. 237.

76. Ibid., p. 138.

77. Stangneth describes the West German authorities' concerns about Eichmann's political plans as "well founded." Ibid., p. 326.

78. Ibid., p. xxii, 118. Klaus Wiegrefe has written that "Eichmann could have been caught – if the Federal Republic had wanted it." Klaus Wiegrefe, "Triumph der Gerechtigkeit," *Der Spiegel*, May 1960, p. 37.

79. Wiegrefe, "Triumph der Gerechtigkeit," *Der Spiegel*, May 1960, p. 37.

80. Wiesenthal, *The Murderers among Us*, p. 97.

81. The trend also shaped art and architecture, as was seen in Anselm Kiefer's paintings of Hitler salutes and Leon Krier's celebration of Albert Speer's architecture. See Andreas Huyssen, "Anselm Kiefer: The Terror of History, the Temptation of Myth," *October*, spring, 1989, pp. 22–45; Leon Krier, *Albert Speer: Architecture, 1932–1942* (New York, 1985).

82. Daniel Magilow, Elizabeth Bridges, and Kristin T. Van der Lugt, eds., *Nazisploitation! The Nazi Image in Low-Brow Cinema and Culture* (New York, 2012).

83. James J. Ward, "This is Germany! It's 1933!' Appropriations and Constructions of 'Fascism' in New York Punk/Hardcore in the 1980s," *Journal of Popular Culture*, winter, 1996, pp. 155–84.

84. Susan Sontag, "Fascinating Fascism," in *Under the Sign of Saturn* (New York, 1980), pp. 73–105 (originally published in *The New York Review of Books* on February 6, 1975). See also Saul Friedlander, *Reflections of Nazism: An Essay on Kitsch and Death* (New York, 1982); George Mosse observed that as "Hitler has been taken over by the entertainment industry, books about his victims are in less demand." George Mosse, "Hitler Redux," *The New Republic*, June 16, 1979, p. 21.

85. Wyden, Peter, *The Hitler Virus: The Insidious Legacy of Adolf Hitler* (New York, 2001).

86. Other works included Werner Maser's monograph *Hitler* (1973) and Sebastian Haffner's study *The Meaning of Hitler* (1978); the film *Hitler: The Last Ten Days* (1972); and Beryl Bainbridge's novel *Young Adolf* (1979). See also Robert Harris, *Selling Hitler: The Story of the Hitler Diaries* (New York, 1986).
87. See, for example, Robert Hughes, "The Hitler Revival: Myth v. Truth," *Time,* May 21, 1973, pp. 81–82.
88. See Ian Kershaw, *The Nazi Dictatorship: Problems and Perspectives of Interpretation* (London, 1985), chapter 2.
89. Robert S. Levine, "The Hitler Vogue," *The Nation*, June 29, 1974, p. 807.
90. Paul Weingarten, "Nazis Still Fighting War – In Literary Blitz," *The Chicago Tribune*, March 3, 1977, p. A1.
91. Craig Whitney, "Der Führer Who?" *The Courier-Journal & Times Magazine* (Louisville, KY), November 11, 1973, pp. 40–48.
92. Neo-Nazi groups did not entirely disappear during this period, however, as was shown by the activities of Manfred Roeder and Michael Kühnen (see chapter 6).
93. Howard Blum, *Wanted! The Search for Nazis in America* (New York, 1977); John Loftus, *The Belarus Secret* (New York, 1982); Tom Bower, *The Pledge Betrayed: America and Britain and the Denazification of Postwar Germany* (New York, 1982); Allan A. Ryan, Jr., *Quiet Neighbors: Prosecuting Nazi War Criminals in America* (New York, 1984). See, more recently, Eric Lichtblau, *The Nazis Next Door: How America Became a Safe Haven for Hitler's Men* (New York, 2014).
94. As was shown by the documentary film *The California Reich* (1976), the "powerless" people who joined Rockwell's successor parties were partly motivated by the "popularization of the Nazis through movies and television." "American Nazis: Are They More Than Just a Curiosity?" *U.S. News & World Report*, November 7, 1977, pp. 57–58. Betty Liddick, "Profile of California's Fourth Reich," *Los Angeles Times*, March 23, 1976, p. E1.
95. Wyden, *The Hitler Virus*, chapter 25.
96. See Deborah Lipstadt, *Denying the Holocaust: The Growing Assault on Truth and Memory* (New York, 1993), chapter 8.
97. "American Neo-Nazis Aid German Fourth Reich," *The Sarasota Journal*, January 10, 1979, p. 12.
98. An East German example was the television series, *Ich, Axel Cäsar Springer* (1968), which portrayed the West German media baron Axel Springer as guiding the Federal Republic from "the Third Reich to the Fourth." Stefan Wolle, *Der Traum von der Revolte: Die DDR 1968* (Berlin, 2008), pp. 25–26.
99. Patterson first published the novel under the pseudonym Martin Fallon in 1962. It was later re-released under Patterson's best-known pseudonym, Jack Higgins. Quotations from the novel come from the following edition: Jack Higgins, *The Testament of Caspar Schultz* (New York, 1985).
100. David Ray, *The End of the Fourth Reich: A Rat Catcher's Adventure* (London, 1966).
101. For further information on the television shows and films, see imdb.com.
102. Harris Greene, *Canceled Accounts* (New York, 1976), p. 7.
103. Manning O'Brine, *No Earth for Foxes* (New York, 1976), p. 200.
104. William Craig, *The Strasbourg Legacy* (New York, 1976).
105. Madeline Duke, *The Bormann Receipt* (London, 1977), p. 145.
106. Adam Hall, *The Quiller Memorandum* (New York, 1965). The novel was originally published in Great Britain as *The Berlin Memorandum*.
107. Martin Hale, *The Fourth Reich* (London, 1965), pp. 44–46.
108. Frederick Forsyth, *The Odessa File* (New York, 1972).

109. Thomas Gifford, *The Wind Chill Factor* (New York, 1994), pp. 413–14, 424.

110. Ben Stein, *The Croesus Conspiracy* (New York, 1979).

111. Ludlum, *The Holcroft Covenant*, p. 180.

112. Andrew Kaplan, *Hour of the Assassins* (New York, 1980), p. 433.

113. Mike Pettit, *The Axmann Agenda* (New York, 1980).

114. The episode was called "Divorce Venusian Style."

115. Red Skull debuted in 1941 in the comic *Captain America*. See John H. Moser, "Madmen, Morons, and Monocles: The Portrayal of the Nazis in Captain America," in Robert G. Weiner, ed., *Captain America and the Struggle of the Superhero: Critical Essays* (Jefferson, NC, 2009), pp. 24–35.

116. In late 1965 and early 1966, the comic book *Tales of Suspense*, issues 72–74, featured Red Skull making good on his wartime prophecy that "if Nazism didn't conquer the world," he would "use its power to destroy all of earth!" In June of 1980, issues 16–17 of *Super-Villain Team-Up* portrayed Red Skull and a Hitler clone, known as the "Hate Monger," battling an Israeli Nazi hunter named Yousuf Tov over a "cosmic cube."

117. Geoff Taylor, *Court of Honor* (New York, 1967), p. 301.

118. Harry Patterson, *The Valhalla Exchange* (Greenwich, CT, 1977).

119. Ib Melchior, *Sleeper Agent* (New York, 1977), p. 175.

120. Jack Hunter, *The Tin Cravat* (New York, 1981).

121. John Gardner, *The Werewolf Trace* (New York, 1977).

122. George Markstein, *The Goering Testament* (New York, 1978).

123. The episode was entitled "The Deadly Games Affair."

124. *They Saved Hitler's Brain* was originally released under the title *Madmen of Mandoras* in 1963. The film was given new footage and re-released under its better-known title in 1968.

125. Edwin Fadiman, Jr., *Who Will Watch the Watchers?* (New York, 1970), p. 150. The same year, Peter Sellers agreed to play an 80-year-old Hitler in the projected film *The Phantom versus the Fourth Reich*, but it was never completed. A. H. Weiler, "Life with Father Hitler," *The New York Times*, May 21, 1972, p. D15.

126. It was based on the short story by Henry Slesar, "The Rise and Fall of the Fourth Reich," *The Magazine of Fantasy and Science Fiction*, August 1975, 63–75.

127. www.dissolute.com.au/the-avengers-tv-series/new-avengers/no1-the-eagles-nest.html

128. Philippe van Rjndt, *The Trial of Adolf Hitler* (New York, 1978), p. 255.

129. Ira Levin, *The Boys from Brazil* (New York, 1976), p. 245.

130. The episode was entitled "Anschluss '77."

131. Ib Melchior, *The Watchdogs of Abaddon* (New York, 1980), p. 237.

132. Timothy B. Benford, *Hitler's Daughter* (New York, 1983), p. 215.

133. O'Brine, *No Earth for Foxes*, p. 31; Craig, *The Strasbourg Legacy*, pp. 88–89; Forsyth, *The Odessa File*, p. 37.

134. Hale, *The Fourth Reich*, p. 66.

135. Melchior, *The Watchdogs of Abaddon*, p. 234.

136. O'Brine, *No Earth for Foxes*, p. 205; Greene, *Canceled Accounts*, p. 16.

137. Melchior, *Sleeper Agent*, p. 1.

138. O'Brine, *No Earth for Foxes*, p. 282.

139. Melchior, *The Watchdogs of Abaddon*, p. 90.

140. Greene, *Canceled Accounts*, p. 174.

141. Ray, *The End of the Fourth Reich*, p. 128.

142. Neil Jillett, "Thanks to Dr. Goebbels," *The Age* (Melbourne, Australia), June 11, 1966.

143. O'Brine added that "a breed of centuries, from Martin Luther … to Martin Bormann, does not change its id overnight." O'Brine, *No Earth for Foxes*, pp. 13–14, 280.

144. Hale, *The Fourth Reich*, pp. 183–84.

145. The quotations are taken from the unnumbered page between the dedication and acknowledgments. For Melchior's biography, see "about the author," p. 369.

146. "Author Hunts Treasures Stolen by Nazis," *The Toronto Star*, November 2, 1977, p. E5. Duke was the daughter of the prominent Austrian Jewish lawyer, Richard Herzog; she fled to England in 1939.

147. See Greene's obituary in *The Washington Post*, September 1, 1997.

148. See Selby, *The Axmann Conspiracy*, which describes Hunter's role in Operation Nursery.

149. Forsyth, *The Odessa File*, p. 29.

150. I. Levin, *The Boys from Brazil*, p. 60. Instead, Lieberman recommends "remembrance," optimistically insisting that "people are better and smarter now" because they know "history." Ibid., p. 272.

151. Gifford, *The Wind Chill Factor*, p. 272.

152. Markstein, *The Goering Testament*, p. 263.

153. *Captain Britain*, 22. When one bystander exclaims, "No one can be trusted! Any *one* of us could be a Nazi!", another thinks to himself, "You don't know how right you are, chum!"

154. Gifford, *The Wind Chill Factor*, pp. 424, 414.

155. Stein, *The Croesus Conspiracy*, pp. 262, 305.

156. Fadiman, *Who Will Watch the Watchers?* p. 252.

157. Ludlum, *The Holcroft Covenant*, p. 447.

158. Von Kraul helps capture the novel's chief Nazi villain, Nagel.

159. Sir George admits that he still "looks back on the Empire with nostalgia." Higgins, *The Testament of Kaspar Schultz*, p. 29. Post-imperial skepticism was also visible in Giles Cooper's novel *The Other Man* (1964), and Kevin Brownlow and Andrew Mollo's film *It Happened Here* (1964).

160. Gardner, *The Werewolf Trace*, pp. 99, 61–62. It is unclear why Gardner (1926–2007) challenged the finest-hour myth. Like Higgins, he had completed military service for his country (serving during the Second World War in the Home Guard and later in the Royal Navy and Royal Marines), but it is possible that a series of postwar identity crises (he left the priesthood and struggled with alcoholism) led him to adopt a more iconoclastic stance in his writing. He chronicled his disillusionment with organized religion and descent into alcoholism in his book *Spin the Bottle* (London, 1963).

161. Ludlum, who served in the Marines in the Pacific in 1944–45, was open about his liberal political views. He was a supporter of Adlai Stevenson and described himself as opposed to "large corporations," "large governments," and "fanatics of all persuasions." Herbert Mitgang, "Robert Ludlum," *The New York Times*, April 16, 1978, p. 272. Gina Macdonald, *Robert Ludlum: A Critical Companion* (Westport, CT, 1997), pp. 11, 14, 61, 90, 102.

162. Fadiman was the nephew of the famous journalist Clifton Fadiman. Given the latter's membership in the Society for the Prevention of World War III, it is possible that his nephew shared his anti-Nazi views.

163. For an author profile, see "Tim Boxer's Traveling with the Stars," *The New York Jewish Week*, March 1, 1981. Kaplan is best known for his *Homeland* continuation novels.

164. Gifford, *The Wind Chill Factor*, p. 424. Gifford's liberal outlook was suggested by his open criticism of the Catholic Church. See Jack Adrian, "Obituary: Thomas Gifford," *The Independent*, November 11, 2000, p. 6.

165. See Ben Stein, "Watergate: No Big Deal," *USA Today*, June 17, 1992; Bob Woodward and Carl Bernstein, *The Final Days* (New York, 1976), p. 447. David Greenberg, *Nixon's Shadow: The History of an Image* (New York, 2003), p. 386, 95n, and p. 211. Bickel's misanthropic tendencies are signaled by his shared name with the psychotic protagonist of Martin Scorsese's film, *Taxi Driver*.

166. This is the argument advanced by Michael Butter in *The Epitome of Evil: Hitler in American Fiction, 1939–2002* (New York, 2009), pp. 113–17. Benford's precise political leanings are unknown, but his obituary described him as a former "altar boy" and borough "police commissioner." "Timothy B. Benford, 67," *The Westfield Leader and The Scotch Plains – Fanwood Times*, August 14, 2008. www.goleader.com/08aug14/11.pdf He also wrote a variety of patriotic books about World War II. See also Timothy B. Benford, *World War II Quiz and Fact Book*, Volumes I and II (New York, 1982 and 1984); Timothy B. Benford, *World War II Flashback – A Fact-Filled Look at the War Years* (Stamford, CT, 1991). These publications suggest that *Hitler's Daughter* envisioned national unity as the proper response to the crises of the 1970s.

167. "Best Seller List," *The New York Times*, September 23, 1973, p. 422; "1975's Best Sellers," *Chicago Tribune*, December 28, 1975, p. E1; "Best Sellers of the Year," *The New York Times*, December 4, 1977, p. 312; *The New York Times*, August 6, 1978, p. BR7; *The Westfield Leader and The Scotch Plains – Fanwood Times*, August 4, 2008. www.goleader.com/08aug14/11.pdf

168. *The Wind Chill Factor* and *The Valhalla Exchange* were not turned into films.

169. "The Best Seller Who Wants to Stop," *The Times* (London), April 22, 1972, p. 14; "Bormann's False Role as 'Priest' Is Related," *The Bridgeport Telegram*, November 29, 1972, p. 38.

170. Farago had discussions with film studios about selling the movie rights to his book. "Book about Bormann, Nazi War Criminal, to Become a Movie," *The Wall Street Journal*, December 14, 1972.

171. See ad from *The Sydney Morning Herald*, November 26, 1978, p. 109.

172. *The New York Times*, March 22, 1973, p. 41.

173. For television listings for Forsyth, see *Daily Independent Journal* (San Rafael, CA), November 1, 1972, p. 41; for Wiesenthal, see *The Democrat and Chronicle* (Rochester, NY), March 29, 1967, p. 38; for Ludlum, see *Detroit Free Press*, March 22, 1978, p. 50; for Erdstein, see *The Kingsport Times-News* (Kingsport, TN), April 3, 1978, p. 21.

174. A. Kaplan, *The Hour of the Assassins*, p. 287.

175. Ludlum, *The Holcroft Covenant*, pp. 120, 318.

176. Bert C. Martin, "Escape from the Torture Dungeon of the Fourth Reich," *Escape to Adventure*, March 1962, pp. 40, 78–81.

177. The headline was "Nazi Mass Murderer Mengele Shot in Brazil," *Neue Revue*, January 5, 1969.

178. *Gallery*, September 1984. *Playboy* magazine often featured discussions about Nazis. See Alex Haley, "Interview: George Lincoln Rockwell," *Playboy*, April 1966; Eric Norden, "Interview: Albert Speer," *Playboy*, June 1971.

179. Kevin Phillips, "Era Demands New Political Leadership," *The Piqua Daily Call* (Piqua, OH), May 17, 1974, p. 6.

180. In 1965, *The Quiller Memorandum* won the Edgar Award from the Mystery Writers of America for best suspense novel. "Capote's 'Cold Blood' Wins Prize," *The Times Record* (Troy, NY), April 23, 1966, p. 4.

181. Rex Barley, "Books in the News," *The Arizona Republic*, March 28, 1965, p. 66; Robert Baldick, "Bereavement of a Simple Man," *Daily Telegraph*, April 15, 1965, p. 21. Reviews of the film were also positive: R. H. Gardner, "Pinter Can Be Comprehensible," *The Sun*, February 10, 1967, p. B4; Patrick Gibbs, "The Complete Spy," *Daily Telegraph*, November 11, 1966; Dilys Powello, "Gentlemanliness Is Out," *The Sunday Times*, November 13, 1966, p. 23.

182. "'Jackal' Author Does It Again," *The Des Moines Register*, November 12, 1972, p. 11C; Don Keown, "Frederick Forsyth Proves 'Day of Jackal' No Fluke," *Daily Independent*, November 11, 1972. The film version was praised in David Robinson, "Invention Scuppered by Reality," *The Times* (London), October 18, 1974, p. 14.

183. Robert Clere, "The Creation of the Fourth Reich," *The Cincinnati Enquirer*, April 25, 1976, p. 105; Jeremy Brooks, "Strong-Arm Storytelling," *The Sunday Times*, April 11, 1976, p. 38.

184. Nancy Tipton, "Books & Art," *Clarion-Ledger* (Jackson, MS), August 14, 1977, p. 103. See also H. R. F. Keating, "Crime," *The Times* (London), February 24, 1977, p. 12; Frank White, "Goebbels Son Alive?" *The Atlanta Constitution*, August 28, 1977, p. 7E.

185. Roger Lupton, "Crime Corner," *The Age* (Melbourne, Australia), September 29, 1965; "Science Fiction," *The Observer*, March 28, 1965, p. 26.

186. "Packed with Action," *Guardian*, August 17, 1978, p. 7; Newgate Callendar, "Criminals at Large," *The New York Times*, February 1, 1976, p. BR7; Edward Warre, "Thrillers," *The Sydney Morning Herald*, June 28, 1980, p. 24.

187. Herbert Luft, "Germany's Past and Present on the Screen," *Jewish Advocate*, September 15, 1966, p. 16B. The directors originally hoped to include real footage of an NPD rally in the film. See "'Quiller' Photographs New Nazi Strutters," *Variety*, June 29, 1966, p. 1.

188. Shirley Murray, "What if . . . ? War Yields Four Thrillers," *The Courier-Journal* (Louisville, KY), August 30, 1979, p. 35.

189. "Mission Became Thriller," *The Lincoln Star* (Lincoln, NE), May 3, 1970, p. 75.

190. Newgate Callendar, "Crimes," *The New York Times*, December 24, 1978, p. BR10.

191. Violet Grant, "One Man vs. the SS," *Daily Telegraph*, September 28, 1972, p. 8; Jeremy Brooks, "Strong-Arm Storytelling," *The Sunday Times*, April 11, 1976, p. 38; Bill Hayden, "Robert Ludlum Produces His Most Intricate Plot Yet," *The Morning News* (Wilmington, DE), March 26, 1978.

192. Robert Clere, "The Creation of the Fourth Reich," *The Cincinnati Enquirer*, April 25, 1976, p. 105.

193. Don Keown, "Frederick Forsyth Proves 'Day of Jackal' No Fluke," *Daily Independent*, November 11, 1972.

194. Joseph McLellan, "Evils of Hitler and the World," *The Washington Post*, January 30, 1979, p. B4.

195. Greil Marcus, *The Dustbin of History* (Cambridge, MA, 1995), pp. 60, 63, 68. The essay originally appeared in *Rolling Stone* in 1976 under the title "Götterdämmerung after Twenty-One Years."

196. "Return of Hitler," *The Stage and Television Today*, May 30, 1963, p. 15.

197. Alan Brien, "Wrong Side of the Footlights," *Sunday Telegraph*, May 26, 1963, p. 14.

198. Carol Kennedy, "Adolf Hitler Returns to London Stage," *The Brandon Sun*, June 12, 1963.

199. "Wie sie Deutschland sehen," *Die Zeit*, May 31, 1963.

200. "Germans Seek BBC's Script of Hitler Play," *The Globe and Mail* (Canada), May 9, 1962, p. 9.

201. "Protest Anti-German Brit. Vidfilm," *Variety*, May 23, 1962; "Hitler Play Leads to Embassy Protest," *The Age* (Melbourne, Australia), May 9, 1962.

202. See Brian C. Etheridge's discussion of the "anti-German wave" of the 1960s in chapter 4 of his *Enemies to Allies*.

203. "Neuentdeckte Satire," *Neue Zeit*, January 25, 1963, p. 4; the East German state television network broadcast the program on state television with the title "Comeback bei Nacht." "Lorbeer für Robert Müller," *Neue Zeit*, January 18, 1963, p. 4.

204. "Braune Katacomben," *Der Spiegel*, February 27, 1967; "'Quiller Memorandum' Cuts Neo-Nazi Scenes in Germany," *The New York Times*, February 28, 1967, p. 32.

205. "Brauner Pfiff," *Neues Deutschland*, March 12, 1967, p. 10. Ernst Wendt, "Entnazifizierung," *Die Zeit*, March 3, 1967.

206. Tom Nugent, "Hitler's Baby: Junk from Brazil," *The Sun*, March 7, 1976, p. D7.

207. Christopher Lehmann-Haupt, "A Couple of Good Explosions," *The New York Times*, October 24, 1972, p. 41.

208. *Kirkus Reviews*, June 28, 1978.

209. Review of *The Watchdogs of Abaddon*, in *Science Fiction and Fantasy Book Review*, January 1980, p. 14.

210. "Porno and the Swastika," *The Anniston Star* (Anniston, AL), April 2, 1978, p. 56; John Leonard, "Thrillers," *The Sun*, March 14, 1978, p. B2; "Robert Ludlum," *The Times* (London), March 14, 2001, p. 25; David Shaw, "Another Digger in the Mother Lode of Villainy," *The Los Angeles Times*, April 2, 1978, p. L4.

211. Margaret Manning, "The SS Lives – With Same Purpose," *The Boston Globe*, October 26, 1972, p. 48.

212. Bill Frank, "End of Trilogy Disappointing," *The Morning News* (Wilmington, DE), p. 16.

213. "Today's Video Tips," *The Arizona Republic*, October 20, 1964, p. 31; see also *The Decatur Daily* (Decatur, IL), January 4, 1965, p. 3.

214. *The Tucson Daily Citizen*, January 4, 1965, p. 36.

215. Robert Kirsch, "Forsyth's Second Novel Misfires Badly," *The Tucson Daily Citizen*, November 4, 1972, p. 46.

216. Joseph Gelmis, "'Memorandum' Flashes Style, Flubs Message," *Newsday*, December 16, 1966, p. 2A.

217. Allan A. Ryan, Jr., "Triple Word Score," *The Washington Post*, March 19, 1978.

218. "Blind General Presides over Secret Nazi Court," *The Bridgeport Post*, June 12, 1966. See also Harry Themal, "Books in the News," *The Morning News* (Wilmington, DE), March 30, 1966, p. 25.

219. Richard Lipe, "The Archfiend and Debussy," *Newsday*, March 6, 1977, p. B23.

220. Sterlin Holmsley, "Forsyth Novel Hard to Swallow," *Express/News*, November 12, 1972, p. 15.

221. "Terrorists, Mad Scientists, and Neo-Nazis," *The Chicago Daily Tribune*, May 21, 1978, p. 112; Stuart Byczynski, "A Nazi behind Every Bush and Stone," *The Sun*, April 16, 1978, p. D4; Hope Hewitt, "Intrigues and Suspense," *The Canberra Times* (Australia), February 9, 1980, p. 15; see also Jack Zaiman, "Big Theme," *The Hartford Courant*, March 26, 1978, p. 6G.

222. Louise Sweeney, "'Quiller Memorandum,'" *The Christian Science Monitor*, December 30, 1966, p. 4; review of *The Quiller Memorandum*, *The Monthly Film Bulletin*, January 1, 1967, p. 34; Richard L. Coe, "Neo-Nazis Are Latest in Heels," *The Washington Post*, January 28, 1967, p. C6.

223. John Breitlow, "Destructive Female, Nazis Provide Thriller Fodder," *The Winona Daily News*, October 31, 1965, p. 39.

224. "Crime and Suspense," *The Anniston Star* (Anniston, AL), January 5, 1975, p. 37.

225. Wolf Donner, "Erbarmen mit den Nazis," *Die Zeit*, 8, 1975; Hellmuth Karasek, "Angst vorm einstmals Schwarzen Mann," *Die Zeit*, April 13, 1973.

226. Review of *Search for the Evil One*, *The Monthly Film Bulletin*, January 1, 1978, p. 162.

227. *The Oneonta Star* (Oneonta, NY), October 20, 1964, p. 9.

228. *The Daily Mail* (Hagerstown, MD), January 7, 1967, p. 21; *The News Journal* (Wilmington, DE), January 7, 1967, p. 19.

229. David Shaw, "Another Digger in the Mother Lode of Villainy," *The Los Angeles Times*, April 2, 1978, p. L4.

230. Alex Hamilton, "Back to the Bunker," *Guardian*, January 31, 1977, p. 8.

231. Tom Shales, "Back in the Bunker," *The Washington Post*, January 27, 1981, p. B1.

232. George Warren, "Soft Cover," *The Los Angeles Times*, January 25, 1981, K8; Stuart Elliott, "Familiar Spy Plot Tingles with New Twists," *Detroit Free Press*, March 8, 1981, p. 21.

233. Joseph Rosenberger, #39 in the *Death Merchant* series, entitled *The Fourth Reich* (Los Angeles, 1980); *Nick Carter: Plot for the Fourth Reich* (New York, 1977); *Nick Carter: The Israeli Connection* (New York, 1982); John Gardner, *Icebreaker* (New York, 1983).

234. Richard Brickner, "'The Odessa File'," *The New York Times*, November 5, 1972, p. BR5.

235. Gloria Whelan, "'Odessa File' is Too Convincing," *Detroit Free Press*, November 12, 1972.

236. Christopher Lehmann Haupt, "Great Experiments in Living," *The New York Times*, March 10, 1976, p. 33.

237. Tom Nugent, "Hitler's Baby: Junk from Brazil," *The Sun*, March 7, 1976, p. D7.

238. Elliott Fremont-Smith, "Two for the Show," *The New York Times*, March 30, 1966, p. 43.

239. Gene Lyons, "Intriguing Intrigue," *The New York Times*, May 15, 1977, p. 231.

240. Owen Findsen, "We Have Ways of Making You Talk," *The Cincinnati Enquirer*, March 4, 1979, p. 110.

241. David Shaw, "Another Digger in the Mother Lode of Villainy," *The Los Angeles Times*, April 2, 1978, p. L4.

242. "'Wind Chill Factor' a Deft Work," *The Winona Daily News*, January 5, 1975.

243. George Perry, "Screen: Crying Out for Truth," *The Sunday Times*, September 22, 1985; David Robinson, "Cinema: Painful Perspectives on the Recent Past," *The Times* (London), September 20, 1985.

244. Michael Wilmington, "'Holcroft': Out-of-Kilter Thriller," *The Los Angeles Times*, October 18, 1985, p. G4.

245. Review of *The Holcroft Covenant*, *Variety*, October 9, 1985.

Re-Germanizing the Fourth Reich: From Reunification
to the Reich Citizens' Movement

1. Conor Cruise O'Brien, "Beware the Reich is Reviving," *The Times* (London), October 31, 1989, p. 18.

2. "Jackson Tours Europe," *Jet*, June 3, 1985. During a visit to the Natzweiler-Struthof concentration camp, Jackson said that "the fourth Reich is in South Africa." "Jackson Tours Nazi Camp," *Philadelphia Inquirer*, May 8, 1985, p. A17.

3. See also "Jackson Compares Botha to Hitler," *The New York Times*, August 30, 1986, p. 4; "75,000 Protesters March on Capitol," *The Boston Globe*, April 26, 1987, p. 22; "Jackson's Radical Platform Woos the Voters," *The Canberra Times* (Australia), March 31, 1988, p. 4. Black newspapers condemned white racists for seeking to "establish ... a fourth Reich" in the US: "Hitlerism in Our Country," *Tri-State Defender* (Memphis, TN), August 20, 1986, p. 5.

4. "Anti-Reagan Rally Draws 75,000 Marchers," *The Toronto Star*, April 26, 1987, p. H2. "Candidate Says Reagan Runs Politburo," *The Times* (Shreveport, LA), October 8, 1982, p. 7. Right-wing supporters of Lyndon La Rouche made similar comments; "Reagan Budget's 'Warped Vision,'" *The Los Angeles Times*, January 13, 1985, p. 4.

5. "Armed Men Close Paper in Panama," *Philadelphia Inquirer*, February 20, 1988, p. A8.

6. "Perceptions and Realities," *The Financial Post* (Toronto), December 30, 1988, p. 10. The reference was to "Quebec's Fourth Reich."

7. The band's founders added that the name had "no political connotations." www .trakmarx.com/2007_02/16_sun.html

8. www.lyricsmatch.com/the-lookouts/fourth-reich-(nazi-amerika); www.ouvirmusica .com.br/the-lookouts/1564817/

9. The strip can be found in *The Southern Illinoisan* (Carbondale, IL), September 11, 1987, p. 15.

10. The strip debuted in 1977. Oakland Ross, "The Mighty Pens of Mexico," *The Globe and Mail* (Canada), June 28, 1983; "Mexico's Troubled Masses Can Laugh at Powerful," *The Atlanta Constitution*, April 8, 1984, p. 19C.

11. Quoted in "Daytona Engines Salute Free Life in the Fast Lane," *The Washington Post*, February 18, 1979, p. D1.

12. "Losers of 1984 Deserve Special Awards for Feats," *The Sun*, January 1, 1985, p. 1B.

13. "Sockers Face a Revamped Sting Tonight," *The San Diego Union Tribune*, November 9, 1985, p. C1.

14. Edwin Hartrich, *The Fourth and Richest Reich* (New York, 1980).

15. Ibid., pp. 6–7.

16. David Schoenbrun, "Economic Miracle," *The New York Times*, March 23, 1980, p. BR4.

17. Lee McGowan, *The Radical Right in Germany: 1870 to the Present* (London, 2002), pp. 158–59.

18. Ibid., pp. 160–69. The Republikaners received 8.7 percent and 14.6 percent in European parliamentary elections in Baden-Württemberg and Bavaria, respectively.

19. "Folksy Kohl Attracts Votes Despite Contempt of Media," *The Globe and Mail* (Canada), January 23, 1987; "Moscow's Deep-Seated Fear – A Fourth Reich," *Guardian Weekly*, March 22, 1987, p. 4.

20. Conor Cruise O'Brien, "Beware, the Reich Is Reviving," *The Times* (London), October 31, 1989.

21. Conor Cruise O'Brien, "Taking Germany's Nationalist Pulse," *The Times* (London), November 17, 1989, p. 18. In this essay, the writer admitted that his original essay had exhibited too much "hyperbole," yet insisted that "the Fourth Reich ... will ... resemble ... Hohenzollern Germany," declaring that was "chilling enough."

22. See "The Freedom March That May Create a Fourth Reich," *Daily Express*, November 6, 1989. Alex Brummer, "All Change for EC as It Ponders Birth of the Fourth Reich," *Guardian*, November 10, 1989, p. 16.

23. "Keine Angst, aber Sorgen," *FAZ*, March 10, 1990, p. 12. See also "Die Furcht vor dem 'Vierten Reich,'" *FAZ*, December 13, 1989, p. 16.

24. "Als ob Kohl das vierte Reich gründen wolle," *Berliner Zeitung*, March 13, 1990, p. 5. This was the claim of the former French Interior Minister, Michel Poniatowski. See also the claim of former French foreign policy adviser to Jacques Chirac, Claude Lellouche, as reported in "Müssen wir lernen, Europäer zu werden?" *Neues Deutschland*, January 9, 1990, p. 6.

25. Dominique Moïsi, "Germany's Unity, Europe's Rebirth," *The New York Times*, November 20, 1989, p. A23.

26. On Sweden, see "Gelassene Zustimmung in Norden," *FAZ*, March 6, 1990, p. 6; Jochen Reinert, "Die Dänen, die Deutschen und Europa – Sorgen und Hoffnungen," *Neues Deutschland*, May 11, 1990, p. 7; on Italy, see *Bezeichungen für "Deutschland" in der Zeit der "Wende": Dargestellt an ausgewählten westdeutschen Printmedien* (Göttingen, 1997), p. 239; "Auf der Geisterbahn," *FAZ*, March 16, 1990, p. 16; "A Bit of Warmth amid Tensions of Germans, Poles," *Philadelphia Inquirer*, March 31, 1990, p. A2.

27. Quoted in Matthias Morgenstern, "Vor der 'deutschen Intifada' zum 'vierten Reich,'" Andrea Kaiser and Tobias Kriener, eds., *Normal ist das besondere: Streiflichter aus 30 Jahren deutsch-israelischer Beziehungen* (Schwalbach/Taunus, 1996), p. 54; see also "Israel Haunted by Specter of 'Fourth Reich,'" *The Tennessean*, February 20, 1990. "Getting Their Act Together?" *The Jerusalem Post*, November 20, 1989, p. 8.

28. "Das Gespenst des Vierten Reiches," *Der Spiegel,* 39, December 18, 1989, p. 21.

29. "Europakonzept der PDS," *Neues Deutschland*, February 6, 1990, p. 6. Later that month, PDS leader Gregor Gysi asked in a speech, "Should a Fourth Reich be rushed into existence after three have already collapsed?" "Gute Gründe, die PDS zu wählen," *Neues Deutschland*, February 26, 1990, p. 8.

30. "Gemeinsam gegen rechts," *Berliner Zeitung*, January 5, 1990, p. 1.

31. In October of 1990 5,000 left-wing opponents of reunification demonstrated against the creation of a "Fourth Reich." "Symbols of the Past Linger as Protesters Strike Note of Dissent," *The Times* (London), October 4, 1990, p. 15. In July, the radical left-wing group SpAD (Spartakist-Arbeiterpartei Deutschlands) charged that West German plans to expropriate communist party property signaled the "dawning of a Fourth Reich." "Nein zur Enteignung," *Neues Deutschland*, July 21, 1990, p. 6.

32. "Terrorists Declare War on the 'Fourth Reich,'" *The Times* (London), August 1, 1990, p. 7. "Terrorist Group Threatens Unified Germany," *The Washington Post*, August 1, 1990.

33. Heleno Saña, *Das vierte Reich: Deutschlands später Sieg* (Hamburg, 1990).

34. Ibid., pp. 230, 234.

35. Ibid., pp. 234, 235.

36. Ibid., p. 236.
37. Ibid., p. 238.
38. Ibid., p. 241.
39. Ibid., p. 242.
40. "Britische Bangen vor 'Viertem Reich,'" *FAZ*, November 9, 1989, p. 5.
41. "Eine Hitler-Statue in jeder Stadt," *FAZ*, November 2, 1989, p. 4.
42. Theo Sommer, "Germans Want to Be Good Neighbors," *The Observer*, November 12, 1989, p. 16.
43. Günther Nonnenmacher, "Falsche Angst vor Deutschland," *FAZ*, December 16, 1989, p. 1.
44. Peter Grubbe, "Furcht vor Deutschen," *Die Zeit*, August 24, 1990. "Brechen die Deutschen nun auf ins Vierte Reich?" *Berliner Zeitung*, December 7, 1990, p. 13.
45. "Kohl Rallies German Reunification Hope," *The Times* (London), December 21, 1989, p. 10.
46. "Kohl Rejects Soviet Call for Reunification Referendum," *The Los Angeles Times*, February 4, 1990, p. 1.
47. "Kohl: Es wird kein viertes Reich geben," *FAZ*, March 7, 1990, p. 2.
48. "Ein viertes Reich wird es nicht geben," *Berliner Zeitung*, February 21, 1990, p. 5.
49. Josef Joffe, "One-and-a-Half Cheers for German Unification," *Commentary*, June 1, 1990, pp. 29–31.
50. One skeptic was William Safire, who in 1989 attacked "[Soviet] apologists in the West's disarmament lobby," such as "West Germany's devious Foreign Minister, Hans-Dietrich Genscher," who was allegedly envisioning "a Fourth Reich rising from NATO's ashes." William Safire, "Bush's 'New Path,'" *The New York Times*, May 15, 1989. *Der Spiegel* responded by saying the US's economic problems were leading the country to scapegoat Germany in the same way it was scapegoating Japan. "Viertes Reich," *Der Spiegel*, 21, 1989, pp. 23–25.
51. "Wiedervereinigung unausweichlich," *Der Spiegel*, 48, 1989, p. 39.
52. "Zu gross für Europa?" *Der Spiegel*, 46, 1989, p. 187.
53. William Tuohy, "Allies Wary as Bonn Plays Host to Gorbachev," *The Los Angeles Times*, June 12, 1989, p. 1.
54. Walter Russell Mead, "United Germany Must Confront Chaos," *The Los Angeles Times*, September 30, 1990, p. 2.
55. J. P. Stern, Diary, *The London Review of Books*, December 7, 1989. Letters to the editor critiqued O'Brien's essay as "far from reality." "German Unity a Threat to Europe?" *The Times* (London), November 2, 1989, p. 15. See also Peter Pulzer, "East Berlin Diary," *The London Review of Books*, April 19, 1990.
56. Lord Weidenfeld, "All Roads Lead to German Unity," *The Times* (London), January 19, 1990, p. 12.
57. "What Experts Told Maggie," *Daily Mail* (London), July 16, 1990, pp. 6–7; Stone later changed his mind in an article entitled "'Germany? Maggie Was Absolutely Right?'" *The Sunday Times*, September 29, 1996, p. 9.
58. McGowan, *The Radical Right in Germany*, p. 173.
59. The number of Germans who joined neo-Nazi groups swelled to around 2,000 in the former east – twice the number that existed in the much more populous western half of the country; ibid., p. 189. Between 1990 and 2007, 130 people were killed in various attacks; Gerard Braunthal, *Right-Wing Extremism in Contemporary Germany* (Basingstoke, UK, 2009), pp. 96–103. The worst attack against a Jewish target was the firebombing of a Jewish synagogue in Lübeck in 1994. For general reflections on the trend, see Robert Gerald Livingston and Volkmar Sander, eds., *The Future of German Democracy* (New York, 1993).

60. "German Attacks Rise as Foreigners Become Scapegoat," *The New York Times*, November 2, 1992, pp. A1, A6.

61. "New Clashes in Germany as Politicians Voice Alarm," *The New York Times*, October 4, 1992, p. 15.

62. "Germans Stage Rally against Neo-Nazis," *The St. Louis Post-Dispatch*, November 9, 1992, p. 1A.

63. "Kriegerdenkmäler schüren Angst," *Berliner Zeitung*, December 10, 1992, p. 7.

64. Christine Toomey, "Women Dreaming of Fourth Reich Swell German Neo-Nazi Ranks," *The Sunday Times*, December 13, 1992, p. 21.

65. Sabine Reichel, "A Legacy of Hate Revives in the East," *The Los Angeles Times*, May 10, 1991, p. B7. See also "Germany Creating Police Unit Aimed at Rightist Groups," *The New York Times*, November 29, 1992, p. 1.

66. Thomas Pfeiffer, "Avantgarde und Brücke," in Wolfgang Gessenharter and Thomas Pfeiffer, eds., *Die neue Rechte – eine Gefahr für die Demokratie?* (Wiesbaden, 2004), pp. 51–69.

67. Hartmut Herb, Jan Peters, and Mathias Thesen, *Der neue Rechtsextremismus: Fakten und Trends* (Lohra-Rodenhausen, 1980), p. 52.

68. Manfred Roeder, *Ein Kampf um's Reich* (Schwarzenborn, 1979), p. 11.

69. The claim appears in Roeder's 1975 letter to Doenitz. See Roeder, *Ein Kampf um's Reich*, pp. 22–24.

70. Ibid., p. 61.

71. Ibid., p. 15.

72. Ibid., pp. 24, 16.

73. Ibid., p. 41.

74. Ibid., p. 34.

75. Ibid., pp. 61–63.

76. "Miese Weise," *Der Spiegel*, 26, 1982, pp. 77–78.

77. In 1995, Roeder delivered a guest lecture at a leadership academy of the Bundeswehr, which caused controversy when news of it broke in 1997. "30 German Army Officers Attended '95 Speech by Right-Wing Terrorist," *The Los Angeles Times*, December 30, 1997, p. A6. "Hitlerjunge mit Tränensäcken," *Der Spiegel*, 18, 1998, pp. 69–76. In 1996, he made headlines for vandalizing the Crimes of the Wehrmacht exhibition in Erfurt. "Neonazis und CSU kämpfen für die Ehre der Wehrmacht," *TAZ*, February 20, 1997. In 1997, he ran for office on the NPD ticket in Stralsund, but lost. Braunthal, *Right-Wing Extremism in Contemporary Germany*, p. 59.

78. Lee, *The Beast Reawakens*, pp. 195–201.

79. Michael Kühnen, *Die Zweite Revolution* (1982). The book was originally published by Thies Christophersen's Kritik Verlag and later by Gary Lauck's NSDAP/AO.

80. Ibid., pp. 84, 86.

81. Ibid., p. 27.

82. Ibid., p. 119.

83. Ibid., pp. 88–93.

84. "Mit Todesmut," *Der Spiegel*, March 27, 1989.

85. https://archive.org/details/LexikonDerNeuenFront

86. McGowan, *The Radical Right in Germany*, pp. 180–88; "Schon gehuscht," *Der Spiegel*, 3, 1990, p. 76; Braunthal, *Right-Wing Extremism in Contemporary Germany*, pp. 31–32.

87. https://openjur.de/u/211744.html Although Kühnen named the Austrian neo-Nazi Gottfried Küssel his successor as the head of the GdNF, the latter never made much

progress on the Fourth Reich, being imprisoned by the Austrian authorities in 1992. See "Hitlerjugend ohne Partei," *Der Spiegel*, 50, 1992, p. 28. Braunthal, *Right-Wing Extremism in Contemporary Germany*, p. 85.

88. Hans-Dietrich Sander, *Der nationale Imperativ: Ideengänge und Werkstücke zur Wiederherstellung Deutschlands* (Essen, 1990).

89. Ibid., p. 18.

90. Ibid., pp. 19, 30.

91. The East German press condemned Sander's book as symptomatic of a revanchistic West German agenda in 1982. See "Ein Aufbruch ohne Ankunft," *Berliner Zeitung*, January 28, 1982, p. 9. See also Ludwig Elm, *Aufbruch ins Vierte Reich?* (Berlin, 1981). Peter Glotz criticized the book in *Die Deutsche Rechte* (Stuttgart, 1989).

92. Sander, *Der nationale Imperativ*, p. 150.

93. Ibid., p. 192.

94. Ibid., pp. 191–94.

95. Sander later observed: "I realized in 1989 that the Allies intended to bring about a final solution of the German question by unifying [merely] ... their two occupation states." The *Staatsbriefe* intended to counteract this. As he put it, "one of the preconditions for reviving the Reich is overcoming the Reich dualism between Berlin and Vienna." Hans-Dietrich Sander and Jürgen Maass, *Im Banne der Reichsrenaissance* (Kiel, 2011), pp. 85, 88.

96. Sander, *Der nationale Imperativ*, p. 16.

97. The phrase *Staatsbriefe* harkened back to Wolfram von den Steinen's description of Frederick II's various printed decrees. Sander and Maass, *Im Banne der Reichsrenaissance*, p. 87.

98. The journal published many articles on the Reich from a variety of perspectives, including Kühnen's essay "Vom Reichsmythos zum Vierten Reich."

99. Hans-Dietrich Sander, "Die Ghibellinische Idee," *Staatsbriefe*, 1, 1990, pp. 24–31 and Hans-Dietrich Sander, "Das Reich als politische Einheit der Deutschen," *Staatsbriefe*, 1, 1991, pp. 25–33.

100. Sander, "Die Ghibellinische Idee," *Staatsbriefe*, 1, 1990, p. 26.

101. Sander employed the sacred idea of the *Katechon*, which Carl Schmitt employed to refer to a bulwark that wards off threats. Ibid., p. 29.

102. Sander, "Das Reich als politische Einheit der Deutschen," *Staatsbriefe*, 1, 1991, p. 29.

103. Ibid.

104. Sander, "Die Ghibellinische Idee," *Staatsbriefe*, 1, 1990, p. 31.

105. Sander, "Das Reich als politische Einheit der Deutschen," *Staatsbriefe*, 1, 1991, p. 33.

106. http://brd-ende.com/

107. See http://brd-ende.com/ See also Manuel Seitenbecher, *Mahler, Maschke, & Co.: Rechtes Denken in der 68er-Bewegung?* (Schöning, 2013), p. 339. The DK grew out of a reading group sponsored by the conservative journal, *Junge Freiheit*.

108. Thomas Grumke and Bernd Wagner, *Handbuch Rechtsradikalismus: Personen – Organisationen – Netzwerke von Neonazismus bis in die Mitte der Gesellschaft* (Opladen, 2002), p. 293.

109. Seitenbecher, *Mahler, Maschke, & Co.*, p. 346. Oberlercher coined the memorable anti-Nazi phrase "Unter den Talaren, Muff von 1000 Jahren" (loosely: "Under the [professors'] robes lurks the musty smell of a thousand years" – a reference to Hitler's "thousand-year Reich").

110. This shift partly reflected Oberlercher's difficulties landing a permanent academic job. After his *Habilitation* was rejected, he became a Privatdozent in Hamburg running study groups. Ibid., pp. 348–50.

111. He joined the anarchist Freie Arbeiter Union (FAU) and thereafter joined various right-wing splinter groups. Ibid., pp. 292–93.

112. Hans Kundnani, *Utopia or Auschwitz? Germany's 1968 Generation and the Holocaust* (New York, 2009), pp. 46, 76–77, 137–38, 223–34. Braunthal, *Right-Wing Extremism in Contemporary Germany*, pp. 66–70. George Michael, "The Ideological Evolution of Horst Mahler: The Far Left–Extreme Right Synthesis," *Studies in Conflict and Terrorism*, 32, 2009, 346–66.

113. Reinhold Oberlercher, "Die Neuschöpfung des Deutschen Reiches," September 12, 1992. www.oberlercher.de/blog/neuschoepfung-des-deutschen-reiches

114. "Reichsverfassungsentwurf," *Staatsbriefe* 1, 1992, pp. 23–26. For the updated 1999 version, see www.reich4.de/1999/11/reichsverfassungsentwurf-rverfe99/

115. Only certain Germans (those who performed military or civil service) were eligible to vote (*Reichsdeutsche* as opposed to *Volksdeutsche*).

116. https://reichstr.eu/1993/01/das-100-tage-programm/

117. https://reichstr.eu/die-fahne-weht/

118. Reinhold Oberlercher, "Die Zerstörung der Demokratie durch die Verfolgung der Patrioten," *Staatsbriefe*, 4, 1997, pp. 9–11, www.vho.org/D/Staatsbriefe/Oberlercher8_4.html

119. Horst Mahler, Günter Maschke, and Reinhold Oberlercher, "Kanonische Erklärung zur Bewegung von 1968," December 24, 1998, https://reichstr.eu/1998/12/kanonische-erklaerung-68/

120. They rechristened the SDS the "Waffen-SDS." Kundnani, *Utopia or Auschwitz?* p. 227.

121. Michael Fischer, *Horst Mahler: Biographische Studie zu Antisemitismus, Antiamerikanismus, und Versuchen deutscher Schuldabwehr* (Karlsruhe, 2015), 329–31. Grumke and Wagner, *Handbuch Rechtsradikalismus*, p. 293.

122. Two different versions can be found here: https://web.archive.org/web/20070927230236/; www.verfassungsschutz-hessen.de/bilder/kolleg.jpg; and www.luebeck-kunterbunt.de/Judentum/Aufstand_Anstaendigen.htm

123. https://reichstr.eu/2002/06/petition-an-die-deutschen-fuersten/

124. https://reichstr.eu/2002/06/sozialordnungsgesetz-sozog/ and https://reichstr.eu/2002/06/arbeitsdienstgesetz-arbdg/

125. Grumke and Wagner, *Handbuch Rechtsradikalismus*, p. 293; Seitenbecher, *Mahler, Maschke, & Co.*, pp. 338–39.

126. Sander and Maass, *Im Banne der Reichsrenaissance*, pp. 102–06. Two articles in 1995 drew attention: one involving Germar Rudolf and a satirical article entitled "The Miracle of Technology" by a pseudonymous (and pun-obsessed) author, "Ole Caust."

127. Brigitte Mihok, ed., *Handbuch des Antisemitismus: Judenfeinschaft in Geschichte und Gegenwart: Band VI Publikationen* (Berlin, 2013), p. 667.

128. Grumke and Wagner, *Handbuch Rechtsradikalismus*, p. 293.

129. Mahler actually quit the party as being insufficiently radical in 2003.

130. "Das Gericht als Bühne," www.netz-gegen-nazis.de/artikel/das-gericht-als-buehne-horst-mahlers-revisionismus-kampagne

131. Mahler ran into resistance from Oberlercher after seeking to privilege the interests of Holocaust deniers (*Verein zur Rehabilitierung der wegen des Bestreiten des Holocaust Verfolgten*, VRBHV), instead of forming a broader coalition. Seitenbecher, *Mahler, Maschke, & Co.*, pp. 339–40.

132. Grumke and Wagner, *Handbuch Rechtsradikalismus*, p. 407.
133. Fabian Virchow and Christian Dornbusch, eds., *88 Fragen und Antworten zur NPD* (Schwalbach, 2008), p. 60.
134. www.hagalil.com/archiv/2000/12/npd.htm
135. Grumke and Wagner, *Handbuch Rechtsradikalismus*, p. 320. See Mahler's manifesto in defense of the NPD, "Appell an die Bürger des deutschen Reiches," from 2000. https://groups.google.com/forum/#!topic/de.sci.geschichte/5bL77sueC68
136. "Ziel ist die BRD abzuwickeln," *Junge Freiheit*, September 24, 2004. www.jf-archiv.de/archiv04/404yy08.htm
137. The NPD exploited dissatisfaction with the curtailment of welfare benefits associated with the Hartz IV reforms. Rainer Burger, "Da waren es nur noch neun," *FAZ*, December 23, 2005.
138. "Sie wollen ein viertes Reich und fressen dafür Kreide," *Sächsische Zeitung*, September 7, 2004. www.sz-online.de/nachrichten/sie-wollen-ein-viertes-reich-und-fressen-dafuer-kreide-598885.html See also Hajo Funke, *Paranoia und Politik* (Berlin, 2002), p. 88. See also Jan Rübel, "Der Kampf um die Strasse," *Die Welt*, November 2, 2004.
139. "Das waren es nur noch neun," *FAZ*, December 23, 2005.
140. "Rep-Chef eröffnet zweite Volksfront," *TAZ*, November 2, 2004. www.taz.de/!678959/
141. "Demonstrationen der NPD und Gegendemonstrationen in Frankfurt," *FAZ*, July 7, 2007, p. 4.
142. David Crossland, "Neo-Nazi Threat Growing Despite NPD Cash Woes," *Spiegel Online*, March 19, 2009.
143. The myriad small groups making up the movement are discussed in Andreas Speit, ed., *Reichsbürger: Die unterschätzte Gefahr* (Berlin, 2017).
144. He made this clear as early as 1998 in his essay "Der Globalismus als höchstes Stadium des Imperialismus erzwingt die Auferstehung der deutschen Nation." Fischer, *Horst Mahler*, pp. 327, 514, 59n. See the document at www.scribd.com/document/230495275/Mahler-Horst-Der-Globalismus-Als-Hochstes-Stadium-Des-Imperialismus-Erzwingt-Die-Auferstehung-Der-Deutschen-Nation
145. Mahler's group later staged a demonstration at the Wartburg in Eisenach in late July 2003. *Handbuch des Antisemitismus*, pp. 726–77. "Der Aufstand für die Wahrheit begann auf der Wartburg," 2003. https://germanenherz.files.wordpress.com/2015/07/horst-mahler-aufstand-fuer-die-wahrheit-2003–11-s-text.pdf
146. Horst Mahler, *Ehre Wahrheit Heimat* (2009). https://germanenherz.files.wordpress.com/2015/07/horst-mahler-ehre-wahrheit-heimat-eine-programmschrift-2006-20-doppels-text.pdf; http://web.archive.org/web/20091014181155/; www.voelkische-reichsbewegung.org/Ehre_Wahrheit_Heimat_runter.pdf
147. Ibid., p. 8.
148. Ibid., pp. 8, 9, 22, 23.
149. Members of the RBB insist that the Weimar constitution was neither abolished by the Nazis nor the Allies. They refer to the Federal Republic of Germany as the OMF, "Organisationsform einer Modalität der Fremdherrschaft."
150. Kai Biermann and Astrid Geisler, "Ein Volk, viele Reiche, noch mehr Führer," *Die Zeit*, April 16, 2016; Thomas Schade, "Eins, zwei, drei – falsche Polizei," *Sächsische Zeitung*, December 16, 2015, p. 3.
151. Verfassungsschutzbericht Brandenburg 2012; see also the website, "Gelber Schein," www.gelberschein.net/

152. Speit, ed., *Reichsbürger*, p. 9.
153. Seitenbecher, *Mahler, Maschke, & Co.*, p. 344.
154. www.npd-berlin.de/tag/uwe-meenen/ "Unrecht behalten," *Die Zeit*, September 22, 2016, p. 11.
155. Oberlercher, moreover, remains active. See David Begrich and Andreas Speit, "'Heiliges Deutsches Reich': Reichsidee und Reichsideologie der extremen Rechte," in Speit, ed., *Reichsbürger*, pp. 22–40.
156. Florian Gathmann and Severin Weiland, "Die unterschätzte Gefahr," *Der Spiegel*, October 20, 2016. www.spiegel.de/politik/deutschland/reichsbuerger-bewegung-die-unterschaetzte-gefahr-a-1117575.html
157. The former leftist Jürgen Elsässer has endorsed the Reich idea in his online journal, *Compact*. "Ein Netzwerk für Putin und Pegida," *Der Tagesspiegel*, August 16, 2015. The popular musician Xavier Naidoo caused controversy by supporting the Reich Citizens' Movement in 2014. "Naidoo bekräftigt Thesen über 'unfreies Deutschland,'" *Die Welt*, March 11, 2015. The same is true of the far-right musician Frank Rennicke, who penned the song "Das Reich." Begrich and Speit, "Heiliges Deutsches Reich," 39–40. Peter Fitzek made headlines for proclaiming a "Kingdom of New Germany" in 2012 and for being indicted for financial crimes in 2016. See "'König von Deutschland' zu Haftstrafe verurteilt," *Der Spiegel*, March 15, 2017. See Tobias Ginsburg, *Die Reise ins Reich: Unter Reichsbürgern* (Berlin, 2018).
158. Glenn Meade, *Brandenburg* (New York, 1997), p. 462.
159. Robert Ludlum, *Apocalypse Watch* (New York, 1995), pp. 736–42.
160. Alan Folsom, *The Day after Tomorrow* (New York, 1995).
161. "The $5 Million Thriller," *The Boston Globe*, April 26, 1994, p. 65.
162. Interview with Folsom in *January* magazine, www.januarymagazine.com/profiles/afolsom.html
163. "Ludlum Goes Full Circle in 4 Hours," *The News Journal* (Wilmington, DE), March 1, 1997, p. E8; Linda Marx, "Robert Ludlum: On a Mission with the Spy Novelist," *The Orlando Sentinel*, May 21, 1995, p. 196.
164. Folsom's novel made it to number two on the *New York Times* bestseller list. *The New York Times*, February 12, 1995, p. BR36. Ludlum's *Apocalypse Watch* made it onto the *London Times* top ten bestseller list. *The Sunday Times*, April 23, 1995, p. 11. Gifford's book, *The First Sacrifice*, had an initial print run of 100,000 copies. *Brandenburg* had a first printing of 125,000. *Publishers' Weekly*, April 28, 1997.
165. Robert Ward, "Right for the Jugular," *The Los Angeles Times*, April 10, 1994; George Hackett, "First Time Novelist Delivers Smashing Thriller," *Santa Cruz Sentinel*, May 20, 1994, p. 57.
166. *Kirkus Reviews*, April 1, 1995.
167. *Booklist*, October 1, 1994; *Library Journal*, July 1994. See also Mary Danforth, "'Sacrifice' Revives Nazi Threat after 20-Year Hiatus," *South Florida Sun Sentinel*, November 13, 1994, p. 88.
168. *Booklist*, June 1997; *Kirkus Reviews*, June 1, 1997. See also Zannah Lyle, "Uncovering New Mysteries," *The Tallahassee Democrat*, July 13, 1997, p. 2E.
169. Review in *The Desert Sun* (Palm Springs), July 14, 1993, p. 15; Ann Hellmuth, "Excitement, Intrigue Aplenty to Liven Up a Lazy Summer," *The Orlando Sentinel*, June 27, 1993, p. 49.
170. The former aired on ABC in 1997, while the latter was split into two films, *Thunder Point* and *The Windsor Protocol* (both starring Kyle MacLachlan), and aired on TMC in 1996 and 1998.

171. Guy Powers, "Ludlum Disappoints in 'Watch,'" *The Hartford Courant*, July 7, 1995, p. 4.

172. "Two Presidents, One Big Problem," *The Chicago Tribune*, October 23, 1994.

173. Ann Hellmuth, "The Hunter Becomes the Hunted," *The Orlando Sentinel*, June 8, 1997, p. F-9.

174. Mike Kent, "Author Treads Water with His Latest Work," *The Indianapolis Star*, July 29, 1993, p. 27. Ron Weiskind, "Thunder Point Makes Noise But Has Little Depth behind It," *The Pittsburgh Post-Gazette*, August 29, 1993, p. 86.

175. The television broadcast was described as "implausible." "'Apocalypse' Centers on Neo-Nazi Plot," *The Los Angeles Times*, March 1, 1997, p. F19.

176. Harry Levins, "Complicated Conspiracy Chapter Makes Entertaining Reading," May 22, 1994, p. 25; Lawrence DeVine, "Folsom Novel a Movie Just Waiting to Happen," *The Times* (Shreveport, LA), April 30, 1994. Newgate Callendar, "Spies and Thrillers," *The New York Times*, May 22, 1994.

177. *Kirkus Reviews*, April 6, 1994.

178. Review of *The Day after Tomorrow* in *New York Magazine*, April 4, 1994, p. 69.

179. "New Front Opens in German War with Hollywood," *The Times* (London), January 14, 1997, p. 14.

180. Steve Martin, *L.A. Story and Roxanne: Two Screenplays* (New York, 1997), pp. 74–75.

181. *Spy Magazine*, January 1990; *Spy Magazine*, April 1990. Two years later, the magazine reported that the "Fourth Reich" came in sixth (out of 100) in its "annual catalog of the most annoying, alarming, and appalling people, places, and things." "The 1992 Spy 100," *Spy Magazine*, December 1992–January 1993.

182. "Secret German plot to start World War III," *The Weekly World News*, December 9, 1997; "Nazi Army Lies Frozen in Antarctic Ice," *The Weekly World News*, October 15, 2002.

183. Certain British observers called the EEC a Fourth Reich already in 1974. "Argwohn und gespannte Neugier schlagen Schmidt entgegen," *FAZ*, December 2, 1974, p. 3. So did Sweden: "Ein mehr als bedrückendes Schauspiel," *Der Spiegel*, August 22, 1987.

184. "The Fourth German Reich," *The Sunday Times*, November 12, 1989, p. 2.

185. "The Future for Britain," *The Sunday Times*, November 19, 1989, p. 2.

186. "Keine Angst, aber Sorgen," *FAZ*, March 10, 1990, p. 12. See also "Die Furcht vor dem 'Vierten Reich,'" *FAZ*, December 13, 1989, p. 16; Henri Froment-Meurice, "Ein Starkes Deutschland, den Nachbarn verpflichtet," *FAZ*, October 2, 1990, p. 10.

187. "Griechische Terrorgruppe droht deutschen Firmen," *FAZ*, November 24, 1990, p. 6. See also "Brüssel und Delphi orakeln um die Wette," *Berliner Zeitung*, December 30, 1993, p. 8.

188. "Wenn die Geschichte zur Waffe wird," *Tageszeitung* (*TAZ*), November 7, 1991, p. 10.

189. "Belgrade Whips Up Fear of Croatia," *The Times* (London), September 18, 1991, p. 12.

190. "Deutschfeindliche Ausfälle Belgrader Blätter häufen sich," *Nürnberger Nachrichten*, July 8, 1991. "In den Medien der jugoslawischen Teilrepublik Serbien häufen sich antideutsche Berichte," *Nürnberger Nachrichten*, August 3, 1991, p. 2.

191. www.marxists.org/history/etol/document/icl-spartacists/periodicals/spartakist/088_July_1991_Spartakist.pdf "Germany Denies Charges of 'Fourth Reich,'" *Northwest Herald* (Illinois), July 9, 1991, p. 7.

192. "When Horror Stories Are Just Another Weapon," *The Globe and Mail* (Canada), August 12, 1992.

193. www.welt.de/print-welt/article646955/Belgrad-fuerchtet-das-Vierte-Reich.html

194. "Nach dem Vierten Reich die Katastrophen-Republik," *FAZ*, April 13, 1991, p. 3.

195. Martin Walker, "Overstretching Teutonia: Making the Best of the Fourth Reich," *World Policy Journal*, spring, 1995, p. 4.

196. Niall Ferguson, "The Golden Mirage of Helmut's Fourth Reich," *The Sunday Times*, June 15, 1997, p. 5.

197. Brian Reading, *The Fourth Reich* (London, 1995).

198. Ibid., pp. 3–4.

199. Ibid., p. 237.

200. Ibid., p. x.

201. Ibid., p. 3.

202. Harold James, "Should We Fear a German Europe?" *The Times* (London), July 1995, p. 36. Diethelm Prowe called it a "lucid" study, *German Studies Review*, February 1999, pp. 172–73. Quentin Peel, "Smokescreen of the British Obsession," *The Financial Times*, July 27, 1995. See also "Viertes Reich und Europäische Union," *FAZ*, August 21, 1995, p. 10.

203. Richard Bernstein, "In World Cup Surprise, Flags Fly with German Pride," *The New York Times*, June 18, 2006, p. 3. Roger Cohen, "Germany and the Cup: A Liberating Normality," *The New York Times*, June 17, 2006, p. 2.

204. Under Schroeder, Germany cut real wages and pensions in the effort to make its economy more competitive. Workers were hit substantially, but Germany's inflation remained modest, while prices soared in Greece, Spain, Portugal, and Italy. This helped German goods outcompete the more expensive goods of the GIPSI nations and promoted Germany's major trade surplus. Mark Blyth, "A Pain in the Athens: Why Greece Isn't to Blame for the Crisis," *Foreign Affairs*, July 7, 2015, www.foreignaffairs.com/articles/greece/2015-07-07/pain-athens; Eduardo Porter, "Germans Forget Postwar History Lesson on Debt Relief in Greece Crisis, *The New York Times*, July 8, 2015, p. B1.

205. "For Germany's Angela Merkel Storm and Stress in Greece," *The Globe and Mail* (Canada), October 10, 2012.

206. Some protesters inserted a swastika inside the flag's twelve stars, while others grouped miniature EU stars to form a giant swastika. www.welt.de/politik/ausland/article13439625/Deutsche-werden-zum-Suendenbock-fuer-die-Griechen.html

207. "77 percent der Griechen glauben: Deutschland will das Vierte Reich," *Deutsche Mittelstands Nachrichten*, February 23, 2012.

208. Michael Martens, "Widerstand gegen das Vierte Reich," *FAZ*, March 20, 2012.

209. Dikos Dimou, "The Bailout Crisis: Why Greece Is Content to Put the Blame on Germany," *The Observer*, March 26, 2015.

210. Michael Martens, "Widerstand gegen das Vierte Reich," *FAZ*, March 20, 2012.

211. Eduardo Porter, "Germans Forget Postwar History Lesson on Debt Relief in Greece Crisis," *The New York Times*, July 8, 2015, p. B1. See also Peter Casey, "Dig Deep to Find the Real Meaning of Debt Forgiveness," *Sunday Independent*, February 8, 2015, p. 7.

212. "Greek Lawmaker Compares Debt Crisis to Holocaust," *The New York Times*, June 24, 2015; "Berlin Faces Austerity Challenge in Brussels," *Spiegel Online*, February 10, 2015; "Tsipras Raises War Reparations Claim at Berlin Press Conference with Merkel," *Guardian*, March 23, 2015.

213. "Italy's Monti Takes Gloves Off in Euro Fight," *The Times & Transcript* (New Brunswick), August 9, 2012.

214. "Von Hitler-Merkel bis Terminator," *Süddeutsche Zeitung*, March 20, 2015.
215. www.ilgiornale.it/news/quarto-reich-827668.html "Antideutsche Stimmung in Italien," *FAZ*, August 7, 2012, p. 11.
216. "What Some Europeans See When They Look at Germany," *Der Spiegel International*, March 23, 2015. www.spiegel.de/international/germany/german-power-in-the-age-of-the-euro-crisis-a-1024714.html; "Italienische Zeitung zeigt Merkel mit Hitler-Bart," *Die Welt*, August 8, 2011. www.welt.de/politik/ausland/article13532791/Italienische-Zeitung-zeigt-Merkel-mit-Hitler-Bart.html
217. Simon Heffer, "Rise of the Fourth Reich," *Daily Mail* (London), August 17, 2011. www.dailymail.co.uk/news/article-2026840/European-debt-summit-Germany-using-financial-crisis-conquer-Europe.html
218. Ibid.
219. Frederick Forsyth, "New Deal Is a Charter for the Fourth Reich," *Sunday Independent*, July 24, 2011.
220. Richard Littlejohn, "Springtime for Merkel!" *Daily Mail* (London), November 18, 2011.
221. "Wir überleben auch noch das Vierte Reich," *FAZ*, September 12, 2008, p. 1.
222. "Tales from the Coffee Shop," *Cyprus Mail*, January 13, 2013.
223. www.wsws.org/en/articles/2016/07/01/unio-j01.html
224. "Russian TV talk show predicts cold war," *BBC Worldwide Monitoring*, December 11, 2014. www.pravdareport.com/opinion/columnists/08-06-2016/134656-russia_fourth_reich-0/; http://novorossia.today/150391-2/ *Novorussia Today* attacked Merkel's "Fourth Reich" for her government's criticism of "fake news." http://europe.newsweek.com/max-keiser-interview-britain-epicentre-financial-fraud-327254: RT's popular show *The Keiser Report*, by web broadcaster Max Keiser, about Germany becoming a "Fourth Reich."
225. Catherine MacMillan, "The Return of the Reich? A Gothic Tale of Germany and the Eurozone Crisis," *Journal of Contemporary European Studies*, 1, 2014, pp. 31–35.
226. "Über den Merkiavellismus," *FAZ*, January 17, 2013, p. 25. "Ulrich Beck im Gespräch," *Goethe Institut*, April 2013. www.goethe.de/ins/gr/de/kul/mag/20572701.html
227. Karlheinz Weissmann, "Der häßliche Deutsche," *Junge Freiheit*, February 19, 2012.
228. Dirk Schümer, "Eine Welle von Deutschenhass rollt durch Europa," *Die Welt*, July 19, 2015. See also Thomas Steinfeld, "Der Zorn des Südens auf das 'Vierte Reich,'" *Süddeutsche Zeitung*, December 15, 2014.
229. Michael Martens, "Und willst du nicht mein Bruder sein," *FAZ*, July 28, 2013, p. 5.
230. Frank Vollmer, "Italiens Zorn auf Deutschland," *Rheinischer Post*, March 10, 2015.
231. Konrad Putzler, "Das vierte Reich – Deutschland erobert Europa," *Die Welt*, August 19, 2011. www.welt.de/politik/ausland/article13554379/Das-vierte-Reich-Deutschland-erobert-Europa.html
232. Harald Martenstein, "Über Deutschlands Image," *Die Zeit Magazin*, August 6, 2015, p. 10.
233. "Kritik an 'Spiegel'-Cover mit Merkel und Nazis," *Die Welt*, March 22, 2015.
234. Dominic Lawson, "Cease Fire! Merkel Isn't Building a Fourth Reich," *The Sunday Times*, November 13, 2011, p. 24.
235. Richard Evans, "The Shackles of the Past," *The New Statesman*, November 21, 2011, p. 24.

236. Martin Ivens, "It's 'Never Again' That Made This Euro Mess," *The Sunday Times*, November 20, 2011.

237. Derek Scally, "Language of 'Perpetrator' and 'Victim' Fuels EU Crisis," *The Irish Times*, July 18, 2015, p. 13.

238. Fareed Zakaria, "Germany's Road to Redemption," *The Washington Post*, September 10, 2015.

Conclusion

1. Leonard Pitts, Jr., "Mr. President," *The Miami Herald*, February 14, 2017.

2. "Welcome to the Fourth Reich," *Democracy Now*, December 6, 2016. www.democracynow.org/2016/12/6/welcome_to_the_fourth_reich_legendary

3. Stacey Patton, "How Donald Trump Is Building a Fourth Reich," *Dame*, November 21, 2016, www.damemagazine.com/2016/11/21/how-donald-trump-building-fourth-reich

4. Mike Rivage-Seul, "'Fourth Reich' Is Coming to Incinerate the Planet," *Lexington Herald-Leader*, December 25, 2016. Jacob Rubashkin, "Trump's Fourth Reich," *The Cornell Daily Sun*, November 23, 2015, https://issuu.com/cornellsun/docs/11–24-15_entire_issue_hi_res_3637854916e22c; "Sieg Heil," *The Collegian*, February 22, 2016, http://collegian.csufresno.edu/2016/02/22/donald-trump-is-going-to-get-us-all-killed/

5. See https://twitter.com/JennyTwist1/status/840128399477620736 and https://twitter.com/search?q=%22fourth%20reich%22&src=typd; see http://fightfascism.tumblr.com/; www.pinterest.com/cbest55/trump-the-fourth-reich/?lp=true; www.reddit.com/r/EnoughTrumpSpam/comments/5cvgv1/america_2016_the_dawn_of_the_fourth_reich/ www.reddit.com/duplicates/4r8qa7/welcome_to_donald_trumps_nascent_fourth_reich/

6. http://abcnews.go.com/US/anonymous-claims-hack-donald-trump/story?id=37730049; www.maciverinstitute.com/2016/12/protesters-fail-to-derail-trump-election-at-wisconsin-electoral-college/

7. Warren Blumenfeld, "The Fourth Estate as Antidote for the Fourth Reich," *The Good Men Project*, November 18, 2017. https://goodmenproject.com/featured-content/the-fourth-estate-as-antidote-for-the-fourth-reich-wcz/

8. https://medium.com/return-of-the-reich

9. They include Frank Gaffney, who heads the Center for Security Policy, Pamela Geller of Atlas Shrugs, and Robert Spencer of Jihad Watch.

10. Bernard Goldberg, "The New Party of No," *Rapid City Journal*, February 15, 2017. http://rapidcityjournal.com/news/opinion/columnists/national/goldberg-the-new-party-of-no/article_00566bff-8424-5204-bf41-fe3353654b16.html

11. William McGurn, "Who's 'Normalizing' Donald Trump Now?" *The Wall Street Journal*, February 7, 2017, p. A13.

12. Ann Coulter, "Pundits and the Fourth Reich," *The St. Augustine Recorder*, March 13, 2016. http://staugustine.com/opinions/2016-03-13/ann-cokulter-pundits-and-fourth-reich

13. Christine Flowers, "Hitler References to Trump Are Lazy, Offensive," *The Winona Daily News*, February 9, 2017. www.winonadailynews.com/news/opinion/columnists/other/christine-flowers-hitler-references-to-trump-are-lazy-offensive/article_53281f28-36da-541e-9f81-577804fbbe08.html

14. "Racist, Anti-Semitic signs Placed at Dumfries Church," *Fox5 News*, August 28, 2017. www.fox5dc.com/news/local-news/racist-anti-semitic-signs-placed-at-dumfries-church

15. www.usatoday.com/story/news/nation-now/2017/05/22/what-alt-reich-nation-facebook-group-fbi-investigating-possible-hate-crime-university-maryland/335961001/

16. "Florida Nazi Leader Gets Five Years for Having Explosive Material," *NBC News*, January 9, 2018. www.nbcnews.com/news/us-news/florida-neo-nazi-leader-gets-5-years-having-explosive-material-n836246

17. www.stormfront.org/forum/t951387/; www.stormfront.org/forum/t923534/ See https://angrywhitemen.org/2016/02/16/stormfront-users-predict-that-donald-trump-will-usher-in-the-fourth-reich/

18. Kimi Yoshino, "Fresh Muslim–Jewish Discord on Campus," *The Los Angeles Times*, May 12, 2006, p. B3. See also "Sabiqun and Anti-Semitism on Campus." http://archive.adl.org/main_anti_israel/sabiqun_anti-semitism250d.html

19. "Remembrance Day – A Delusional Escape to a Time When Fascists Were the Enemy," *Canadian Arab News*, November 9, 2006.

20. Robert Horenstein, "The Ultimate Abuse," *The Jerusalem Post*, March 16, 2009, p. 46. Sherri Muzher, "Turning the Palestinian Cause into Medusa," *The Arab American News*, September 27, 2008, p. 13: "Israel is now the Fourth Reich."

21. This was true of Doc Jazz's 2013 song, "Hungry," www.docjazz.com/damned-fourth-reich/; https://twitter.com/moderate_rabble/status/777324354216624128 and https://twitter.com/communicipalist/status/772719520477765633 See the 2017.3 reference on Mondoweiss to "the burning of Palestinian civilians with illegal white phosphorous by The Fourth Reich." http://mondoweiss.net/2012/04/english-effort-to-boycott-israeli-theater-is-likened-to-nazi-book-burning/

22. Marc Perelman, "False Report Triggers Rush of Iranian-Nazi Comparisons," *The Forward*, May 26, 2006, p. 1.

23. Mathew Wagner, "Jesus's Zionists," *The Jerusalem Post*, May 1, 2009, p. 14.

24. "A Grotesque Love of Propaganda," *Daily Mail* (London), March 21, 2015.

25. www.pravdareport.com/opinion/columnists/01-04-2015/130153-boys_from_brussels-0/#sthash.hvQ8xDh6.dpuf

26. www.strategic-culture.org/news/2014/06/19/a-fourth-reich-is-already-under-construction-in-ukraine.html

27. "USA Creates Fourth Reich to Destroy Russia," *Pravda Report*, February 9, 2015. www.pravdareport.com/world/americas/09-02-2015/129738-0/

28. www.express.co.uk/news/world/841539/EU-news-European-Union-fourth-reich-Germany-communism-Poland; www.sueddeutsche.de/politik/ungarn-wer-hat-angst-vor-dem-fremden-mann-1.3088398

29. Adam Lebor, *The Budapest Protocol* (London, 2011).

30. Cotton Levi Grove, *4th Reich of Antarctica: Secrets of South America* (2012), Patrick Parker, *Treasures of the Fourth Reich: A Novel of Suspense* (2012), and Gary Compton, *The Fourth Reich – Head of the Snake* (2016).

31. http://dc.wikia.com/wiki/Fourth_Reich

32. See Gavriel D. Rosenfeld, *Hi Hitler! How the Nazi Past Is Being Normalized in Contemporary Culture* (Cambridge, UK, 2015), pp. 198–203.

33. www.salon.com/2017/02/04/the-end-of-the-world-as-we-know-it-the-donald-trump-white-house-is-set-to-destroy-decades-of-u-s-foreign-policy/ In 1998, Rage Against the Machine released a song, "No Shelter," that included the line: "Cinema, simulated life, ill drama; Fourth Reich Culture – Americana." www.azlyrics.com/lyrics/rageagainstthemachine/noshelter.html

BIBLIOGRAPHY

Adorno, Theodor W., "What Does Coming to Terms with the Past Mean?" in Hartman, ed., *Bitburg in Moral and Political Perspective*, pp. 114–29.

Allemann, Fritz René, *Bonn ist nicht Weimar* (Cologne, 1956).

Allen, Charles, *Heusinger of the Fourth Reich* (New York, 1963).

Andreas-Friedrich, Ruth, *Berlin Underground: 1938–1945* (New York, 1947).

Anglo-Jewish Association, *Germany's New Nazis* (1951).

Appelius, Claudia, *"Die schönste Stadt der Welt"*: *Deutsch-jüdische Flüchtlinge in New York* (Essen, 2003).

Backes, Uwe and Jesse Eckhard, *Politischer Extremismus in der Bundesrepublik Deutschland*, Volume III (Cologne, 1989).

Baldow, Beate, *Episode oder Gefahr? Die Naumann–Affäre* (Ph.D. Dissertation, Freie Universität Berlin, 2012).

Banchoff, Thomas, *The German Problem Transformed: Institutions, Politics, and Foreign Policy, 1945–1995* (Ann Arbor, 1999).

Barbian, Nikolaus, *Auswärtige Kulturpolitik und "Auslandsdeutsche" in Latinamerika, 1949–1973* (Wiesbaden, 2013).

Bark, Dennis and David Gress, *A History of West Germany: From Shadow to Substance, 1945–1963* (Oxford, 1989).

Barker, Jennifer Lynde, *The Aesthetics of Antifascist Film: Radical Projection* (New York, 2013).

Bärsch, Claus-Ekkehard, *Die politische Religion des Nationalsozialismus* (Munich, 1998).

Bayer, Karen, *"How Dead Is Hitler?" Der Britische Starreporter Sefton Delmer und die Deutschen* (Mainz, 2008).

Becker, Manuel and Christoph Studet, *Der Umgang des Dritten Reiches mit den Feinden des Regimes* (Berlin, 2010).

Beevor, Antony, *The Fall of Berlin 1945* (New York, 2002).

Begrich, David and Andreas Speit, "'Heiliges Deutsches Reich': Reichsidee und Reichsideologie der extremen Rechte," in Speit, ed., *Reichsbürger*, pp. 22–40.

Ben-Menahem, Yemima, "Historical Necessity and Contingency," in A. Tucker, ed., *A Companion to the Philosophy of History and Historiography*, pp. 110–30.

Benford, Timothy B., *Hitler's Daughter* (New York, 1983).

   World War II Quiz and Fact Book, Volumes I and II (New York, 1982 and 1984).

   World War II Flashback – A Fact-Filled Look at the War Years (Stamford, CT, 1991).

Bernhard, Georg, "Entwurf einer Verfassung für das 'Vierte Reich,' Januar/Februar 1936," in Langkau-Alex, ed., *Dritter Band*, pp. 25–34.

Berning, Cornelia, *Vom 'Abstammungsnachweis' zum 'Zuchtwart': Vokabular des Nationalsozialismus* (Berlin, 1964).

Bernstein, Matthew H., "Unrecognizable Origins: 'The Song of the Dragon' and Notorious," in Palmer and Boyd, eds., *Hitchcock at the Source*, pp. 139–59.

Bernstein, Michael André, *Foregone Conclusions: Against Apocalyptic History* (Berkeley, 1994).

Bess, Michael, *Choices under Fire: Moral Dimensions of World War II* (New York, 2008).

Biddiscombe, Perry, "Donald and Me: The Iraq War and the 'Werewolf' Analogy," *International Journal*, summer, 2004, 669–80.

   The Last Nazis: Werewolf Guerilla Resistance in Europe, 1944–1947 (Stroud, UK, 2006).

   "Operation Selection Board: The Growth and Suppression of the Neo-Nazi 'Deutsche Revolution' 1945–47," *Intelligence and National Security*, 1, 1996, 59–77.

   Werwolf!: The History of the National Socialist Guerrilla Movement, 1944–1946 (Toronto, 1998).

Biess, Frank, Mark Roseman, and Hanna Schissler, *Conflict, Catastrophe, and Continuity: Essays on Modern German History* (New York, 2007).

Blum, Howard, *Wanted! The Search for Nazis in America* (New York, 1977).

Bodroghkozy, Aniko, *Equal Time: Television and the Civil Rights Movement* (Urbana, IL, 2012).

Bollmus, Reinhard, *Das Amt Rosenberg und seine Gegner: Studien zum Machtkampf im nationalsozialistischen System* (Munich, 2006).

Bower, Tom, *Klaus Barbie: The "Butcher of Lyons"* (New York, 1984).

The Pledge Betrayed: America and Britain and the Denazification of Postwar Germany (New York, 1982).

Bowler, Peter, *Darwin Deleted: Imagining a World without Darwin* (Chicago, 2013).

Bracey Jr., John H., August Meier, and Elliott Rudwick, eds., *Black Nationalism in America* (Indianapolis, 1970).

Bracher, Karl Dietrich, "Democracy and Right Wing Extremism in West Germany," *Current History*, May 1, 1968, 281–87.

The German Dictatorship: The Origins, Structure and Effects of National Socialism (New York, 1970).

Brandes, Ina, "Kurt Schumacher: Der Kandidat aus Weimar," in Forkmann and Richter, eds., *Gescheiterte Kanzler-Kandidaten*, pp. 27–44.

Braunthal, Gerard, *Right-Wing Extremism in Contemporary Germany* (Basingstoke, UK, 2009).

Brendle, Franz, *Das konfessionelle Zeitalter* (Berlin, 2015).

Brinton, Laurel J., "Historical Discourse Analysis," in Tannen, et al., eds., *The Handbook of Discourse Analysis*, pp. 222–43.

Brochhagen, Ulrich, *Nach Nürnberg: Vergangenheitsbewältigung und Westintegration in der Ära Adenauer* (Hamburg, 1994).

Broszat, Martin, ed., *Deutschlands Weg in die Diktatur* (Berlin, 1983).

Buchna, Kristian, *Nationale Sammlung an Rhein und Ruhr: Friedrich Middelhauve und die nordrheinwestfälische FDP 1945–1953* (Munich, 2010).

Buchstab, Günter, Brigitte Kaff, and Hans-Otto Kleinmann, eds., *Verfolgung und Widerstand, 1933–1945: Christliche Demokraten gegen Hitler* (Düsseldorf, 1986).

Busch, Otto and Peter Furth, *Rechtsradikalismus im Nachkriegsdeutschland: Studien über die Sozialistische Reichspartei (SRP)* (Berlin, 1957).

Buscher, Frank M., "Kurt Schumacher, German Social Democracy and the Punishment of Nazi Crimes," *Holocaust and Genocide Studies*, 3, 1990, 261–73.

Buschke, Heiko, *Deutsche Presse, Rechtsextremismus und nationalsozialistische Vergangenheit in der Ära Adenauer* (Frankfurt, 2003).

"Die Sozialistische Reichspartei im Raum Lüneburg 1949–1952," in Weisbrod, ed., *Rechtsradikalismus in der politischen Kultur der Nachkriegszeit*, pp. 87–107.

Butter, Michael, *The Epitome of Evil: Hitler in American Fiction, 1939–2002* (New York, 2009).

Caplovitz, David and Candace Rogers, *Swastika 1960: The Epidemic of Anti-Semitic Vandalism in America* (New York, 1961).

Carr, Caleb, "VE Day – November 11, 1944," in Cowley, ed., *What If?* 2, pp. 333–43.

Chamberlin, William Henry, *The German Phoenix* (New York, 1963).

Childs, David and Jeffrey Johnson, *West Germany: Politics and Society* (New York, 1981).

Clark, Delbert, *Again the Goose Step* (New York, 1949).

Cocks, Geoffrey, "Hollywood über Alles: Seeing the Nazis in American Movies," *Film & History*, 45.1, summer, 2015, 38–54.

Collier, David S. and Kurt Glaser, *Berlin and the Future of Eastern Europe* (Chicago, 1963).

Conant, James Bryant, *Germany and Freedom: A Personal Appraisal* (Cambridge, MA, 1958).

Connor, Ian, "The Radicalization that Never Was? Refugees in the German Federal Republic," in Biess, Roseman, and Schissler, eds., *Conflict, Catastrophe, and Continuity*, pp. 221–36.

Constantine, Alex, ed., *The Essential Mae Brussell: Investigations of Fascism in America* (Port Townsend, WA, 2014).

Cook, Barnard A., *Europe since 1945: An Encyclopedia*, Volume I (New York, 2001).

Cowley, Robert, ed., *What If? 2: Eminent Historians Imagine What Might Have Been* (New York, 2001).

Craig, William, *The Strasbourg Legacy* (New York, 1976).

Dabringhaus, Erhard, *Klaus Barbie: The Shocking Story of How the U.S. Used This Nazi War Criminal as an Intelligence Agent. A First-Hand Account* (Washington, DC, 1984).

Dahrendorf, Ralf, *Society and Democracy in Germany* (London, 1965).

Davidson, Eugene, *The Death and Life of Germany* (New York, 1959).

Davies, Norman, *Rising '44: The Battle for Warsaw* (New York, 2004).

Delgado, Mariano, Klaus Koch, and Edgar Marsch, eds., *Europa, Tausendjähriges Reich und Neue Welt: Zwei Jahrtausende Geschichte und Utopie in der Rezeption des Danielbuches* (Freiburg, Switzerland, 2003).

Demshuk, Andrew, *The Lost German East: Forced Migration and the Politics of Memory, 1945–1970* (New York, 2012).

Denton, Robert E., "The Rhetorical Functions of Slogans: Classifications and Characteristics," *Communication Quarterly*, spring, 1980, 10–18.

Dettke, Dieter, *The Spirit of the Berlin Republic* (New York, 2003).

Di Tella, Guido and D. Cameron Watt, eds., *Argentina between the Great Powers, 1939–1946* (Pittsburgh, 1990).

Dirks, Walter, "Der restaurative Charakter der Epoche," *Frankfurter Hefte*, 9, 1950, 942–55.

Domarus, Max, *Hitler: Speeches and Proclamations, 1932–1945, The Chronicle of a Dictatorship* (Wauconda, IL, 1990).

Donald, David, *Liberty and Union* (Boston, 1978).

Donohoe, James, *Hitler's Conservative Opponents in Bavaria: 1930–1945* (Leiden, Netherlands, 1961).

Dornberg, John, *Schizophrenic Germany* (New York, 1961).

Dorril, Stephen, *MI6: Inside the Covert World of Her Majesty's Secret Intelligence Service* (New York, 2000).

Drachkovitch, Milorad M. and Branko Lazitch, *The Comintern: Historical Highlights, Essays, Recollections, Documents* (Palo Alto, 1966).

Dubiel, Helmut, *Niemand ist frei von der Geschichte* (Munich, 1999).

Dudek, Peter and Hans-Gerhard Jaschke, *Entstehung und Entwicklung des Rechtsextremismus in der Bundesrepublik: Zur Tradition einer besonderen politischen Kultur* (Opladen, 1984).

Duffett, John, *Against the Crime of Silence: Proceedings of the International War Crimes Tribunal* (New York, 1970).

Duke, Madeline, *The Bormann Receipt* (London, 1977).

Ebach, Jürgen, *Neue Schrift-Stücke: Biblische Passagen* (Gütersloh, 2012).

Edinger, Lewis Joachim, *Kurt Schumacher: A Study in Personality and Political Behavior* (Palo Alto, 1965).

Eisenhower, Dwight D., *Crusade in Europe* (Baltimore, 1997).

Elliott, J. H., *Empires of the Atlantic World: Britain and Spain in America, 1492–1830* (New Haven, 2006).

Elm, Ludwig, *Aufbruch ins Vierte Reich?* (Berlin, 1981).

Emmet, Christopher and Norbert Muhlen, *The Vanishing Swastika: Facts and Figures on Nazism in West Germany* (Chicago, 1961).

Erdstein, Erich, *Inside the Fourth Reich* (New York, 1977).

Ermarth, Michael, ed., *America and the Shaping of German Society, 1945–1955* (New York, 1993).

Etheridge, Brian C., *Enemies to Allies: Cold War Germany and American Memory* (Lexington, KY, 2016).

Evans, Richard, *Cosmopolitan Islanders: British Historians and the European Continent* (Cambridge, UK, 2009).

The Third Reich at War (New York, 2009).

Fadiman Jr., Edwin, *Who Will Watch the Watchers?* (New York, 1970).

Farago, Ladislas, *Aftermath: Martin Bormann and the Fourth Reich* (New York, 1974).

Finkenberger, Martin, "Johann von Leers und die 'faschistische Internationale' der fünfziger und sechziger Jahre in Argentinien und Ägypten," *Zeitschrift für Geschichtswissenschaft*, 6, 2011, 522–43.

Fischer, Michael, *Horst Mahler: Biographische Studie zu Antisemitismus, Antiamerikanismus, und Versuchen deutscher Schuldabwehr* (Karlsruhe, 2015).

Flanagan, Thomas, "The Third Reich: Origins of a Millenarian Symbol", *Journal of European Ideas*, 3, 1987, 283–95.

Folsom, Alan, *The Day after Tomorrow* (New York, 1995).

Forkmann, Daniela and Saskia Richter, eds., *Gescheiterte Kanzler-Kandidaten: Von Kurt Schumacher bis Edmund Stoiber* (Wiesbaden, 2007).

Forsyth, Frederick, *The Odessa File* (New York, 1972).

Frei, Norbert, *Adenauer's Germany and the Nazi Past: The Politics of Amnesty and Integration* (New York, 2002).

"Das Problem der NS-Vergangenheit in der Ära Adenauer," in Weisbrod, ed., *Rechtsradikalismus in der politischen Kultur der Nachkriegszeit*, pp. 19–31.

"Vergangenheitsbewältigung or 'Renazification'? The American Perspective on Germany's Confrontation with the Nazi Past in the Early Years of the Adenauer Era," in Ermarth, ed., *America and the Shaping of German Society*, pp. 47–59.

Friedlander, Saul, *Reflections of Nazism: An Essay on Kitsch and Death* (New York, 1982).

Friedrich, Otto, *Before the Deluge: A Portrait of Berlin in the 1920s* (New York, 1995).

Fritz, Stephen, *Endkampf: Soldiers, Civilians, and the Death of the Third Reich* (Lexington, KY, 2004).

Fritzen, Florentine, *Gesünder leben: Die Lebensreformbewegung im 20. Jahrhundert* (Stuttgart, 2006).

Fulbrook, Mary, *A History of Germany 1918–2014: The Divided Nation* (Chichester, UK, 2014).

Funke, Hajo, *Paranoia und Politik* (Berlin, 2002).

Gaddis, John Lewis, *The Cold War: A New History* (New York, 2005).

The Landscape of History: How Historians Map the Past (Oxford, 2004).

Gamm, Hans-Jochen, *Der Flüsterwitz im Dritten Reich* (Munich, 1963).

Gardner, John, *Spin the Bottle* (London, 1963).

The Werewolf Trace (New York, 1977).

Gassert, Philipp, "The Specter of Americanization: Western Europe in the American Century," in *The Oxford Handbook of Postwar European History*, pp. 182–200.

Gat, Azar, *Victorious and Vulnerable: Why Democracy Won in the Twentieth Century and How It Is Still Imperiled* (Lanham, MD, 2010).

Gaupp, Friedrich, *Deutsche Fälschung der abendländischen Reichsidee* (Bern, 1946).

Geppert, Dominik, *Die Ära Adenauer* (Darmstadt, 2002).

Gessenharter, Wolfgang and Thomas Pfeiffer, eds., *Die Neue Rechte – eine Gefahr für die Demokratie?* (Wiesbaden, 2004).

Giersch, Herbert, et al., *The Fading Miracle: Four Decades of Market Economy in Germany* (Cambridge, UK, 1992).

Gifford, Thomas, *The Wind Chill Factor* (New York, 1994).

Gimbel, John, *The American Occupation of Germany: Politics and the Military, 1945–1949* (Palo Alto, 1968).

Ginsburg, Tobias, *Die Reise ins Reich: Unter Reichsbürgern* (Berlin, 2018).

Gisevius, Hans Bernd, *Bis zum bitteren Ende: Vom Reichstagsbrand bis zum 20. Juli 1944*, Volume II (Hamburg, 1959).

Glaeßner, Gert-Joachim, *Politik in Deutschland* (Wiesbaden, 2006).

Glienke, Stephan Alexander, Volker Paulmann, and Joachim Perels, eds., *Erfolgsgeschichte Bundesrepublik? Die Nachkriegsgesellschaft im langen Schatten des Nationalsozialismus* (Göttingen, 2008).

Glotz, Peter, *Die Deutsche Rechte* (Stuttgart, 1989).

Görtemaker, Manfred, *Geschichte der Bundesrepublik Deutschland: Von der Grundung bis zur Gegenwart* (Munich, 1999).

Thomas Mann und die Politik (Frankfurt, 2005).

Greenberg, David, *Nixon'sShadow: The History of an Image* (New York, 2003).

Greene, Harris, *Canceled Accounts* (New York, 1976).

Griffin, Des, *Fourth Reich of the Rich* (Clackamas, OR, 1976).

Griffin, Roger, *The Nature of Fascism* (New York, 1996).

Grumke, Thomas and Bernd Wagner, *Handbuch Rechtsradikalismus: Personen – Organisationen – Netzwerke von Neonazismus bis in die Mitte der Gesellschaft* (Opladen, 2002).

Gunst, Dieter, "Hitler wollte kein 'Drittes Reich,'" *Geschichte, Politik, und ihre Didaktik*, 17, 1989, 299–305.

Gurock, Jeffrey, *The Holocaust Averted: An Alternate History of American Jewry, 1938–1967* (New Brunswick, 2015).

Guy, Stephen, *After Victory: Projections of the Second World War and Its Aftermath in British Feature Films, 1946–1950* (Ph.D. Dissertation, Queen Mary, University of London, 2002).

Habe, Hans, *Our Love Affair with Germany* (New York, 1953).

Hagen, William W., *German History in Modern Times: Four Lives of the Nation* (Cambridge, MA, 2012).

Hale, Martin, *The Fourth Reich* (London, 1965).

Hall, Adam, *The Quiller Memorandum* (New York, 1965).

Hanrieder, Wolfram, *Germany, America, Europe: Forty Years of German Foreign Policy* (New Haven, 1989).

Hansen, Henning, *Die Sozialistische Reichspartei (SRP): Aufstieg und Scheitern einer rechtsextremen Partei* (Düsseldorf, 2007).

Harris, Robert, *Selling Hitler: The Story of the Hitler Diaries* (New York, 1986).

Hartman, Geoffrey, ed., *Bitburg in Moral and Political Perspective* (Bloomington, IN, 1986).

Hartrich, Edwin, *The Fourth and Richest Reich* (New York, 1980).

Hassell, Agostino von and Sigrid MacRae, *Alliance of Enemies: The Untold Story of the Secret American and German Collaboration to End World War II* (New York, 2006).

Heideking, Jürgen and Christof Mauch, *American Intelligence and the German Resistance to Hitler* (Boulder, CO, 1996).

Henke, Klaus Dietmar, "Die Grenzen der politischen Säuberung in Deutschland nach 1945" in Herbst, ed., *Westdeutschland 1945–1955*, pp. 127–33.

Herb, Hartmut, Jan Peters, and Mathias Thesen, *Der neue Rechtsextremismus: Fakten und Trends* (Lohra-Rodenhausen, 1980).

Herbert, Ulrich, *Best: Biographische Studien über Radikalismus, Weltanschauung und Vernunft, 1903–1989* (Bonn, 1996).

A History of Foreign Labor in Germany (Ann Arbor, 1990).

"NS-Eliten in der Bundesrepublik," in Loth and Rusinek, eds., *Verwandlungspolitik: NS-Eliten in der westdeutschen Nachkriegsgesellschaft*, p. 114.

"Rückkehr in die Bürgerlichkeit: NS-Eliten in der Bundesrepublik," in Weisbrod, ed., *Rechtsradikalismus in der politischen Kultur der Nachkriegszeit*, pp. 157–73.

Herbst, Ludolf, ed., *Westdeutschland 1945–1955: Unterwerfung, Kontrolle, Integration* (Munich, 1986).

Herf, Jeffrey, *Divided Memory: The Nazi Past in the Two Germanys* (Cambridge, MA, 1997).

"The Holocaust and the Competition of Memories in Germany, 1945–1949," in Michman, ed., *Remembering the Holocaust in Germany*, pp. 9–30.

"Multiple Restorations: German Political Traditions and the Interpretation of Nazism, 1945–1946," *Central European History*, 26, 1, 1993, 21–55.

Reactionary Modernism: Technology, Culture, and Politics in Weimar and the Third Reich (Cambridge, UK, 1984).

Hermand, Jost, *Old Dreams of a New Reich: Volkish Utopias and National Socialism* (Bloomington, IN, 1992).

Hertfelder, Thomas, "Ein Meistererzählung der Demokratie? Die großen Ausstellungshäuser des Bundes," in Hertfelder, Lappenküper, and Lillteicher, eds., *Erinnern an Demokratie in Deutschland*, pp. 139–78.

"'Modell Deutschland' – Erfolgsgeschichte oder Illusion?" in Hertfelder and Rödder, eds., *Modell Deutschland*, pp. 9–27.

Hertfelder, Thomas and Andreas Rödder, eds., *Modell Deutschland – Erfolgsgeschichte oder Illusion?* (Göttingen, 2007).

Hertfelder, Thomas, Ulrich Lappenküper, and Jürgen Lillteicher, eds., *Erinnern an Demokratie in Deutschland: Demokratiegeschichte in Museen und Erinnerungsstätten der Bundesrepublik* (Göttingen, 2016).

Heukenkamp, Ursula, ed., *Schuld und Sühne? Deutsche Kriegserlebnis und Kriegsdeutung in deutschen Medien der Nachkriegszeit (1945–1961)* (Amsterdam, 2001).

Higgins, Jack, *The Testament of Caspar Schultz* (New York, 1985).

Hilton, Stanley E., "The United States and Argentina in Brazil's Wartime Foreign Policy, 1939–1945," in Di Tella and Watt, eds., *Argentina between the Great Powers*, pp. 158–80.

Hirsch, Kurt, *Kommen die Nazis Wieder? Gefahren für die Bundesrepublik* (Munich, 1967).

Hitler, Adolf, *Mein Kampf* (Boston, 1971).

Hixson, Walter L., ed., *The American Experience in World War II*, Volume XII (New York, 2003).

    The United States and the Vietnam War: Volume III, Leadership and Diplomacy in the Vietnam War (New York, 2000).

Hockerts, Hans Günter, ed., *Koordinaten deutscher Geschichte in der Epoche des Ost-West Konflikts* (Munich, 2004).

Hoenicke Moore, Michaela, *Know Your Enemy: The American Debate on Nazism, 1933–1945* (Cambridge, UK, 2010).

Hoffmann, Johannes Friedrich, *Antiochus IV. Epiphanes, König von Syrien: Ein beitrag zur allgemeinen und insbesondere israelitischen Geschichte, mit einem Anhange über Antiochus im Buche Daniel* (Leipzig, 1873).

Höhn, Maria, *GIs and Fräuleins: The German–American Encounter in 1950s West Germany* (Chapel Hill, NC, 2002).

Höper, Wilhelm, *Die drei Reiche: Von der Kaiserkrone zum Hakenkreuz* (Breslau, 1934).

Horne, Alistair, *Return to Power: A Report on the New Germany* (New York, 1956).

Hughes, Michael, *Shouldering the Burdens of Defeat: West Germany and the Reconstruction of Social Justice* (Chapel Hill, NC, 1999).

Hunter, Jack, *The Tin Cravat* (New York, 1981).

Huyssen, Andreas, "Anselm Kiefer: The Terror of History, the Temptation of Myth," *October*, spring, 1989, 22–45.

Jarausch, Konrad, *After Hitler: Recivilizing Germans, 1945–1995* (New York, 2006).

    "The Federal Republic at Sixty," *German Politics and Society*, March, 2010, 10–29.

Jarausch, Konrad and Michael Geyer, *Shattered Past: Reconstructing German Histories* (Princeton, 2009).

Jelinek, Gerhard, *Nachrichten aus dem 4. Reich* (Salzburg, 2008).

Juling, Peter, *Programmatische Entwicklung der FDP 1946 bis 1969: Einführung und Dokumente* (Meisenheim am Glan, 1977).

Kahn, Arthur D., *Experiment in Occupation: Witness to the Turnabout: Anti-Nazi War to Cold War, 1944–1946* (University Park, PA, 2004).

Kailitz, Steffen, *Politischer Extremismus in der Bundesrepublik Deutschland: Eine Einführung* (Wiesbaden, 2004).

Kaplan, Andrew, *Hour of the Assassins* (New York, 1980).

Kaplan, Jeffrey and Tore Bjørgo, eds., *Nation and Race: The Developing Euro-American Racist Subculture* (Boston, 1998).

Kaplan, Lawrence S., "NATO after Forty-Five Years: A Counterfactual History," in Papacosma and Heiss eds., *NATO in the Post-Cold War Era: Does It Have a Future?* (New York, 1995), pp. 3–21.

Kershaw, Ian, *The Nazi Dictatorship: Problems and Perspectives of Interpretation* (London, 1985).

Kettenacker, Lothar, *Germany 1989: In the Aftermath of the Cold War* (New York, 2009).

Kiani, Shida, "Zum politischen Umgang mit dem Antisemitismus in der Bundesrepublik: Die Schmierwelle im Winter 1959/1960," in Glienke, Paulmann, and Perels, eds., *Erfolgsgeschichte Bundesrepublik?* pp. 115–45.

Kielmansegg, Peter Graf, *Lange Schatten: Vom Umgang der Deutschen mit der nationalsozialistischen Vergangenheit* (Berlin, 1989).

Kinane, Karolyn and Michael Ryan, eds., *End of Days: Essays on the Apocalypse from Antiquity to Modernity* (Jefferson, NC, 2009).

Kirkpatrick, Ivone, *The Inner Circle: Memoirs of Ivone Kirkpatrick* (New York, 1959).

Kisatsky, Deborah, *The United States and the European Right, 1945–1955* (Columbus, OH, 2005).

Kitchen, Martin, *A History of Modern Germamy* (Malden, MA, 2006).

Kittel, Manfred, *Die Legende von der zweiten Schuld: Vergangenheitsbewältigung in der Ära Adenauer* (Berlin, 1993).

"Peripetie der Vergangenheitsbewältigung: Die Hakenkreuzschmierereien 1959/60 und das bundesdeutsche Verhältnis zum Nationalsozialismus," *Historisch-Politische Mitteilungen,* 1, 1994, 49–67.

Klapp, Orrin E., *Inflation of Symbols: Loss of Values in American Culture* (New Brunswick, NJ, 1991).

Klemperer, Victor, *I Will Bear Witness: A Diary of the Nazi Years, 1933–1941* (New York, 1998).

The Language of the Third Reich: LTI, Lingua Tertii Imperii: A Philologist's Notebook (London, 2000).

The Lesser Evil: The Diaries of Victor Klemperer, 1945–1959 (London, 2003).

Kleßmann, Christoph, *Die doppelte Staatsgründung: Deutsche Geschichte, 1945–1955* (Bonn, 1991).

Koch, Klaus, "Europabewusstsein und Danielrezeption zwischen 1648 und 1848," in Delgado, et al., eds., *Europa, Tausendjähriges Reich und Neue Welt*, pp. 326–84.

Koch-Weser, Erich, *Hitler and Beyond: A German Testament* (New York, 1945).

Kogon, Eugen, *The Theory and Practice of Hell* (New York, 1964).

Kommunistiche Partei Deutschlands, *Viertes Reich fällt aus: Das Urteil des Bundes-Verfassungsgerichtes über die SRP* (Hilden, 1952).

König, Helmut, "Das Erbe der Diktatur: Der Nationalsozialismus im politischen Bewusstsein der Bundesrepublik," *Leviathan*, 2, 1996, 163–80.

Koop, Volker, *Himmlers letztes Aufgebot* (Cologne, 2008).

Kosthorst, Daniel and Michael Feldkamp, *Akten zur Auswärtigen Politik der Bundesrepublik* (Munich, 1997).

Kotkin, Steven, *Stalin: Volume I, Paradoxes of Power, 1878–1928* (New York, 2014).

Kowalsky, Wolfgang and Wolfgang Schroeder, eds., *Rechtsextremismus: Einführung und Forschungsbilanz* (Opladen, 1994).

Krier, Leon, *Albert Speer: Architecture, 1932–1942* (New York, 1985).

Kruse, Kevin M. and Stephen Tuck, eds., *Fog of War: The Second World War and the Civil Rights Movement* (New York, 2012).

Kühnen, Michael, *Die Zweite Revolution* (1982).

Kulish, Nicholas and Souad Mekhennet, *The Eternal Nazi: From Mauthausen to Cairo, The Relentless Pursuit of SS Doctor Aribert Heim* (New York, 2014).

Kundnani, Hans, *Utopia or Auschwitz? Germany's 1968 Generation and the Holocaust* (New York, 2009).

Langkau-Alex, Ursula, ed., *Dritter Band: Dokumente zur Geschichte des Ausschusses zur Vorbereitung einer deutschen Volksfront* (Berlin, 2005).

Lebor, Adam, *The Budapest Protocol* (London, 2011).

Lebow, Richard Ned, *Archduke Franz Ferdinand Lives! A World without World War I* (New York, 2014).

   "Counterfactuals, History and Fiction," *Historical Social Research*, 2, 2009, 57.

   Forbidden Fruit (Princeton, NJ, 2010).

Lee, Martin A., *The Beast Reawakens: Fascism's Resurgence from Hitler's Spymasters to Today* (Boston, 1997).

Lemons, Russell, *Goebbels and der Angriff* (Lexington, KY, 1994).

Lessner, Erwin, *Phantom Victory: A Fictional History of the Fourth Reich, 1945–1960* (New York, 1944).

Levin, Harry, *Memories of the Moderns* (New York, 1982).

Levin, Ira, *The Boys from Brazil* (New York, 1976).

Levsen, Sonja and Cornelius Torp, "Die Bundesrepublik und der Vergleich," in Levsen and Torp, eds., *Wo liegt die Bundesrepublik?* pp. 9–28.

Levsen, Sonja und Cornelius Torp, eds., *Wo liegt die Bundesrepublik? Vergleichende Perspektiven auf die Westdeutsche Geschichte* (Göttingen, 2016).

Lewis, Rand C., *A Nazi Legacy: Right-Wing Extremism in Postwar Germany* (New York, 1991).

The Neo-Nazis and German Unification (Westport, CT, 1996).

Lichtblau, Eric, *The Nazis Next Door: How America Became a Safe Haven for Hitler's Men* (New York, 2014).

Linklater, Magnus, Isabel Hilton, and Neal Ascherson, *The Nazi Legacy: Klaus Barbie and the International Fascist Connection* (New York, 1985).

Lipstadt, Deborah, *Denying the Holocaust: The Growing Assault on Truth and Memory* (New York, 1993).

Livingston, Robert Gerald and Volkmar Sander, eds., *The Future of German Democracy* (New York, 1993).

Loewenstein, Hubertus zu, *After Hitler's Fall: Germany's Coming Reich* (London, 1934).

Loftus, John, *The Belarus Secret* (New York, 1982).

Long, Wellington, *The New Nazis of Germany* (Philadelphia, 1968).

Lorenz, Karl, *Methodenlehre und Philosophie des Rechts in Geschichte und Gegenwart* (Berlin, 2010).

Loth, Wilfried and Bernd-A. Rusinek, "Einleitung," in Loth and Rusinek, eds., *Verwandlungspolitik: NS-Eliten in der westdeutschen Nachkriegsgesellschaft*, pp. 7–11.

eds., *Verwandlungspolitik: NS-Eliten in der westdeutschen Nachkriegsgesellschaft* (Frankfurt, 1998).

Frankfurt on the Hudson: The German Jewish Community of Washington Heights, 1933–1983, Its Structure and Culture (Detroit, 1989).

Lübbe, Hermann, "Der Nationalsozialismus im politischen Bewusstsein der Gegenwart," in Broszat, ed., *Deutschlands Weg in die Diktatur*, pp. 329–49.

Hermann Lübbe im Gespräch (Munich, 2010).

Ludlum, Robert, *Apocalypse Watch* (New York, 1995).

The Holcroft Covenant (New York, 1978).

MacDonald, David B., *Thinking History, Fighting Evil: Neoconservatives and the Perils of Analogy in American Politics* (Lanham, MD, 2009).

Macdonald, Gina, *Robert Ludlum: A Critical Companion* (Westport, CT, 1997).

MacMillan, Catherine, "The Return of the Reich? A Gothic Tale of Germany and the Eurozone Crisis," *Journal of Contemporary European Studies*, 1, 2014, 24–38.

Macrakis, Kristie, Thomas Wegener Friis, and Helmut Müller-Enbergs, eds., *East German Foreign Intelligence: Myth, Reality and Controversy* (New York, 2010).

Magilow, Daniel, Elizabeth Bridges, and Kristin T. Van der Lugt, eds., *Nazisploitation! The Nazi Image in Low-Brow Cinema and Culture* (New York, 2012).

Mahler, Horst, *Ehre Wahrheit Heimat* (2009).

Maier, Charles, *The Unmasterable Past: History, Holocaust, and German National Identity* (Cambridge, MA, 1988).

Manning, Paul, *Martin Bormann: Nazi in Exile* (Secaucus, NJ, 1981).

Marcus, Greil, *The Dustbin of History* (Cambridge, MA, 1995).

Markstein, George, *The Goering Testament* (New York, 1978).

Marrs, Jim, *The Rise of the Fourth Reich: The Secret Societies That Threaten to Take over America* (Solon, OH, 2008).

Martin, Steve, *L.A. Story and Roxanne: Two Screenplays* (New York, 1997).

Mauch, Christof and Jeremiah Riemer, *The Shadow War against Hitler: The Covert Operations of America's Wartime Secret Intelligence Service* (New York, 2002).

Maulucci, Jr., Thomas W., "Comparing the American Occupations of Germany and Iraq," *Yale Journal of International Affairs*, winter, 2008, 120–30.

McAleer, Kevin, *Dueling: The Cult of Honor in Fin-de-Siècle Germany* (Princeton, 2014).

McBride, Joseph, *Whatever Happened to Orson Welles? A Portrait of an Independent Career* (Lexington, KY, 2006).

McGilligan, Patrick, *Alfred Hitchcock: A Life in Darkness and Light* (New York, 2003).

McGowan, Lee, *The Radical Right in Germany: 1870 to the Present* (London, 2002).

Meade, Glenn, *Brandenburg* (New York, 1997).

Meding, Holger, *Der Weg: Eine deutsche Emigrantenzeitschrift in Buenos Aires, 1947–1957* (Berlin, 1997).

Meier, Christian, *Das Gebot zu vergessen und die Unabweisbarkeit des Erinnerns: Vom öffentlichen Umgang mit schlimmer Vergangenheit* (Munich, 2010).

Melchior, Ib, *Sleeper Agent* (New York, 1977).
  The Watchdogs of Abaddon (New York, 1980).

Meskil, Paul, *Hitler's Heirs* (New York, 1961).

Messenger, David A. and Katrin Paehler, eds., *A Nazi Past: Recasting German Identity in Postwar Europe* (Lexington, KY, 2015).

Michael, George, "The Ideological Evolution of Horst Mahler: The Far Left–Extreme Right Synthesis," *Studies in Conflict and Terrorism*, 32, 2009, 346–66.

Michman, Dan., ed., *Remembering the Holocaust in Germany, 1945–2000: German Strategies and Jewish Responses* (New York, 2002).

Middleton, Drew, *The Renazification of Germany* (New York, 1949).

Mihok, Brigitte, ed., *Handbuch des Antisemitismus: Judenfeinschaft in Geschichte und Gegenwart: Band VI Publikationen* (Berlin, 2013).

Mill, John Stuart, *On Liberty* (London, 1864).

Miller, Moses, *Nazis Preferred: The Renazification of Western Germany* (New York, 1950).

Milliken, Jennifer, *The Social Construction of the Korean War: Conflict Possibilities* (Manchester, UK, 2001).

Minott, Rodney G., *The Fortress That Never Was: The Myth of Hitler's Bavarian Stronghold* (New York, 1964).

Mitchell, Arthur, *Understanding the Korean War: The Participants, the Tactics, and the Course* (Jefferson, NC, 2013).

Mitelberg, Louis, Walter Heynowski, and Hans Picard, *Das Vierte Reich* (Berlin, 1955).

Mohler, Armin, *Die konservative Revolution in Deutschland 1918–1932: Ein Handbuch* (Graz, 1999).

Montagu, Ivor, *Germany's New Nazis* (London, 1967).

Morgan, Roger, *The United States and West Germany, 1945–1973: A Study in Alliance Politics* (London, 1974).

Morson, Gary Saul, *Narrative and Freedom: The Shadows of Time* (New Haven, 1994).

Moses, Dirk, *German Intellectuals and the Nazi Past* (Cambridge, UK, 2009).

Mühlberger, Detlef, *Hitler's Voice: The Völkische Beobachter, 1920–1933: Volume II, Nazi Ideology and Propaganda* (Bern, 2004).

Muhlen, Norbert, *The Return of Germany* (Bern, 1953).

Murphy, Brendan, *The Butcher of Lyon: The Story of Infamous Nazi Klaus Barbie* (New York, 1983).

Nagle, John David, *The National Democratic Party: Right Radicalism in the Federal Republic of Germany* (Berkeley, 1970).

Namier, Lewis, *Avenues of History* (London, 1952).

Naumann, Klaus, "Die neunziger Jahre, ein nervöses Jahrzehnt am Ende der Nachkriegszeit," in Heukenkamp, ed., *Schuld und Sühne?*, pp. 801–11.

"Selbstanerkennung: Nach 40 Jahren Bundesrepublik: Anstöße zur Bewältigung einer 'Erfolgsgeschichte,'" *Blätter* 9, 1988, 1046–60.

Newton, Ronald, "The United States, the German-Argentines, and the Myth of the Fourth Reich, 1943–47," *The Hispanic American Historical Review*, 1, February, 1984, 81–103.

Nicholls, A. J., *The Bonn Republic: West German Democracy 1945–1990* (New York, 1997).

Niven, Bill, *Facing the Nazi Past: United Germany and the Legacy of the Third Reich* (London, 2002).

Noethen, Stefan, "Pläne für das Vierte Reich: Der Widerstandskreis im Kölner Kettelerhaus 1941–1944," *Geschichte in Köln*, 39, 1996, 51–73.

Novick, Peter, *That Noble Dream: The "Objectivity Question" and the American Historical Profession* (Cambridge, UK, 1989).

O'Brine, Manning, *No Earth for Foxes* (New York, 1976).

Olick, Jeff, *In the House of the Hangman: The Agonies of Germany Defeat, 1943–1949* (Chicago, 2005).

Pagden, Anthony, *The Enlightenment: And Why it Still Matters* (New York, 2013).

Palmer, R. Barton and David Boyd, eds., *Hitchcock at the Source: The Auteur as Adapter* (Albany, 2011).

Papacosma, S. Victor and Mary Ann Heiss, eds., *NATO in the Post-Cold War Era: Does It Have a Future?* (New York, 1995).

Patterson, Harry, *The Valhalla Exchange* (Greenwich, CT, 1977).

Pauwels, Jacques, *The Myth of the Good War: America in the Second World War* (Toronto, 2002).

Perels, Joachim, *Das juristische Erbe des Dritten Reiches* (Frankfurt, 1999).

Peterson, Edward, *The American Occupation of Germany: Retreat to Victory* (Detroit, 1977).

Peterson, Walter F., *The German Left-Liberal Press in Exile: Georg Bernhard and the Circle of Émigré Journalists around the Pariser Tageblatt–Pariser Tageszeitung, 1933–1940* (Ph.D. Dissertation, State University of New York at Buffalo, 1982).

Pettit, Mike, *The Axmann Agenda* (New York, 1980).

Pfeiffer, Thomas, "Avantgarde und Brücke," in Gessenharter and Pfeiffer, eds., *Die neue Rechte – eine Gefahr für die Demokratie?* pp. 51–69.

Phillips, Gene D., *Out of the Shadows: Expanding the Canon of Classic Film Noir* (Lanham, MD, 2012).

Pikart, Eberhard and Wolfram Werner, eds., *Das Parlamentarische Rat, 1948–1949*, Volume V (Boppard, 1993).

Pinson, Koppel and Klaus Epstein, *Modern Germany: Its History and Civilization* (New York, 1966).

Popp, Valerie, *Aber hier war alles anders…; Amerikabilder der deutschsprachigen Exilliteratur nach 1939 in den USA* (Würzburg, 2008).

Posner, Gerald, *Case Closed: Lee Harvey Oswald and the Assassination of JFK* (New York, 2003).

Mengele: The Complete Story (New York, 1986).

Prittie, Terence, *Germany Divided: The Legacy of the Nazi Era* (New York, 1960).

Pulzer, Peter, *German Politics, 1945–1995* (Oxford, 1995).

Rauschning, Hermann, *The Conservative Revolution* (New York, 1941).

Ray, David, *The End of the Fourth Reich: A Rat Catcher's Adventure* (London, 1966).

Reading, Brian, *The Fourth Reich* (London, 1995).

Redles, David, *Hitler's Millennial Reich: Apocalyptic Belief and the Search for Salvation* (New York, 2005).

"Nazi End Times: The Third Reich as Millennial Reich," in Kinane and Ryan, eds., *End of Days*, pp. 173–96.

Reed, Douglas, *Nemesis? The Story of Otto Strasser and the Black Front* (Boston, 1940).

Rempel, Gerhard, *Hitler's Children: The Hitler Youth and the SS* (Chapel Hill, NC, 1990).

Richards, Rashna Wadia, *Cinematic Flashes: Cinephilia and Classical Hollywood* (Bloomington, IN, 2013).

Riess, Curt, *The Nazis Go Underground* (New York, 1944).

Ringer, Fritz, "Max Weber on Causal Analysis, Interpretation, and Comparison," *History and Theory*, May, 2002, 163–78.

Ritter, Gerhard, *The German Problem: Basic Questions of German Political Life, Past and Present* (1965).

Robin, Corey, *Fear: The History of a Political Idea* (New York, 2004).

Rödder, Andreas, "Das 'Modell Deutschland' zwischen Erfolgsgeschichte und Verfallsdiagnose," *Vierteljahrshefte für Zeitgeschichte*, 3, 2006, 345–63.

Roeder, Manfred, *Ein Kampf um's Reich* (Schwarzenborn, 1979).

Rogers, Daniel E., *Politics after Hitler: The Western Allies and the German Party System* (New York, 1995).

Rosenberg, Alfred, *The Myth of the Twentieth Century* (Ostara, 2000).

Rosenberg, Emily, "'Foreign Affairs' after World War II: Connecting Sexual and International Politics," *Diplomatic History*, January, 1994, 59–70.

Rosenfeld, Gavriel D., *Hi Hitler! How the Nazi Past Is Being Normalized in Contemporary Culture* (Cambridge, UK, 2015).

"The Reception of William L. Shirer's The Rise and Fall of the Third Reich in the United States and West Germany, 1960–1962," *Journal of Contemporary History*, January, 1994, 95–129.

"The Ways We Wonder 'What If? Towards a Typology of Historical Counterfactuals,'" *The Journal of the Philosophy of History*, 3, 2016, 382–411.

Rudolph, Hermann, ed., *Den Staat denken: Theodor Eschenburg zum Fünfundachtzigsten* (Stuttgart, 1989).

Russell, Lord, *Return of the Swastika?* (New York, 1969).

The Scourge of the Swastika (London, 1954).

Ryan, Jr., Allan A., *Klaus Barbie and the United States Government: A Report to the Attorney General of the United States* (Washington, DC, August, 1983).

Quiet Neighbors: Prosecuting Nazi War Criminals in America (New York, 1984).

Saña, Heleno, *Das vierte Reich: Deutschlands später Sieg* (Hamburg, 1990).

Sander, Hans-Dietrich, *Der nationale Imperativ: Ideengänge und Werkstücke zur Wiederherstellung Deutschlands* (Essen, 1990).

Sander, Hans-Dietrich and Jürgen Maass, *Im Banne der Reichsrenaissance* (Kiel, 2011).

Schaber, Will, ed., *Thinker versus Junker* (New York, 1941).

Schildt, Axel, *Ankunft im Westen: Ein Essay zur Erfolgsgeschichte der Bundesrepublik* (Frankfurt, 1999).

Schissler, Hannah, *The Miracle Years: A Cultural History of West Germany, 1949–1968* (Princeton, 2000).

Schletter, Christian, *Grabgesang der Demokratie: Die Debatten über das Scheitern der bundesdeutschen Demokratie von 1965 bis 1985* (Göttingen, 2015).

Schlosser, Hans Dieter, *"Es wird zwei Deutschlands geben": Zeitgeschichte und Sprache in Nachkriegsdeutschland 1945–1949* (Frankfurt, 2005).

Schmidt, Helmut and Fritz Stern, *Unser Jahrhundert: Ein Gespräch* (Munich, 2010).

Schmidt, Peer and Gregor Weber, eds., *Traum und res publica: Traumkulturen und Deutungen sozialer Wirklichkeiten in Europa von Renaissance und Barock* (Berlin, 2008).

Schmitz-Berning, Claudia, *Vokabular des Nationalsozialismus* (Berlin, 1998).

Schneppen, Heinz, *Odessa und das Vierte Reich: Mythen der Zeitgeschichte* (Berlin, 2007).

Scholtyseck, Joachim, *Robert Bosch und der liberale Widerstand gegen Hitler 1933 bis 1945* (Munich, 1999).

Scholz, Michael F., "Active Measures and Disinformation as Part of East Germany's Propaganda War, 1953–1972," in Macrakis, Friis, and Müller-Enbergs, eds., *East German Foreign Intelligence*, pp. 113–34.

Schrafstetter, Susanna, "Siegfried Zoglmann, His Circle of Writers, and the Naumann Affair," in Messenger and Paehler, eds., *A Nazi Past*, pp. 113–38.

Schwarz, Hans-Peter, *Die Ära Adenauer: Gründerjahre der Republik, 1949–1957* (Stuttgart, 1981).

"Die ausgebliebene Katastrophe: Eine Problemskizze zur Geschichte der Bundesrepublik," in Rudolph, ed., *Den Staat denken*, p. 151.

Schwarz, Michael, *Vertriebene und "Umsiedlerpolitik,"* (Munich, 2004).

Seaman, L. C. B., *Post-Victorian Britain 1902–1951* (London, 1966).

Seidel, Carlos Collado, *Angst vor dem "Vierten Reich": Die Allierten und die Ausschaltung des deutschen Einflusses in Spanien, 1944–1958* (Paderborn, 2001).

Seitenbecher, Manuel, *Mahler, Maschke, & Co.: Rechtes Denken in der 68er-Bewegung?* (Schöning, 2013).

Selby, Scott, *The Axmann Conspiracy: The Nazi Plan for a Fourth Reich and How the U.S. Army Defeated it* (New York, 2012)

Sereny, Gitta, *Into That Darkness: From Mercy Killing to Mass Murder, a Study of Franz Stangl, the Commandant of Treblinka* (New York, 1974).

Shirer, William L., *The Rise and Fall of the Third Reich* (New York, 1960).

Shulman, Charles, *Europe's Conscience in Decline* (Chicago, 1939).

Simonelli, Frederick J., *American Fuehrer: George Lincoln Rockwell and the American Nazi Party* (Urbana, IL, 1999).

"The World Union of National Socialists and Postwar Transatlantic Nazi Revival," in Kaplan and Bjørgo, eds., *Nation and Race*, pp. 34–57.

Simpson, Christopher, *Blowback: America's Recruitment of Nazis and Its Effects on the Cold War* (New York, 1988).

Slesar, Henry, "The Rise and Fall of the Fourth Reich," *The Magazine of Fantasy and Science Fiction*, August, 1975, 63–75.

Small, Melvin, *Antiwarriors: The Vietnam War and the Battle for America's Hearts and Minds* (Wilmington, DE, 2002).

Sontag, Susan, "Fascinating Fascism," in Sontag, ed., *Under the Sign of Saturn*, pp. 73–105.

ed., *Under the Sign of Saturn* (New York, 1980).

Speit, Andreas, ed., *Reichsbürger: Die unterschätzte Gefahr* (Berlin, 2017).

Stahl, Daniel, *Nazi-Jagd: Südamerikas Diktaturen und die Ahndung von NS-Verbrechen* (Göttingen, 2013).

Standley, Fred L. and Louis H. Pratt, eds., *Conversations with James Baldwin* (Jackson, MS, 1989).

Stangneth, Bettina, *Eichmann before Jerusalem* (New York, 2014).

Starr, Kevin, *The Dream Endures: California Enters the 1940s* (New York, 1997).

Stein, Ben, *The Croesus Conspiracy* (New York, 1979).

Steinacher, Gerald, *Nazis on the Run: How Hitler's Henchmen Fled Justice* (Oxford, 2011).

Stephan, Pierre, *Thomas Harlan: Das Gesicht deines Feindes: Ein deutsches Leben* (Berlin, 2007).

Stern, Fritz, *The Politics of Cultural Despair: A Study in the Rise of the Germanic Ideology* (Berkeley, 1961).

Sternberger, Dolf, *Dreizehn politische Radio Reden* (Heidelberg, 1947).

Stevenson, William, *The Bormann Brotherhood* (New York, 1973).

Stone, Dan, *The Oxford Handbook of Postwar European History* (Oxford, 2012).

Stöss, Richard, *Die extreme Rechte in der Bundesrepublik: Entwicklung – Ursachen – Gegenmaßnahmen* (Opladen, 1989).

Strasser, Otto, *Deutschlands Erneuerung* (Buenos Aires, 1946).

Germany Tomorrow (London, 1940).

Hitler and I (Boston, 1940).

Sugrue, Thomas, "Hillburn, Hattiesburg, and Hitler: Wartime Activists Think Globally and Act Locally," in Kruse and Tuck, eds., *Fog of War*, pp. 87–102.

Tannen, Deborah, Heidi E. Hamilton, and Deborah Schiffrin, eds., *The Handbook of Discourse Analysis* (Oxford, 2015).

Tauber, K. P., *Beyond Eagle and Swastika* (Middletown, CT, 1967).

Taylor, Frederick, *Exorcising Hitler: The Occupation and Denazification of Germany* (New York, 2011).

Taylor, Geoff, *Court of Honor* (New York, 1967).

Tent, James F., *Mission on the Rhine: Reeducation and Denazification in American-Occupied Germany* (Chicago, 1982).

Tetens, T. H., *Germany Plots with the Kremlin* (New York, 1953).
   The New Germany and the Old Nazis (New York, 1961).

Tetlock, Philip E., Richard Ned Lebow, and Geoffrey Parker, eds., *Unmaking the West: "What-If?" Scenarios That Rewrite World History* (Ann Arbor, MI, 2006).

Tooze, Adam, "Reassessing the Moral Economy of Post-War Reconstruction: The Terms of the West German Settlement in 1952," *Past and Present*, 2011, 47–70.

Trevor-Roper, Hugh, *History and Imagination* (Oxford, 1980).

Trittel, Günter J., "Die Sozialistische Reichspartei als Niedersächsische Regionalpartei," in Weisbrod, ed., *Rechtsradikalismus in der politischen Kultur der Nachkriegszeit*, pp. 67–85.
   "Man kann ein Ideal nicht verraten ... " Werner Naumann – NS-Ideologie und politische Praxis in der frühen Bundesrepublik (Göttingen, 2013).

Tucker, Aviezer, ed., *A Companion to the Philosophy of History and Historiography* (Chichester, 2009).

Tucker, Jonathan B., ed., *Toxic Terror: Assessing Terrorist Use of Chemical and Biological Weapons* (Cambridge, MA, 2000).

US Department of State, *Blue Book on Argentina: Consultation among the American Republics with Respect to the Argentine Situation* (New York, 1946).
   Foreign Relations of the United States, Diplomatic Papers, 1945: European Advisory Commission, Austria, Germany, Volume III (Washington, DC, 1945).

van Dijk, Ruud, "The 1952 Stalin Note Debate: Myth of Missed Opportunity for German Unification?" *Working Paper No. 14, Woodrow Wilson International Center for Scholars*, May 1996.

van Dijk, Teun A., "Critical Discourse Analysis," Tannen, et al., eds., *The Handbook of Discourse Analysis*, pp. 466–85.

van Emsen, Kurt, *Adolf Hitler und die Kommenden* (Leipzig, 1932).

van Laak, Dirk, "'Nach dem Sturm schlägt man auf die Barometer ein ... ' Rechtsintellektuelle Reaktionen auf das Ende des 'Dritten Reiches,'" *WerkstattGeschichte*, 17, 1997, 25–44.

van Rjndt, Philippe, *The Trial of Adolf Hitler* (New York, 1978).

Vials, Chris, *Haunted By Hitler: Liberals, the Left, and the Fight against Fascism in the United States* (Amherst, MA, 2014).

Virchow, Fabian and Christian Dornbusch, eds., *88 Fragen und Antworten zur NPD* (Schwalbach, 2008).

Vollmer, Bernhard, *Volksopposition im Polizeistaat: Gestapo- und Regierungsberichte, 1934–1936* (Stuttgart, 1957).

Von Hodenberg, Christina, "Of German Fräuleins, Nazi Werewolves, and Iraqi Insurgents: The American Fascination with Hitler's Last Foray," *Central European History*, 41, 2008, 71–92.

Von Miquel, Marc, *Ahnden oder amnestieren?: Westdeutsche Justiz und Vergangenheitspolitik in den sechziger Jahren* (Göttingen, 2004).

Waldeck, R. G., *Meet Mr. Blank: The Leader of Tomorrow's Germans* (New York, 1943).

Walters, Guy, *Hunting Evil: The Nazi War Criminals Who Escaped and the Quest to Bring Them to Justice* (New York, 2010).

Ward, James J., "'This is Germany! It's 1933!' Appropriations and Constructions of 'Fascism' in New York Punk/Hardcore in the 1980s," *Journal of Popular Culture*, winter, 1996, 155–84.

Weber, Jürgen, *Germany, 1945–1990: A Parallel History* (Budapest, 2004).

Weber, Wolfgang E. J., "... oder Daniel würde zum Lügner, das ist nicht möglich: Zur Deutung des Traums des Nebukadnezar im frühneuzeitlichen Reich," in Schmidt and Weber, eds., *Traum und res publica*, pp. 203–26.

Wedemeyer-Kolwe, Bernd, *"Der neue Mensch": Körperkultur im Kaiserreich und in der Weimarer Republik* (Würzburg, 2004).

Weinberg, Gerhard, "Who Won World War II and How?" in Hixson, ed., *The American Experience in World War II*, Volume XII, pp. 1–13.

Weiner, Robert G., ed., *Captain America and the Struggle of the Superhero: Critical Essays* (Jefferson, NC, 2009).

Weisbrod, Bernd, "Einleitung," in Weisbrod, ed., *Rechtsradikalismus in der politischen Kultur der Nachkriegszeit*, pp. 7–18.

ed., *Rechtsradikalismus in der politischen Kultur der Nachkriegszeit: Die verzögerte Normalisierung in Niedersachsen* (Hanover, 1995).

Wenzlhuemer, Roland, "Counterfactual Thinking as Scientific Method," *Historical Social Research*, 2, 2009, 27–54.

Werner, Wolfram, ed., *Das Parlamentarische Rat, 1948–1949*, Volume IX (Munich, 1996).

West Side Committee against Renazification of Germany, *Shadow of the Swastika: German Rearmament & Renazification. The Road to World War III* (1950).

Wetzel, Juliane, "Der parteipolitische Rechtsextremismus," in Kowalsky and Schroeder, eds., *Rechtsextremismus*, pp. 89–102.

Wiesenthal, Simon, *The Murderers among Us* (New York, 1967).

Wilson, John, "Political Discourse," in Tannen, et al., eds., *The Handbook of Discourse Analysis*, pp. 775–94.

Winkler, Heinrich August, *Germany: The Long Road West: Volume II, 1933–1990* (New York, 2007).

Wittlinger, Ruth and Steffi Boothroyd, "A 'Usable' Past at Last? The Politics of the Past in United Germany," *German Studies Review*, October, 2010, 489–502.

Wolfrum, Edgar, *Die geglückte Demokratie: Geschichte der Bundesrepublik Deutschland von ihren Anfängen bis zur Gegenwart* (Munich, 2006).

    Geschichte als Waffe: Vom Kaiserreich bis zur Wiedervereinigung (Göttingen, 2001).

Wolle, Stefan, *Der Traum von der Revolte: Die DDR 1968* (Berlin, 2008).

Würffel, Stefan Bodo, "Reichs-Traum und Reichs-Trauma: Danielmotive in deutscher Sicht," in Delgado, et al., eds., *Europa, Tausendjähriges Reich und Neue Welt*, pp. 407–11.

Wyden, Peter, *The Hitler Virus: The Insidious Legacy of Adolf Hitler* (New York, 2001).

Yeadon, Glen, *The Nazi Hydra in America: Suppressed History of a Century – Wall Street and the Rise of the Fourth Reich* (Joshua Tree, CA, 2008).

Zamoyski, Adam, *Phantom Terror: Political Paranoia and the Creation of the Modern State, 1789–1848* (New York, 2015).

Zentner, Christian and Friedemann Bedürftig, *Das Grosse Lexikon des Dritten Reiches* (Munich, 1985).

Ziemke, Earl Frederick, *The U.S. Army in the Occupation of Germany: 1944–1946* (Washington, DC, 1975).

Zink, Harold, *The United States in Germany* (Princeton, 1957).

INDEX